T0287761

A History of the Ozarks

Volume 3

THE OZARKERS

A History of the Ozarks

Volume 3
THE OZARKERS

Brooks Blevins

UNIVERSITY OF ILLINOIS PRESS
Urbana, Chicago, and Springfield

This project is supported in part by a grant
from the Arkansas Humanities Council and
the National Endowment for the Humanities.

Cataloging data available from the Library of Congress
ISBN 978-0-252-04405-2 (cloth : alk)
ISBN 978-0-252-05299-6 (ebook)

For Ollie (Beck) Trivitt and
in memory of Junior Trivitt

Contents

Acknowledgments

Having spent the better part of a decade working on this trilogy, I could probably dedicate a fourth volume to all of you whose help made this possible, from the countless people at small-town libraries and historical societies to the hundreds of scholars and writers whose work on the Ozarks and Appalachia paved the way for my contribution to the history of upland Southerners. I'll do my best to thank as many of you as I can. Some of my research was made possible by a grant from the Graduate College of Missouri State University (MSU), and I thank Dean Victor Matthews and the MSU College of Humanities and Public Affairs for the yearlong sabbatical that helped launch this series.

Archivists and librarians provided valuable assistance. They include Anne M. Baker, Tracie Gieselman-Holthaus, and Shannon Mawhiney of the MSU Special Collections; Geoffery Stark and the staff at the University of Arkansas Special Collections in Fayetteville; Susan Young, Allyn Lord, Carolyn Reno, Marie De-meroukas, and the rest of the staff at the Shiloh Museum of Ozark History in Springdale; John Bradbury, Carole Goggin, Katie Seale, Erin Smither, Gary Kremer, Kimberly Harper, Laura Jolley, the late Beth Lane, and many others at the various research centers of the State Historical Society of Missouri; Connie Yen at the Greene County Archives; Michael Price, Brian Grubbs, and Renee Glass at the Library Center in Springfield; Jane Wilkerson, Brian Irby, Darren Bell, Rebecca Ballard, and Elizabeth Freeman at the Arkansas State Archives; Sophia Skinner, Neva Parrott, Rose Scarlet, and the late Sylvia Kuhlmeier at the Garnett Library at MSU–West Plains; Holly Hasenfratz of the Oklahoma State Archives; Glenn Gohr of the Flower Pentecostal Heritage Center in Springfield; Kathy Whittenton, Camille Beary, Rob Austin, and Brenda Lindsey at Lyon College's Mabee-Simpson Library; Twyla Wright, Laura Reed, Terri Crawford, and Amelia Bowman at the Old Independence Regional Museum in Batesville;

Daniel Lindsey at the Paul Weaver Library of Ozarka College; Vincent Anderson at the Donald W. Reynolds Library in Mountain Home; Tom Peters, Shannon Conlon, Nathan Neuschwander, and the rest of the staff at MSU's Meyer Library; and staff members at the Missouri State Archives, Missouri Historical Museum and Archives, the John Vaughan Library at Northeastern State University in Tahlequah, the Butler Center for Arkansas Studies in Little Rock, the Murray State University Special Collections and Archives, the Southern Historical Collection at the University of North Carolina at Chapel Hill, the Tennessee State Library and Archives, and the Rubenstein Library at Duke University.

For the many hours he spent crafting maps, I thank Jim Coombs. For compiling statistical data, I thank Zachary Beck, Jordan Webb, and Elizabeth Smith. For a variety of reasons, I owe a debt of gratitude to Blake Perkins, Andrew Cole, Jay Jenkins, Wayne Glenn, James Johnston, Nese Nemec, Bob Besom, Crystal Payton, Leland Payton, Jared Phillips, Phil Howerton, Jason McCollom, Tom Kersen, Kathleen Morrissey, Leigh Adams, Alex Primm, Ed McKinney, Frank Priest, John Chuchiak, Kathleen Kennedy, Craig Albin, Gordon McCann, Amos Bridges, Lisa Rau, Mary Lou Holmes, Trevor Martin, Gary Buxton, Daniel Woods, Tom Neumeyer, and Kris Sutliff. For reading the manuscript and offering sound advice, I thank Dan Pierce, Lynn Morrow, and an anonymous reviewer. The staff at the University of Illinois Press has been terrific, as usual. I appreciate editor James Engelhardt's vision of this project as a viable trilogy, Alison Syring's role in seeing it to completion, Tad Ringo's project management, Jill R. Hughes's expert copyediting, and the efforts of Dustin Hubbart and the art department in securing rights to the beautiful works of the Society of Ozark Painters and using them in the wonderful cover designs.

For their patience with my long hours working and writing in my shed, I thank my wife, Sharon, and my children, Bryan and Annie, who were kids when I started this trilogy and are now plumb growed. I dedicate this book to my grandma, Ollie (Beck) Trivitt, and to my grandpa, the late Junior Trivitt. They lived much of this story.

Introduction

A fancy banquet hall in a swanky hotel seems an unlikely venue to kick off the first regionwide folk festival in the Ozarks—unless, that is, none of the *folk* are actually there. When festival organizers and local dignitaries gathered in the Crystal Room of Springfield's Kentwood Arms on the evening of April 16, 1934, there were no overall-clad fiddlers, no basket weavers with tobacco-stained beards, nairy a bonnet or snuff stick on a woman in sight. No one in the Crystal Room looked like they were standing beneath a chandelier for the first time.

Scheduled to start the next morning, the Ozarks Folk Festival was Missouri's penultimate jamboree in a season of shindigs for the unsophisticated. Converging on the "Queen City of the Ozarks" were the "winners" from a series of small-town regional festivals. Those deemed best of show in Springfield would advance on up Route 66 to appear in the first-ever National Folk Festival in St. Louis. The performers may have been noticeably absent on the evening of April 16, but among the esteemed guests at the Kentwood Arms was St. Louisan Sarah Gertrude Knott, the thirty-nine-year-old force of nature behind the National Folk Festival. Visiting all the way from North Carolina was Bascom Lamar Lunsford, the "Minstrel of the Appalachians," who had launched Asheville's Mountain Dance and Folk Festival half a dozen years earlier.

Lunsford was big stuff in those mountains back east, but in southwestern Missouri his star was eclipsed by the woman who referred to herself as "Queen of the Hillbillies." A native of the small town of Galena, Missouri, and author of the popular "Hillbilly Heartbeats" column in a Springfield newspaper, middle-aged May Kennedy McCord was the only Ozarker serving on the national festival's advisory council. She was accompanied at the Kentwood Arms by Vance Randolph, the self-taught folklorist who was well on his way to becoming the mouthpiece and interpreter of the realm, a regular "Mr. Ozark." Like Lunsford,

Randolph was in Springfield as a judge of talent and authenticity. And like his Appalachian counterpart, Randolph was an adept judge of feminine charms, the two married men vying for the affections of the unmarried Knott. But the finer points of male preening slipped into afterthought when the evening's welcome address proved anything but hospitable.[1]

There had already been pushback from a few of the men in the Crystal Room. A month earlier a closed-door meeting of the directors of the Springfield Chamber of Commerce produced a sharp rebuke of any event "advertising to the world that we're ignorant." Business leaders feared the region's biggest city would "get into the same predicament" that had long plagued Missouri's neighbor to the south. "They've been trying to live down that hill-billy stuff in Arkansas for years," warned the chamber secretary. Celebrating the nobler deeds of ancestors was one thing, noted another chamber director, "but there are a lot of fool things I'd like to see people forget." When McCord assured the chamber that "we're not trying to present freaks or ignoramuses . . . just trying to preserve some of the old, lovely, beautiful, wonderful things that went into the making of this country," the chamber's president doused the flames of discord. "We can't ignore . . . the traditions of a people," declared entrepreneur John T. Woodruff. "To pass them up would be to throw away something of real value."[2]

The calming words of the powerful Woodruff seemingly put the matter to rest, but it wouldn't stay that way. As chamber president—not to mention owner of the Kentwood Arms—it was Woodruff who was tasked with welcoming festival visitors that evening in the Crystal Room. Given Woodruff's deft diplomacy a month earlier, McCord was flabbergasted by what happened next. The sixty-six-year-old businessman leveled his sights on "carpetbagger" writers whose fascination with the backwoodsy characters of the region colored perceptions of the Ozarks. *The Shepherd of the Hills* author, Harold Bell Wright, claimed Woodruff, knew next to nothing about the region, and if "measured by any standard of a literary man, he couldn't pass the third grade." Literary scholars shared Woodruff's estimation, but it was shocking to hear such blunt criticism of the book that had become the sacred centerpiece of the tourism industry in southwestern Missouri. The chamber president was just warming up.[3]

Woodruff next took aim at a closer target, Vance Randolph, accusing him of "consorting with some of the undercrust" and presenting "them as typical." But the folklorist's worst sin was "his association with the author of *The Woods Colt*," a novel released just months earlier by a major New York publisher. Woodruff proceeded to give said author, Thames Williamson, the most thorough dressing down of any carpetbagger, dismissing his Ozarks-set book as "the rottenest, nastiest stuff I've ever seen in print." Williamson was nowhere close to the Ozarks, but the person to whom he had dedicated *The Woods Colt*, Randolph, was by now the object not just of the chamber president's wrath but of everyone's rapt attention. The perpetually scowling Woodruff concluded this awkward roast with a final plea that the organizers not "go to St. Louis and stage any rough stuff." Shocked and chastened, Randolph declined to offer a rebuttal. He would take a parting jab at the chamber in a Springfield newspaper two days later. The remarkable thing about the showdown between Woodruff and Randolph is that both were motivated by a love of the Ozarks. But their definitions of the Ozarks conjured up two very different places. In lifestyle and philosophy, you could scarcely have engineered more perfect opposites. Each worked diligently to craft an Ozarks in his own image.[4]

Vance Randolph and the Ozarks have been more closely entwined than possibly any other individual and region in the United States. But "Mr. Ozark" was no native. Raised in a conservative, middle-class family in Pittsburg, Kansas, he took to the margins early on, rubbing elbows with immigrant miners and labor radicals before earning a master's degree in psychology at Clark University in Massachusetts. When Columbia University anthropologist Franz Boas rejected Randolph's dissertation proposal on white mountaineers, the contrarian romantic gave up his dream of an academic career and landed in little Pineville, Missouri, in the 1920s. There Randolph married the daughter of a local physician and began a career as a hack writer of cheap paperbacks who devoted as much time as he could to cataloging a dying way of life among the plain people of the backwoods. Analyzing the peculiarities of regional dialect and collecting folk songs and stories, Randolph emerged in the Depression decade as a sort of Margaret Mead for the Ozarks, an outsider gone native who interpreted the eccentricities of an exotic region for mainstream American readers. His dispatches from this "primitive" land came forth as magazine and journal articles, nonfiction books, and even a few novels. In the decade preceding Pearl Harbor, Randolph did more than anyone else to bring wide recognition to a heretofore obscure region.[5]

In many respects John T. Woodruff represented everything the iconoclastic Randolph found abhorrent about small-town conformity and boosterism. An attorney for the Frisco Railroad, Woodruff had settled in Springfield thirty years earlier. And to claim he had been involved in the city's subsequent development would be like claiming the pope is involved in the church. Practically every significant civic and commercial milestone in the Queen City of the Ozarks after 1904 bore Woodruff's imprint. He built three hotels and the first "skyscraper" in the Ozarks and spearheaded efforts to create Springfield's first golf course and country club. Woodruff played a leading role in the establishment of the city's first municipal airport and was among those responsible for the creation and naming of Route 66. Despite his own limited formal education, Woodruff served on the board of trustees of Drury College, securing a fifty-thousand-dollar grant from John D. Rockefeller's General Education Board and an additional fifty thousand from another tycoon, Andrew Carnegie. It was banter over a shared love of golf that broke the ice with the Scottish-born philanthropist.[6]

But in the Crystal Room on this night in April 1934, it wasn't the divergent career paths that drove a wedge between the über-booster Woodruff and the outsider Randolph. It was their divergent visions of the Ozarks. Randolph's Ozarks was a place of anachronism, where old women in bonnets dipped snuff, sang ancient ballads, and knew their way around a spinning wheel. It was a place where old men in overalls listened for the bay of a fox hound and told stories punctuated with phrasings unintelligible to the average American. Randolph knew there was a world of town dwellers and valley farmers barely distinguishable from their counterparts elsewhere around the nation—and that this Ozarks would gradually force his into oblivion. But Randolph was also aware that his Ozarks—where old-timers "believe firmly in witchcraft and all sorts of medieval superstitions"—was eminently more titillating and marketable to the American public. If he couldn't preserve a dying world, at the very least he could record its artifacts for posterity.[7]

Despite his country club membership and three-piece suits, Woodruff was no stranger to Randolph's Ozarks. Born on a farm in Crawford County, Missouri, Woodruff was raised in a dogtrot log house at the head of Boone's Creek before his parents moved to the edge of Bourbon, where his father operated a store. The polymath Woodruff maintained a lifelong interest in horticulture and animal husbandry, but in public he pitched his tent in the camp of the forward-looking champions of modernization. Woodruff's Ozarkers were "high-minded, patriotic and God-fearing." "Never get the idea that is rampant today," he scolded the folklorists, "that [Ozarkers] are uncouth, illiterate and . . . possessed of none of the finer sensibilities."[8] In fact, at the very moment banjoists and balladeers bum-rushed the Queen City in the spring of 1934, citizens of "finer sensibilities" were busy creating the Springfield Symphony Orchestra. Randolph had no truck with Wagner, woodwinds, or Woodruff's defense. He simply preferred to highlight the kind of people who would take the stage in duckins the next day, not the kind who would don tuxedos and file into Drury College's Clara Thompson Hall ten months later for the symphony's inaugural performance.[9] Woodruff's modern and progressive Ozarks was good for the business of business. Randolph may not have shared the chamber's concern for the damage a hillbilly image could do to the bottom line, but his conception of the Ozarks was not without its own financial rewards, as tourism entrepreneurs in the Shepherd of the Hills Country had already discovered. "If the local chamber of commerce doesn't appreciate this publicity," he shot back on his way out of Springfield, "then so much the worse for the local chamber of commerce."[10]

While the effects of the long Civil War era colored the region for decades, it was a different conflict that defined Ozarks history in the twentieth and early twenty-first centuries. The kerfuffle in the Kentwood Arms laid bare a struggle playing out among those who would define the Ozarks and Ozarkers. By the time John T. Woodruff took aim at Vance Randolph, the fog of anonymity that long cloaked the hills of middle America had burned away, exposing the region to the intense light of the national gaze. Inspired by the stories of Harold Bell Wright and other local colorists, Randolph and fellow romantics scoured the ridges and hollers for the residue of a lost world, the survival of a priceless primitivism. In the years between the world wars the romanticizers found their Ozarkers in crossroads stores, on viney porches, behind mule-drawn harrows in narrow creek bottoms. They found them in one-gallused overalls and Mother Hubbard dresses, in callused bare feet in one-room schoolhouses with homemade benches and potbellied wood-burning stoves. Their Ozarkers paid no mind to the caterwauling on the radio but held fast to the old "ballets" that grandma sang. They didn't cotton to the city feller's love of mammon. They made do with what they had and had only what they needed.

Woodruff, too, found the building blocks to construct the Ozarks in his image. His Ozarkers were prairie farmers with Jersey cattle and silos of grain. They were engineers and educators, superintendents and salesmen. They spent long hours in aprons in main street mercantiles, pencils tucked behind ears. They drove Plymouths and Buicks to the English Gothic church house on the corner and stayed dressed for the band concert that evening. They attended Rotarian conventions and ladies' aid meetings; drank their coffee from cups, not saucers; took float-fishing trips on the White or Current; sent their daughters to piano lessons and their sons to Boy Scouts. Woodruff's Ozarkers knew when the stock market crashed. They graduated from high school, occasionally from college. They didn't disagree when St. Louisans declared the hills full of hicks, but they resented the hicks for dragging everyone else down with them. They criticized novelists, travel writers, and Hollywood for showing favoritism to Randolph's Ozarkers.

It was bad news for Woodruff and other townsfolk who spent years picking hayseeds from their hair, but Randolph's romantic vision of the Ozarks was the easier sell in the national marketplace of stereotype and caricature. Human nature draws our gaze toward the unusual within any group. So it is no surprise that the minority who clung to the old days and old ways disproportionately influenced the creation of the *idea* of the Ozarks. It is understandable that they dominated the social construct that would color every depiction of the region for decades to come. Randolph's ridge runners—their characteristics boiled down to the essentials of the sturdy mountaineer or the hillbilly—were more interesting and entertaining. Woodruff's strivers were too familiar, too tainted with

Babbittry and doomed to anonymity. Randolph's "deliberately unprogressive" Ozarkers were colorful and unique.[11] They offered an alternative to the droning acquisitiveness of modern American life. Woodruff's money and power—not to mention his ownership of the venue—carried the evening in the Crystal Room, but it was Randolph's Ozarkers who represented the region not only on the National Folk Festival stage but in the national consciousness as well. And it is Randolph's memory, not Woodruff's, that still looms in the twenty-first century. Standing on the dais in the Crystal Room in 1934, Woodruff sensed the fight was already lost.

There was no shortage of Randolph's backwoodsmen or Woodruff's better sort, but a majority of Ozarkers resided somewhere between those poles. Most of the Ozark region was less fertile, more rugged, less populated, and poorer than surrounding places, but only rarely did these challenges fleece Ozarkers of the common desire for things newer and better, the hope of achieving some semblance of the American dream. Continuing a theme of *The Old Ozarks* and *The Conflicted Ozarks*, this third volume of *A History of the Ozarks* presents the history of the post–Civil War era as a regional variation of an American story, the Ozarkers as people whose experiences have not diverged from the currents of mainstream American life as sharply and consistently as the mythmakers would have it. But viewing the region's past through a more unexceptional lens—somewhere between Randolph's romantic vision and Woodruff's progressive dream—does not render the Ozarks a bland, rural echo of the national experience. In some ways the twentieth-century Ozarks strayed from the continuum of American historic progression more noticeably than did the old Ozarks. For much of the period under study, significant portions of the Ozarks seemed always to be a generation behind the standard American story. It was this time lag, after all, that supplied Randolph and other romantics with their subjects. Yet the time lag was more a product of poverty and physiographic barriers than a result of conscious rejection of Woodruff's modern world and its progressive spirit. It was more pronounced in the most rugged and inaccessible subregions of the Ozarks, where the terrain proved especially challenging to transportation and communication.

These subregional differences in the Ozark uplift reflect the other issue informing *The Ozarks*. Randolph and the romanticizers found their Ozarkers more plentiful in the backwater neighborhoods of the poorest and most remote areas, subregions like the White River Hills, the Boston Mountains, and the Courtois Hills. It was Ozarkers in these places—where folk traditions held on longer and technological change caught on later than elsewhere across the continent—who came to represent the region in popular culture. The Springfield Plain, on the other hand, had been an Ozarks oasis of prosperity since before the Civil War. The "hillbillies" and anachronistic old-timers who populated

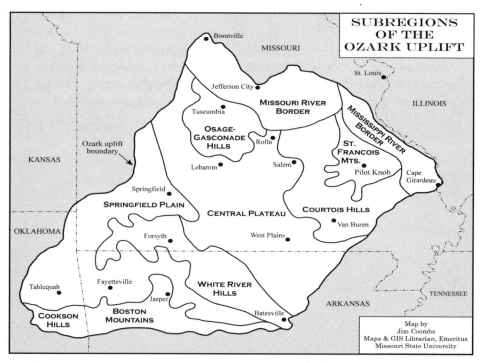

Ozarks Subregions. Courtesy of Jim Coombs and Emilie Burke, Missouri State University, Springfield.

the nation's books, magazine articles, and movies about the Ozarks were not extinct in the Springfield Plain, but they composed only a small minority. The Springfield Plain was home to the region's cities and largest towns, the seat of most Ozarks colleges and cultural institutions, the territory of its most prosperous farms and largest industries. In short, this gently rolling prairie expanse was the primary habitat of Woodruff's Ozarkers. To a lesser degree, similar contrasts delineated railroad towns and more vibrant county seats from their hinterlands. Such economic cleavages were almost never depicted in popular portrayals of Ozarkers. The divide between the haves and the have-nots—between the residents of the comparatively prosperous Ozarks and those of the poor Ozarks—remains a defining characteristic of the region today.

The fight between the chamber of commerce and the romanticizers in 1934 was in essence a struggle to determine which of these two groups would define the Ozarks—the haves or the have-nots. But neither definition was broad and inclusive enough to encompass the people of a meandering hill country stretching from the outskirts of St. Louis to the Cherokee Nation in Oklahoma.

Whether in the depths of the Great Depression or more than two decades into the twenty-first century, the Ozarkers are a people with no single story to tell. Beyond the quaint and anachronistic folkways of Randolph's Ozarkers, and beyond the modern American lifestyles of Woodruff's Ozarkers, lie the stories of a people who share a connection to this ancient, weathered plateau we call the Ozarks. They are stories shrouded by the simplistic imagery that has clung to the hill folks for more than a century. They are the stories of the famous and the obscure. They are the stories of the Ozarkers.

1 CHANGE AND CONTINUITY

"'Before many years a railroad will find its way yonder. Then many will come, and the beautiful hills that have been my strength and peace will become the haunt of careless idlers and a place of revelry. I am glad that I shall not be here.'"[1] So spoke Daniel Howitt, the titular character of the most influential book ever written about the Ozarks, Harold Bell Wright's *The Shepherd of the Hills*. Set in the White River country of southwestern Missouri and released in 1907, the novel introduced hundreds of thousands of Americans to a little-known place in the heart of the nation. The local color movement that dominated American literature during the last quarter of the nineteenth century was on its downslope by the Teddy Roosevelt era, pushed to the margins by the grittier, more realistic voices of young modernists. It was fitting that a genre of literature most fully at home in the Victorian sensibilities of the previous century was only now finding its way into one of the continent's last unexplored populations of regional distinctiveness, a full generation after local colorists began penning magazine stories of mountaineers in the Appalachians of Tennessee and Kentucky. The Ozarkers have long lived in the shadow of their kinfolk in the expansive highlands east of the Mississippi, developments in Appalachia eventually making their way westward like hand-me-downs between siblings.

The Shepherd of the Hills was inspired by the author's convalescence in the bucolic countryside of which he wrote. A thirty-something parson of solid Yankee stock, Wright gave up his ministry temporarily in 1905 to recover his health on a farm in the hills west of Branson. Immersed in tales of the exploits of the Bald Knobbers and enamored with the earthy genuineness of his hosts, Wright crafted the romantic story of big-city minister Daniel Howitt's retreat to the rural Ozarks and his physical and spiritual rejuvenation amid the beauty and serenity of nature. Infused with the young writer's own preoccupation with such trends as muscular Christianity and eugenics and the back-to-the-land movement's belief in rural living's innate superiority over the urban lifestyle, the melodramatic novel struck a chord with readers. The book sold two million copies within a decade and motivated untold numbers of literary tourists to venture into the hills in search of the real-life people who inspired Wright's characters and the natural beauty that saved Dad Howitt.[2]

At least some of those early tourists must have recognized the irony as they stepped off the passenger cars at the shiny new Branson depot. Wright's novel was, after all, an elegy for a lost world, a paean to a pre-railroad arcadia. His arrival in Taney County coincided with the laying of the last few miles of track for the White River Railway. Within months the entire line was in operation. Wright saw the arrival of the railroad as a bold line of demarcation between a premodern and a modern Ozarks, between a land of isolated, independent subsistence farmers and one of markets and modernization. The railroad signaled fundamental and lasting change, and not for the better. Like Dad Howitt, Wright was apparently glad he was not around for the drastic transformation to come, relocating to California before the novel came out.[3]

Wright lived to see the maturation of the idea of the Ozarks that he played such a central role in creating. Given his wistful romanticizing of a presumed premodern Ozarks, perhaps he could take solace in knowing that the popular image of the region remained in large part true to his vision of a rural Shangri-la in *The Shepherd of the Hills*. Writers and travelers continued to mourn the passing of an age in the Ozarks backcountry. Their primitivist and nostalgic yearnings suspended in amber Wright's arcadian vision and its persistent counter-vision: dual stereotypes of sturdy, antimaterialistic pioneers and slovenly, ignorant hillbillies.

It is no coincidence that the creation and evolution of the idea of the Ozarks took place in the years following the appearance of that great symbol of modernity in the most rugged and inaccessible sections of the Ozark uplift. Historian Ronald D. Eller observes the same phenomenon in Appalachia, where the image of a static and isolated region emerged at the very moment that industrial and social forces transformed life in the mountains in the late nineteenth and early twentieth centuries. Scholars of regionalist literature of the late nineteenth century have argued that it was the critical juncture at which local economies and cultures began to succumb to nationalizing forces that sparked the regionalists' fascination with the premodern idiosyncrasies of life in the backwaters of North America. More accurately, it was the *perception* of drastic economic and social transformations that fueled the preoccupation with groups on the margins of American society. Though regions like Appalachia and the Ozarks had long been incorporated into national and international markets and into the broad currents of American culture, anachronistic elements of mountaineer life—log cabins, dialects, moonshining—survived in sufficient quantities to bolster preconceptions of old-timey otherness.[4]

At the heart of the enterprise, however, was something more universal. Undergirding the regionalist fascination with hill folks was the primitivist spark that for ages has enlivened the modern's interaction with the less modern. Regionalist literature, according to scholar Richard H. Brodhead, was spurred by the elite's quest for "inhabitable backwardness."[5] Premodern places unsullied by the homogenizing ways of modernity satisfied the streetcar suburbanite's longing to connect his own life with something more primal and authentic, something exotic yet safely domesticated. In the early twentieth century, Ozarkers took their place alongside the nation's other domestic exotics. How little or how much the socially constructed *idea* of the Ozarks favored reality was beside the point.

Opening the Ozarks

So we begin our history of *The Ozarkers* with a dichotomy at the heart of their creation: the arrival of that symbol of nineteenth-century modernization and the simultaneous construction of a backward-looking regional mythology. The arcadian world perpetuated by novelists and other searchers never existed in the static purity they suspected. As in more progressive and integrated areas of the United States, society in the nineteenth-century Ozarks evolved along an American continuum. It was an evolution that took place on a periphery, certainly, and one that often lagged behind mainstream currents, but it was ultimately an evolution that produced historic progression before the coming of the railroad as well as after. The railroad may not have signaled the stark divide between the old days and the new world that Wright imagined, but its arrival in the rural Ozarks, as elsewhere around the country, was momentous. Almost constant construction of railroads in the final three decades of the nineteenth century crisscrossed the Missouri Ozarks, so the dawning of the twentieth century found much of the Ozarks moderately well covered by railroad service, with one notable exception. The White River watershed of north-central Arkansas remained the region's last extensive virgin territory.

As if making amends for so long neglecting the area, railroaders built not one but two lines through the heart of the Arkansas Ozarks in the first decade of the twentieth century. Responding to geologist John C. Branner's glowing 1892 report of minerals in north-central Arkansas, former Arkansas governor Powell Clayton and the St. Louis investors who owned the Eureka Springs Railway reorganized their line as the St. Louis and North Arkansas Railroad. Built largely by Austrians, Bulgarians, and other immigrants with assistance from local farmers and their sons, the line reached the town of Harrison in April 1901 and from there extended southeastward to Leslie (formerly Wiley's Cove) on

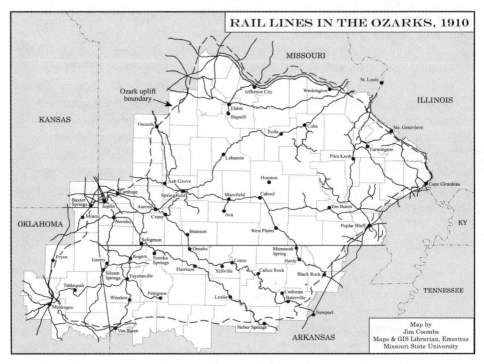

Rail Lines in the Ozarks, 1910. Courtesy of Jim Coombs, Missouri State University, Springfield.

the Middle Fork of the Little Red River in September 1903. When completed in early 1909, the newly reorganized Missouri & North Arkansas (M&NA) stretched almost 360 miles from Joplin through the Ozarks and across the Delta to Helena, Arkansas, on the Mississippi River.[6]

As usual, the expansion of rail service into a new country created winners and losers. Harrison, whose business owners raised forty thousand dollars to ensure the road's timely construction, celebrated the arrival of the first train with a parade and cannonade. Down the line in Searcy County, the merchants in the community of Duff boarded up their shops and relocated to the new town of Gilbert when the railroad missed their neighborhood by less than a mile. Leslie flourished as a lumber manufacturing center and for a few years boasted a nineteen-mile spur, nicknamed the Dinky Line, designed to fetch white oak logs for the town's barrel factories. The M&NA's decision to move its general offices to Harrison in 1914 established the Boone County seat as north-central Arkansas's largest and most influential town. Timber boomtowns sprang up along the M&NA in the hardwoods of Arkansas, from Pindall to Pangburn, though the bonanza had largely played itself out by the end of World War I.[7]

Paralleling the M&NA to the east, sometimes as close as 10 miles away, was a second road through the heart of the Arkansas Ozarks. Incorporated in 1901 as a branch of the St. Louis, Iron Mountain, and Southern, the White River Railway obtained charters to build a road connecting two of its main lines. Beginning construction at Batesville in the spring of 1901, contractors hired local workers for up to $1.50 per day and men with teams of horses or mules for as much as $3.00 per day. Nevertheless, labor shortages during planting and harvesting seasons necessitated the importation of workers—Austrians, Italians, Greeks, Macedonians, and other immigrants. Hugging the east bank of the White River—a route that required the blasting of the famed Calico Rock and other picturesque bluffs—the railroad extended through hilly country to Lake's Ferry (renamed Cotter) by August 1903. There the line bridged the White River and continued toward the northwest while construction of the Missouri section commenced in January 1904, reaching Aurora ("Summit City of the Ozarks") in late summer and Galena, on the James Fork of the White River, in the fall. In June 1905 a southbound train chugged down the Roark Creek valley within earshot of a convalescing Harold Bell Wright, pulling into the new station at Branson. Full service commenced in January 1906 on the new 239-mile route between Carthage and Batesville.[8]

Several towns along the White River Railway prospered. Aurora, which also lay on the main line of the St. Louis–San Francisco Railway, or the Frisco, became a thriving crossroads and served as headquarters of the White River Railway. A few miles down the line, the town of Crane blossomed after the building of a round-house and locomotive repair shop. Located roughly midway between Carthage and Newport, Arkansas, Cotter became a division point for the line. Eventually rechristened the White River Division of the Missouri Pacific Railroad, the line thrived in the early years on timber products and, during times of high prices, on shipments of zinc from the Yellville district. But the promise of mineral wealth that played such a crucial role in the creation of both lines ultimately proved a disappointment, petering out after the boom years of World War I.[9]

Barely more than a decade into their existence, the rail lines scrambled for survival, each clinging to residual mining and lumber industries and promoting various agricultural commodities in a region ill-suited to commercial farming. "'Long on scenery but short on revenue,'" the White River Line tried to boost its sagging fortunes with excursion trains, but outside of Eureka Springs and Branson the region's tourism industry remained a minor affair until after World War II. Ultimately, the heart of the Arkansas Ozarks simply generated too little shipping to support two major lines. Structurally inferior to the White River Line, the M&NA struggled from its inception. Beset by strikes, negative publicity from deadly crashes, and the crippling of the Ozarks barrel industry by Prohibition, the M&NA limped through the Depression and World War II

Missouri Pacific railyards and roundhouse, Crane, Missouri. Courtesy of Lynn Morrow Papers (R1000), folder 910, State Historical Society of Missouri, Rolla.

before ceasing operations in 1946. Reopened as the Arkansas & Ozarks Railway, the sixty-mile section from Seligman to Harrison functioned for another decade without passenger service before shutting down for good in the spring of 1960. The White River Line survived on the slimmest of profits. Both roads were important to the economic and cultural lives of the communities and towns along their routes in the first half of the twentieth century. Their coming was eagerly anticipated by farmers, merchants, and townsfolk, and, in the case of the M&NA, the railroad's removal was a devastating event that threatened economic and cultural regression.[10]

The decade and a half preceding World War I also witnessed a nationwide expansion of short lines. "Interurbans" connected the various towns of the mining districts of southeastern Missouri and the Tri-State region. Planned as an interurban connecting Ava, Missouri, with the Frisco at Mansfield, the Kansas City, Ozarks & Southern Railroad instead launched operations in 1910 as a steam-powered short line. Like countless other citizens in countless other towns, the people of Ava welcomed the inaugural run of the line's locomotive with a musical greeting from a cornet band, another mandatory institution of small-town progressivism in a hopeful age. The editor of the *Douglas County Herald* was almost beside himself with optimism on the eve of the line's inauguration. "It has been the evangel of progress," he waxed, "of religion and of education, of material prosperity and moral betterment wherever its whistle is heard." But for so many marginal towns, the railroad failed to make good its utopian promises. "Little did those cheering hundreds dream of the disappointments and disillusionments that were to follow," intoned a local historian almost half a century later, long after the Ava depot had been shuttered and the rolling stock sold for scrap. Douglas County's modest export economy of timber, produce, and livestock could not sustain even so minor an outfit as the Ozark Southern Railway, as the line was renamed in 1915.[11]

At least Ava got its shot. Many other small towns and hamlets watched as railroad routes avoided them or waited for chartered roads that never advanced beyond blueprint stage. The late nineteenth and early twentieth centuries produced dozens of these "paper lines." Lack of capital was the usual culprit. One of the region's most notable near misses was the "Ozark Short Line," the moniker given to a paper line that began life in 1908 as the Missouri, Inland, and Southern. Looking to connect the towns of Rolla and Cabool with a sixty-five-mile electric interurban, Elbert Young, an adventuresome Texas County native, and Houston druggist "Doc" Herrington secured rights-of-way, sold town lots, and oversaw the completion of a poorly constructed hydroelectric dam on the Big Piney River. By the time Young landed in prison and Herrington moved to Idaho under a cloud of suspicion, a few miles of track had already been laid south of Rolla and a depot built at Houston. The Ozark Short Line sold for a hundred dollars at the Phelps County courthouse in 1913, and the Houston station remains an architectural oddity to this day, a depot without a railroad.[12]

Local Color

The Ozark Short Line fiasco proved a colorful and ongoing saga, but robber baron finances and courthouse intrigue were not the stuff of Ozarks legend. As far as railroads were concerned, the ridiculousness of Thomas W. Jackson's 1903 *On a Slow Train through Arkansaw* was closer in spirit to the emerging Ozarks stereotype. The evolution of the idea of the Ozarks, like the creation of any social construct, owed something to reality, though it wasn't beholden to it. Despite the explosion of railroad building and extractive industry in the post–Civil War years, the Ozark region remained comparatively rural and remote. Like other such places, the Ozarks contained progressive and modernizing towns amid vast stretches of farmland and timber. It encompassed subregions of widely varying terrain, soil qualities, and economic demographics. Some, such as the Springfield Plain of southwestern Missouri and northwestern Arkansas, fostered an agricultural and commercial prosperity that bore little resemblance to the backwoods image that emerged in the early twentieth century. Most other places sheltered at least a few pockets of anachronism. Not all or even most Ozarkers in these places maintained old-timey lifestyles, but enough did so to attract the attention of travel writers, missionaries, novelists, and folklorists. Enough did so to paint the region with the tint of exoticism and otherness.

The idea of regional uniqueness was no new development in the postwar years. The South in general had emerged as an American Other in the antebellum era. The Old Southwest in particular gained renown as a land of uncouth, unbridled, proudly independent backwoodsmen. Among the prominent fictional characters imagined by the period's humorists was at least one resident of the Ozark uplift, C.F.M. Noland's Pete Whetstone of the Devil's Fork of Arkansas's Little Red River. Whetstone's backwoods antics contributed to a developing nineteenth-century "Arkansaw" image that predated and presaged any conscious recognition of an Ozarks type. The Arkansas Traveler story, in which an urbane wanderer encounters a backwoods squatter with predictably humorous results, may have been inspired by someone's sojourn in the Ozarks. But it remained an Arkansas, not an Ozarks, story, as did other creative expressions that portrayed the old Bear State as a haven for proto-hillbillies.[13]

In the latter decades of the nineteenth century, the Arkansaw image, with its dual connotations slandering or promoting the collective otherness of a state's population, helped pave the way for the social construct of the Ozarks. The Arkansaw image was not alone, for the last quarter of the century also witnessed the creation of *Appalachia*, the idea of the southern mountains and mountaineers in the national consciousness. Sharing historic connections with the Ozarks and thus cultural and social commonalities, Appalachia emerged as an Other within an Other, an allegedly unique subregion of the exotic South. Appalachia's regional singularity rested on many of the same characteristics and anachronistic survivals that would later come to describe the Ozarks, from log cabins and moonshiners to bucolic valleys and feuding rustics. The crafting of an Appalachian construct by writers, missionaries, and other outsiders who ventured into the mountains provided a blueprint a generation later when the same kinds of people began defining the Ozarks and Ozarkers.

Will Wallace Harney's 1873 *Lippincott's Magazine* article, "A Strange Land and a Peculiar People," is often cited as the first nationally published work to treat Appalachians as a unique and definable population. At least a generation would pass before the Ozarks received a written treatment wielding the socially constructive powers of Harney's piece, but hints of a nascent idea of the Ozarks appeared in occasional stories in the final third of the nineteenth century. Investigating the historic 1865 shootout between James "Wild Bill" Hickok and David Tutt on the public square of Springfield, Missouri, journalist George Ward Nichols traveled to the Ozark region's largest town to watch "the coming and going of the strange, half-civilized people . . . dressed in queer costumes . . . made of skin, but so thickly covered with dirt and grease as to have defied the identity of the animal." Nichols observed groups of indolent men leaning on posts and lying on sidewalks. "The most marked characteristic of the inhabitants seemed to be an indisposition to move," he noted in his article for *Harper's New Monthly Magazine*. Yet, for Nichols, who never once used the word "Ozarks," Springfield was part and parcel of an amorphous Wild West emerging from the ashes of war. In succeeding decades reporters continued to lurch toward a regional construct as they chronicled the most sensational stories emanating from the hills. Detailing revenuer raids and Ku Klux Klan nightriding in southeastern Missouri, the *St. Louis Globe-Democrat* assured its readers that the people of the remote hills "are generally ignorant and reckless, living in log cabins and cultivating small patches of corn, which they think is of little use unless made into whisky." It was national coverage of another band of masked vigilantes, the Bald Knobbers, that ultimately produced the embryo of a social construct, the idea of the Ozarks as a land of "unsophisticated mountaineers" trapped in ignorance and superstition.[14]

More crucial than hit-and-run reporting to the development of the idea of a region was the late nineteenth-century's predominant genre of popular literature. Regionalist, or local color, fiction filled the pages of magazines and found its way into novels and plays. It required little more than "a zone of backwardness where locally variant folkways still prevail," according to literary scholar Richard H. Brodhead. Relying on the recreation of local dialects and other "heavily conventionalized . . . formulas," the local colorist needed only a cursory "acquaintance with a way of life apart from the culturally dominant." Led by such nationally recognized writers as Charles Egbert Craddock (née Mary Noailles Murphree) and John Fox Jr., Appalachian local color hit its stride in the 1880s and 1890s, painting portraits of isolated mountaineers and the outsiders who encountered them.[15]

Ozarkers made only rare appearances in the early years of local color. The earliest known contribution to the regionalist genre that used the Ozarks as a setting was an 1884 novella, *Parson Brooks: A Plumb Powerful Hard Shell, A Story of Humble Southern Life*. Written by John Monteith, a Yale-educated "carpetbagger" in Missouri's state government, *Parson Brooks* represents a sort of transitional stage in the evolution of the idea of the Ozarks. Monteith crafts now-familiar descriptions of the proto-hillbilly Brooks and his windowless log cabin that shelters no fewer than seventeen family members. "A square, bony, skinny frame," long nose, beady blue eyes peering from beneath heavy eyebrows, and a thin growth of unshaven beard contributed to a classic look topped off by a sartorial ensemble that would remain en vogue on the backsets of *Hee Haw* a century later: "a checked woolen shirt, and jean pantaloons of butternut hue . . . [and] a hat of drab-colored felt, with a low crown [and] a broad brim."[16]

Despite his use of some of the most common visual motifs of mountaineer local color, however, Monteith viewed the Brookses not as specimens of a distinctive Ozarks but as run-of-the-mill, poor white Southerners. In the author's dialectic of clashing American cultures, the uneducated parson represents the "affable, sedate, and . . . picturesque" Southerner in opposition to the "progressive but . . . angular, nervous, radical, and irritative" Yankee. Monteith's tortured attempt to convey regional dialect has Parson Brooks speaking in a Foghorn-Leghorn-meets-*Slingblade* mélange of southernisms that could have seemed plausible only to someone who had never met an Ozarker. Monteith makes use of other devices that would become commonplace in Ozarks local color—the comely and intelligent daughter who springs inexplicably from the loins of backwoodsmen, for instance—but *Parson Brooks* was a story *in* the Ozarks, not *of* the Ozarks.[17]

More than a decade would elapse before a local colorist conceptualized the Ozarks as a unique region containing a distinctive and definable population. That singular accomplishment appears to have been the work of a long-forgotten writer named Mary Stewart, whose 1897 novel, *Unspotted from the World*, appeared ten years before Harold Bell Wright's *The Shepherd of the Hills* and presaged some of the latter book's themes. At the center of *Unspotted from the World* are the Grays, a family of unusual educational and artistic attainments living in a remote valley in the Missouri Ozarks that they share only with the Fosters, their tenant-farming, hardworking neighbors whose ways and accents reveal them to be the only *real* Ozarkers of the story. The Grays and Fosters remain blissfully shut off from the world beyond the ridges until the arrival of a St. Louis pastor who has retreated to the countryside to recover his declining health in the "pure and invigorating" atmosphere of the Ozarks.[18]

Even more consciously and stridently religious than Wright, Stewart shared the pastor's faith in the efficacy of the social gospel and a healthy respect for the tenets of muscular Christianity. *Unspotted from the World* also unflinchingly embraced the arcadian spirit, the conviction that the city was a place of wretchedness and evil and that the only true cure for urban ills was a retreat to the bucolic countryside. Her novel abandoned the Ozarks setting about one-third of the way into the story, but Stewart made a clear case for Ozarks exceptionalism, an announcement that its people embodied the same otherness, deviance, and timelessness that pervaded descriptions of Appalachians:

> The natives of the Ozarks are a people peculiar unto themselves. . . . As civilization approaches, they recede until the fastnesses of the mountains become their stronghold, where they persistently refuse to tolerate any innovation, and progress is an unknown quantity among them. . . . They regard education as pernicious, and woe be unto the reformer that seeks to press upon them the adoption of his modern ideas of progress and civilization. . . . They . . . are content if they know where the next meal is coming from, and have enough tobacco to last through the day. Seldom do the smoldering fires of ambition break out among them to consume even a single individual of a household.[19]

Stewart's brief synopsis of the people of the Ozarks, like most usable regional constructs, reduced the average Ozarker to a set of essential characteristics, traits that would have been in greatest supply in the rugged backcountry and among the poor. But we never meet these true, essentialized Ozarkers in *Unspotted from the World*. The unseen masses of natives who populate the hills and hollers surrounding the Grays' secluded valley almost certainly carry forth the uninspired and unambitious ways of their forebears. Yet Stewart's obvious condescension barely masked the same envy felt by Monteith's Colonel Payne in *Parson Brooks*, the modern's inchoate longing for the presumably carefree and contented existence of the savage.

More than the natives' lifestyle, the middle- and upper-class men and women who wrote regionalist stories and those for whom they were written coveted the Ozarkers' surroundings. Even before the emergence of the idea of the Ozarks in local color literature, the few writers who set stories in the region found the Ozark uplift's physical features more endearing than the Ozarkers who inhabited the place. If the verdant hills and clear streams of the Ozarks possessed an almost mystical power to restore physical vitality and spiritual strength to those brought low by the poisons of the city and the burdens of modernity, the people who called them home were at best quaint diversions, at worst lamentable excrescences blighting a divine landscape. In *Sally of Missouri*, a 1903 novel by Missouri Valley native Rose Emmet Young, a New Yorker first viewing the hill country is unable to suppress a primal howl atop the crest of a ridge. His first encounter with natives along a wilderness path, however, elicits not ecstasy but revulsion, and he hastily escapes the "hill tribe."[20]

Four years later an obscure author named Grover Clay hammered home the almost irredeemable otherness and irreversible declension of the tribe of native Ozarkers. *Hester of the Hills: A Romance of the Ozark Mountains* is significant in that it was likely the first East Coast–published novel to feature the word "Ozark" on the cover, a clear indication that the social construct of the region had advanced beyond the stage of infancy. It is also noteworthy as one of the most unrelentingly harsh depictions of native Ozarkers. Tracing the well-worn path of literary convention, *Hester of the Hills* follows a wealthy St. Louis businessman, Sidney Stanton, as he travels to the Ozarks to oversee a massive land transaction, only to take a shine to a beautiful girl who is trapped, again inexplicably, in a bestial and ignorant backwoods clan. Once Stanton's cousin whips Hester into passable shape for the city's high society, the two wed, but Hester soon discovers Sidney's caddish ways and hightails it back to the Ozarks. Here, in the slovenly cabin of her youth, the boorish depravity and putrid filthiness of her home folks come into sharp relief, sending her on a mad dash for the first train back to civilization. Trapped between two worlds, this transformed Hester from the hills concludes that life as a neglected trophy wife in the city is far superior to a lifetime sentence among the hillbillies at home.[21]

Clay's cynical novel gained no devoted followers, but another local color yarn published the same year, 1907, found a receptive audience. Harold Bell Wright's *The Shepherd of the Hills*—with its nonsectarian spirituality and back-to-the-land vibe—seemed the antidote to *Hester of the Hills*. Like other arcadian novels of the day, *The Shepherd of the Hills* drips with disdain for the city. "Small wonder our lives have so little of God in them," intones Daniel Howitt, the title character weakened by years as a Chicago minister, "when we come in touch with so little that God has made." In the Ozarks, "almost supernatural in its beauty," Howitt recovers his health and rediscovers his higher purpose in life. *The Shepherd of the Hills* is rich in literary convention. Howitt takes under his wing a comely, vivacious mountain girl, Sammy Lane, educating her academically, socially, and morally. And Sammy finds herself in a love triangle, her growing attraction to strapping farm boy "Young Matt" Matthews undermining her betrothal to Ollie Stewart, whose life as a clerk in a city has rendered him weak and effeminate. Toss in the nightriding terror of the Bald Knobbers, an elfin woods child who communicates with trees, and Howitt's long-lost son living in a nearby cave, and there's a little something for anyone's taste.[22]

The Shepherd of the Hills became one of the most popular books of its era, launching Wright on a career that would cement his place among the best-selling American authors of the first half of the twentieth century. The one-two punch of Wright's novel and the completion of Powersite Dam on the White River half a dozen years later sparked a tourism boom in the Branson area, "Shepherd of the Hills Country," that continues to evolve in the twenty-first century. The massive popularity and economic influence of *The Shepherd of the Hills* has, in fact, obscured the dark secret of the novel that did more than anything else to solidify and popularize the social construct of the Ozarks. For Wright, the Ozark uplift contained within its hills and valleys the elixir of rejuvenation, but the potion seems to have had no effect on the real mountaineers, the bona fide natives of the Ozarks. If anything, the isolation that produced the serenity craved by the educated and affluent of the cities bred only ignorance and backwardness in most Ozarkers. Wright didn't bludgeon the natives as had Grover Clay. He simply fanned them to the peripheries of his story, banishing the marginalized to the margins.

He sets the tone in the opening pages when Daniel Howitt first encounters a true youngster from the hills, Jed Holland. From the stranger's tailored clothing and well-groomed hair to his "marvelously pure, deep, and musical" voice, Jed senses something different about Howitt. "The boy looked at the speaker in wide-eyed wonder; he had a queer feeling that he was in the presence of a superior being." Like Jed Holland, the novel's other natives are minor characters who only briefly intersect with the storyline, with two notable exceptions: the aforementioned Ollie Stewart, whose physical degeneration after leaving the hills for the city reinforces Wright's anti-urban theme, and Wash Gibbs, a hulking, brutish mountain man and leader of the Bald Knobbers. But what about the Lanes and the Matthews family? Influenced by the eugenics theories increasingly occupying the minds of middle- and upper-class whites of Protestant, northern European descent, Wright goes out of his way to establish the non-Ozarks lineage of the families that produce the nubile youngsters who "owed it to the race" to marry and procreate. Jim Lane, Sammy's father, is identified as the scion of a distinguished old family of the Deep South whose coupling with her mountain maiden mother—like breeding a Hereford bull to a scrub heifer—has significantly improved Sammy's bloodline. The Matthewses, as it turns out, came from Illinois, a migration pattern that Wright employs to reinforce their Yankee descent, an even stronger link with a heralded Anglo-Saxon heritage. In Wright's universe the superior bloodlines of Young Matt and Sammy render them amenable to the cultivation of the learned outsider, the only method by which the salvation of the Ozarker is possible.[23]

The literary tourism sparked by *The Shepherd of the Hills* put money in the pockets of entrepreneurial Ozarkers, some of whom snookered visitors into believing they were the inspirations for characters in the book. Still, Harold Bell Wright held no particular affinity for those he would have considered the true hill people of the Ozarks. The natives were interesting in a quaint way, with their superstitions and Saturday night shindigs, and they could be rendered useful with the right kind of cultivation by knowledgeable outsiders. But they were superfluous to the central function of the Ozarks in the world of the local colorist: region as refuge from the ills and anxieties of urban life. Only those with the money, education, and "breeding" to appreciate the unique, restorative qualities of the Ozarks could claim its benefits and in turn extol its virtues to its ignorant rural natives. It was the land itself that was special. As for the rural dwellers of the ridges and the hill country whom the outsiders considered the true Ozarkers, they could be mocked on one hand as the isolated declensions of a noble race and exalted on the other as the independent children of the natural world.

Elements of this imagery appeared in stories and novels that sought to capitalize on the suddenly marketable Ozarks. In the decade following the publication of *The Shepherd of the Hills*, publishers released at least ten novels set in the region. Most followed Wright's arcadian blueprint and hued to his bundle of eugenics-laced racism, do-gooder impulses, and broad spirituality. The same era introduced a new breed of publications disseminating regional imagery in nonfiction accounts of life in the Ozarks. Most such stories in the years before World War I emanated from the pens of travel writers drawn to the region by the romantic descriptions of local colorists. New Englander Clifton Johnson, the premiere American travel writer of his generation, was perhaps the first to document the region just emerging from obscurity years after the "discovery" of Appalachia. His brief illustrated account of a visit to the railroad village of Cedar Gap, Missouri, appeared in a 1906 issue of the magazine *Outing*.[24]

Johnson and other travel writers generally sought out the same colorful rural regions and populations that infused regionalist fiction. They were documenting endangered rural folkways and other romantic relics of the nineteenth century sure to be obliterated in the twentieth. Nevertheless, given their dependence on the railroad for transportation, the travel writers' version of the rustic, backwoods Ozarks could not avoid the taint of iron-horse modernity. The truly remote areas remained so and escaped notice by the travel writer until the automobile age of the post–World War I years. Johnson, for one, was stripped of his romantic fancies by the "lack of wildness" at Cedar Gap, a small village nestled atop an eminence where the rugged Central Plateau flattened into the rolling Springfield Plain. Served for more than two decades by a railroad and inhabited by a comparatively prosperous if plain-living population, Cedar Gap nonetheless provided a few nuggets of color for Johnson's urban readers, including hogs wallowing beneath a whitewashed schoolhouse and an emotional "graveyard sermon" from a "red-faced, sweating" preacher. Johnson even spent a couple of nights in a log house, though his hosts were newcomers from Iowa who volunteered their less-than-favorable impressions of the true natives among whom they had settled.[25]

If Johnson splashed around the edges of Ozarks otherness, journalist Victor H. Schoffelmayer dove in headfirst. Describing a camping trip on the upper reaches of the White River for *New Age Magazine*, Schoffelmayer portrayed his journey into the Ozarks as "a visit to foreign lands." There was no mistaking his fascination with Ozarkers. "No more original, odd and picturesque people are to be found in America than the hill dwellers of the Ozark uplift," he marveled, "a race combining the shiftlessness of the Gypsy with the hardihood of the Puritan and the carefree indifference to work of the Neapolitan." Amused by the "quaint manners and picturesque speech" of the patrons at a "primitive" store, Schoffelmayer and his party "penetrated more deeply into the interior, and came face to face with the squalor and poverty which long has stigmatized the Ozark hills. Once when invited to partake of the noon-day meal in a 'Hill Billy's' shack, the filth was so revolting that none of us could eat." Schoffelmayer foresaw a day when outside pressures would eliminate the region's distinctiveness, though the journalist evinced none of the wistful angst of the Arcadian. "The 'Hill Billy' is slowly being displaced by the northern settler who is transforming the Ozark hills into apple and peach orchards and goat and cattle ranches. . . . His extinction is but a matter of time."[26]

Like so many reports of stark and unavoidable transformation, the prediction of the "Hill Billy's" extinction was greatly exaggerated. Had Schoffelmayer been granted a peek into the Ozarks of the twenty-first century, he may have been satisfied that this backwoods species still exists, despite the ribbons of blacktop and the massive concrete dam that drowns the gravel bars on which his party camped. In the short term, the upheaval of World War I did not expunge the

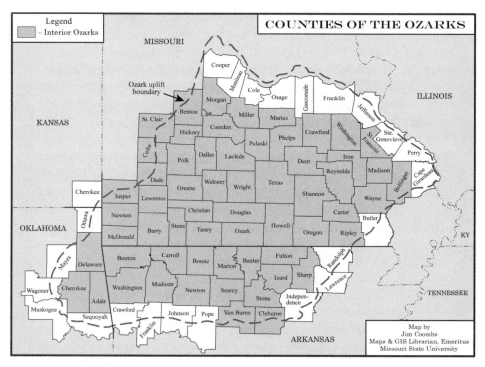

The Interior Ozarks. Courtesy of Jim Coombs, Missouri State University, Springfield.

backwoodsmen from the rural hill country, nor did the mad modernization of the 1920s eliminate fascination with the anachronistic way of life in the Ozarks, whether real or merely perceived. Technological innovations and Jazz Age youth culture worked feverishly to banish antiquarian ways and attitudes to oblivion, but evolution's conspiracy to erase the vestiges of the past only heightened interest in the people and places being left behind.

Becoming Ozarkers

Except for a smattering of magazine travelogues and an occasional newspaper feature, the Ozarks remained undiscovered territory for nonfiction readers at the dawn of the 1920s. It was in the interwar years that the social construct of the Ozarks matured before a national audience. By the latter half of the 1920s, prominent magazines and urban newspapers began documenting the lives of rural Ozarkers, from the quaintness of their speech to the seeming incongruity of their hellfire religion and ancient superstitions. For any marginal region, it was these kinds of exotic qualities that usually garnered attention. But in an age when the old white Protestant establishment fretted the loss of its exalted place, it was the rather unexotic demographic profile that drew first notice. The region's overwhelming whiteness flashed a lighthouse beam to those grown uneasy in a nation awash in ethnic and racial diversity. Like Harold Bell Wright, many later chroniclers of the Ozarkers were preoccupied with bloodlines and breeding, imbuing the idea of the Ozarks with a racial specificity that excluded anyone who didn't look the part. Writing in *The Outlook*, Lawrence F. Abbott recorded the heroic efforts of students at Arkansas's College of the Ozarks, "whose families, of pure Anglo-Saxon strain, have for several generations been residents of the agricultural highlands of the Ozarks." Detouring into eugenics territory, Abbott praised the region for producing "representatives of fine old American stock whose physique, crania, and profiles would not have been out of place among the Greek athletes in the stadium at Athens." Photojournalist Charles Phelps Cushing assured readers that off the well-traveled roads lived a "splendid stock of sturdy American humanity, rare and racy of the soil, last survivors of a hardy race of mountaineers, whose virtues and whose vices alike, contrasted with those of the Jazz Age."[27]

If the Ozarkers' "pure" racial and ethnic heritage supposedly linked them with the earliest European settlers of North America, their lifestyles—allegedly frozen in time by physical isolation and a cultural disposition to conservatism—likewise hearkened back to the days of America's ancestors. Visiting a backwoods bachelor in Taney County, Missouri, Charles Morrow Wilson found the "place untouched by the ways of a modern world." Seventeen wolf pelts provided rustic adornment for a cabin "built of logs, hand-hewn and chinked with valley mud." For Cushing, "the very word 'Ozarks' itself [had] a romantic sound; implying remoteness, wild and rugged scenery; and . . . truly primitive conditions of living." Invoking the era's "contemporary ancestors" romanticism, Cushing promised visitors to the Ozarks that they would "feel there the actual sinews of American pioneer humanity." It was this alleged timeless quality that more than anything else satisfied the primitivist yearnings of the age and inspired F. M. Van Natter's proclamation that in the Ozarks "one may still hear a pack of hounds open-up on the hot end of a fox trail . . . [and see] women beside their spinning wheels still walk back and forth drawing out the thread."[28]

There is a fine line between romance and ridicule. The very characteristics that endeared the quaint Ozarker to one writer could strike another as evidence of ignorance and cultural regression. Veteran Missouri newspaperman William R. Draper, for one, was immune to the primitive charms of the rural residents of the upper Osage River country. "The Ozarkians, if such the tribe could be called," observed Draper in a piece for *The Outlook*, "have lived lazy, kin marrying, morally clean, but none too God-loving lives. . . . The crop tenders are none too active in the growing season, and to them winter is a delight because they can group around the fireplace—and loaf." Like many observers who took a dim view of Ozarkers, Draper encountered them only in the context of their resisting modernization—in this case the building of Bagnell Dam and creation of the massive Lake of the Ozarks. Draper's observation that the landowners displaced by the reservoir were "hillside farmers [who] spent most of their time converting their corn crops into liquid form" no doubt salved the consciences of urban readers.[29]

An anonymous reporter in the *New York Times* marveled at the luxury hotels in the hills once inhabited by "barefoot hillbillies" but predicted that the shelf life for stereotypes was a long one: "Of course, vaudeville performers, imaginative playwrights and some journalists will not be affected by this change for years to come. The old jokes will still be told."[30] The primitive imagery associated with the more positive romantic interpretations of Ozarks life was likewise scarcely affected by real-life transformations in the region. Yet the modernizing developments of the era prodded into action those who would preserve vestiges of a disappearing lifestyle, if only in print. No one responded more urgently to the primitivist impulse to embrace and chronicle a threatened way of life than did a trio of young men whose combined efforts put the finishing touches on the idea of the Ozarks. Had no other writers given a whit about the region, the sheer volume of words churned out by Otto Ernest Rayburn, Charles Morrow Wilson, and Vance Randolph would have introduced millions of American readers to Ozarkers in the years between the world wars. Keeping to the backroads and isolated hollers, each harbored his own reasons for cherishing the last of a doomed breed. Their persistent spotlight on cantankerous individualists and intractable old-timers presented an image of a region blissfully behind the times and a people unconcerned with their failure to conform.[31]

Raised on a Kansas farm, Rayburn first grew enamored of the Ozarks after reading *The Shepherd of the Hills* as a college student. When his back-to-the-land experiment in southwestern Missouri was cut short by military service in World War I, Rayburn returned to the region in the early 1920s, paying the bills as an educator and magazine publisher. While teaching at a mission school in Kingston, Arkansas, he established *Ozark Life* in 1925, the first of several regional magazines that Rayburn would publish over the next three and a half decades. Providing much of the content for the romantic, boosterish magazine himself—with special emphasis on folklore and racial heritage—Rayburn also wrote regular Ozark-themed columns for Sunday newspapers in Little Rock and Tulsa. Like his later and most lasting contribution to the public's perception of the Ozarks—his 1941 book, *Ozark Country*—Rayburn's *Ozark Life* and other ruminations on the magical qualities of his adopted region were infused with his "spirit of romanticism."[32]

A "spirit of romanticism" is probably too timid a description for the thematic ribbon winding through the works of the trio's youngest writer and only member who could claim roots in the Ozarks. A native of Fayetteville and 1926 graduate of the University of Arkansas, Charles Morrow Wilson began writing as an understudy to Charles J. Finger, a British-born adventurer who published a well-regarded literary journal, *All's Well*. Introduced to the outsider's view of the unique Ozarks by Finger and others in his Fayetteville coterie of artists and intellectuals, Wilson possessed a deep and romantic appreciation for the authentic, rural Ozarkers of the backcountry. Proclaiming that appreciation as only the idealistic and youthful can, he penned a bevy of articles focusing on the primitive qualities of an almost mystical land. In "Moonshiners" Wilson reassessed illegal distillers as a fraternity of colorful, honest men pushed into wildcatting by infertile lands and economic necessity. In "Backwoods Morality" he described individualistic, clannish Ozarkers as "surprisingly well informed on legal procedure and craftiness" and more neighborly and generous than one might think. In "Elizabethan America" Wilson explored the then-popular notion that the peculiar speech patterns and vocabulary of the South's mountaineers was the outcome not of cultural degeneration but of the survival of Elizabethan English among an isolated population. "Husbandmen and ploughmen of Shakespeare's England and present-day upland farmers," claimed Wilson, "could very likely have rubbed shoulders and swapped yarns with few misunderstandings."[33]

In the late 1920s and early 1930s, no writer contributed more to the maturation of the social construct of the Ozarks than did Wilson, whose entertaining articles appeared in some of the nation's most popular magazines. But he was not the one to bring the Ozarks most fully into the national consciousness. More than a quarter century after the appearance of Emma Bell Miles's groundbreaking look at life in Appalachia, the Ozark region received its first book-length, ethnohistorical treatment when New York's Vanguard Press issued *The Ozarks: An American Survival of Primitive Society*. Its author, folklorist and iconoclast Vance Randolph, was relatively unknown at the time (1931) but would go on to supplant Wilson as the leading voice in defining a region and its people for half a century.

The Ozarks was more a reflection of Randolph's contrariness than a balanced portrait of life in the region. And the author made no attempt to conceal his biases, admitting that he was "not concerned with the progressive element in the Ozark towns, nor with the prosperous valley farmers, who have been more or less modernized by recent contacts with civilization." Like Horace Kephart, whose *Our Southern Highlanders* served as an inspiration for *The Ozarks*, Randolph was interested not in the ties that bound region to nation but in the peculiarities that differentiated them, the "diverting and picturesque."[34] After all, what editor rushed to publish stories about teachers in Fayetteville or mechanics in Springfield when their lives bore no perceptible differences from those of their peers elsewhere around the nation? Superstitious ridge runners, ballad-singing grannies, and moonshiners? That was more like it. Though not unique to the Ozarks, such characters were at least unknown to urban readers across the country. Randolph's book was also a product of its era. Published by a leftist press more than a year into the worst depression in American history, *The Ozarks* reflected not only Randolph's rejection of his middle-class upbringing but also the fellow traveler's rebuke of the capitalistic paradigm at the heart of American society. In his own ornery way, Randolph dismissed the vacuity of the bourgeois machine by embracing the real people thrown clear of its gears and belts. He praised "famous men" and condemned the society that ignored them with a wink instead of the cudgel wielded by James Agee and Walker Evans a decade later.[35]

The Ozarks covered a variety of topics that by 1931 had become standard fare in discussions of Appalachians and Ozarkers: dialect, folk songs, foxhunting, moonshining, play parties, and superstitions. Randolph also took on weightier subjects such as woman's role in the rural Ozarks and the sometimes-deleterious effects of tourism in a chapter he called "The Coming of the 'Furriners.'" Long before social scientists talked of granting agency, Randolph did just that for his rural subjects. Randolph's Ozarkers were not the downtrodden, preternaturally aged peasants whose fate the leftists bemoaned and whose children the progressives looked to rescue. His Ozarkers were not victims. His Ozarkers lived the lives they lived on purpose. "With the possible exception of some remote districts in the southern Appalachians," wrote Randolph, "the 'hill-billy' section of the Ozark country is the most backward and deliberately unprogressive region in the United States."[36]

The publication of *The Ozarks* marked the coming of age of *the* Ozarks. A social construct that found its legs almost a quarter century earlier in Harold Bell Wright's *The Shepherd of the Hills* reached maturity at the hands of the chroniclers of the Ozarks in the days of Charles Lindbergh and Babe Ruth. Wilson, Rayburn, and Randolph's shared vision of a unique and charmingly primitive Ozarks coexisted with a less savory image of a land of isolated, inbred, ignorant hillbillies more coarse than arcadian. But it was the former vision that held sway through the years of the Depression. It was Randolph's vision of the Ozarkers' independence and dogged persistence in the face of steep slopes and steeper odds that served as inspiration for a nation down on its luck. Whether the picturesque, Elizabethan-talking contemporary ancestor of the back hills or the slightly more picaresque moonshiner, the Ozarks had its identity. For good or bad, it was the place that time had forgotten, a land where the primitive pervaded the present. Like most images, it was shorthand, an essentialized definition of a regional population based on that population's most unusual and colorful cohort. Regardless of how poorly or perfectly the idea of the Ozarks reflected the real Ozarkers, a place had become a people.

2 LIVING OFF THE LAND

Of all the writers who ever penned a word about the Ozarks, there remains one whose fame and endurance are unmatched. Yet she received not a single mention in the previous chapter, for almost none of her readers has ever read anything she wrote about the region she called home for more than sixty years. Long before she became America's most beloved author of juvenile literature, generations before her simple yet engrossing stories of life on the western frontier inspired an iconic television series, Laura Ingalls Wilder was a regular correspondent for the *Missouri Ruralist*. For thirteen years she dispensed advice and spun yarns for the farming magazine's readers, encouraging good old Yankee industry and frugality, providing lessons on poultry raising and care for orchards, and sharing homey anecdotes from life on the farm. Given the abiding popularity of her *Little House* books, the writer's *Missouri Ruralist* output is viewed as little more than a training ground for the astonishingly productive years of her retirement. But in the annals of the Ozarks, it is the pre–*Little House* experiences of Laura Ingalls Wilder that provide our window into agricultural life between the Civil War and the Great Depression.[1]

Born in the Wisconsin woods less than two years after the end of the Civil War to parents of Puritan heritage, Laura Ingalls accompanied her family on its peripatetic wanderings around the heart of North America. The Ingallses' search for a place to call home finally ended in the eastern Dakota Territory in the early 1880s, but Laura's marriage to Almanzo Wilder led to still more restlessness, with brief sojourns in Minnesota and Florida. The final relocation took place in 1894 after neighbors came back from a trip to Missouri bearing a railroad's promotional booklet, *Among the Ozarks: Land of the "Big Red Apples."* Leaving South Dakota in July perched atop a two-seat hack, Laura, Almanzo, and their seven-year-old daughter, Rose, made the journey of roughly 650 miles in six weeks.

A lifelong farmer on flatter, more fertile terrain, Almanzo found southwestern Missouri unpromising at best, "ridges rolling in every direction and covered with rocks and brush and timber." But anyone with a passing knowledge of the Wilders knew that tiny, indomitable Laura made the decisions, and she deemed this alien landscape of stone and wood a veritable mound of clay waiting to be shaped into a thing of beauty and utility by someone as determined as she.[2]

Like other immigrants attracted by railroad boosterism, the Wilders eschewed the vast expanses of the "inland" Ozarks in favor of a location near the modernizing iron horse. Laura and Almanzo promptly bought a forty-acre tract of land a mile east of Mansfield, a town of fewer than five hundred souls that had sprouted thirteen years earlier when the Kansas City, Fort Scott, and Memphis Railroad laid tracks on its way from Springfield to the Mississippi River. Still only twenty-seven years old, Laura dubbed their little piece of the Ozarks Rocky Ridge Farm, a most apt moniker that foretold hard times to come. Rocky Ridge was almost completely covered in woods, with the exception of a four-acre clearing on which the previous owner had left an infant orchard whose big red apples were at least a couple of years in the future. Living in town until Almanzo could finish a tailor-made house for Laura, the Wilders survived a hand-to-mouth existence peddling firewood and eggs to neighbors.[3]

At first glance, it seems odd that Laura and Almanzo—two young adults with the prairie in their blood—would have chosen this spot. Just a few miles to the west lay one of the starkest demarcations between geographic subregions in all the Ozarks. There an even smaller railroad town, Cedar Gap, sat on the highest eminence in southwestern Missouri, the fertile Springfield Plain to its west, the more rugged, less yielding Central Plateau to its east and south. But 1894 was late in the game for immigration to the Ozarks. The better lands along the railroads had been claimed by early arrivals, and any prairie farms for sale on the Springfield Plain would certainly have cost the Wilders significantly more than the ten dollars per acre they forked over for Rocky Ridge. While their near neighbors on the prairies to the west developed extensive grain, fruit, and dairy industries in the half century following the railroad's arrival, the Wilders survived only through a diversified strategy that was more typical of farm families on the ridges and in the hollers beyond the Springfield Plain. Over the decades, the Wilders relied on Laura's expert hand with her poultry flock; on sales of apples from their modest orchard; on slight but marketable crops of strawberries, onions, and grapes; and on regular sales of cream from a few dairy cows. "Perhaps we have not made so much money as farmers in a more level country," Laura informed her *Missouri Ruralist* readers, "but neither have we been obliged to spend so much for expenses."[4]

For the Wilders and most other farm families in the Ozarks in the years between the Civil War and the Great Depression, farming consisted of a long series of experiments with potential commercial commodities. It was made up of challenges from rugged terrain and poor soil, from unpredictable weather and a regional marketplace increasingly integrated into national currents. The Wilders resided within earshot of a train whistle, but for many Ozarkers prosperity lay beyond reach due to the challenges of remoteness. For these families, life on the farm promised little more than subsistence. "This Country is a hard place," observed a farmer in Arkansas's Boston Mountains. "The man can make plenty hear to live on and hav reasonable helth but ther is no big money."[5] In such hard places the familiar patterns of pioneer life persisted deep into the twentieth century, convincing observers of hog killings, sorghum makings, and barn raisings that the world of the Ozarker plodded on in unbreakable rhythm, unperturbed by the modern age beyond the pastures and fencerows. It was, in fact, the great era of agricultural diversity in the Ozarks, when this region tying the Midwest to the South and hitching both to the West counted within its fifty-thousand-square-mile expanse wheat farms and dairies, orchards and cotton fields, truck patches and razorbacks. Life on the farm provided a common point of reference for most Ozarkers, but what was raised on the farm differed from ridge to ridge across the diverse landscape that is the Ozarks. The region's gradual integration into the national marketplace rendered farmers' collective pursuit a precarious one, demanding an adaptability and resourcefulness that would become hallmarks of rural life in the Ozarks.

Southern Staples

The steeper taxes of the Reconstruction era, coupled with a serious wartime reduction in livestock numbers, created an urgency among farmers to produce cash crops. In the southern reaches of the region, many farmers turned to cotton, though a slumping market and the intensive labor demands of this strange new crop in the hill country left more than a few Ozarkers dismayed. Exhausted from three summer days of hoeing his four-acre patch, in 1867 an Izard County, Arkansas, farmer regretted that he had not completely destroyed his crop (as had most of his neighbors) and declared that "from this time forward others may raise the cotton or all Yankeydom may do without." A drop in prices that fall prompted a farmer in the uplands of neighboring Independence County to write to his nephew that "cotin is wirth nothing and them that raised hit is brok."[6]

Still, more and more Ozarkers devoted acres to the South's leading staple crop. "Our little valleys that have been in cultivation for fifteen to twenty-five years in corn," wrote a Searcy Countian to the *Arkansas Gazette* in the summer of 1872, "now yield a bale of good cotton per acre." In the quarter century following the Civil War, a wave of cotton cultivation immersed a broad swath of the Ozarks. At the zenith of its geographic expanse in the late 1800s, the cotton

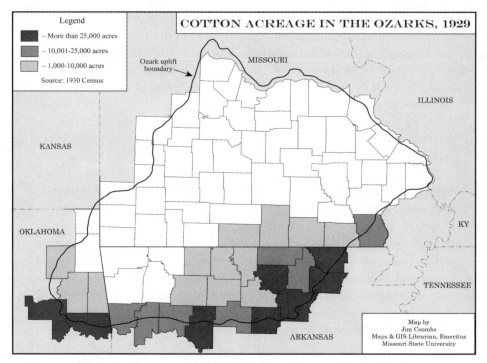

Cotton Acreage in the Ozarks, 1929. Courtesy of Jim Coombs, Missouri State University, Springfield.

flood inundated the eastern two-thirds of the Arkansas Ozarks and extended into the southern tier of counties in Missouri. Though the production of fiber on this fringe of the South paled in comparison to that in Dixie's warmer areas, by 1880 farmers in both Howell and Oregon counties in Missouri produced more than one thousand bales. Even in the remote Buffalo River country, the arrival of cotton introduced farmers to the world of furnish merchants, crop liens, and sharecropping. At the height of Buffalo River cotton raising in the 1890s, the Richland Creek valley boasted no fewer than four cotton gins.[7]

In Taney County, on the far northwestern margin of the Cotton South, Douglas Mahnkey lived a childhood experienced by few other Missourians. In addition to owning the general store in tiny Mincy, Mahnkey's parents operated a cotton gin and press in the early twentieth century. The fall harvest season was a hectic time that required the hiring of three temporary workers who often labored deep into the night. Teenage Douglas had charge of weighing customers' cotton and writing out their receipts, which, if they were fortunate, covered their year's expenses at the Mincy store. But cotton farming was a precarious endeavor on either side of the Arkansas-Missouri line, where killing frosts in late spring and early fall were not unheard of. This latitudinal challenge accounted for the almost complete disappearance of cotton in the Missouri Ozarks before the Depression.[8]

Acreage devoted to cotton expanded in gradual fashion in the southeastern Ozarks until World War I's bonanza prices convinced farmers to break new ground for crops. Herman and Frances Lewis, newlywed tenant farmers in Izard County, did well enough with small cotton crops in 1918 and 1919 that they not only covered their bills at the local store but also paid off two mules, a cultivator, and a new wagon. Buoyed by several years of high prices, the Lewises borrowed six hundred dollars to buy forty acres of rough woodland in early 1920. Beset by plunging postwar cotton prices, the young couple barely made enough to pay their taxes before selling their farm two years later and moving in with Frances's widowed mother. Many of their neighbors, however, found themselves caught up in the vicious cycle of the crop lien system, planting more acres in cotton in hopes of paying off rising debts. As a result, the decade following World War I witnessed a tremendous increase in the amount of land devoted to cotton in the southeastern Ozarks, almost all of it marginal and subject to erosion.[9]

Between 1919 and 1929, cotton acreage in the Ozarks increased by more than 50 percent, with farmers in four interior counties planting more than twenty thousand acres of the crop by the latter year. In those counties—Izard, Cleburne, Van Buren, and Sharp—more than four out of five farmers raised cotton at the onset of the Great Depression. In addition, cotton farming saw a resurgence in the counties on the western margins of Ozarks cotton country as acreage in Searcy County jumped two-thirds and Stone County's crop almost doubled. Cotton culture also brought higher rates of farm tenancy to the southeastern Ozarks. Though farmers in the Ozarks were still much more likely to own their own land than were those in Arkansas in general, at the beginning of the Great Depression more than 40 percent of farm operators in the Ozark region's cotton-dependent counties worked someone else's land.[10]

Another southern staple crop enjoyed brief interest from Ozarkers after the Civil War, though it never achieved the staying-power of cotton. The region's most dynamic tobacco-producing locale emerged on the prairie lands of the far western Ozarks. Capitalizing on legal ambiguities, Cherokee entrepreneur Elias Boudinot established a plug tobacco factory on Wet Prairie about one hundred yards west of the Arkansas state line in 1868. Producing some five thousand pounds of grape juice–sweetened plug tobacco per day at a complex employing more than one hundred laborers, the Cherokee businessman prospered as he easily outsold excise-taxed tobacco from the St. Louis market. Eventually, however, St. Louis manufacturers lobbied Congress to extend the excise tax to the Indian Territory, and in late 1869 agents from the Internal Revenue Service (IRS) seized the Cherokee factory and arrested Boudinot. Not only did the government's actions ruin Boudinot's business, but the U.S. Supreme Court's ruling in the *Cherokee Tobacco* case the following year ultimately brought an end to the federal government's long-standing practice of treaty making with American Indian nations and quashed any notion of tribal sovereignty.[11]

The demise of Cherokee tobacco did not spell the end of tobacco raising for Ozarkers. It was across the line in northwestern Arkansas that the region's tobacco industry reached its pinnacle in the late nineteenth century. In the 1870s many farmers used logs to construct two-story curing barns and devoted small patches to Virginia Golden Leaf, White Burley, and other varieties. At decade's end Benton County produced more than three hundred thousand pounds of tobacco, one-quarter of the entire crop of the Ozarks. At the peak of production, buyers came down from factories in St. Louis and southwestern Missouri, and county seat Bentonville boasted four manufacturers turning out cigars as well as plug, twist, and smoking tobacco. The Arkansas Tobacco Company's closure in the 1890s signaled the demise of Benton County's modest tobacco economy, as farmers began shifting to edible commodities that could now be shipped by rail. A few years after World War I, an agricultural agent for the White River Division of the Missouri Pacific Railroad established a White Burley demonstration farm at Branson, sparking a minor tobacco revival. Farmers in Taney County looking for an alternative to cotton planted some fifteen hundred acres of tobacco by 1924. Small patches provided a modest cash income for a few farmers into mid-century.[12]

Breadbasket with Long Sweetening

Tobacco's limited appeal and cotton's relegation to the southeastern Ozarks reflected a region with limbs extending into a variety of staple-crop territories but always in marginal fashion. A study of U.S. agricultural regions in the 1920s placed most of the Ozarks within a transition zone extending from southern New Jersey to the Flint Hills of Kansas dubbed the Corn and Winter Wheat Belt.[13] A key money crop for many farmers in this transition zone was wheat, which occupied the attention of thousands of Ozarkers for much of the period between the Civil War and the Great Depression. The swath of the Ozarks most devoted to commercial wheat raising fell short of the production levels on the prairies and plains to the north and west. Nevertheless, wheat remained a crucial commodity for many Ozarkers until the rationalization of national markets left the region's grain farmers unable to compete with more-efficient producers elsewhere.

On some of the region's poorer and more remote farms, the ancient methods of harvesting and threshing (or "thrashing," as it was called in the Ozarks) survived into the twentieth century. As a girl growing up in the hills of Fulton

County, Arkansas, in the World War I era, Erma Humphreys watched her father expertly cut down "swaths" of wheat with a cradle scythe, which her mother hand-tied into sheaths using bindings made from handfuls of straw. The sheaths were then stood on end and arranged in tipi-like shocks and left to dry in the open field for two or three weeks before being threshed. The ability to wield a cradle scythe was already an outdated skill by then, as a series of technological advancements had gradually mechanized the reaping and binding process.[14]

The evolution of labor-saving breakthroughs in the threshing process—separating grain from straw—was just as significant. Mechanical threshers appeared in the Ozarks as early as the 1850s, and by the 1870s most families in the region had access to a "groundhog" thresher, a stationary machine powered by oxen or horses on a sweep mill. The time and labor saved by a mechanical thresher was a source of joy and relief for farmers, while the extra income it promised its owner was cause enough for elation. "We can do more Thrashing and do it better than any Thrasher has ever done in the State of Arks," an excited new owner in Washington County claimed. "It would make the hair rise on your head to Stand by and see it thrash." Thresher owners transported the machine from neighborhood to neighborhood during season and received a portion of the grain as payment.[15] By the time portable threshers powered by steam engines began to replace animal-fueled contraptions around the turn of the century, threshing had developed into an annual social event for families and communities. Women and girls prepared meals for large crews of men and boys from the neighborhood, some of whom went from farm to farm during season, bunking in neighbors' attics and barns until the sheaths were all gone.[16]

High postwar wheat prices spurred interest among Ozarkers. Wheat farming experienced its most substantial growth on the prairies of the Springfield Plain, especially in the counties traversed by the new railroad lines in southwestern Missouri. By the turn of the twentieth century, the Ozark region's top three wheat-producing counties (Lawrence, Jasper, and Greene) lay in this subregion, where wheat production increased a staggering 400 percent in the final three decades of the nineteenth century. When abundant crops intersected with favorable prices, farmers on the prairies of the Ozarks gained access to material prosperity unmatched in other parts of the region. Recounting his boyhood in Dade County, Missouri, John K. Hulston recalled that money from the wheat harvest of 1904 paid for his grandparents' new Overland automobile.[17]

Advances in technology certainly played a role in the emergence of this breadbasket in the Ozarks, but more crucial was the growth of local and regional markets. With comparatively minor amounts of wheat shipped out of the region, the marketplace depended on the proliferation of commercial flouring mills. Within a decade of the arrival of the railroads, commercial steam-powered mills began to emerge in the booming towns of the Springfield Plain. One of the earliest was

North Springfield's Queen City Flouring Mill, built in 1879 by a group of local investors headed by German immigrant John Schmook. Capable of milling 150 barrels (almost fourteen and a half tons) of flour in twenty-four hours, Queen City found ready markets in the East and South. Five years later another German immigrant established the Eisenmayer Milling Company in North Springfield. By the early twentieth century, Eisenmayer's forty-six-thousand-square-foot facility turned out one thousand barrels of Spotless and Royalty brand flour per day.[18]

Across the Springfield Plain, Joplin pioneer John B. Sergeant established the booming mining city's first commercial mill in 1882; the Joplin Flouring Mill was capable of producing three hundred barrels per day at the turn of the century. Beginning in the latter half of the 1880s, merchant mills of various sizes sprang up along the rails in southwestern Missouri and northwestern Arkansas. Most of these small-town mills served a local and regional clientele of wholesalers and merchants. Southwestern Missouri shoppers in Barry, Stone, and Christian counties, for example, grew accustomed to seeing the Nancy Hanks and White Satin brands of the Crane Milling Company. An Ozark, Missouri, mill sold its Fancy, Daisy, and Snowball brands to local merchants and to customers as far away as Texas. Consolidation in the early twentieth century narrowed the truly national mills to a handful of companies in the region's largest cities. On the eve of World War I, Springfield contained just three commercial millers, but the eighty-seven employees of the firms produced a combined thirty-three hundred barrels per day, many of them destined for the European market.[19]

Despite its locus in the Springfield Plain, the flour-mill trend made its way into plenty of more unlikely locales in the Ozarks. Investors in little Marshall, Arkansas, hauled some twenty-five tons of materials seventy miles by wagon train for the construction of a roller mill—to provide farmers an alternative to cotton and to "show the outside world how Marshall is improving notwithstanding we are so far from the railroad."[20] But wheat farming was not to be the solution to the agricultural conundrum in Marshall, nor in the Springfield Plain over the long haul, for that matter. Falling prices after 1919 and the forces of national market efficiency narrowed commercial wheat's territory to the Great Plains and the upper Midwest, bringing about a rapid demise of wheat farming and flour milling in the Ozarks in the 1920s. Springfield saw its milling industry consolidated into a single producer by the mid-1930s. The massive old "Model" mill operated by the Colorado Milling and Elevator Company continued to produce flour until 1951, but it did so with carloads of wheat transported from the Great Plains.[21]

Another grain crop that became increasingly common throughout the decades between the Civil War and the Great Depression was grown for its juice. An African plant introduced to the United States in the late antebellum period, *Sorghum bicolor* is a tall, cane-like grass that thrives in the hot, dry summers

Cassville Milling Company, Cassville, Missouri. Courtesy of Lynn Morrow Papers (R1000), folder 757, State Historical Society of Missouri, Rolla.

of the Ozarks and whose cooked juices provided generations of Ozarkers an alternative to store-bought cane sugar. Sorghum syrup—or "molasses," as most Ozarkers called it—became a common treat in the region's homes after the Civil War, though a widespread commercial market never developed. Its cooking process remains a symbol of a romanticized, simpler Ozarks. And a master sorghum maker lived on in community memory long after his demise. On rare occasions he received his accolades on this side of the grave, as when Wayne County's Jade Melton won first prize for his molasses at the 1904 Louisiana Purchase Exposition in St. Louis.[22]

Most early sorghum mills were portable affairs consisting of little more than a cane press, a guide pole, and a long copper pan with wooden sidings. In late summer or early fall, makers transported their equipment to a level spot, built a makeshift furnace of stone and mortar to hold the pan, and harnessed a horse or mule to the pole that connected to gears perched on an elevated tripod. Farmers brought wagonloads of stripped cane to feed into the press as the animal's circular path powered the rollers that squeezed juice into a trough leading to a large barrel, whence a tube conveyed it via gravity flow to the evaporator pan. As the juice cooked and frothed in the hot pan, the maker skimmed green scum from the seething surface with a flat-bottomed wooden scoop and gradually moved the thickening juice through a series of baffles until it was cooked to the consistency and color preferred by the customer. The finished syrup was drained through a hole at the end of the pan into a crock, jar, or barrel. The sweetness drew stinging yellow jackets. It also attracted human visitors who conversed over glasses of the tangy, yellow "cider" made from the water used to clean the pan. Children played in the mound of squeezed stalks, or "plummies." A good crop of sorghum promised a winter of popcorn balls and molasses cookies and a year's worth of "long sweetening" on biscuits, to say nothing of the green scum and plummies that fattened hogs.[23]

No part of the harvesting and processing of the region's most ubiquitous grain, corn, inspires the nostalgic reverence reserved for bygone sorghum making, though the few old gristmills that survive in the twenty-first century remain objects of romantic curiosity. On the social side, corn generated the occasional husking bee, in which neighbors gathered in a shed or barn to remove ears from shucks amid singing and storytelling. Whatever dignity there was at a husking dissipated when a young man discovered a reddened ear beneath the shucks, for tradition dictated that the finder of crimson corn be rewarded with a kiss from the girl of his choice. Corn's myriad uses and its high caloric content made it far and away the most universal and essential crop on an Ozarks farm. Ozarkers turned the grain into hominy and cornmeal. They fed the grain and fodder to livestock and converted corn into batches of wildcat whiskey. They found the materials for artistic expression in this most mundane product of the farm, from corn-shuck hats to delicate dolls. In rural Fulton County, Arkansas, shy Everett Sutton devoted solitary hours to the creation of an elaborate, miniature cornstalk-village model of the now-forgotten hamlet of Flora on the smooth white-sand floor of an abandoned chicken house. Even the crop's refuse held value, for no roost pole or outhouse was well supplied without its pile of cobs.[24]

"Put a turn of corn on my horse and took my gun and led my horse to the mill 2 miles distant," reads young farmer and Confederate veteran John J. Sitton's account of an October day in Oregon County, Missouri, in 1869.[25] The trip to the mill with a "turn of corn"—or a wagonload for those who faced a longer journey—was a common occurrence, a reflection of cornmeal's crucial role in the Ozarker's diet and the gristmill's central function in Ozarks society. A place for trading horses, swapping stories, and disseminating news, mills of various sizes and grinding capacities appeared throughout the region in the last third of the nineteenth century. Many relied on water power, of which there was no shortage in the karst Ozark upland, while steam-driven mills became increasingly common as the twentieth century neared.

Farmers of the Springfield Plain grew prodigious amounts of corn. By 1889, a year in which Ozarkers harvested well over fifty million bushels, nine of the top ten corn-producing counties lay in this subregion. Farmers on the Springfield Plain continued to pace the region two decades later when corn production in the counties of the Ozark upland peaked at more than sixty million bushels.[26] Though corn was more likely to generate significant cash payments in fertile areas, it was more integral to farming operations among Ozarkers in marginal, rugged places. In hilly subregions with few level fields, farmers depended on corn's versatility and hardiness, often devoting most of their cropland to maize. A study conducted in the World War I era, for instance, revealed that farmers in poor, sparsely populated Carter and Reynolds counties in Missouri's rugged Courtois Hills planted over 90 percent of their tilled land in corn. It was often in such remote places that converting corn into whiskey was a more efficient and profitable use, for a wagonload of wildcat liquor was worth a lot more money than a wagonload of corn. More commonly, Ozarkers in remote areas with limited access to markets sent their corn to town on four legs. In the late fall in mountainous Newton County, Arkansas, in the 1880s, Joseph Moss and a neighbor drove their corn-fattened hogs over the Boston Mountains into the Arkansas Valley, butchered them, and sold the meat.[27]

Razorback's Range

The marketing of animals and meat was not as dominant in the postwar agricultural economy as it had been in antebellum days, but livestock raising remained an integral part of the rural Ozarker's livelihood. Though the Civil War took a terrible toll on hogs and other livestock, the region's swine population rebounded quickly, exploding to an all-time recorded high of almost two million by 1880, or about two and a half pigs for each person living in the Ozarks. With the Ozarkers' pork-heavy diet, many if not most of these animals ended up in the smokehouse. Catching a free-range razorback pig was no simple task but one made easier with the assistance of a good hog-catching dog trained to clamp hold of an animal's ear or leg and hold on until the master arrived. Once caught in autumn, hogs were penned and fattened for a month to ten weeks on corn, wheat shorts and bran, sorghum scum, and sometimes purslane, a nutritious plant that Ozarkers dubbed "pigweed" and considered a rank imposter in gardens.[28]

The fall or winter hog killing was one of the most important communal labor events of the rural calendar. When the first "solid cold" arrived, neighbors and extended families converged for several days of hard work, reminiscing, and fancy eating. Men got the process started by killing the hog and dipping the carcass in a barrel of scalding water to loosen the hair. The scraped pig was suspended on a gambrel stick for gutting and transferred to a scaffold for butchering. The expert butchers of the bunch removed hams, shoulders, and sides and salted them away in a "meat box" for up to two months, at which point they were hung inside the smokehouse to season over a smoldering pile of hickory shavings and corn cobs. Women mixed fat with meat from the ribs and backbone to make sausage, some of which they stuffed in long white cloth stockings sealed by dipping them in boiling lard. They fried the rest of the sausage and sealed it in crocks or jars. For several days after a killing, the host family and their helpers dined on the parts always consumed fresh: ribs and backbone, liver, melt (spleen), heart, jowl, and brains, the latter almost always cooked and served with eggs, as were squirrel brains. Few Ozarkers made chitlins from the animal's intestines, though head cheese, or "souse," always found a taker. Made by seasoning the boiled meat scraped from the head and feet, head cheese was sometimes fried in pancake batter to make it less offensive to the finicky or, among those of German descent, mixed with liver to make liverwurst. Women rendered lard by boiling the pig's fat in large kettles; they skimmed off the tiny bits of meat that floated to the surface for use as cracklings in cornbread. The lard was stored away for use as cooking grease and for the home manufacturing of lye soap.

When a hog killing came to an end, a single family might have processed and put away the meat of as many as half a dozen pigs dressing out at an average of three hundred pounds. The rest of the fattened pigs were destined for market. For most farmers in the Ozarks, this meant waiting for the arrival of the hog drovers. "Hog drovers, hog drovers, hog drovers / We're courting your daughter so rare, so fair / Can we get lodgin' here, O here / Can we get lodgin' here?" ask the shady traveling men of an old play-party song with Irish roots. No wonder George Washington Woodruff sequestered drovers in his barn loft when they lotted their animals overnight at his Crawford County, Missouri, farm in the 1870s. Given the drover's reputation as a "pretty low outfit," it is no surprise that the farmer of the song denied them so much as a barn loft for rest, for "this is my daughter that sits by my side / No hog drover can make her his bride." No matter the probity or infamy of their drovers, passels of hogs crisscrossed the Ozarks on their way to be sold and butchered in St. Louis, Kansas City, and Little Rock or to the nearest railroad holding pen. Drovers traveled with multiple wagonloads of corn, a surefire way to coax hogs into following the trail from one farm to the next. On particularly long treks, the drove of pigs could expand to dangerous size. Drover Ben Elder and his crew gathered a mass of more than thirteen hundred hogs one drought-stricken summer and drove them all the way to Kansas, where the animals broke free from their pens in Olathe and enjoyed a night on the town.[29]

Butchering hogs, Des Arc, Missouri, c. 1909. Courtesy of John F. Bradbury Jr. Collection, RA1652 (unprocessed at time of publication), State Historical Society of Missouri, Rolla.

In the remote Boston Mountains of southern Madison County, Arkansas, farmer William Asbury Green Smith and his neighbors did not wait for the drovers, choosing instead to drive their own hogs the fifty miles to Mulberry on the Little Rock and Fort Smith Railroad in the 1870s. Relying on dogs and older boys to handle the herding chores, the farmers loaded down wagons with corn and a variety of other products to sell to Mulberry merchants, including hides, ginseng, tallow, sorghum, maple syrup, dried fruits, and quilts. On the back half of the three-week journey, the drovers turned teamsters, hauling neighbors' orders back to the mountains.[30]

Drives became less common in the early twentieth century as stock laws began to close the open range, first in more prosperous and progressive areas and eventually in more rugged places as well. Webbed wire enclosures and highbred swine—Durocs, Berkshires, and Poland Chinas—were the marks of progressive farming. These highbreds lacked the old razorback's toughness and adaptability, but they made more efficient use of feed by putting on weight more rapidly. Overall, hog raising in the Ozarks entered a period of slow decline in the 1880s as the pig population in the region dipped by about 30 percent in the next four decades.[31]

The steady destruction of forests—ideal razorback habitat—was one reason for the decline in hogs. Beyond the woods on the prairie lands and treeless plateaus, the abundance of wild grasses created ideal habitats for sheep and cattle. Sheep were valued for their wool, but few Ozarkers developed a taste for mutton. Soldiers and bushwhackers apparently had little appetite for lamb or hogget as well, for the 1870 census found sheep outnumbering cattle in the Ozarks. Sheep raising in the region experienced a dramatic rise in the early twentieth century as railroads and university experts promoted wool and lamb production as a logical use of the landscape in the infertile uplands of the Central Plateau and the cutover riverine hills. Flocks in the Ozarks grew by more than one-third in the first decade of the new century, with sheep outnumbering cattle and people in rugged interior Missouri areas like Laura Ingalls Wilder's Wright County. The era witnessed ambitious attempts by newcomers to convert denuded forest lands into massive sheep ranches. Beset by ecological abuse and limited marketing opportunities, most failed, as did Robert Hopson Tate's early twentieth-century venture to run thousands of Angora goats in the Boston Mountains of Arkansas. On the positive side, Hop Tate's daughters proved to be skillful goatherds, and one of them met her future husband on the job. It was a romantic origin story that perhaps no other couple in the region could claim.[32]

The effort to establish a lasting sheep-raising industry in the Ozarks failed as well. By 1920 cattle numbers in the region dwarfed those of sheep by more than four to one. The year 1920 also marked the first census in which the cattle population exceeded the number of pigs in the Ozarks. It was a marked reversal from forty years earlier, when hogs outnumbered cows almost three to one. The Ozark region may not have qualified as cattle country just yet, but it had made great strides in that direction.[33]

It would take more than half a century for the region to approach its prewar per capita production numbers, but the cattle population of the Ozarks mushroomed in the late nineteenth century, growing by more than 250 percent alone in the two decades following 1870. By 1890 Ozarkers owned well over one million head, twice the number of cattle found in the region on the eve of the Civil War. Existing outside the popular romance of western cowboy culture, the cattle industry occupied a rather stealthy prominence in the Ozarks. As one cattle drover noted in the late nineteenth century, livestock buyers "scatter more money over the country among the farmers and stock growers than all other men put together." While farmers in the Springfield Plain and the livestock-heavy northern Ozarks ranked among the region's leaders in cattle production, counties in rugged, less fertile areas also produced large numbers for market, with cows outnumbering people by more than two to one in such marginal Missouri counties as Ozark, Taney, and Hickory by 1920.[34]

The cattle drover or cowboy escaped the public opprobrium reserved for the lowly hog drover. Yet the two characters played essentially identical roles in their respective livestock systems, traveling well-worn trails at designated times of the year and paying cash for animals to add to their market-bound menageries. Returning to his home in Searcy County, Arkansas, after the war, Union veteran John Morris bought cattle from neighbors and profited from long drives to Fort Scott, Kansas, and Sedalia, Missouri. To the west in Madison County, James Wilson groused to a brother that "my Stock has Et moor this winter than I cold sell the Stock for at this time," but ten months later, after a successful drive to Argenta (North Little Rock), he promised to commence "buying young cattel as soon as I go home." Like hog drovers, cattle buyers traveled with hired hands and wagonloads of provisions, lotting their cattle at night and purchasing feed at farms noted as "stock pits." At Gainesville, Missouri, John Harlin maintained a stock pit for cattle drives on their way to West Plains. Drives through Ozark County continued well into the twentieth century. John's son Hugh recalled making a three-day drive to West Plains with his brother in the early days of the Depression, the teenagers spending nights in Tecumseh and Pottersville along the way.[35]

The Harlins's destination was the stockyard at the Frisco Railroad. As rail lines penetrated farther into the remote Ozarks in the decades after the Civil War, cattle drives contracted, most of them heading no farther than the nearest depot with livestock facilities. The McCaskill brothers began driving herds of cattle from Shannon and Texas counties to Springfield or to the railhead at Salem, Missouri, in the early 1880s. When the Current River Railroad dissected Shannon County later in the decade, the McCaskills built a large barn at the railroad town of Low Wassie, bringing an end to their long drives. Situated on a branch line of the Frisco south of Springfield, the town of Ozark, Missouri, developed into a major magnet for drovers in the White River hill country to the south, reportedly eclipsing all other Frisco stations in cattle shipping by the early 1900s.[36]

Different factors contributed to the expansion of cattle populations, and the oppositional styles of cattle raising ultimately led to friction within communities. In the 1890s and early 1900s, farmers in some of the region's most marginal and remote areas turned to cattle as a more efficient alternative to staple crops. An 1898 correspondent from Wiley's Cove in the Boston Mountains of Arkansas informed readers of the *Arkansas Gazette* that area farmers had recently abandoned cotton, resulting in a "conversion of everything into live stock for the market." The Boston Mountains, White River Hills, and other rugged Ozark subregions teemed with free-range cattle bearing the brands of their owners, some of whom owned not an acre of land. Raised in Ripley County, Missouri,

Harry Thaxton recalled driving herds of cattle to Doniphan from the rugged country between Buffalo and Brier creeks, where as many as three thousand head roamed the open range in the World War I era. In the Boston Mountains of northern Pope County, Arkansas, Scott Page "had no idea how many cows and hogs he owned and often where they were to be found," recalled his grandson. "When the cattle buyers came, and most of the cattle were driven in out of the woods, the numbers were astounding."[37]

Even as rugged, infertile stretches of the Ozarks filled with cattle, "progressive" agriculturists began importing Shorthorn, Angus, Hereford, and other purebred animals to improve the bloodlines of the region's scrub stock. Such a financial investment motivated progressive farmers to push for stock laws that closed the range in a designated area. Often pitting haves against have-nots, the stock law controversy generated intense emotions and resentments on both sides. "The pride of the elite was often cramped by the lack of a stock law," noted one chronicler of turn-of-the-century life in northern Arkansas. The elite, aided by their much more numerous middling kinfolk and neighbors, gradually carried the day in prosperous subregions like the Springfield Plain. By 1901 the rural Spring River country of eastern Jasper County, Missouri, was off limits to roaming livestock, allowing a Bowers Mill farmer to corral cattle trespassing in his cornfield and charge their owners fifty cents per head in damages. At the height of the Progressive Era in the decade before World War I, stock law debates even penetrated more rugged areas of the Ozarks. In the hills of Douglas County, Missouri, the small town of Ava passed a stock law in 1908. Seven years later five Douglas townships followed suit in a tight vote, becoming the first rural areas in the county to close the range. In 1928 a controversial referendum closed the range throughout the county, despite the efforts of voters in three remote townships to fight the order.[38]

Douglas County may have taken a "progressive" turn in the early twentieth century, but broad swaths of the Ozarks remained open-range territory at the onset of the Great Depression—some southeastern Missouri districts into the 1960s. Like their razorback peers, the scrub cattle that populated the range tended to be smaller and leaner than their purebred cousins but sturdier and less prone to disease as well. No threat to bovine fitness generated more legislation, lost revenue, and social unrest than did *babesiosis*, better known as Texas fever, an ailment caused by protozoa living inside ticks that sickened and sometimes killed cattle. The purebred stock of progressive Ozarkers and midwestern cattlemen was highly susceptible to *babesiosis*, prompting the U.S. Department of Agriculture (USDA) to impose a quarantine on infected areas in 1891. In the Ozarks the quarantine line tended to follow the state line, which meant that during most of the year it was illegal to ship or drive Arkansas cattle northward into Missouri. Taking no chances, the Missouri General Assembly enacted a year-round ban on imports of Arkansas cattle, prompting a war of words between the two states and a retaliatory Arkansas bill that limited the importation of Missouri mules.[39]

Looking to alleviate a budding sectional conflict by ridding the South of the disease-carrying arachnids, in 1906 Congress appropriated funds to the USDA for an extensive tick-eradication program to be administered by the Bureau of Animal Industry (BAI). Not surprisingly, farmers in the prosperous Springfield Plain responded most positively to the BAI's voluntary program. After building concrete dipping vats under the direction of BAI agents and the state veterinarian, farmers in northwestern Arkansas and in the counties bordering Missouri brought their cattle to designated dipping locations to be dunked in solutions of poison and water. Not all Ozarkers reacted so favorably to a program that seemed to cater to the interests of more prosperous agriculturists and that was almost always coordinated on a local level by these same farmers. In some neighborhoods open-range cattle owners objected to the burdensome task of rounding up animals that were most likely immune to the ravages of Texas fever and driving them to the nearest dipping vat. Fines levied on undipped cattle did not improve the skeptic's disposition. In a few extreme cases, opponents dynamited dipping vats, and in the White River Hills of Izard County nightriders drove a "tick inspector" from his home. The aggression reached its crescendo amid a renewed dipping movement after World War I, when suspected aggrieved cattlemen ambushed two farmers-turned-tick-inspectors on Hutchinson Mountain in Independence County, leaving one dead and another wounded. The struggle over tick eradication continued for another year or so until all the Arkansas Ozarks counties saw their quarantine lifted.[40]

The controversy over cattle tick eradication was the region's most colorful example of the introduction of government- and industry-supported scientific agriculture and the class animosities that it sometimes stirred. Though often portrayed as a symbol of backwoods Ozarkers' cultural predisposition to fight government intervention and reject modernity, opposition to the dipping program, according to historian J. Blake Perkins, more accurately reflected "the rural dispossessed's populist defiance against 'well-bred' locals." Besides, it was the Ozarkers' willing participation in the agricultural marketplace that motivated the strongest reactions.[41] In the years that followed the murder of the tick inspector, Vance Randolph and other seekers of anachronism would construct a vision of the Ozarks around the folks of the backcountry who seemed to stubbornly hold on to the past. They weren't likely to enamor folklorists and travel writers, but progressive-minded Ozarkers were just as integral to the story of the region. The conflicts among Ozarkers themselves—between local elites and their poorer neighbors—were ultimately more crucial than an imagined cultural rejection of the outside world.

Land of the Big Red Apple

Nothing exercised a greater influence on agricultural change in the period between the Civil War and the Great Depression than the progressive agricultural establishment, which was anchored in the nation's land-grant university system and allied with railroad companies and emerging agribusiness interests. In the Ozarks the establishment had its earliest and most immediate impact in the Springfield Plain of northwestern Arkansas, where the state university served as a beacon of scientific farming. When federal funding supported the creation of the university-allied Arkansas Agricultural Experiment Station in Fayetteville in 1888, Ozarkers in the Springfield Plain benefited from the station's scientific reports and from institutes conducted by station personnel. The federal government's creation of the cooperative extension service on the eve of World War I promised to disseminate scientific-farming knowledge to farm families across the nation using county agents employed by land-grant universities. Still, because these agents had to be partially funded by the counties themselves, years passed before extension and home demonstration agents became commonplace in the region's poorest counties.[42]

Before the regularization of the cooperative extension service, railroad agricultural agents largely filled the void as disseminators of scientific agriculture. It was railroad promotion that led to the Ozark region's second experiment station. Upon the completion of the Kansas City, Fort Scott, and Memphis Railroad (KCFS&M) in the early 1880s, the line's agents incessantly boosted south-central Missouri to potential immigrants as the "Land of the Big Red Apple." The tree fruit industry expanded so rapidly in the region in the late nineteenth century that the Missouri General Assembly ordered the building of the Missouri State Fruit Experiment Station in 1899 just north of the small railroad town of Mountain Grove. Within a few years, farmers in this subregion—or at least those who, like the Wilders, lived comparatively near the railroad—could attend institutes on orchards and ground fruits and view educational displays transported up and down the line in railroad cars.[43]

Nothing in the story of the post–Civil War Ozarks better exemplified the influence of progressive agriculture and railroad promotion than fruit farming. Interest in fruits, especially orchards, emerged in the early years of the postwar era. In Texas County, Missouri, Billy West maintained small orchards of apple, peach, pear, and plum trees, kept bee gums near the orchards, and built a shed equipped with a woodstove for use as a drying kiln. In remote Newton County, Arkansas, Union veteran Isaac Coonrod Wishon ordered seedlings from a Nashville mail-order nursery and invested in an evaporator and kiln. The wagon ride out of Low Gap was too long and treacherous to market fruit, but the Wishons made apple butter and preserves and canned and dried fruit for winter.[44]

But the Wests, Wishons, and anyone else with dreams of profitable fruit farming were simply in the wrong place before the arrival of the railroad. The marketing potential opened up by rail service was the key to this profitable new endeavor. Within five years of the 1869 arrival of the railroad at Lebanon, Missouri, Union veteran Charles Draper was hard at work developing his Laclede County fruit farm, putting in rows of pear, plum, and cherry trees and a dizzying array of now-forgotten apple varieties, from Rambos and White Winter Pearmains to Red Junes and Yellow Bellflowers. Down the tracks in Greene County, Ira Sherwin Haseltine, a Vermont-born immigrant from Wisconsin, began buying land along the rails in 1871, where he and his sons set out some seven thousand apple trees during their first three years in the Ozarks. A new peach tree might start paying back its owner in its third year, and an apple tree generally took eight to ten years to turn a profit for the first time, making the orchard business off limits to all but the most prosperous agriculturists.[45]

The extension of a Frisco line into northwestern Arkansas and the completion of the KCFS&M across south-central Missouri in the early 1880s provided the boost needed to spark a regional transformation. A commercial orchardist who couldn't hear a locomotive's whistle was as rare as a September frost. The last two decades of the nineteenth century ushered in an age of corporate outside investment in the rural Ozarks as capitalists from St. Louis and Kansas City and from as far away as New York gobbled up tens of thousands of acres along the rails. Perhaps the largest such endeavor involved the Ozark Plateau Land Company. Owned by a group of investors from Buffalo, New York, the company eventually held rights to roughly one hundred thousand acres spread across four Missouri counties, from Camden southward to Webster. New York native Absalom Nelson came to Missouri to manage the firm's marketing efforts in 1882 and became one of the most powerful voices for the orchard industry in the Ozarks. Settling on a farm on the outskirts of Lebanon, he produced award-winning fruit through his Nelson's Apple House and reportedly landed an order from the British royal family. More importantly, he promoted orchards on the tens of thousands of acres of farmland sold by the company and became one of the premier spokespersons for the Ozarks apple industry through his involvement in the Missouri State Horticultural Society and the Missouri Board of Agriculture.[46]

This corporate element also promoted conformity in the name of economic efficiency. Louis Erb, a German immigrant who established a large orchard and summer resort at Cedar Gap, Missouri, became an early champion of the Ben Davis, a sturdy, deep-red variety that wintered well and lent the region its "Land of the Big Red Apple" moniker. Admitting that the Ben Davis was "really not a fine eating apple," he nonetheless urged fellow promoters to "impress upon the minds of your fruit growers to plant only a few varieties of apples,

Wickersham Orchard, Koshkonong, Missouri. Courtesy of Lynn Morrow Papers
(R1000), folder 816, State Historical Society of Missouri, Rolla.

... always having an eye to large fruit." By the early twentieth century, the Ben
Davis accounted for perhaps 75 percent of the trees in commercial orchards, its
ubiquity inspiring the name of a village just a few miles north of the Missouri
State Fruit Experiment Station. The adoption of the Ben Davis as the apple of
choice ultimately had a negative effect on the region's orchard industry, as the
development of freezer cars and cold storage facilities gave preference to tastier,
more delicate apples and led to a backlash against the big red apple of the Ozarks
and against its champion, Louis Erb.[47]

Nowhere was the impact of outside investment more obvious than along the
route of the KCFS&M, especially south of Willow Springs, where the "southern
slope of the Ozark range" was touted as the nation's next great peach-producing
area. The orchard lands of Howell and Oregon counties were almost wholly
owned by post-railroad newcomers to the region or by absentee developers. Near
Koshkonong—named by a railroad employee for a lake in Wisconsin—several
large orchards produced peaches and apples by the turn of the century, including such corporate entities as the Iowa Fruit Company, Frisco Fruit Company,
and St. Elmo Fruit Farm. Eight miles north sat Brandsville, creation of wealthy
Chicagoan Michael Brand, who purchased seventeen thousand acres on which
to set an orchard and vineyard and raise livestock. Located in the "center of
the Missouri Peach Belt" was West Plains, a town of almost four thousand
people whose fruit-related industries included cold storage facilities, a dried fruit
warehouse, and vinegar and cider factories. A few miles north of West Plains,

Hector D. Mackay, a New York–born Kansan, entered the fruit business near the railroad stop he named Pomona in honor of the Roman goddess of fruitful abundance. No orchard developer on the "southern slope" left a more colorful legacy than Col. Jay L. Torrey, a Wyoming rancher and onetime St. Louis attorney who bought more than ten thousand acres west of Koshkonong. Torrey promoted his European-style planned community as perfect for orchards and ideal "for the cultivation of the mind by a residence in the village" of Fruitville. When his utopian vision failed to take shape, he tried unsuccessfully to have the Missouri state government relocated to Fruitville after fire destroyed the capitol in Jefferson City in 1911.[48]

Northerners and other newcomers to the Ozarks dominated the affairs of horticultural societies and marketing associations. They also dictated the narrative that underlay much of the fruit industry's promotion, a familiar discourse calling on Yankee know-how and industry to supplant the ignorance of the native population. "All that is now wanting to make Southwest Missouri the leading fruit-growing locality of the world," Absalom Nelson informed the mostly northern readers of a boosterish tract for the KCFS&M, "is live, wideawake, energetic and progressive men, who will force the old fogy element into the last ditch." Though fellow New Yorker George T. Powell declared that "agriculture is yet in a primitive condition" in southern Missouri in the early 1890s, he observed that "in 60 or 90 days from the time a Northern settler has come in here he has from 10 to 40 acres of land cleared . . . and orchards set, where so short a time previous the forest stood."[49]

The Central Plateau of southern Missouri, with its recent devastation during the Civil War, provided a blank slate to newcomers. But the situation across the region in the Springfield Plain of northwestern Arkansas was more complex. It was there, in the counties of Benton and Washington, that the orchard industry of the Ozarks reached its pinnacle. In antebellum days this agricultural oasis had gained a reputation for fruit production, and even before the arrival of the railroad, commercial orchards dotted the landscape. Visiting the area in 1872, a Methodist bishop witnessed "magnificent" orchards, the apples from which were the "boast of everybody." Three years later a Fayetteville man expressed his intention to send a barrel of the region's finest apples to a Wisconsin editor to boost the area's "reputation abroad, for fruit raising."[50]

By the time the Frisco's St. Louis, Arkansas, and Texas Railway penetrated northwestern Arkansas in 1881, Benton and Washington counties were poised to take their places among the nation's great fruit producers. Northwestern Arkansas also attracted its share of transplants. Goldsmith Davis found his way from Minnesota to Benton County in 1867 and twenty-two years later owned the county's largest orchard and nursery. More than other fruit-producing Ozarks locales, however, Benton and Washington counties reflected a balance between newcomers and old settlers. Representing the latter cohort, brothers Lee and George Britt established a nursery midway between Bentonville and Rogers in 1888, from which they eventually shipped fruit seedlings across the United States and to Europe. To the south in Washington County, former planter and slaveholder Dick Bean looked to tap the new market with his Cane Hill Canning and Evaporating Company.[51]

Unlike the territory along the KCFS&M, northwestern Arkansas was not dominated by massive corporate orchards. In Benton County, the most fruit-dependent county in all the Ozarks, small owner-operated farms were the norm. An early twentieth-century promotional pamphlet for the Kansas City Southern Railway observed thick settlement in the vicinity of the railroad town of Gentry, where some twenty-five hundred people clustered into farmsteads averaging only forty acres. The same booklet described the area around the county's largest town, Rogers, as "a country of small holdings, intensely cultivated." Of all the counties of the interior Ozarks, only Greene County, Missouri, had a smaller average farm size than Benton's 93.1 acres in 1910.[52]

In 1889 Washington County produced more apples than any other county in the state or region, while neighboring Madison County ranked as the leading peach-growing county in the Ozarks. Buoyed by experiment station research and railroad promotion, fruit production in Benton and Washington counties and in the prairie portions of Carroll and Madison counties exploded in the subsequent thirty years. By the turn of the century, practically every railroad town claimed fruit-shipping warehouses, an evaporator plant, and local marketing associations. Larger towns boasted canneries, cold storage facilities, and vinegar plants, as well as ancillary industries such as barrel factories and stave mills. The burgeoning fruit industry also spurred the building of additional rail lines. After years of clamoring by orchardists, the Ozark and Cherokee Central connected Fayetteville and Okmulgee, Oklahoma, providing convenient shipping for farmers in Farmington, Prairie Grove, and other towns along the route. The Kansas City and Memphis Railroad built a short line from Fayetteville to Cave Springs. With canneries springing up along its tracks and its heavy cargoes of apples, grapes, and strawberries, the shipper was known as the "Fruit Belt Line" until its demise during World War I.[53]

Despite the fickle nature of fruit farming, it had become the cash-crop focus for farm families in northwestern Arkansas by the turn of the century. In 1899 Washington and Benton counties combined to produce more than 1.17 million bushels of apples, 25 percent of the entire output of the Ozarks. A bumper crop two years later sent more than four hundred carloads of apples rolling out of Rogers alone, and the 2.5 million bushels harvested in Benton County was reputed to be the largest yield for a single U.S. county to that time. The 1904 Louisiana Purchase Exposition (World's Fair) in St. Louis only enhanced

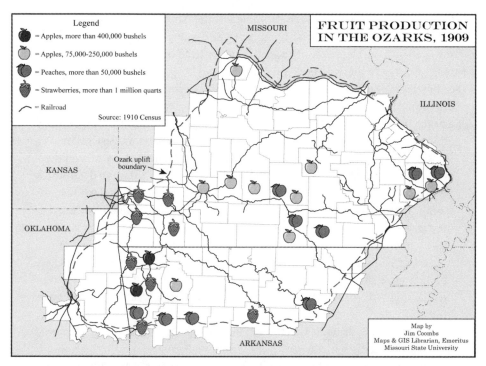

Fruit Production in the Ozarks, 1909. Courtesy of Jim Coombs, Missouri State University, Springfield.

the growing legend, as northwestern Arkansas orchards dominated the apple prizes. Two years later the area's booming orchard industry prompted U.S. senator James H. Berry to secure a branch of the U.S. Weather Bureau for his hometown of Bentonville—reportedly the smallest town in the nation to claim a first-order office. Census takers recorded gargantuan apple numbers in 1919. Benton County's 3.18 million bushels alone made up 40 percent of the output of the Ozarks.[54]

No one made greater use of the "Land of the Big Red Apple" slogan than did the boosters of the KCFS&M. But much of this line's orchard space was devoted to the peach and not the apple. Even more subject to untimely frosts and disease than were apples, peaches tended to produce all-or-nothing crops in the Ozarks. But the bumper crops could be so profitable that orchardists tolerated the more numerous bust years. In the corporate farm–dominated "Peach Belt" of Oregon and Howell counties, successive bonanza crops between 1912 and 1915 necessitated the recruiting of thousands of temporary laborers and filled hundreds of train cars with brimming peach crates. But the run of good luck offered false hope in a place whose latitude and elevation rendered it too susceptible to late freezes. The area that had been promoted as the "southern slope of the Ozark mountains" was in fact too far north, and the commercial peach industry that survived into the Depression era was located instead on the true southern slope of the Ozarks in the Arkansas Valley.[55]

Beset with San Jose scale, cedar rust, codling moths, and years of climatic unpredictability, Ozarkers in the post–World War I era faced a future without a peach belt or the big red apple. With production falling after the bumper crop of 1919, the town of Rogers launched its annual Apple Blossom Festival in 1923, featuring a parade, beauty queens, a carnival, and anything else you would expect to encounter at a small-town celebration. But the festival was a deathwatch for a once-vibrant world that burst into fragrant greens, pinks, and whites each spring. Town fathers pulled the plug after the fifth one. Ultimately, the commercial orchard industry of the Ozarks experienced a long, slow demise. There was no mistaking the symbolism in 1939 when the image of an apple that had long adorned license plates for Rogers residents was replaced with a chicken. The U.S. government issued its own decree on the death of the region's commercial orchards three years later when it shuttered the Weather Bureau office in Bentonville.[56]

As much as anything, it was the gradual process of market integration that doomed orchardists in the Ozarks. Climatic advantages and irrigation advances granted growers in the Pacific Northwest the upper hand. Relying on Wenatchee's now-iconic Red Delicious, the state of Washington laid claim to 20 percent of the U.S. market by the end of World War I, far outdistancing the production of the Ozarks. Like cotton and wheat farming in the Ozarks, the region's orchard industry ultimately succumbed to the jumble of forces operating to ensure market efficiency across the sprawling but increasingly integrated landscape of the United States. Thousands of farm families in the Ozarks went back to the drawing board, searching for the next big thing to bring prosperity to the region. Thousands of Ozarkers hit the migrant trails to supply a generation of cheap labor to the winners in the nation's orchard race.[57]

Truck Crops

The commercial production of tomatoes accompanied the orchard boom in the region. Among the earliest tomato farmers in the Ozarks were orchardists who planted tomatoes among their fruit trees for a few years until the trees became productive. It was such farmers who found a market for their tomatoes at a new cannery in Springdale, Arkansas, in 1885, the earliest-known commercial canning operation in the region. In the following years, small canneries sprang up along the rails. By 1900 one out of every five cans of tomatoes in the United States originated in the Ozarks. Commercial canning was such a major concern in the early twentieth century that a canning factory *factory* opened in Springfield in 1904. Thomas Brown's Canning Factory Company manufactured and sold five different sizes of portable canners, ranging from a small model capable of only eight hundred cans per day to a machine cranking out fifty-five hundred. The availability of Brown's small canners provided ambitious entrepreneurs an affordable path to the position of rural industrialist. In 1905, for instance, young Roy Nelson invested one thousand dollars in machinery and facilities and packed his father's large tomato crop on their Webster County farm. Nelson opened about a dozen other canneries in the years to come, and by 1924 the factories belonging to the "Tomato King of the Ozarks" produced 18 percent of the region's product.[58]

The number of tomato canneries operating in the Ozarks exploded at the very moment Roy Nelson was establishing himself in the industry. By 1908 Nelson's native Webster County contained dozens of canning operations, and small canneries sprang up from corner to corner in the region, from Cincinnati, Arkansas, to Ellsinore, Missouri. The plentiful farmer-canners of the early years gradually gave way to fewer, larger canning factories that supplied seed and fertilizer to contract growers who agreed to sell their crops at a predetermined price. One attraction of the system was that farm families could earn additional income as factory workers. Operating up to four months a year, canneries hired boys to wash tomatoes and load them into wire baskets for scalding. From there the tomatoes were taken in wooden buckets to an assembly line of girls who cored them and removed the skin. Women packers filled the cans, which were then sealed, bathed in hot water, crimped, labeled, and boxed. With the abundant supply of labor in the Ozarks, fillers and packers still routinely received only a nickel a bucket at the end of the Depression. Hourly employees brought home as little as a dollar for an eight-hour day. But any cash was precious cash in poor places like Missouri's Stone and Taney counties, which together contained about sixty seasonal canneries by the 1920s.[59]

Tomato farming increased after World War I as national consumption soared and commission brokers continued to find buyers for Ozarks-canned tomatoes from the Great Lakes to the Gulf of Mexico. Nowhere was this trend more noticeable than in southwestern Missouri and northern Arkansas, where agriculturists looked for crops to replace orchards. By 1925 farmers in McDonald County, Missouri, devoted three thousand acres to tomatoes. The cannery in the railroad town of Anderson pumped seventy-five thousand dollars into the local economy through factory wages and payments for crops. It and the county's seventeen other canning factories shipped more than two hundred carloads of canned tomatoes that year, a total value of more than three hundred thousand dollars. Even greater was production in the rugged White River Hills to the east. In 1926 the White River Division of the Missouri Pacific Railroad shipped

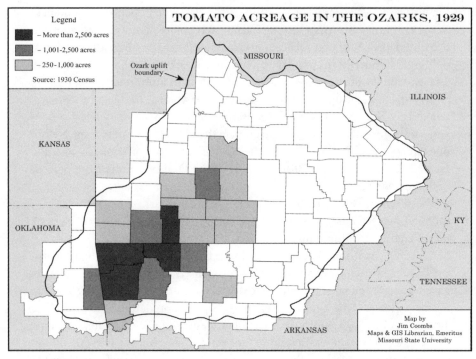

Tomato Acreage in the Ozarks, 1929. Courtesy of Jim Coombs, Missouri State
University, Springfield.

sixteen hundred carloads of canned tomatoes from canneries up and down the
line between Crane, Missouri, and Cotter, Arkansas.[60]

By the 1930s the tomato patch had become an apt symbol for life in the
hardscrabble Ozarks. A tough plant with deep roots that held fast to rocky,
thin-soiled hillsides through hot, dry summers, the tomato provided little more
than a barebones income, but it rarely left a hardworking clan with nothing. An
army of struggling families continued to supply local canners into the heart of
the Depression. By the end of the 1930s, the Ozark region's share of the national
canned tomato market had dropped from 12 percent at the onset of the Depression to less than 7 percent, but it remained a viable industry for the time being.
The poor farmer's desperation to earn cash income and the ability of small-scale
canners to turn a modest profit assured tomato farming's survival into the mid-
twentieth century.[61]

As a poor man's crop, tomatoes received less attention from scientific experts
and promoters than did fruits. Among the earliest fruits under study at the
experiment stations were grapes and strawberries, both of which made great

strides on Ozarks farms in the early twentieth century. Outside of the Ozark uplift's German fringe along the Missouri and Mississippi valleys, vineyards had never been a conspicuous part of Ozarks farming, but the interior Ozarks could lay claim to one of the nineteenth century's most renowned vintners. From his farm and vineyards in a rural community just east of Neosho, Missouri, Swiss immigrant Hermann Jaeger spent years grafting old-world cultivars to wild grape rootstocks to develop hardy vines. His disease-resistant rootstock saved the French wine industry from the devastating phylloxera root louse in 1880, an act for which he was later knighted into the French Legion of Honor. The other rare instances of nineteenth-century vineyard success in the interior Ozarks tended to be the work of farmers of German-speaking heritage as well. In the White River Hills southeast of Rogers, the Starck brothers established northwestern Arkansas's most notable early vineyard on their Vinola Wine Ranch, their products winning medals in the United States and in Europe.[62]

But it was immigrants from southern Europe who built the foundation of the region's grape-growing industry in the early twentieth century. Looking for a healthier climate and an opportunity for greater independence, a group of Italians recruited to labor on an Arkansas Delta plantation found their way to the northwestern part of the state and purchased land five miles west of Springdale in 1898. Within a decade about seventy Italian families owned more than fourteen hundred acres of prairie land in and around Tontitown, much of it devoted to vineyards. The first carloads of Tontitown grapes left Springdale in 1909. Far up the Frisco tracks in Phelps County, Missouri, another colony of Italians from the Arkansas Delta settled at Knobview in 1900 and that same year began their own vineyards with Concord cuttings from the gardens of Dillon, a tiny French settlement established a decade earlier about ten miles away. Knobview (later renamed Rosati) was smaller than Tontitown, but it followed its Arkansas sister with its own *festa della vendemmia* (festival of the grape harvest) and a local grape growers association.[63]

In an unusual twist, the onset of national prohibition in 1920 coincided with a period of tremendous growth in Ozarks vineyards. That same year the Welch Grape Juice Company began construction of a large plant in Springdale. Promoted by experiment station personnel and extension agents, grape growing experienced dramatic expansion in the 1920s, extending beyond Tontitown onto hundreds of non-Italian farms. Within three years Washington and Benton counties were home to five thousand acres of vineyards, more than 90 percent of them devoted to Welch's favored Concord grape. By 1926 the Welch plant received almost twelve hundred carloads of grapes from northwestern Arkansas growers alone, with additional shipments from southwestern Missouri and Rosati. Within a few years, two additional grape juice factories opened in Springdale, as well as two wineries in the post-Prohibition era.[64]

More widespread than grape growing in the early twentieth century was strawberry raising. For more than half a century, farmers of the Ozarks were major strawberry producers, and for much of that period no crop in the region provided a greater and more consistent return on investment. At the height of the strawberry industry, growers associations popped up around the Ozarks, but the heaviest production came from a corridor stretching from Crawford County, Arkansas, to Jasper and Lawrence counties in Missouri. Bolstered by the efforts of the Benton County Fruit Growers and Shippers' Union, the Fayetteville Fruit Growers' Association, and the Shippers' Union of Springdale, in 1899 pickers harvested almost four million quarts of strawberries from more than forty-one hundred acres in Arkansas's Benton and Washington counties.[65]

In southwestern Missouri the small town of Sarcoxie took an early lead in strawberry production. Its path to becoming "the most important strawberry shipping point in the west" owed much to one family. A German-born immigrant from Wisconsin, Herman Wild developed a small business that his sons expanded into James B. Wild & Bros. Nursery just a few years after the arrival of the railroad. By the early 1880s, the Wilds and their thirty-three employees shipped seedling trees and berry plants around the country. In 1883 James B. Wild persuaded local farmer John Carnahan to put strawberry beds in his apple orchard, and Carnahan's success convinced other Sarcoxie farmers to invest in plants from Wild & Bros. Within a few years the town began shipping carloads of berries. It was around the same time that James B. Wild's son Gilbert imported European rootstock and began a profitable flower business that would grant Sarcoxie the nickname "Peony Capital of the World" in the twentieth century.[66]

Railroad towns across southern Missouri became strawberry shipping points in the early twentieth century. A labor-intensive type of agriculture requiring long, late-winter days of building beds and setting plants, strawberry growing was epitomized by small acreages. In 1914 Missouri's leading strawberry producing county, Lawrence, counted 370 commercial strawberry farmers averaging just over three acres apiece. Still, profits could be substantial. A 1915 survey in Newton County, Missouri, discovered that strawberry farmers routinely cleared between $250 and $650 per acre. No wonder the residents of a rural neighborhood on the edge of Oliver's Prairie dubbed their community Aroma after the region's most popular variety of the fruit. Neosho became a major strawberry shipping point. Among the town's industries in the early twentieth century were a large cannery and a box factory that made strawberry crates from sycamore and black gum. The town's first annual Strawberry Festival, in June 1904, celebrated the harvest's shipment of 125 cars, each holding more than twelve thousand quarts. A preserving plant went up in Neosho in 1913, producing specifically for the soda fountain and ice cream parlor market.[67]

Strawberry pickers near Mount Vernon, Missouri, 1905. Courtesy of Lynn Morrow Papers (R1000), folder 834, State Historical Society of Missouri, Rolla.

In 1919 strawberry production in the region exceeded 15 million quarts, roughly 80 percent of which came from half a dozen contiguous counties stretching from Lawrence County, Missouri, down to Washington County, Arkansas. By this time Springdale, Arkansas, had become the Ozark region's preeminent fruit-shipping town, establishing an agricultural marketing foundation that would begin to transition into poultry and cattle a generation later. But in the days before World War II, it was strawberry pickers, not poultry plant workers, who flocked to the region in search of work, creating tent cities and forcing local authorities to deal with migrant worker issues.[68]

Local growers associations advertised in newspapers for the hundreds of pickers needed in each community. Made up of nearby town dwellers, school kids dismissed in early May for the harvest, or itinerant laborers who followed the nation's harvest trails, pickers received one to three cents per quart. For most of the region's strawberry growers, marketing involved the formidable Ozark Fruit Growers Association (OFGA), formed in Springfield in 1903 as an umbrella organization that could translate a much larger membership into a more powerful voice. The OFGA maintained a full-time secretary-treasurer's office on the Frisco in Rogers, Arkansas, and a seasonal general manager's office up the line at Monett, Missouri, and hired seasonal inspectors, graders, and field agents to maintain a quality crop. Representing members from around the Ozarks (including Almanzo Wilder), the OFGA contracted with commission agents in cities, while buyers from New York, Chicago, Boston, and other metropolitan centers set up shop in Monett during the harvest season. Eventually, the "most powerful force in Mississippi valley fruit marketing" expanded into apples, peaches, blackberries, tomatoes, and other crops.[69]

The high-powered marketing of fruit farmers in the prosperous Springfield Plain bore little resemblance, of course, to the farming activities of thousands of marginal families populating the more inaccessible portions of the Ozarks. In fact, farming on the westernmost reaches of the Springfield Plain differed significantly from that in southwestern Missouri and far northwestern Arkansas. In the old Cherokee Nation, where native and white farmers began acquiring ownership of individual allotments of land only five years after passage of the federal Curtis Act of 1898, orchard culture and truck farming made little headway before the Depression. The boundary separating Oklahoma from Arkansas and Missouri represented a "cultural fault line," according to geographer Leslie Hewes. On the west side of this line, farmers were much less likely than their Arkansas and Missouri neighbors to own the land they worked and much more likely to live in log houses and scratch out subsistence-style livings. This was especially true of Ozarkers who were at least one-half Cherokee by blood, the largest numbers of whom lived in the rugged Cookson Hills west of the Arkansas line.[70]

Such a marginal existence was just as common in other parts of the region. For many farmers in the Courtois Hills, Boston Mountains, and White River Hills, life was more about making do than making money. Even into the twentieth century, survival strategy in such areas included a diverse range of activities, from raising a few open-range pigs and hunting wild game to cutting timber and gathering marketable forest products. In the 1910s and 1920s, at his small store at Ponca in the rugged Buffalo River watershed of Arkansas, Lester Young bought from his customers black walnut meats, haw bark, and ginseng and golden seal roots. Ozarkers dug and sold a variety of other wild roots coveted for medicinal purposes—red puccoon, lady slipper, may apple, wild ginger, and snake root. But "buying the wild roots by the pound also was ticklish business," recalled the son of early twentieth-century rural storekeepers, "lest the merchant be 'taken in' by some sharp old hill woman who mixed some worthless roots with the 'sang' or golden seal."[71]

Sang, or ginseng, was the most sought after of all the products of the wild, and many families laid claim to at least one "sanghoe" for digging roots on rocky hillsides. So valuable was ginseng in the late nineteenth century that a few entrepreneurs tried to turn the wild plant into a domesticated cash crop. When Houston, Missouri, native Tom Millard moved to China and wrote back home to tell his uncle about the great demand for the root in the Orient, it set off a ginseng-farming craze in Texas County in 1889. Frank Millard bought sixteen thousand dollars' worth of roots to plant on his Big Piney River land and sent a squadron of young men and boys to roam the hills of the Ozarks as far south as Arkansas's Boston Mountains in search of ginseng. Millard's excitement coaxed other locals into ginseng cultivation, and Texas County exported thousands of pounds of roots to China and New York. A steep drop in prices brought a quick end to root farming, but the spirit of experimentation and entrepreneurship remained alive and well—in the forests, in the fields, and even in the factories of the Ozarks.[72]

3   INDUSTRY AND IMAGE

James L. Dalton stared out at readers of *Hearst's Magazine* in the autumn of 1920. If ever there was a picture of the titan of industry, Dalton's was it. Piercing eyes, aquiline nose, gray-flecked Van Dyke, white collar, and black tie. A middle-aged man at the height of success, atop a multimillion-dollar corporation with sales offices around the globe. Though only half a dozen years removed from living in a small town on the edge of the Missouri Ozarks, here was Dalton—his life story featured in one of America's glitziest magazines alongside a series of sketches of the business world's most powerful movers and shakers. Here he was in the company of men whose names resonate to this day—Rockefeller, du Pont, Swift, Eastman. Here was James L. Dalton, American inventor and entrepreneur—"A Barefooted Boy in the Ozarks."[1]

Dalton's wasn't the only titan story lacking old money, prep schools, and the Ivy League, but his was the only biography in which region became a central character. The Ozarks was just beginning to emerge in the public consciousness as an identifiable cultural region—the kind of place that should produce fiddlers and moonshiners, not millionaire industrialists. The article's author, B. C. Forbes, was not one to overlook the Horatio Alger echoes of any success story that traced its origins to such an unlikely place. Neither was sensationalist publishing tycoon William Randolph Hearst, whose parents were born and raised in the same geographic region that produced Dalton. For Forbes, Dalton's rise was nothing less than "Lincolnesque." The rolling hills of his boyhood became isolating mountains, the seventeen miles to the nearest railroad a formidable forty-mile journey. Like the remarkable souls who occasionally sprang from inferior native bloodlines in the local color novels of the Ozarks, Dalton's intelligence and skills could only have been the gifts of a gracious god or the result of natural accident. "Although he was never in his life taught to 'parse' a sentence, he is now a brilliant speaker and writer, the recipient of requests from leading chambers of commerce."[2]

But Forbes need not have resorted to exaggeration and regional stereotype to stress the unlikely life journey of James Lewis Dalton. Born in rural Ripley County, Missouri, a year and a half after his Confederate father returned home from the war, Dalton grew up on a farm in the Eleven Point River valley of neighboring Randolph County, Arkansas. A precocious and mechanically inclined child, Dalton spent long hours experimenting with machinery and crafted a working wooden model of his mother's sewing machine. When his father's death left the family in straitened circumstances, James received a rudimentary education in local one-room schoolhouses and later trekked more than sixty miles through the hills to attend the Lacrosse Collegiate Institute, an academy where he may have parsed a few Latin sentences. At the age of eighteen, Dalton took the sixty dollars he cleared from a small cotton crop and rode the rails northward, finding work at a dry goods house in St. Louis. After a brief apprenticeship, he returned to the Ozarks and a job as a store clerk in Doniphan, Missouri, soon mastered the business and married the sister of his employers, and at age twenty relocated to Poplar Bluff to run a branch of his employers' enterprise. Buying out his brothers-in-law, Dalton capitalized on Poplar Bluff's location on Jay Gould's St. Louis, Iron Mountain, and Southern Railway and built up southeastern Missouri's largest department store.[3]

It was around the dawn of the new century that the former mechanical wunderkind took an interest in developing a smaller, simpler adding machine. Collaborating with a St. Louis inventor, Dalton received a patent for a ten-key device and launched the Dalton Adding Machine Company in a little shed in Poplar Bluff in 1904. He poured all of his energy into growing the new company, even serving as traveling salesman. In 1914, with the rapidly expanding firm outgrowing its facilities and marketing capacity in Poplar Bluff, Dalton moved his operations to a Cincinnati suburb. By 1920 the company was the second-largest of its kind on the planet, with annual sales of $12 million, and various models of Dalton adding machines could be found in offices around the world. Following his untimely death from a burst appendix in 1926, James L. Dalton's successors sold the company to a conglomerate soon renamed Remington Rand. The new corporation continued to manufacture Dalton adding machines into the 1950s.[4]

Despite stereotypes that threatened to reduce even the most successful Ozarkers to caricature, industry and commerce provided regional links with national and international markets. But Ozarks society was not monolithic. Some Ozarkers thrived amid a new world of railroads and steam engines. Others lived lives little different from those of their parents and grandparents. It was this dichotomy that contributed to stereotypes and provided a foundation for one of the region's chief industries, tourism. Above all, the Ozarks remained a region where geography, history, and access to markets created real and lasting subregional differences.

Industry on the Periphery

The pre-Depression Ozarks was a largely rural region with only a handful of small cities and towns worthy of the designation. Nevertheless, industrial activity increased significantly in the years following the Civil War. The arrival of the Atlantic and Pacific Railroad in North Springfield spurred the establishment of a cotton textile mill, a woolen mill, an iron foundry, flour mills, and a tobacco factory. Most manufacturers were extensions of the region's agricultural base and rarely achieved anything more than a regional clientele. Some small towns also boasted firms that catered to a local farming population or capitalized on the region's raw materials, producing everything from saddles and brooms to furniture and wagons. On the eve of World War I, Neosho, Missouri—a town of fewer than four thousand people—claimed an industrial roster of three flour mills, two cigar factories, four wagon shops, a planing mill, iron foundry, plow factory, bottling works, creamery, candy factory, cannery, and a marble works. But none of them found customers far beyond the confines of Missouri's southwestern corner.[5]

Businesses like the Dalton Adding Machine Company—firms that added value to raw materials or achieved a market beyond the Ozarks—were extremely rare in the pre-Depression years. Most such industries were offshoots of St. Louis shoe and garment corporations that sprouted along rail lines in the 1920s. The Rice-Stix Dry Goods Company, for example, established garment factories in Lebanon, Richland, Bonne Terre, and other regional towns, presaging a dramatic expansion of that industry in the post–World War II era. The best example of a homegrown manufacturer was the Springfield Wagon Company, founded in 1872 and operated for seventy years by the Fellows family. Initially successful due to its attractive yet sturdy wagons that were designed to withstand the rugged, rocky terrain of the Ozarks, by the 1890s the thirteen-acre plant's one hundred workers built twenty-five "Old Reliables" per day in a variety of specialized models and shipped them as far away as South America. Securing the show wagon market—Buffalo Bill's Wild West Show and Ringling Brothers were customers—the company expanded its workforce to three hundred in the early twentieth century. By 1925, the year it introduced its "Ozark" model, the Springfield Wagon Company was the nation's dominant wagon manufacturer. Facing declining sales in an automobile age, Springfield Wagon expanded into tractor- and truck-drawn trailers.[6]

Perhaps it is fitting that a nineteenth-century firm like the Springfield Wagon Company held on in the Ozarks until the middle of the twentieth century while the Dalton Adding Machine Company abandoned the region for a more modern location in a midwestern suburb. Industrial activity in the Ozarks of the late nineteenth and early twentieth centuries, after all, remained a reflection of the region's still-peripheral status within the nation's economy. Despite the region's integration into broader markets and cultural currents, the Ozarks was nevertheless a place that exploited and exported its natural resources, a place that more often than not exported its most able and ambitious people along with their ideas and their creations. The extraction of raw materials and low-skill processing dominated Ozarks industry during the era. Sometimes this created unusual and now long-forgotten fad industries, such as pearling and its associated mussel shell button factories on the Osage, Black, and White rivers in the early 1900s. But the region's chief extractive industries capitalized on extensive stands of virgin forests and plentiful subterranean deposits of minerals.

Timber Boom

The Conflicted Ozarks charted the emergence of the postwar commercial timber and lumber business in the Ozarks, but it was the quarter century or so after the arrival of the first rail cars in the Missouri Lumber and Mining Company's (MLM's) town of Grandin in 1889 that witnessed the boom years of the industry. Importing most of its skilled laborers from older timber regions up north and relying on the local population to supply unskilled workers, the MLM controlled more than three hundred thousand acres in Carter, Reynolds, and Ripley counties and built more than one hundred miles of tram lines into the hills and hollers for use by its seven locomotives and three hundred log cars. At peak production in the early 1900s, the insatiable Grandin mill operated twenty hours per day, six days each week, and consumed some seventy acres of pine daily to produce 250,000 board feet of Beaver Dam Soft Pine lumber. Before the area's timber supply played out, annual profits for the company exceeded seven hundred thousand dollars, and the workforce topped fifteen hundred, most of whom lived in company-owned Grandin.[7]

Like many large firms, MLM also contracted logging operations to middlemen who hired woodcutters, skinners, loaders, and teamsters to deliver wagonloads of logs to the company's tram lines. These workers lived in tents or wooden huts in remote logging camps that relocated farther up a tram line once the pine trees of at least a foot in diameter had been harvested from the camp's surroundings. Residents of the town of Grandin, which ballooned to more than three thousand people shortly after the turn of the twentieth century, enjoyed decidedly more modern conditions than did the inhabitants of the rustic forest camps. A prime example of corporate paternalism in the Ozarks, Grandin featured company-owned rental houses with electric lights and telephones, a first-rate high school, library, churches, company store, and hospital, which at one time offered the services of six doctors and two nurses, all paid for by a monthly family deduction of $1.25 per employee.[8]

Grandin experienced the short life typical of the timber boomtown. After only two decades, the once expansive yellow pine forests of Carter and Ripley counties were gone. Anticipating this development, MLM started buying up virgin timber lands to the north in Shannon County just after the turn of the century, constructing a short line into their new territory in 1907. Closing the factory at Grandin two years later, MLM moved its milling machinery to its new company town on Mahans Creek about a mile west of the Shannon County seat. At this new location, dubbed West Eminence, the familiar story played out once again, this time lasting only ten years before MLM signaled the end of the region's yellow pine boom by selling its facility and pulling out of Missouri altogether.[9]

The Missouri Lumber and Mining Company was only the largest of several corporate firms rushing to exploit the latest forest bonanza in a continental trail that stretched back through the decades to the woods of the upper Midwest, the Great Lakes, and upstate New York and New England. Like MLM, most of the other companies were controlled by outside investors, often stockholders and managers from previous bonanza regions. The construction of the Current River Railroad across southern Shannon County spurred the establishment of two large milling facilities. In 1889 the Cordz-Fisher Lumber Company built its mill on the new line at Birch Tree. The mill produced eighty thousand board feet per day and provided its almost three hundred employees with electricity and running water at a time when no one in the rural Ozarks enjoyed such amenities. Ten miles east of Birch Tree an even larger plant sprang up adjacent to the town of Winona. The Ozark Land and Lumber Company (OLL) established a corporate village named Fishertown in 1888. With his astute wife, Georgia, overseeing OLL's company stores at Fishertown and four logging camps, Iowan John H. Berkshire built the company into the region's second-largest lumber producer by the turn of the century. Employing more than four hundred workers at two mills, OLL owned or leased some three hundred thousand acres and milled more than 36 million board feet of lumber annually in the early 1900s. Not to be outdone by Grandin or Birch Tree, Fishertown boasted a hospital, a town band, a semiprofessional baseball team, a croquet field with electric lights, and a gargantuan company store with thirty-five employees.[10]

In the fifteen years between 1888 and 1903, MLM, Cordz-Fisher, and OLL combined to produce almost 1.34 billion board feet of pine lumber. So powerful were the three companies that in 1898 they and the region's fourth-largest producer, Holladay-Klotz Land and Lumber Company, agreed to work together to decrease costs and increase profits through a Kansas City trust corporation

Ozark Land and Lumber Company mill, Fishertown/Winona, Missouri. Courtesy of Priscilla Evans Photograph Collection (P0545), State Historical Society of Missouri, Columbia.

known as the Missouri Land and Lumber Exchange. Organized by MLM's general manager, John Barber White, and presided over by OLL's Berkshire, the exchange was a product of the Progressive Era's search for corporate efficiency. Following the lead of other major industries such as coal and oil, the firms in the exchange pooled their resources for marketing and promotion purposes and agreed to a predetermined share of the market.[11]

The corporate mills wasted little time stripping southeastern Missouri of its pineries. By 1910 the mills in Grandin, Birch Tree, and Fishertown were silent. MLM's operation at West Eminence came to an end in 1919, and the last of the big pine mills, Bunker-Culler Lumber Company's facility on the Dent-Reynolds county line, shut down in 1921, spelling the end of the fifty-year yellow pine boom in Missouri's Courtois Hills. Company towns like Grandin and Bunker grew doty in the absence of their corporate creators. Even older settlements rotted with the departure of the timber boom's colorful characters and cash money. Greenville, one of the oldest towns in the Ozarks, saw its fortunes wax and wane with the rise and fall of the Holladay-Klotz Land and Lumber Company. An unlikely partnership between native Ozarker Hiram Holladay and

Alsatian immigrant Eli Klotz, the company transformed Greenville into a mill town with the establishment of a new plant in 1892. Perhaps the most colorful and memorable of the era's lumber barons, the tall, muscular, mustachioed, pistol-packing Holladay reigned over 130,000 acres in addition to his mills, company stores, and rental houses from a Victorian mansion in the Wayne County seat. The six-shooter proved of no use, however, when he was gunned down in the spring of 1899 in the bedroom of his sister-in-law.[12]

It is likely that few Holladay-Klotz employees shed a tear for their imperious boss, whose decision to arm himself may have stemmed more from a history of mistreatment of workers than from a reputation for philandering. In 1889 Holladay underwent an investigation by Missouri's Bureau of Labor Statistics into numerous complaints stemming from paying workers in "checks" that could be used only at the company store and could not be redeemed at face value. This "truck system" produced an atmosphere in which workers often sold their pay coupons for as little as half of their face value to boardinghouse managers or other minions of Holladay. Abuses of this kind came with the territory of "cut-and-get-out" extractive industries and lingered throughout most of the timber boom era. In Ripley County in the 1890s, for instance, the King Bee mill on the Little Black River continued to pay its workers only in company store coupons. As late as 1907, the MLM temporarily converted its Grandin workforce to the truck system and threatened to shut down the mills if employees protested. Only in 1912 did state legislation effectively bring an end to the truck system. But there is little evidence of unionizing or organized protest in the lumber industry. As one mill worker at Grandin recalled, if anyone complained to management there was always someone else waiting to take his place.[13]

The delicate cost analysis between exploitation on the one hand and paternalism on the other was one of the key equations in the operation of a company town. In Grandin the MLM looked to occupy its employees' downtime with baseball games, band concerts, a gymnasium, and a long list of clubs and organizations. Like other corporate overseers at the time, the company also attempted to maintain a sober, dependable workforce by inculcating a Victorian, middle-class morality. During its two decades in Grandin, the MLM provided churches for workers and actively discouraged drinking and gambling. In addition to its social control efforts, the company on occasion waived rental fees for injured but dependable workers and provided various kinds of financial assistance to the widows and families of workers killed on the job. The fact that such concerns for widows were not rare underscored the hazardous nature of the industry and provided some explanation for the drunkenness and violence that continually concerned management.[14]

It may be tempting to portray life in the region's company towns as a cultural conflict between the worker's essentially premodern mind-set and the modern, capitalistic vision of the corporations and their management. The Ozarker's employment in such a setting has been pictured as a grim and grudging acceptance of a new world order, as if there were no alternative but to succumb to the soul-sapping fate of industrialism.[15] But the agency exercised by rural Ozarkers was more likely reflected in their willingness to enter the wage-earning workforce, more so than in psychological or cultural struggles with management. After all, the surest way to reject the factory whistles and time clocks of the company town was to stay on the farm. For many rural Ozarkers, the modern amenities of a company town and a job with a steady paycheck—even a low-paying, labor-intensive job—was preferable to life on a hardscrabble farm.

The story of the company town in the rural Ozarks is certainly too complex to be encapsulated within the hackneyed model of cultural conflict. Company towns brought together a small group of educated managers with skilled laborers who generally followed the migrating lumber industry, locals hired for unskilled jobs, and many transient men and families who tended to populate these mushrooming villages. Companies like the MLM even recruited young single women from metropolitan business colleges to occupy clerical and secretarial positions. In such a stew of humanity, it is probable that native Ozarkers constituted a minority of residents in some company towns, a likelihood that would seem to be supported by burgeoning populations in the pine belt during the lumber boom. In the five counties in the heart of the yellow pine bonanza of the 1890s and early 1900s (Carter, Oregon, Reynolds, Ripley, and Shannon), the combined population increased by an astounding 136 percent between 1880 and 1900, well over twice the overall regional rate of growth.[16] While the region was known for producing large families in this era, much if not most of this increase was the result of immigration. Any study purporting to reveal deep cultural divisions between natives and newcomers must first establish which actors fell into which category, and that nuanced study waits to be written.

Financial abuses were not limited to the employees of corporate industries in company towns. One year after investigating Holladay's truck system, Missouri's Bureau of Labor Statistics received complaints from railroad-tie hackers in Miller County. In this instance, the alleged abuses were carried out by storekeepers who served as tie-buying contractors for railroad companies. Miller County hackers accused tie contractors of inducing them into debt by expediting the grading and sale of ties delivered by hackers who owed money to the storekeeper but delaying payment for men whose accounts were in the black. Storekeepers denied any sinister motives, claiming instead that it was simply sound business practice to see to it that the ties of their debtors were the first ones sold to the railroad.[17]

Many of the complaints in Miller County came from farmers who cut ties as a sideline. Among poor families in the most rugged areas of the Ozarks, tie-hacking developed into a key component of survival in the years between the

Civil War and the Great Depression. A class of full-time tie hackers also emerged in the Ozarks by the turn of the twentieth century. Between them, farmers and professional tie hackers hewed tens of millions of railroad ties, usually of white or red oak or some other hardwood. Scoring, or hewing, the sides and removing the clinging wood chips, called "juggles," required great skill with both a broadax and a double-bitted ax. A "scantling," or homemade measuring stick, ensured the tie's standard dimensions of eight to eight and a half feet in length and six by eight inches in width. Finished ties were hauled to the nearest tie-buying location and were promptly marked with a branding hammer, indicating to which of the large tie companies or railroads they belonged.[18]

Tie-hacking season was generally in the winter and spring, but tie drives and rafts on the streams of the Ozarks usually took place in the fall. Drives—in which thousands of ties were dumped into a river to follow the current downstream—often moved at the glacial pace of a mile per day, prompting a state law that limited them to fifty thousand ties per drive in 1909. Guiding "rafts" of connected ties down the Big Piney, Gasconade, Current, and other rivers was the chore of a breed of character known as the tie rafter. A skilled tie rafter could handle a raft of three hundred ties using only a long set pole for steering and a snub pole for breaking, but larger rafts required teams of rafters who carried food and supplies with them and camped nights on sandbars. Tie hackers were not devoid of folklore—legend had it that John Henson, a sort of Paul Bunyan of the hardwoods, had once hacked a superhuman fifty-seven ties in a single day and could carry four ties (up to eight hundred pounds) on his shoulders—but it was rafters who tended to dominate stories told around the stoves at the end of a river boom. They carried a well-earned reputation for rowdiness, none more so than Reynolds County native Nathaniel "Stub" Borders, a heavy drinker and frequent brawler who received his moniker when a dynamite explosion cost him his right hand and left eye. Working primarily on the Big Piney and the Gasconade, Borders abandoned his first wife and spent five years behind bars for killing a man who allegedly hit his second one. He was approaching fifty years of age by the time he ran his last raft down the Big Piney in 1922.[19]

Borders did much of his tie rafting for the Abeles & Taussig Tie Corporation of St. Louis, one of many tie-buying firms operating in the Ozarks between the Civil War and the Depression. Other companies buying from hackers in the region included Schneider Brothers, Louis F. Pillman, and Hobart-Lee. No tie buyer in the Ozarks was larger than the T. J. Moss Tie Company of St. Louis. At the time of his premature death in 1893, Thomas Jefferson Moss, hailed as the "Tie King," had grown his business into one of the nation's largest tie-buying companies in little more than a decade. Incorporated after his death and operated by his lieutenant and childhood friend, John Wallace Fristoe, the T. J. Moss Tie Company bought more than one hundred thousand cutover acres from

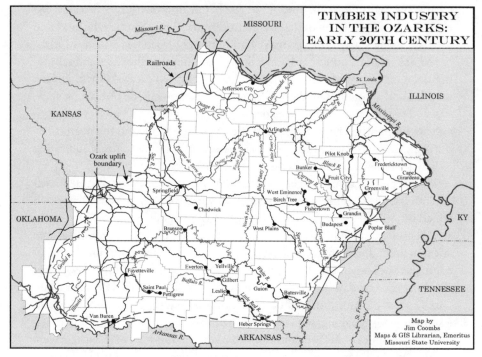

Timber Industry in the Ozarks, early twentieth century. Courtesy of Jim Coombs, Missouri State University, Springfield.

the Ozark Land and Lumber Company after World War I. Moss's purchase of former pine lands reflected a popular development in the timber and lumber industry, as hardwood companies frequently moved into areas only after large mills harvested the more lucrative yellow pine.[20]

Though the pine industry may have viewed the hardwooders as scavengers, the voracious demand for railroad ties and other uses for oak and hickory made the hardwood industry an important element of the region's industrial saga. In the old pine region, hardwood mills tended to be smaller, portable operations specializing in hubs, staves, barrels, handles, or charcoal. Factories manufacturing wooden hubs for wagon and automobile wheels sprang up at Piedmont, Lesterville, and other communities in the Black and Current River watersheds. The same region hosted small hickory handle factories and hardwood flooring manufacturers. Fredericktown's Pioneer Cooperage Company maintained stave mills in several Bollinger and Wayne County communities in the early 1900s. An even larger enterprise, H. D. Williams Cooperage Company, operated farther south at Poplar Bluff. Williams's move to northwestern Arkansas in the early twentieth century signaled the region's most significant hardwood boom in the heart of its most extensive deciduous forests.[21]

The hardwood lumber bonanza of northwestern Arkansas followed the expansion of the railroad. East and south of the rolling prairies of northwestern Arkansas, the Boston Mountains and White River Hills contained large stands of old-growth white oaks, red oaks, and other marketable timber. The arrival of the Frisco in 1881 spurred a boom in the westernmost reaches of Arkansas's hardwood forests. The region's first lumber baron, Ohio native Hugh McDanield, built a short line from Fayetteville to the hamlet of St. Paul in the Boston Mountains in 1886. This "St. Paul Branch" was eventually extended to Pettigrew, forty-five miles from Fayetteville, near the headwaters of the White River. In its boom years at the end of the branch, Pettigrew boasted mills producing tongues, axles, and spokes for wagons; barrel staves; plow handles; furniture; and lumber shipped to Michigan to be turned into floorboards for Ford automobiles. Major tie companies stationed field agents in Pettigrew, and markets developed for other woods—dogwood for loom shuttles, cherry for furniture squares, and beech for the flooring of skating rinks and gymnasiums. Fayetteville also blossomed into a major lumber manufacturing town, with factories producing wagons and wagon parts, wheel spokes, and barrel staves.[22]

Hardwood and cedar production in the White River watershed hit high gear shortly after the turn of the century with the construction of parallel rail lines through the heart of the region. By 1910 Branson, Missouri, and its environs contained a cedar mill and factories for manufacturing wagons, veneer, spokes, handles, and pencils. The 1920s saw the establishment of a baseball bat manufactory in Mountain Home and a hickory golf stick factory in the Izard County railroad town of Guion. Eighty-five miles to the west, the hamlet of Everton, just off the Missouri & North Arkansas (M&NA), sported its own golf club plant. It was this westernmost of the two railroads that generated the most intensive timber processing. The Houston, Ligett & Canada Cedar Company began harvesting Newton County trees as soon as the locomotives chugged into Buffalo River country, and the Eagle Pencil Company of New York built a spur from the hamlet of Gilbert to the banks of the river, where logs floated from the interior were loaded directly onto cars.[23]

But it was white oak that received the lion's share of attention along the M&NA. The line's first lumber boomtown was Leslie, which received railroad service in 1903 and soon hosted stave mills, hub plants, and handle factories. Relocated to Leslie from Poplar Bluff, Missouri, in 1906 the H. D. Williams Cooperage Company could manufacture five thousand barrels per day at its sixty-eight-acre plant, becoming the town's major employer during the boom years. With its thirteen portable sawmills, its 17.5-mile branch line, and its company-owned hotels, houses, and stables, Williams employed a total of twelve hundred workers before a fire gutted the factory in 1912. Rebuilt at a smaller capacity, Williams Cooperage continued to anchor employment in Leslie—which at its apex boasted four banks, four newspapers, and a hospital—until national prohibition forced its closure in the mid-1920s.[24]

In both the pine hills of Missouri and the hardwood hollers of Arkansas, the decade of the 1920s found much of the Ozarks a cutover wasteland. The end of the region's forests may have arrived earlier than most expected, but it was a foregone conclusion nonetheless. In 1892, even before the timber boom engulfed his area, an editor in Shannon County warned readers that "the time will come—must come—when your mammoth saw mills all depart, and with them goes your vast forests of pine and oak, and in their place will be left a barren waste of stumps and brush." There was little the timber cutters, farmers, and mill workers could do to remedy the situation. Corporate lumber interests and their native brokers owned or leased most of the land, after all, and the run of Shannon's residents were willing to enjoy the steady paychecks while they lasted. If it was corporate management to which he spoke, he need not have bothered. The American lumber industry had operated by the same strategy for generations—get in, get out, and move on.[25]

In rare instances clear-cutting left hillsides and hollers denuded of everything save thousands of stumps. Such drastic cases were generally the work of the minerals industry, especially the iron furnaces that revived briefly during World War I. The Mid-Continent Iron Company's furnace in Carter County, Missouri, stripped thousands of acres as it burned through 180 cords per day before shutting down in 1921. The MLM, the OLL, and other pine lumber corporations did not engage in clear-cutting, but their policy of harvesting marketable logs as quickly as possible did not include replanting forests. Consequently, what had once been six and a half million acres of pine and oak-pine forests in southern Missouri largely grew back as scrub oak woodlands. Loggers generally discarded any part of the tree above the limb line, leaving tops to rot or burn on the forest floor. With this massive loss of cover and mast, Missouri's whitetail deer population declined to an estimated two thousand animals by the beginning of the Depression. Less than half that many survived in Arkansas, and turkeys fared little better. The loss of the region's forests also took its toll on an already declining open-range hog farming culture, and the detritus littering the hills provided wildfire tinder during the annual spring burnings that many Ozarkers still practiced.[26]

The massive exodus of timber companies in the 1910s and 1920s also left behind a trail of human detritus, thousands of workers and their families whose choices boiled down to following the lumber industry on its migration elsewhere or staying in the rural Ozarks. For transients and other landless laborers, remaining in the Ozarks brought dependence on unsteady work in a declining extractive resources industry. For those who owned land, the postwar agricultural depression promised little more than a bare existence. The experience of wage earning and modern, consumer culture exercised powerful mojo on the psyche. For thousands of families, the old ways on the farm seemed suddenly archaic. Tate C. Page recalled his own Arkansas family's brush with modernity during World War I, when a stave company leased land from his grandfather in the Boston Mountains. Earning cash by supplying lumber for the company's structures and selling goods to workers out of a makeshift store, the Pages underwent a "change in attitudes." When the stave company pulled out two years later, "the Pages tried to put their world back together but the glue was gone."[27]

At least the Pages had a farm to return to. That was rarely an option for the thousands of laborers who had no deep roots in the Ozarks and whose livelihoods had been completely tied to the timber and lumber industry. For the large companies, transient families represented little more than the cheap labor that secured profit margins. Management had little doubt that the same class of humanity would materialize in the woods of the next bonanza region. When queried about the fate of hundreds of low-wage workers in the wake of the MLM's exodus from Grandin, general manager John Barber White rationalized his company's sudden loss of corporate paternalism by reasoning that his former employees would be better off living "in small log houses and rais[ing] their living . . . than working around a sawmill and paying rent."[28]

This self-serving, bottom-line approach was evident in a lumber industry sideline. To avoid paying property taxes on unproductive acreage, the MLM and other companies attempted to sell cutover lands as quickly as possible. Following precedents set in the Great Lakes region a generation earlier, they marketed their ridges and hollers as ideal agricultural real estate. The MLM and OLL established model farms to tout the area's prospects for orchards, stock raising, and dairy farming. A Minneapolis firm with grand visions of a fifty-thousand-head cattle ranch purchased a large block of MLM land, while a Texas rancher bought OLL acreage for sheep raising. Both dreams came to naught. In 1906 the MLM settled a colony of Hungarian families in what once had been woods a few miles southeast of Grandin. Today only the place-name Budapest on topographical maps commemorates this ruse. The Munger Securities Company engineered an elaborate scheme on former MLM property around a small railroad town a few miles north of Grandin. Munger promised an attractive package of goods for anyone forking over three hundred dollars—a plot of orchard land, shares of stock in two canneries, and town lots in Hunter—before dissolving amid a shower of lawsuits in 1920. A few years later, the Eastern Slope Fruit Farms Company attempted to transform some of Reynolds County's ravaged forests into an agricultural oasis, with model communities called Fruit City and Dairyville.

But this impenetrable land along the upper Black River was not destined for metamorphosis into a midwestern model of prosperous family farms.[29]

The forests have returned to Reynolds County over the past century, though not the majestic stands of giant yellow pine that once shaded the ridges. The rails were pulled up years ago. Time has erased most signs of man's mad rush to profit from nature's bounty. Time has had the same effect—with a little help from the National Park Service—225 miles across the region in a place that may be even more remote and rugged than Reynolds County. No place in the Buffalo National River is more popular with tourists than the Boxley Valley in Newton County, Arkansas. Boxley's white-frame church house, log barns, and old homes remind visitors of days gone by in this isolated little nook of the Ozarks, just as they are supposed to. It's the closest thing the region has to the popular Cades Cove section of Tennessee's Great Smoky Mountains National Park, except in Boxley's case a few humans remain in the valley.

Like Cades Cove, the Boxley Valley that greets tourists is a butterfly in amber, a place where the conscious decisions of image crafters have erased the signs of industrial ambition. In 1882 the Carthage and Arkansas Mining Company arrived in this Newton County valley looking to capitalize on the area's deposits of lead and zinc ore. After building a smelter, the company's organizer laid out a town named for a local merchant. Like most in his line of business, he harbored few doubts that Boxley would become the booming seat of a prosperous mining district. Yet the organizer was an unlikely father of a town in the rural Ozarks, sharing as he did almost nothing in common with the agricultural settlers of the valley. A rare Swedish immigrant in rural Arkansas, Eric Hedburg had been trained as a mining engineer and iron master in the Bergslagen region of his home country before landing in the United States two years earlier. His sojourn in the Buffalo Valley proved a brief one. After about a year, "the long wagon-haul of [fifty] miles to the nearest railroad proved a fatal disadvantage, and the project was abandoned until better conditions of transportation could be enjoyed." The wait continues for those better conditions.[30]

Ozark Ores

Mining constituted the other half of the region's extractive industry in the years between the Civil War and the Depression. Most places in the Ozarks contained marketable minerals, though digging them up and transporting them profitably was no easy task. The industry's failures always outnumbered its successes, but at times and places when prices were high and ore was plentiful, minerals proved a far more lucrative natural resource than timber. The era's two most notable American natural resources—coal and oil—played only a minimal role in the story of the Ozarks, accounting for the region's near anonymity in the annals of digging and drilling. Yet the Ozark uplift and its environs led the nation in the production of multiple minerals, most notably lead and zinc.

Only a few of the more than three dozen minerals found in the Ozarks actually generated income and jobs. World War I spurred a minor resurgence in iron smelting, but the story of iron in the Ozarks is primarily a nineteenth-century one. In Greene County, Missouri, the Ash Grove Lime and Portland Cement Company claimed to be the largest manufactory of its kind west of the Mississippi. On the eve of World War I, Ash Grove's dozen kilns produced up to seventeen hundred barrels of lime per day. The company's miserly pay scale may have been a reflection of the substantial number of black employees at the plant, an uncommon development in the industrial Ozarks. It was another limestone product that brought recognition to Jasper County. In an outcropping north of Carthage in 1880, stone cutters discovered hard rock suitable for construction yet capable of taking a high polish. The first shipments of Carthage White Marble rolled out five years later, and a building boom—highlighted by the construction of Jasper County's Romanesque revival-style courthouse—brought in orders from around the Midwest. Jasper County also emerged as a leading manufacturer of finished, interior marble, and a Carthage company secured the contract to supply marble for Missouri's new capitol building in Jefferson City in 1913.[31]

Newton County emerged in the postwar era as Missouri's leader in the production of tripoli, mining more than four million pounds a year by the end of the nineteenth century. In Arkansas silica mines profited from the friable St. Peter sandstone at Guion on the Missouri Pacific's White River Line and at Everton on the M&NA. Miners in southeastern Missouri dug fireclay and nickel, while barite and granite emerged as lucrative products for St. Louis investors. Barite revived the mining heritage of Potosi's Washington County, once the home of Moses Austin's territorial lead-mining plantation. In the late nineteenth century, the use of barite (known locally as "tiff") in modern industrial products—explosives, asbestos, and linoleum, to name a few—created heavy demand for the colorless, high-gravity mineral. Relying on French patois–speaking descendants of the area's old Creole population to mine tiff using the pick-and-shovel methods of their lead-mining ancestors, St. Louis–based De Lore Baryta Company held a virtual monopoly on barite extraction by the early 1900s.[32]

To the south and east of Washington County, in the heart of the ancient St. Francois Mountains, the granite industry emerged in the late nineteenth century. The rock of the region's pre-Cambrian core was used for building stone, monuments, and paving blocks. St. Louisan Philip W. Schneider's operation at Graniteville in Iron County supplied stone for the buildings and bridges of his city's postwar expansion. In the 1870s and 1880s, the Syenite Granite Company, Sheahan Brothers, and smaller concerns established quarries in a granite belt

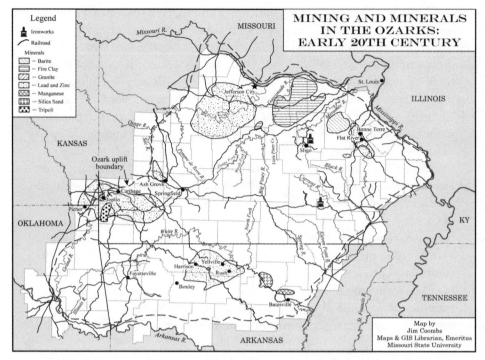

Mining and Minerals in the Ozarks, early twentieth century. Courtesy of Jim
Coombs, Missouri State University, Springfield.

extending from St. Francois County southward to Wayne and Carter counties.
Graniteville's various shades of red granite found its way into some of St. Louis's
most notable structures—the U.S. Custom House and Post Office, the Mercantile
Library Building, and the Anheuser-Busch Brewery—as well as buildings from
Baltimore to San Francisco. During the height of the region's granite industry
in the late nineteenth century, when millions of blocks paved the streets of St.
Louis, the Syenite Granite Company employed fifteen hundred workers at its
Graniteville facility.[33]

   The granite and marble industries left a more aesthetic record of their seasons
of prosperity, but it was the massive chat piles littering the landscape of the
region's mineral areas that commemorated the most valuable products: lead
and zinc. In the post–Civil War years, even after almost a century and a half
of mining activity in the Ozarks, lead continued to generate immense profits,
send men to early graves, and scar an already pockmarked landscape. Since
the 1850s, lead mining in Missouri had centered on two separate and quite dis-
tinct locations in the Ozarks—the Lead Belt of southeastern Missouri and the
southwestern Missouri district that eventually centered on Joplin. Both areas

continued producing into the twentieth century, but the Ozark uplift's lead and zinc map expanded to include parts of Arkansas, Oklahoma, and Kansas, the latter two states helping constitute the Tri-State District. While the methods and economics of mining in the Lead Belt and the Tri-State District reflected striking dissimilarities in the late nineteenth century, corporate consolidation and market rationalization gradually created a somewhat uniform mining culture that came to define two areas on opposite sides of the Ozark plateau.

An outside-owned mining corporation helped southeastern Missouri regain its dominance after the Civil War. Created by New York investors to exploit a plot of St. Francois County mineral land, the St. Joseph (St. Joe) Lead Company responded to a destructive fire at its Bonne Terre plant in 1883 by rebuilding with about ten times its previous smelting capacity, buying up rival companies, and constructing a railway to Herculaneum, Moses Austin's old town on the Mississippi River. St. Joe continued to open rich new shafts in the knobby St. Francois Mountains, creating a series of company towns in the process: Desloge, Rivermines, Elvins, and Doe Run. The Desloge Lead Company, the Federal Lead Company, and at least half a dozen other firms of various sizes joined St. Joe in St. Francois and Madison counties by World War I. But St. Joe controlled over half the area's market and proclaimed itself the world's largest lead-producing company. Lead Belt firms cashed in on inflated wartime prices that approached one hundred dollars a ton in 1917, a year that saw more than three hundred thousand tons of lead leave the area. An unusually robust postwar lead market pushed St. Joe to the peak of its prosperity and production in the mid-1920s.[34]

By World War I the state of Missouri produced about one-third of the lead mined in the United States, and St. Joe and the other mines in the Lead Belt accounted for almost 90 percent of the state's production. Most of the remainder came from the Joplin/Tri-State District of southwestern Missouri. That district's rather measly output of less than thirty-nine thousand tons in 1917 reflected a shift in the area decades earlier from an economy based on lead extraction to one primarily dependent on zinc, a mineral absent from most ore beds in the Lead Belt. Skyrocketing prices in the 1870s, due to increased use in galvanizing barbed wire and other metal products, kick-started the zinc-mining business in southwestern Missouri. Nicknamed "jack" or "black jack" by miners, zinc fueled the rapid growth of the Ozark region's most dynamic late-nineteenth-century boomtown, so much so that Joplin became known as "the town that jack built."[35]

By the end of the century, lead had become jack's overlooked little brother in the Joplin district. A zinc boom commencing in 1896 and ending with the Panic of 1907 triggered an almost region-wide speculative mining frenzy. Between 1890 and 1910, Jasper County experienced a population explosion, growing from fifty thousand people to almost ninety thousand, more than a third of whom resided in the city of Joplin. The Joplin area's industrial base brought its citizens the flavors of the modern, urban world before almost anyone else in the region had a taste. The construction of a dam and hydroelectricity plant at Grand Falls on Shoal Creek introduced the district to electric power in 1890, and the early 1900s saw the building of the Southwest Missouri Electrical Railway. The trolley system allowed workers and their families to enjoy the modern amenities of a city while commuting to work in an outlying mining town.[36]

The interurban railway was accompanied by a certain degree of modernization within the mining industry as well. While St. Joe and its competitors in the Lead Belt adopted the most modern technology and underwent consolidation that left only a few large players in the game, for most of the late nineteenth century mining in the Joplin district was characterized by rather primitive methods and a decentralized market dominated by wildcat entrepreneurs. Beginning in the 1890s, however, economies of scale and market integration began to chip away at Joplin's wide-open mining scene. Before the turn of the century, consolidations reduced the number of lead-smelting companies from seventeen to only three. Steam engines increasingly rendered animal and human muscle obsolete. Black powder, and later dynamite, came into common use for blasting in the early 1900s, as did steam drills for miners. Hand shoveling remained more cost-effective than the mechanical alternative until the eve of World War II, however, and in the early twentieth century a man with a strong back and stamina could earn a robust six to seven dollars for an eight-hour day shoveling ore.[37]

In the early 1900s corporate consolidation took hold in the Tri-State District. The Picher Lead Company dominated the district's lead smelting. All zinc smelting took place in southeastern Kansas, nearer the coal fields that powered the furnaces, but the new century found three vertically integrated companies controlling the flow of zinc: the American Zinc, Lead, and Smelting Company; the New Jersey Zinc Company; and the old Granby Mining and Smelting Company. Following custom, most continued to lease their mineral lands to local mining outfits instead of keeping miners on the company payroll. The emergence of American Zinc and New Jersey Zinc in the Joplin district reflected the market's eastern U.S. locus. The industry's center shifted from London to Boston in the late 1800s, marked by the 1899 incorporation of American Zinc by a group of capitalists led by former Harvard baseball teammates William H. Coolidge and Edward A. Clark. Corporate consolidation and market restriction gradually reduced the district's once-independent operators to laborers as the years wore on.[38]

Like their counterparts in the lead industry, zinc producers enjoyed a spike in prices as World War I limited the exporting capabilities of major suppliers Germany and Belgium. American Zinc raked in massive profits in the war's first three years, but a development elsewhere in the Tri-State changed the

Zinc ore shovelers at the Daisy Belle Mine near Aurora, Missouri, 1910. Courtesy of
Library of Congress.

trajectory of the district. In 1914 a joint exploration by two corporations revealed
an extensive untapped ore bed on the far western periphery of the Ozark uplift
about twenty-five miles southwest of Joplin. Two new Oklahoma boomtowns,
Picher and Cardin, sprang up, and the two corporations merged to form the
Eagle-Picher Lead Company. Though Joplin remained the administrative and
financial center of the zinc-mining industry, the base of activity in the Tri-State
District shifted almost immediately to the northeastern corner of Oklahoma.
By 1918 Oklahoma ranked as the nation's number-one zinc-mining state.[39]

Years before the discovery of zinc in Oklahoma, wildcatters and investors had
tried to develop the industry in Arkansas. After a Fayetteville promoter exhibited
a massive boulder of almost pure zinc at the 1893 Chicago World's Fair, a sort of
mineral madness descended on northern Arkansas. Companies materialized,
shafts were sunk, and would-be tycoons came face-to-face with the realization
that had slammed Eric Hedburg a decade and a half earlier—that without a
railroad, getting ore out of the heart of the Ozarks was no paying proposition.
As one historian of the region observed, the only people making money in this
mining "boom" were those selling land. In Newton County, Arkansas, farmer

Beecher Moss found himself in high cotton when he sold a forty-acre homestead to a zinc-crazed St. Louis shoe salesman for a thousand dollars, a local price unheard of before the boom.[40]

When rail lines were constructed through the White River country in the early 1900s, most of the region's richest mines remained far from either railroad. But wartime prices made zinc mining in Arkansas profitable nonetheless. In the fall of 1915, miners worked more than two hundred mines within a twenty-five-mile radius of Harrison. The Arkansas district's focal point, however, was farther down the river in Marion County, where a boomtown sprouted a couple of miles up Rush Creek at the site of the Morning Star Mine—the mine once proclaimed the "greatest deposit of zinc ever discovered in the world." Amid the frenzy of wartime price jumps in 1916 and 1917—legend has it that the price of zinc shot up by $6.50 over the course of a single Joplin band concert—Morning Star and its neighboring mines produced thousands of tons of zinc ore, all of it hauled out of the holler by wagon. The town of Rush mushroomed, but a drop in zinc prices in late 1917 rendered its ore too costly to mine. Rush was a ghost town at mid-century.[41]

When the war came to an end, the brief Arkansas zinc boom was dead and gone, but the United States had supplanted Germany and Belgium as the world's leader in zinc production. And Picher's Ottawa County, Oklahoma, sat at the center of the industry's universe. Strong postwar protective tariffs rejuvenated zinc prices in the early 1920s, and the industry's mid-decade peak saw Ottawa County miners digging more than half a million tons of zinc. Southwestern Missouri's output declined to insignificance by 1925, but the Tri-State District dominated the American market, generating more than $57 million in zinc and lead sales that year. Eagle-Picher and American Zinc turned profits until the bottom dropped out of the market in the early years of the Depression.[42]

Mining Maladies

By the post–World War II years, at which point American Zinc was under the direction of native Ozarker Howard I. Young, the zinc industry in the Ozarks had been reduced to "small-scale, cleanup mining." Just how much cleaning up American Zinc was doing remains a matter of speculation. Like other forms of mining, the lead, zinc, and iron industries left in their wake a scarred and poisoned landscape. Some effects were obvious to anyone: the thousands of acres of forests stripped to provide fuel for iron furnaces, the pockmarked hills from generations of practically unregulated digging. Some, like the region's earliest dams, were not so obvious. The first impoundment on the White River generated electricity for the mines, and had St. Joe not signed on as a customer of St. Louis's Union Electric Company, plans to build the Osage River dam that created the Lake of the Ozarks would not have materialized so quickly.[43]

One of the "Great Pyramids of St. Francois County, Missouri," Flat River. Courtesy of Lynn Morrow Papers (R1000), folder 885, State Historical Society of Missouri, Rolla.

Most landscape-altering of all mining's environmental impacts were the mountainous chat piles that loomed over every mining town. These piles remained the most visible legacy of the lead and zinc industry at the dawn of the twenty-first century. Because 70 percent or more of the crude ore extracted from mines was unusable, massive amounts of once-subterranean material ended up on the surface as waste. These "tailings," or chat, were eventually dumped into piles by giraffe-necked conveyor belts. Rising up to three hundred feet high and covering as much as thirteen acres, these man-made hills retained just enough metallic content to render them toxic. Nevertheless, communities in the Lead Belt and the Tri-State used these grassless balds for recreation and even resigned themselves, in tongue-in-cheek fashion, to promoting the eyesores as local attractions—"The Great Pyramids of St. Francois County."[44]

Even more toxic than the chat piles were the "slime ponds," man-made reservoirs into which mining companies dumped tailings and chemicals. In some cases companies didn't bother with reservoirs, flushing chat and other refuse into streams. Locals in southeastern Missouri took to calling one particularly polluted stream Slime Creek. In 1911 a group of landowners identifying themselves as the Big River Farmers' Association sued St. Joe and four other lead companies to halt this practice, claiming that the toxic stew flowing through the Big River and its tributaries killed fish and wildlife and endangered soil fertility. The farmers won a temporary injunction against toxic dumping, but the lead companies' delaying tactics prolonged the practice until chat piles and slime ponds largely replaced it during World War I. Taking on a behemoth like St. Joe was a tricky proposition, not only because the company controlled most of the Lead Belt's wealth but also because even the activists challenging the company "all benefited to varying degrees from the expansion of big business." As historian Bob Faust discovered in his examination of Progressive Era campaigns in the area, "many of these people accepted the realities—the paychecks and the discipline—of a new industrial order."[45]

The worst abuse of the region's particular brand of industrialization was the illness visited on its workers. Though cave-ins, explosions, and toxic gases made mining an inherently dangerous occupation, lead and zinc miners faced still more formidable health challenges. Lead poison was a constant concern for miners and others who worked and lived around smelter fumes and drank contaminated water. More insidious were diseases contracted from extended exposure to fine dust particles underground. Living in a ramshackle neighborhood in the northwestern corner of Joplin, surrounded by the families of miners and smelter employees, young Ethel Reed witnessed firsthand the terrible physical and psychological cost paid by the district's workers. "The fathers were a fearsome and depressing lot," she recalled years later. "Most of them had a hacking cough, or a ghastly pallor, or both, and they were listless and unfriendly around the house, even when they were not sick in bed from lead poisoning."[46]

But it almost certainly wasn't lead poison that brought low the fathers of her playmates. The Reeds' neighbors sound like textbook cases of silicosis or pneumoconiosis, known in the vernacular as "miner's consumption." Exposure to underground air heavy with tiny blade-like dust particles eventually scarred the lungs, leaving them fibroid and causing shortness of breath, coughing, and weight loss and making them vulnerable to the contagious malady of tuberculosis. In the early twentieth century, an alarming death rate among Tri-State miners attracted national attention. The U.S. Public Health Service dispatched a young doctor and a "sanitary engineer" to the Joplin district in 1914. The report issued the following year confirmed the "unusual prevalence of tuberculosis" in the mining counties of southwestern Missouri. The Jasper County Antituberculosis Society estimated that 720 southwestern Missouri miners died in 1912 alone, while the society's nurse suggested that the 341 tuberculosis patients she visited in the previous fourteen months represented only one-fifth of the area's total cases. A mine operator estimated that only half of the 750 men he had employed over the previous eight years were still alive. Moving their operation to Webb City in 1915, the Public Health Service investigators examined over seven hundred miners and found that more than three in five suffered from a pulmonary disease related to exposure to mine dust. Focusing on underground workers who spent their days shoveling load after load of crude ore into 1,250-pound "cans," the researchers found that "hard, constant work had broken these men down, so that at the ages of 22 to 30 they were already on the down grade." In 1917 the Public Health Service created the Tri-State Sanitary District under the supervision of Dr. Thomas Parran Jr., who would go on to serve as surgeon general of the United States under presidents Roosevelt and Truman. As late as 1940 an exposé on silicosis in the Tri-State District referred to the main thoroughfare in the mining town of Treece, Kansas, as "The Street of Walking Death."[47]

The same Public Health Service report that called for limiting flint dust in mines also recommended changes to the piece-rate system that encouraged overexertion among shovelers. But the report's authors recognized the unlikelihood of such a change anytime soon. "Any infringement of [the piece-rate system] would meet with opposition," they admitted, "more from the miner in all probability than from the operator." It may have been a curious observation to anyone unfamiliar with the "poor man's camp" ethos that was still alive and well in the Joplin area. Of all the differences between the Lead Belt and the Tri-State District, none was so jarring as their collective stances on unionization and the autonomy of the individual worker. Miners in the Lead Belt had organized years earlier and carried out known strikes in 1905 and 1913, but it was a different story in the Tri-State District.[48]

Joplin's wide-open egalitarian system was beginning to disappear as World War I got under way, but the miners kept faith that they could join the ranks of the producers in the old poor man's camp. "It is a common saying in southwestern Missouri that every miner is a prospective operator," noted the report of the Public Health Service. The decentralized nature of the mining industry in the region had long made it a poor recruiting ground for labor leaders. Even before the turn of the century, the miners of southwestern Missouri had earned a reputation as the West's toughest strikebreakers, beginning with their role in defeating the Western Federation of Miners' strike in the Colorado gold mines in 1896. As historian Jarod Roll observes, this initial foray into strikebreaking was motivated not so much by an innate anti-unionism as by economic concerns during a tough time for miners in southwestern Missouri. Though they were demonized by unions of their era, "their strikebreaking was an informed act, not an ignorant or coerced one, that reflected the careful appraisal of lucid working-class actors informed by the pressures of their time and place." By 1910, according to Roll, this autonomous streak and strikebreaker battles had given birth to "a nativist, working-class anti-unionism." The district's miners steadfastly rejected the industrial unionism of the Western Federation of Miners and the organizing efforts of the Industrial Workers of the World. Only in the 1940s, in the waning days of the region's mining activity, would labor unions successfully organize in what was left of the Tri-State District.[49]

The ethnic makeup of the two Missouri mining regions accounted for yet another significant contrast. Born of collaborations between Native Americans and

French immigrants in the Mississippi Valley, the Lead Belt from its beginnings had been a place marked by diversity, and it continued to be home to a polyglot mix of miners over the generations—enslaved Africans, French Creoles, upland Southerners, the Cornish and Irish, and Germans. After the turn of the twentieth century, St. Joe and other corporate interests began further diversifying the Lead Belt's ethnic profile by recruiting Italians, Poles, Russians, and Hungarians—the latter three reduced to "Hunkies" in nativist lingo. When World War I erupted, the area bore a strong resemblance to other ethnically diverse mining districts around the United States. But not the Joplin district. An anomaly among the nation's extensive mining regions, the Tri-State District's miners were "practically all of American stock." "Like other white men in this age of Jim Crow and imperial aggression," Roll argues, "Tri-State miners asserted their claim of racial authority through violence against perceived enemies." Clearing the Tri-State of those enemies—whether radicals, Blacks, or immigrants—assured the dominance of a brand of white nativist conservatism that chagrined labor leaders and baffled labor historians.[50]

The Lead Belt's diverse workforce was no symbol of cultural and ethnic détente, however. The "new immigrants" of the era often bred suspicion and resentment among their native-born neighbors, as well as among more-established immigrant groups such as the Germans and Irish. "Even the Preachers and the amateur devil-chasers in such towns as Flat River and Bonne Terre devoted their activities principally to spreading the Gospel among the home-bred and let the Hunkies carry on whatever nefarious practices pleased them best," Farmington native Herbert Asbury wryly observed. "We didn't want them in our Heaven, anyhow." Just one year after Asbury penned a blistering account of his home region's oppressive religious atmosphere, he published what is now his best-known book, *The Gangs of New York: An Informal History of the Underworld*, in 1927. Though a work of creative nonfiction and based on little substantial research, the book inspired Martin Scorsese's 2002 film of the same title. Asbury's decision to exaggerate the ethnic violence of nineteenth-century New York City may have emanated, as most suspect, from the sensationalized atmosphere of Al Capone's gangster age in America. But it also could have been inspired by a terrible page in the history of the corner of the Ozarks where he spent his youth.[51]

Asbury had already fled St. Francois County, Missouri, for a career in journalism by the time the Lead Belt Riot erupted in the summer of 1917. It is unclear what percentage of workers in the mines of the Lead Belt were eastern and southern Europeans, but their numbers were substantial and possibly even growing in 1917 as corporations like St. Joe prepared for the likelihood that many of their native-born workers would be drafted into military service. The draft-eligible men were no doubt aware of this potentiality as well, and the anxieties of leaving their families and losing their jobs bred resentment toward their employers and rekindled latent hostilities toward their "Hunky" coworkers.[52]

Exactly what set off the riot remains a matter of speculation. Some chalked it up to the actions of the radical Industrial Workers of the World. Local rumors suggested that a foreigner's quip about taking the Americans' jobs and their women did the trick. Whatever lit the fuse, it detonated during a shift change at a Federal Lead Company shaft in Flat River on the evening of Friday, July 13, when a group of American miners attacked foreigners in the change house. To escape the assault, several foreign miners jumped out a second-story window; one took a bullet in the leg as he fled. Not satisfied with their initial display, a mob of native-born miners went from shaft to shaft driving immigrant miners from their jobs and terrorizing foreigners on the streets. A throng perhaps five hundred strong gathered the next morning and marched behind a U.S. flag to the Federal Lead Company's office, demanding the firing of foreign workers and threatening to hang the company attorney. Receiving no promise of action from corporate officials, the mob looted homes in "Hunky Town," rounded up Italians from nearby "Dago Hill," and herded them toward the depot in Flat River. By the end of the day, several carloads of foreign miners and their families had been shipped out of Flat River destined for St. Louis, reducing the Lead Belt's foreign-born population by an estimated seven hundred to fifteen hundred people.[53]

Arriving the second night of the riot, the state militia provided a safe escape for foreigners who remained in the region, including the family of Polish miner Anthony Pacosz, who barricaded themselves inside the boardinghouse they operated. The militia also arrested dozens of men suspected of taking part in the riots. When federal troops replaced the state militia later in the year to ensure a steady supply of lead for the war effort, the lead companies reimported their foreign laborers, including Anthony Pacosz. But it remained an uninviting place for immigrant workers. The xenophobia of wartime provoked the St. Joe Lead Company to announce in November 1917 that it would remove from its payroll any workers who were not native-born or naturalized citizens, prompting almost five hundred applications for citizenship in Farmington. As for the riot, more than one hundred people received indictments from the St. Francois County grand jury, but any serious charges were eventually dropped. Only four men were found guilty and fined one hundred dollars plus court costs.[54]

"It is important not to mistake the riot for some ill-defined prowar nativist uprising against anyone not 100 percent American," observes historian Christopher C. Gibbs. Resentful of corporate bosses who had recently begun to modernize mining operations, and facing conscription into the military to fight a war that many opposed amid the threat of losing their jobs to immigrants, American miners lashed out at easy targets in "a case of one group of victims punishing another." From this perspective, the Lead Belt Riot appears as a particularly ugly example among many instances of wartime sabotage in Missouri and in the Ozarks. The war's early days saw strike-related violence in St. Louis and Kansas City, and just a few months before the Lead Belt Riot, violence erupted across the region in Springfield between striking streetcar workers and imported strikebreakers.[55]

Politics and Protest

Labor strife continued after the war with prolonged strikes on the region's rail lines following the conversion from wartime government control back to private ownership. Rancor on the M&NA ultimately led to the hanging of a striker near Harrison, Arkansas, a deed attributed to Ku Klux Klansmen and other anti-strike vigilantes. In Springfield, Frisco employees taking part in a nationwide railroad strike in 1922 enjoyed more local support. But, as historian Stephen L. McIntyre illustrates, "national events far beyond the control of Springfield residents ultimately determined the fate of the strike," which came to a halt in the fall of the year when a federal court declared the stoppage a conspiracy under the Sherman Antitrust Act. One of the few bright spots for the region's organized labor in the wake of the failed strikes was the strong bond forged between Democrats and unions. Springfield union leader Reuben Wood, who "did more than any other labor leader in Missouri's history to advance the cause of organized labor," later represented southwestern Missouri's sixth district in congress during Franklin D. Roosevelt's first two administrations. Such sustained Democratic leadership in southwestern Missouri was out of the ordinary in the post–Civil War years, however.[56]

An examination of county voting patterns in presidential elections between 1876 and 1928 illustrates the region's political divisions. With few exceptions, Republican candidates tended to carry the counties of Missouri's southwestern quadrant, while Democrats received the bulk of votes from residents in the counties of the southeast. The two-party system had a better go of it in counties along the Missouri and Mississippi rivers and in a few places where Republican redoubts faded into Democratic domain. Though most Arkansas counties remained firmly rooted in southern Democracy throughout the era, the influx of midwestern immigrants into parts of the Missouri Ozarks gradually increased the Republicans' footprint. Counties along the Frisco such as Webster, Laclede, and Crawford had switched from Democrat to Republican control by the late 1880s, and the first two decades of the twentieth century would see about a dozen others join them in the fold of the Grand Old Party, including once-Democratic strongholds such as Howell, McDonald, Morgan, and Newton counties.[57]

The Ozark uplift's landscape of yeoman farmers and rural miners would seem to have provided a perfect breeding ground for third-party politics during the era of agrarian and labor protests. Greenback Party presidential candidate James B. Weaver ran much stronger in the region than in the country as a whole in 1880, carrying almost one in six voters in the interior counties of the Missouri Ozarks and winning pluralities in Douglas and St. Clair. The same election sent Springfield's Ira Sherwin Hazeltine to congress on the Greenback ticket. The end of the decade found more than two dozen populist-minded newspapers spread across the region, but the number of Ozarkers casting ballots for third-party candidates in 1888 fell to one in twelve. Though most people in the region continued to align themselves with one of the two major parties, the Ozarks made at least two notable contributions to the era's narrative of political dissension. The region provided the birthplace of one of the era's most enduring symbols of farmer protest and produced a politician so closely associated with one of populism's central goals that it granted him an unforgettable nickname.[58]

In Arkansas agrarian political protest was largely the work of two farmers' organizations that sprouted from native soil in 1882: the Agricultural Wheel and the Brothers of Freedom. The latter had its birth on the south slope of the Boston Mountains in the rural community of Ozone in Johnson County. The founder and chief leader of the Brothers of Freedom, a Canadian-born, New England–raised postwar homesteader named Isaac McCracken, espoused a creed that was a "mountain grown blend of scripture, the Declaration of Independence and the Greenback platform." McCracken was one of perhaps fifteen agrarian candidates to win a seat in the Arkansas General Assembly, and the Brothers of Freedom swept county offices in Johnson, Newton, and Van Buren. The Brothers had expanded well beyond the Boston Mountains by the time they merged with the Agricultural Wheel a year later, adopting the latter name for the organization. McCracken became president and brought the political sensibilities of the Brothers with him. Dissatisfied with the futility of relying on endorsed Democrats to do their bidding, McCracken and the Agricultural Wheel joined forces with the Knights of Labor in 1888 under the banner of the Union Labor Party. The party made a strong showing in the face of probable voter fraud on the part of Democrats, but the 1889 general assembly came and went without notable change. "Stolen elections, violence, and disfranchisement killed the third-party movement in Arkansas," notes historian Matthew Hild of the early 1890s, leaving the state securely in the hands of conservative Democrats.[59]

By 1896 two decades of political dissension had lost its steam in the face of major party opposition and chicanery, and third-party protest had been reduced to single-issue politics focusing on expansion of the money supply through the free coinage of silver. Promising that a bimetallic system based on both gold and silver would increase slumping crop prices and relieve debtors, promoters of the silver issue appealed to wage-earning laborers as well as yeoman farmers venturing deeper into market agriculture. In the Ozarks and much of the rest of the nation, Democrats effectively co-opted the silver issue as part of a more populist-oriented Democratic platform. In the process one Missouri Ozarker played a crucial role in the Democrats' embrace of silver coinage.

Though largely forgotten outside his home county of Laclede, longtime Democratic congressman Richard P. Bland was perhaps more closely associated with silver coinage advocacy than was any other politician in the country—so much so that he became "Silver Dick" to constituents and colleagues alike. A Kentucky native who spent the war years in the silver-mining boomtowns of the Comstock Lode in modern-day Nevada, "Silver Dick" Bland cosponsored the Bland-Allison Act of 1878, which required the U.S. Treasury to purchase at least two million dollars' worth of silver per month and convert it to legal tender. The act's overturning fifteen years later set the tone for the election of 1896. The surging popularity of bimetallism made Silver Dick a leading candidate for nomination as president going into the Democratic National Convention. Bland, who followed tradition by skipping the raucous Chicago meeting, emerged as the leading vote-getter in early balloting but was eventually bested by a much younger and more dynamic midwestern silver advocate, William Jennings Bryan, whose impassioned "Cross of Gold" speech made him the new voice of mainstream agrarian discontent. Bryan may not have been an Ozarker, but his message resonated with the region's common man. He captured several dependable Republican counties and made the strongest showing in the Ozarks of any Democratic presidential candidate of the late nineteenth century. To this day, Bryan remains the only Democrat to carry Douglas County, Missouri, in the post–Civil War era.[60]

Not only did Bryan's "Cross of Gold" speech forever alter the relationship between presidential hopefuls and political conventions, but his decision to travel the country stumping on his own behalf revolutionized presidential campaigning. At one point the speechmaking tour brought him through the Ozarks on the Frisco line, where adoring crowds gathered to see and hear the "Great Commoner." Among the various advisers accompanying Bryan on his journey through the region was William Hope Harvey, a Chicago resident who may have been the only person in America more identified with the free silver movement than was Silver Dick Bland. Just two years earlier Harvey had gained nationwide recognition when he authored a booklet presenting the case for ditching the gold standard. Sales of *Coin's Financial School* netted Harvey a small fortune and granted him a new nickname to go along with his sudden fame. Both "Coin" Harvey and his candidate took to the Ozarks. Bryan returned to southwestern

Missouri just two weeks after his defeat to shoot whitetail deer in a remote hunting park on the White River in Taney County.[61]

Watering Holes and Float Fishing

Coin Harvey, not surprisingly, was drawn to a rural community called Silver Springs, located even farther up the White River near the bustling railroad town of Rogers, Arkansas. Harvey bought half a section of land there a few years later and opened a grand tourist resort that he named Monte Ne. (It might seem blasphemous that old Coin would drop "Silver Springs," but Harvey probably suspected the wealthy vacationers he coveted were perfectly happy with the gold standard.) At the height of its popularity in the years before World War I, Monte Ne featured a golf course, dance pavilion, tennis court, and the first indoor swimming pool in Arkansas. Harvey and his backers even imported an authentic Venetian gondola to carry visitors across a slough that separated the Monte Ne depot from the hotels. Among Monte Ne's most sought-after guests were Tulsans bathed in oil money, a clientele Harvey targeted with the resort's Oklahoma Row.[62]

Only in the post–World War II years would tourism come to dominate the economy across much of the Ozarks, but the industry's roots lay in the era between the Civil War and the Depression. The region's tourism industry depended heavily on natural resources. Scenic vistas, caves, and springs lured curiosity seekers and those in search of the romance of nature. Wealthy and middle-class sportsmen from St. Louis and Kansas City retreated to the region's plentiful streams and woodlands to fish and hunt. Tens of thousands of people sought physical and psychological rejuvenation at mineral water spas and hillside lodges that sprang up around the Ozarks. By the second decade of the twentieth century, the region even became a magnet for literary tourists, as fans of Harold Bell Wright flocked to southwestern Missouri in search of the people who inspired his characters and the divine peace that pervaded his pages. Underlying all these endeavors was a spirit of primitivism, the modernist's desire to exchange an increasingly urban, conformist world for one seemingly unburdened with anxiety and pollution. But the search for a preindustrial arcadia in the rural Ozarks paralleled an age of natural resource exploitation that endangered the very physical beauty attracting visitors. The rise of the tourism industry itself—like science's observer effect—invariably altered and sometimes extinguished the very traits sought by tourists.

Springs became popular gathering places in Europe and in the eastern United States in the first half of the nineteenth century, and they were magnets that drew the curious and the ill even in a sparsely settled place like the Ozarks. But it was only in the post–Civil War era that the mineral water fad developed into a full-fledged boom in North America. The Ozarks, one of the nation's great karst regions, played its part in the mineral water craze, and the explosion of spa building proved to be but an early chapter in a long history of Ozarks tourism.

In the populist tradition of the Ozarks, some of the earliest "spa towns" were rude camps that inspired no visions of elite eastern watering holes. Among the earliest primitive spas in the region was Sulphur Springs in the Boston Mountains of Newton County, Arkansas. Hundreds converged on Sulphur Springs each summer in search of rest and recuperation in the hot days after crops were laid by. Before the 1870s were out, Sulphur Springs featured two stores, a schoolhouse, and two boardinghouses charging two dollars per week. More rustic was the situation at Hood's Spring in the Cherokee country of northeastern Oklahoma. As a boy in the 1880s, a rheumatic Ben Greer and a coughing friend were hauled some forty miles from their homes in northwestern Arkansas and left at Hood's with only firearms, a wagon, and pots and pans. For five weeks the young teenagers fed themselves on squirrel and turkey and shared Hood's waters with Cherokees who came to the spring to fill their jugs.[63]

Though incredulous locals familiar with Newton County's Sulphur Springs had no "more confidence in them than any springs they have ever been acquainted with," promoters trumpeted the curative powers of mineral water. And self-appointed experts backed them up. University of Missouri chemistry professor Paul Schweitzer ensured the skeptical that "many of these waters indeed possess virtues of a very high order, which . . . destine them to become sources of relief for suffering mankind." Among a litany of ailments the waters were believed to treat were malaria, heartburn, eczema, liver and kidney disorders, and dyspepsia. Claiming that the water of a spring healed his cut while he was on a hunting trip in rural Christian County, Missouri, the fatefully named Fountain T. Welch promoted the spa town of Ponce de Leon. It and other nearby boomtowns Reno Spring and Eau de Vie Spring blossomed in the 1880s and continued to attract visitors and entrepreneurs until a chemical test of Reno's waters in the 1890s revealed it to be nothing more than an ordinary spring. Many promoters followed Welch's example and chose names that promised rejuvenation. Cedar County, Missouri, boasted spa towns known as El Dorado and Balm. In northwestern Arkansas, Electric Springs and Elixir Springs vowed to quicken the step.[64]

No spa town's name elicited the heady promise and financial potential of the enterprise as surely as did Arkansas's Eureka Springs, the most famous and enduring of the entire region. Locals had long known about the alleged curative powers of a cluster of more than sixty springs, but it was only in 1879, after a prominent local judge claimed the waters cured a sore on his leg, that health seekers rushed to find relief amid the steep hollers in the White River Hills of

Carroll County. Like most spa towns, the earliest years represented a sort of Wild West phase as squatters pitched tents and erected shanties on hillsides and jostled for space in makeshift bathhouses and along muddy stream banks. Even after former Arkansas governor Powell Clayton and a group of his enterprising Republican friends completed an eighteen-and-a-half-mile railroad connecting Eureka Springs to the Frisco in early 1883, the place bore little resemblance to posh resorts back east.[65]

"This is the worst apology for a watering place I ever saw," wrote a visitor from St. Louis in the summer of 1885. Known to posterity only as Ed, he found little to recommend in this dirty, disorganized excuse for a vacation destination. "The houses . . . of all sizes and shapes (except neat or pretty) are scattered all around over the hills and valleys, without any regularity at all," Ed complained. "The streets run in all directions, forming triangles, semi-circles, and various other geometrical figures except right angles, and there are no two houses fronting the same way." Even more troubling than the nonconformist architecture and whomper-jawed layout was the leper-colony clientele, "a motley, dirty, lazy set of people—squatters who have settled here when the fever first struck." Ed found Eureka's streets and springs teeming with invalids and rheumatics hobbling "about with the aid of sticks, people with plaster over their faces or hands, indicating the presence of cancers or ulcers or paralyzed in an arm or foot." The persnickety St. Louisan predicted that it would "require years to exterminate the objectionable classes of people and to get rid of their hovels," thus preventing the "poor, dirty and ignorant" from scaring "off the desirable people from a watering place."[66]

Powell Clayton and the investors in his Eureka Improvement Company wouldn't have said so publicly, but they likely shared Ed's concerns. The goal, after all, was not to cram the hollers full of consumptives and the walking dead but to turn Eureka into an Ozarks version of New York's Saratoga Springs. Their plans were already in full bloom by the time Ed made his way back to the smoggy comforts of St. Louis. On May 1, 1886, the grand five-story, quarried-stone Crescent Hotel opened for business in a twenty-seven-acre park atop West Mountain. Costing more than a quarter of a million dollars, the one-hundred-room hotel featured gaslights, steam heating, and a hydraulic elevator and provided guests a bowling alley, tennis courts, and croquet grounds. The opening of the Crescent Hotel marked a turning point in the history of Eureka. Aided by Frisco promotion, the spa town attracted more and more wealthy patrons from St. Louis. At the dawn of the twentieth century, Eureka Springs boasted an electric streetcar and modern utilities.[67]

Low-rent spa towns continued to attract Ed's undesirables, but many watering holes turned toward posh accommodations for the wealthy. In 1890 St. Louis investors built the imposing Gasconade Hotel at Lebanon, Missouri. Constructed

Eureka Springs, Arkansas, 1914. Courtesy of Library of Congress.

atop a well whose waters displayed magnetic properties, the Gasconade failed to turn a profit and burned to the ground in 1900. In the northwestern corner of Arkansas, the spa town of Sulphur Springs (not the one mentioned earlier) boomed after the Kansas City Southern reached the place in 1889. A dam on Butler Creek created a half-mile-long lake, and bathhouses at each spring declared their waters' unique curative powers. Bottled water from the springs was shipped as far away as Texas, and wealthy patrons from Kansas City and elsewhere summered at one of the town's seven hotels, including the spacious Kihlberg Hotel and Bath House, which could house up to two hundred guests.[68]

Declining public faith in the curative powers of spring water resulted in a rapid demise in the early 1900s. The 1905 completion of the architecturally anomalous Basin Park Hotel—constructed on the side of a steep hill, each of its eight floors had ground-level access—proved to be the last hurrah of the spa era in Eureka Springs. Three years later the town's Crescent Hotel reacted to declining business by renting out its facilities for use as a women's college and taking guests only in the summer months. While the Frisco promoted Eureka Springs and other towns near its lines, rarely did travelers in southeastern Missouri ride the rails to spa towns, which were few and far between. Even the "Big Springs Country" of the Courtois Hills played little role in the region's mineral water craze. Southeastern Missouri's best-known—and perhaps the Ozark region's most unusual—resort appeared during World War I when an Illinois doctor built a native-stone building at the entrance of Welch Cave/Spring on the upper Current River in Shannon County. Convinced that the air issuing forth from the subterranean depths would ease the suffering of asthmatics, the doctor had no cure for his sanitarium's isolation and let the property go for tax forfeiture during the Depression.[69]

The country traversed by the St. Louis, Iron Mountain, and Southern Railway was not devoid of charms for the vacationist, however. Just a train ride of a few hours from St. Louis, Iron County's Arcadia Valley developed into a weekend getaway and summer-home refuge for wealthy urbanites. A popular spot for the retreats of religious denominations, the Arcadia Valley lured generations of affluent St. Louisans with promises of cool mountain breezes and stunning hilltop views of green valleys. No individual played a more crucial role in promoting the valley as a destination and summer abode than did longtime Ironton resident and Union veteran John W. Emerson. Effectively retired in the early 1870s, the New England–born land baron developed his immaculate Sylvan Lake estate just outside Ironton. Featuring a brick Italianate house, summer cottages, manicured trout ponds, and a small lake, all lit by yard lanterns, the Emerson estate became the showplace from which he touted the Arcadia Valley as a western Saratoga Springs to friends in the St. Louis business community. An avid outdoorsman, Emerson also worked with the U.S. Fish Commission to stock the Current and Black rivers and other streams with salmon and trout in 1879. Nonindigenous species that almost never reproduced in the wild Ozarks, Emerson's trout and salmon were likely gone by the time the region's first fishing and hunting clubs sprang up a decade later.[70]

Emerging from its roots in the rural havens of wealthy industrialists, float fishing matured around the turn of the century and anchored outdoor tourism in the Ozarks in the decades preceding World War II. In the late 1880s, railroad executives, lumber company bigwigs, and other wealthy sportsmen from St. Louis, Kansas City, and Springfield founded getaways like the Current River Fishing and Hunting Club in Ripley County and the Carter County Fishing and Shooting Club. Building clubhouses on the swift-moving stream, members bought flat-bottomed boats constructed at sawmills by local craftsmen. Choked for much of the year with massive rafts of ties and lumber, however, the Current, the Black, and other southeastern Missouri streams—where "exploitation rather than recreation was the principal pursuit"—did not develop into popular float-fishing destinations. Other locations in the region filled that void. As early as the 1870s in the northern Ozarks, St. Louis sportsmen had begun bringing their dogs and boats by rail to hunt and fish the Gasconade River and its tributary, the Big Piney. Here, too, private clubhouses and rustic resorts sprang up within a short ride of the Frisco's tracks. St. Louis postal workers established their Kickapoo Lodge while brewers founded Griesedick Lodge. The Gasconade's destinations included the Jerome Hunting and Fishing Club (promoted by sporting goods magnate George H. Rawlings) and the Dixon Hunting and Fishing Club.[71]

Sitting at the center of the Gasconade country's float-fishing region were the twin towns of Arlington and Jerome. By the mid-1890s, the *St. Louis Globe-Democrat*'s "Rod and Gun" column and other urban publications regularly described the outings of prominent sportsmen to the "Catskills of Missouri." Favorite subjects in these accounts were the local fishing and hunting guides, "mythic pathfinders" who knew every shoal and eddy of the river and whose colorful stories enhanced the exotic ambience of the experience. In the Gasconade country, no guide was more respected than Perry Andres. A former tie rafter and market hunter, Andres developed the most extensive guiding service in the watershed, with more than a dozen outfitting camps extending from the upper Big Piney River to the lower Gasconade. Operating out of his headquarters at Arlington and making frequent forays to St. Louis to drum up business, Andres and his guides used wooden boats crafted by his brother and cousin. Ike Sturgeon, the "Natty Bumppo of the Osage," shepherded St. Louis sportsmen down the Ozark region's northernmost river in his twenty-five-foot-long, three-foot-wide, handmade sassafras boat. Another river guide may have indirectly affected the very creation of the social construct of the Ozarks. Visiting the O-Joe Club on the Elk River near Noel, Missouri, with his parents in 1899, a seven-year-old Vance Randolph "perceived at once that a guide named Price Payne was the greatest man in the world." But years before the folklorist began to craft a cussedly anachronistic portrait of his adopted region, the travelogues of wealthy sportsmen "helped 'invent' a mythical Ozarks for an urban readership." Nowhere was this truer than in the White River watershed of southwestern Missouri.[72]

It was only after the completion of the White River Line in 1906 that float fishing in rural southwestern Missouri took off. The two river towns with direct rail access, Galena and Branson, became major hubs. One of the first entrepreneurs to commercialize the float in the newly opened territory was railroad engineer W. H. Schriber, who built the Bonita Hotel Resort at Galena and hired skilled rivermen to pilot boats, cook meals, and provide fishing instructions for patrons on the serpentine float down the James and White rivers to Branson. Local guide and businessman Charlie McCord built Galena Boating Company into the largest commercial outfitter in the Ozark region. From Branson, outfitters offered guided floats of up to 250 miles downriver, as far as the new town of Cotter, Arkansas. Photojournalist Charles Phelps Cushing left one of the earliest accounts of southwestern Missouri's commercial float-fishing business after a four-day trip from Galena to Branson in 1911. Guided by "a plain country boy in faded blue overalls," Cushing paid $2.70 per day for his guide, boat, tent, and bedding, in addition to the costs for food. The photojournalist found "none of the flavor of professionalism and pose that sometimes may be detected in the Maine woods. You simply float, hunt along shore, fish for bass, shoot a few frogs and turtles, and after a camp-cooked meal enjoy your pipe in some such contented state of mind as Huck possessed that night in the cave."[73]

Cushing's young guide may have just been getting his feet wet in the trade. Four days with one of the region's more colorful chaperones—the legendary Tom Yocum, for instance—almost certainly would have inspired the retelling of a local yarn or two. Legends of the Yocum silver dollar and other fantastic tales of buried treasures were favorites. Or maybe the photojournalist and his guide were too physically uncomfortable in a boat "never more than three [feet] broad at the widest point." If Cushing had returned to float the James and White just a few years later, he would have found a craft more to his liking. By World War I the so-called johnboat—the White River country's "most famous folk product"—had evolved into the vessel of choice for the region's outfitters and tourists. A wider craft with more cargo space and leg room, the johnboat of the Ozarks could be as large as thirty-two feet long and six feet wide, though most were about four feet wide and eighteen to twenty-four feet long. By the 1920s, outfitters could be found on just about any navigable stream in the Ozarks. But the heart of the float-fishing empire still lay along the James and White rivers, where outfitters provided almost twice as many boats as did guides on the Current and Gasconade combined. Even in the depths of the Depression, Jim Owen, a former newspaperman from Jefferson City, built the region's most renowned outfitting business from his headquarters in Branson. Relying on "his finely 'trained hillbillies' who spoke a contrived dialect for visitors," Owen carried on a brisk business until the erection of Table Rock Dam on the White River in 1958.[74]

Shepherd of the Hills Country

Long before the Army Corps of Engineers ruined the float-fishing excursion in southwestern Missouri, the greater Branson area had developed into the

Ozark region's preeminent tourist destination. Branson's early attractions were primarily of the natural variety, but the publication of Harold Bell Wright's most famous novel in 1907 and the construction of the region's first man-made lake half a dozen years later elevated the once-remote area to a different plane of popularity. Branson's melding of natural and literary tourism and its complicity in cultural exploitation in the name of financial profit contributed more to the emerging cultural construct of the Ozarks than did any other place in the region. By the time the Great Depression set in, the "Shepherd of the Hills Country" had become something more than just the heart of the Ozarks. In the minds of many tourists, it *was* the Ozarks.

The origins of Branson tourism stretch back to the late nineteenth century, when Canadian William Henry Lynch and his two teenage daughters invited visitors to tour Marble Cave, today a Silver Dollar City attraction known as Marvel Cave. It proved a short-lived effort, however, and it was only after the construction of the White River Line and the completion of Powersite Dam on the White River that the Lynches returned to the Ozarks. Building a lodge and cabins and staging concerts and vaudeville shows in the cave, the Lynches attracted adventure seekers and artists who debarked at the little depot only two and a half miles away. Among the latter were a covey of Midwesterners drawn to the picturesque bluffs and vistas of the White River valley. Carl Rudolph Krafft, Rudolph Ingerle, Frank Nuderscher, and other artists formed the Society of Ozark Painters, exhibiting their work in Springfield, St. Louis, and Chicago. Like the local colorist Wright, these impressionists discovered the Ozarks just as their style was eclipsed by practitioners of more modern, experimental forms. Later adopting the Arcadia Valley as their seat of inspiration, the Ozark Painters rejected many of the tenets of modern art. Their romantic depictions of a rustic land ever so lightly touched by humanity was a perfect complement to the emerging Ozarks image of the interwar years—and the perfect adornments for a trilogy of regional histories a century later.[75]

The Lynches welcomed a new breed of visitor as well: the literary tourist. By the time the cave reopened in 1913, *The Shepherd of the Hills* had captured the imagination of tens of thousands of readers smitten with Harold Bell Wright's characters and his descriptions of the bucolic Ozarks. Longing for a place and a people untouched by the corrupting hand of modernity, tourists from St. Louis, Chicago, and other urban locales made the cave part of a three-pronged expedition that included a visit with the Rosses (local storekeepers who had inspired the good-hearted Matthewses of the novel) and a hike to the tiny post office of Notch. Holding court at the latter was Levi Morrill, an aging New Englander who had provided the model for a minor *Shepherd* character called Uncle Ike. The Rosses and Morrill became willing participants in the area's commercialized efforts to reinvent itself to match the world of Wright's imagination.[76]

It was no mere coincidence that the Lynches chose 1913 as the year to re-open their cave. That was also the year that Joplin's Ozark Power and Water Company completed a modest dam on the White River just upstream from Forsyth. The small lake it created, Taneycomo, quickly became the greatest single tourist attraction in the Shepherd of the Hills Country. Before the year was out, two resorts sprang up on the north side of the lake: the Sammy Lane Resort (named for the novel's ingénue) at Branson and the Cliff House on the bluff overlooking the dam. With its dance hall, tennis court, horseback riding, and float-fishing outfitters, the Cliff House catered to urban sportsmen and their families. Within two years of the dam's completion, a Kansas City couple built Taneycomo's most ambitious resort, Rockaway Beach. Selling cottage lots to affluent families, Rockaway boasted a "Japanese style" dance pavilion with a full-time summer orchestra by the 1920s. Not to be outdone, the Cliff House recruited wealthy members from across the Midwest, including noted Chicago trial lawyer Clarence Darrow.[77]

The agnostic Darrow was an outlier in Shepherd of the Hills Country. Wright's novel—though nonsectarian and perhaps a bit too mystical for fundamental-ists—was nonetheless infused with a broad Protestant spiritualism. The area's early tourism developments seemed to take their cues directly from the author's moralizing conservatism. Across the White River from Branson, Springfield real estate developer William H. Johnson sold land to two institutions that ensured a more staid and sober atmosphere. One was a Chautauqua ground and sum-mer retreat established by the Southwest Presbyterian Assembly. Motivated by the same anti-urban and antimodern spirit that pervaded *The Shepherd of the Hills*, the Presbyterians worked to keep Taney County free of saloons and limited access to their facilities to organizations that shared their sentiments, such as the Women's Christian Temperance Union and the Campfire Girls. The Presbyterians' next-door neighbor was a Young Men's Christian Association summer school, Camp Ozark.[78]

As time went on, the lines between myth and reality, fiction and fact, became more blurred than ever. Pearl Spurlock's Shepherd of the Hills taxi carted eager fans of the novel over the glade rocks and creek beds that passed as backroads west of Branson, pointing out the homes and landmarks that inspired the novel-ist's enduring portrait of the Ozarks. Locals posed for photographs as characters from the novel. On his trip to scout locations for a film version of *The Shepherd of the Hills* in 1918, Wright himself encountered no fewer than three Sammy Lanes, one of whom offered him a pony ride for fifty cents.[79]

Mother Roads and State Parks

Spurlock's "tour bus" may have rattled the innards of anyone looking for "the trail that is nobody knows how old," but it also reflected the most significant development in the tourism industry after World War I. The proliferation of automobiles spurred early highway building efforts, and in turn the improved roadways led to new tourist developments. By most accounts the Ozark region greeted the twentieth century with some of the worst roads in the middle of the continent. Tradition left maintenance to crews of men required to devote a specified number of days each year to road labor. Described by one small-town Arkansas newspaper editor as a "relic of the ignorance, injustice and barbarism of the dark ages," this nineteenth-century holdover came under fire from advocates of the good roads movement in the Progressive Era. Among the most vociferous were businessmen whose livelihoods depended on tourism. Wielding the biggest bullhorn in the Ozarks was Monte Ne proprietor "Coin" Harvey, who launched the Ozark Trails Association (OTA) in 1912 to promote improved roads in the region.[80]

The OTA did not actually build or fund roads but instead channeled its efforts into tourism promotion. Within a few years thousands of delegates gathered at OTA conventions in cities both within the region and far beyond to promote the growing network of trails and ensure their towns a place on a planned main route from St. Louis to Southern California. Ultimately, Harvey's brainchild did little more than publish an atlas and mark telephone poles, roadside barns, and concrete obelisks between Missouri and New Mexico with its familiar green "O.T." against a white backdrop. The OTA was not the only good roads/tourism organization operating in the region. In 1915—almost two decades before his spat with Vance Randolph—Springfieldian John T. Woodruff oversaw the formation of the Inter-Ozark Highway Association, which drafted its own attractive sign—a Maltese cross with the letters I.O.H. painted on a red background. Woodruff also worked with the St. Louis Business Men's League to build the Ozark Highway between the metropolis and Springfield, a road eventually absorbed into the OTA network. Farther east, Mountain Grove, Missouri, banker J. A. Chase served as president of the Ozark Scenic Highway Association, which began promoting the construction of present-day U.S. Highway 60 during World War I. Established in Joplin in 1919, the Ozark Playgrounds Association boosted the sites and scenes of southwestern Missouri and northwestern Arkansas with its slogan "The Land of a Million Smiles."[81]

These tourism-minded associations may not have built roads, but their voices added to the growing chorus of good roads advocates who eventually forced the hand of government. At the height of the Progressive Era in 1916, Congress passed the Federal Highway Act, which laid the groundwork for a national highway system and provided matching funds for state road-building initiatives. Follow-up legislation in Missouri and Oklahoma shifted highway construction and maintenance from county to state oversight with the creation of highway commissions and provided funding for building projects through gas taxes. Arkansas was slower to respond to the federal government's offer of matching funds. Only in the late 1920s did the perpetually impoverished state enact significant improvements, just in time for the Great Depression to let the air out of the program's tires. By then the days of the old road associations had come to an end. In 1926 a joint board of federal and state representatives endorsed a proposal for a uniform nationwide system of numbered highways. The board designated more than half a dozen federal routes through the Ozarks, most of which were graded and graveled by the end of the decade and hard-surfaced by the beginning of World War II. The region's most famous road received its numerical designation at an April 30, 1926, meeting in Springfield amid the hoopla of a Rotarian convention. Route 66, eventually immortalized in song and on screen, connected Chicago with Los Angeles via St. Louis, Tulsa, Amarillo, and Santa Fe. The Ozarks section of the route followed the ancient spine of the uplift, largely paralleling the Frisco's line from the outskirts of St. Louis to Springfield and then westward to Joplin before exiting the region in northeastern Oklahoma.[82]

The completion of Route 66 through the Ozarks in 1931 ushered in a golden age of roadside tourism that lasted into mid-century. Tourist courts, cafés, gift shops, and campgrounds sprouted along the "Mother Road," pumping commerce and adventure into formerly sleepy little hamlets like Hooker, Halltown, and Devil's Elbow. Merchants frequently played up the region's hillbilly image with rustic handicrafts that satisfied urban preconceptions of old-timey folkways in the rural Ozarks. In Pulaski County, near the community of Clementine, a number of families made their livings crafting white oak baskets, straight-backed chairs, and footstools. In 1928 basket maker William F. Childers relocated from Texas County to "Basketville" and built a log house alongside Route 66. Here the extended Childers clan manufactured baskets and other wood products in a large shop filled with belt-driven machines. By the latter years of the Depression, the basket business had become so lucrative for another Basketville family, the Beckers, that they began wholesaling handmade merchandise to popular area tourist stops such as the Novelty House and the Totem Pole.[83]

Despite the tourist trade's penchant for anachronism and the locals' willing complicity in the "selling of tradition," Route 66 was usually the bearer of modernity. In July 1928, Pierce Petroleum opened a state-of-the-art, eighty-thousand-dollar California mission-style terminal on the Mother Road in Springfield. Featuring a bus station, restaurant, soda fountain, filling station, garage, and car wash, the Pierce-Pennant system's twentieth-century tavern may have been the

Postcard for a Route 66 souvenir stop, Strafford, Missouri. Courtesy of John F. Bradbury Jr. Collection, RA1652 (unprocessed at time of publication), State Historical Society of Missouri, Rolla.

most elaborate highway travel complex in the nation. One month later Pierce's second location opened at Rolla—a three-story Colonial Revival building boasting a dance hall and enough "snob appeal" to balance out the rustic cornpone vibe of Basketville just down the road. Like Sam Walton four decades later, Pierce Petroleum saw enough potential in the Ozarks economy to launch what it hoped would become a nationwide chain in one of the country's most rural regions. The company's success at Springfield and Rolla prompted Pierce to build similar Route 66 tavern complexes farther west, but these "visual symbols of refinement" did not wear well in a Depression decade that came to celebrate simplicity and commonness. By the early 1940s, the Pierce Pennant tavern was a thing of the past.[84]

It was the less patrician auto traveler that fueled the emergence of the state park system in the interwar years. In the Ozarks, Missouri assumed an early and active role in the phenomenon, as its initial foray into park creation focused almost exclusively on the hills widely recognized as the playground for the well-to-do of Kansas City and St. Louis. Missouri created its parks program as a division of the state's game and fish department in 1919, just three years after the establishment of the National Park Service. But it was only in 1924 that the state founded its first parks, beginning with Round Spring on the Current River in Shannon County. In fact, the first eight parks initiated into the system were located in the Ozarks, almost all of them in the rugged Courtois Hills. Before the year 1924 came to a close, the state had secured the land around Big Spring, just down the Current from Van Buren, as well as a little summer resort at Alley Spring on the Jacks Fork River. The first state parks emphasized wildlife conservation, fishing, and hunting, but tourism and the promotion of state parks as weekend and summer getaways for suburbanites quickly eclipsed all other considerations under the oversight of Game and Fish commissioner Keith McCanse, who "almost singlehandedly molded the state park image into a vital element of the Ozarkian touristic landscape." A native of southwestern Missouri, McCanse made highly publicized floats on regional streams, boosted the new state parks on Jefferson City's WOS radio station, and stuffed the monthly *Missouri Game and Fish News* with romantic stories of Ozarks lore and locales.[85]

In the Courtois Hills, the state parks movement reflected the central role of the budding tourism industry in a poor area with few viable alternatives in the post–timber boom era. It also reflected a willingness to refashion history and manipulate regional imagery in service to tourists' expectations. In Eminence the boosterish editor of the weekly newspaper published a twenty-one-point list of instructions for interacting with tourists, ranging from keeping livestock off the roads to whitewashing fence posts. Like the residents of *The Andy Griffith Show*'s fictional Mayberry—whose efforts to impress Hollywood visitors almost led them to cut down the town's beloved old oak tree—the *Current Wave*'s editor and his ilk even impressed upon locals the necessity of getting rid of those apparently unsightly rail fences and yard gates that had seen better days. A good dose of modernization seemed to be the elixir for a hayseedy image as far as the progressive sort was concerned, but not everyone agreed that newer and neater was better. Over at Alley Spring, state parks construction engineer A. L. Drumeller ordered the demolition of the park's modern store building with its town-like false façade. In its place workers erected a more rustic-looking, pine-log structure built not in the style of the nineteenth-century Ozarks hewn-log building but in the Craftsman style borrowed from the North Woods, popularized by the National Park Service, and adopted as the motif for Missouri's state parks. In this age of regional image making, the real story of the Ozarks and Ozarkers was always more complex than it seemed.[86]

4 OZARKS SOCIETY

Benjamin Franklin (B. F.) Adams was just a boy when his family arrived in Springfield, Missouri, in the heart of the Civil War. The small town burgeoned with people like the Adamses, refugees from the violent and dangerous interior Ozarks. B. F. recalled scant details from his boyhood in northern Arkansas—a few names of neighbors, a trip by flatboat down the White River with an uncle. His country life behind him, B. F. Adams grew up with the blossoming postwar town, the place that came to call itself the Queen City of the Ozarks. His father and an uncle found steady employment as stonemasons, building the sturdy structures of a hopeful city. Another uncle opened a barber shop, took an active role in the Republican Party, and served multiple terms on Springfield's city council. Taking advantage of opportunities never afforded his parents, B. F. Adams completed high school and launched a short-lived effort as a newspaper owner and editor. For more than forty years, he taught school and conducted summer institutes for fellow teachers throughout southwestern Missouri. An eager joiner and community stalwart, Adams devoted three decades as a leader and lecturer for the Knights of Pythias and the Masons and oversaw financial affairs at the neighborhood Methodist church.[1]

The life of B. F. Adams spanned almost the full eighty years from the Civil War through the Great Depression. At first glance the collective story of B. F. Adams and his extended family was unremarkable and thus representative of tens of thousands of families of the era. Like most Ozarkers, Adams's primary concerns were family, community, and the social institutions that enveloped them—schools, churches, fraternal organizations. The experiences of the Adamses also reflected more specific postwar developments. The family's transition to "urban" life coincided with the growth of towns and small cities in a still overwhelmingly rural region and the economic and social cleavages that accompanied that process. Life beyond the farms, forests, mines, and mills of the Ozarks was a microcosm of the American experience in the era between the Civil War and the Great Depression, with an occasional splash of regional distinctiveness. It was a crucial element to a fuller understanding of what it meant to be an Ozarker in the very age that invented the concept.

African American Life

For the Adams family, there was one more social distinction that played a central role in their day-to-day lives: race. They were among the thousands of formerly enslaved who forged new lives as freedmen and women in the face of discrimination. Race played a role in the evolution of Ozarks society in the post–Civil War years. The region's lily-whiteness (98 percent of the population at the beginning of the Depression) contributed to the developing imagery of both heroic Anglo-Saxon descendants and degenerate hillbillies in an age of Jim Crow segregation and rising nativism. Still, nonwhites carved out their own livelihoods and cultural identities in some locations. When the state of Oklahoma joined the Union in 1907, there were almost forty-two thousand registered Cherokees living in the old Indian Territory, roughly two-thirds of whom resided in the Ozark uplift. The Flint District in the forested Cookson Hills of southern Adair and Cherokee counties was home to the largest concentration of full-blooded Cherokees, those most likely to speak the native tongue at home and use the language in worship services. Much smaller numbers of Senecas, Quapaws, Wyandottes, Shawnees, Peorias, and Modocs resided in the hills just beyond southwestern Missouri's border.[2]

Though fewer in number than Native Americans in the cultural Ozarks, African Americans were more broadly dispersed in the region. Ranging from minuscule or nonexistent throughout large swaths of the region to substantial in a few towns and rural places, their presence created different dynamics from one locality to another. These local dynamics on occasion spawned unexpected stories of racial harmony. They also bred violence and oppression. On the whole they resulted in a Black-and-white world not unlike that in other parts of the border South, a place where the Jim Crow order gained the upper hand but where former enslaved people and their descendants crafted lives of purpose and promise out of challenging circumstances.

Like the Adamses, thousands of freedmen and women relocated during the decade following 1860. Many of them left the Ozarks entirely. In the region's interior counties, the Black population declined by more than one-third during the 1860s, as many left their former masters' homes for places like Kansas and St. Louis. Even with an influx of exodusters that grew the number of African Americans by more than one-third in the 1870s, the interior's Black population

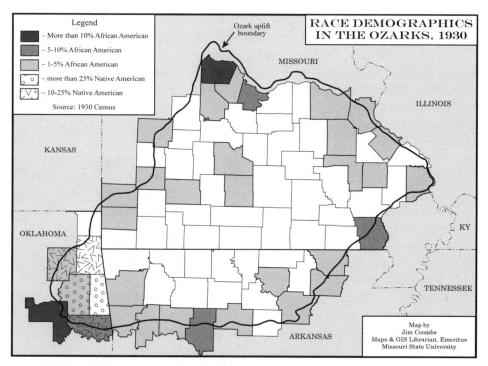

Race Demographics in the Ozarks, 1930. Courtesy of Jim Coombs, Missouri State University, Springfield.

stagnated thereafter. While the overall population of the interior Ozarks topped one million by the early 1900s, the percentage of African Americans steadily declined to statistical insignificance, falling below 1 percent by the end of World War I. One of the few places in the region that experienced a Black influx was Greene County, Missouri, specifically Springfield. Securely in the hands of Union forces for the final three years of the war, Springfield served as a beacon of freedom for hundreds of families like the Adamses. Greene County's Black population grew by more than one-quarter in the 1860s and continued to expand in the following years before plateauing at 3,441 in 1890, accounting for almost one in four African Americans in the interior Ozarks.[3]

Pressure from intolerant whites was a push factor in Black migration, as were the rugged interior's war-torn farms and comparatively infertile land, both of which discouraged the development of the extensive farm tenancy system that emerged in many areas of the South. Some Black families remained on the land in the rural Ozarks. Others arrived as newcomers in the region, claiming homesteads like thousands of their white contemporaries. Most notable of the exodusting homesteaders in the Ozarks was a wagon train of African American families who settled in the vicinity of Hartville, Missouri, ballooning Wright County's Black population from twenty-six in 1870 to more than four hundred by the turn of the century. In the 1890s a similar band of fifteen Black families from North Carolina established the Red River community in the Van Buren County hills north of Clinton, Arkansas. By the early twentieth century, Red River contained its own churches, businesses, and schoolhouse. For most Black Ozarkers, however, towns and cities held the greatest promise for jobs and a sense of community.[4]

The enslaved labor force in the Ozarks possessed a variety of skills, some of which aided freedmen and women in the transition to independence. Peter Van Winkle employed Black workers at his sawmill in northwestern Arkansas, where families lived in remodeled slave quarters but asserted "their humanity and equality through consumption . . . of cheap, mass-produced goods." In southeastern Missouri, freedman Louis Hill worked his way up from miner to "charger" in a Mine La Motte lead furnace, where a white coworker taught him to read between shifts. Will Gatewood, a former enslaved carriage driver in Fayetteville, Arkansas, accompanied Union troops to Springfield with his wife, Narcissa. Opening a grocery store in partnership with another formerly enslaved man, the entrepreneurial Gatewood was successful enough to send a daughter to Oberlin College and a granddaughter to Howard University.[5]

African American society was most fully realized in Springfield, which featured its own professional and business class by the late 1800s. At its height Black Springfield boasted two physicians, two lawyers, a dentist, a druggist, and several African American–owned businesses, including Hardrick Brothers. The city's largest retail grocery, Hardrick Brothers catered to a clientele of affluent whites and maintained a fleet of a dozen delivery wagons. While not as financially successful as the Hardricks, Walter "Ducky" Majors left the most intriguing legacy of the city's Black entrepreneurs. A skilled blacksmith and mechanic, Majors was the proprietor of one of the city's earliest automobile sales and repair shops and is remembered as the builder of Springfield's first horseless carriage, a steam-powered vehicle that he drove around the town square in 1901. Springfield's solidly Republican Black community exercised its influence at the polls as well, electing three different African Americans to the city council in the late nineteenth and early twentieth centuries as well as three school board members. The Greene County Court elected two different Black men to serve as county coroner, including Alfred Adams, B. F.'s uncle.[6]

Typical of African American communities across the nation, preachers and teachers in Springfield played an outsize role in local affairs. By the turn of the twentieth century, at least seven different religious congregations provided ministerial leadership. Many of the church houses doubled as elementary schools in Springfield's Jim Crow educational system, sending students to Lincoln High

Hardrick Brothers Grocery, Springfield, Missouri. Courtesy of Katherine G. Lederer Collection, Special Collections and Archives, Missouri State University, Springfield.

until integration in 1955. Members of the community also created a collection of social institutions that paralleled those of their white neighbors. Lewis Tutt, a freedman from Arkansas whose white half-brother was gunned down by "Wild Bill" Hickok on the public square, organized Springfield's first Black fraternal body, the Eureka Lodge of the Prince Hall Masons. African American women founded the Literary and Musical Society and the Literary Calm Chat Club. The community exercised its patriotic fervor in 1898 by raising Company L of the Seventh Volunteer Colored Infantry Regiment, an outfit whose first lieutenant was Springfield native and Howard University Law School graduate Thomas Campbell.[7]

Only a few other towns in the region—Batesville, Fayetteville, and Joplin among them—contained an African American population substantial enough to foster a vibrant social and institutional life, and none nourished a middle class on par with Springfield's. Beyond Greene County and the border counties fronting the Arkansas, Mississippi, and Missouri rivers, at the turn of the twentieth century only two of the region's counties contained as many as one thousand Black inhabitants. More than two in five counties in the Ozarks interior housed minute populations of fewer than one hundred African Americans.[8]

For Black families living in such isolated circumstances, social activities and even basic education were often beyond reach. In rural Newton County, Missouri, in the 1870s Marion Township lacked the fifteen school-age African Americans required by state law to justify the establishment of a separate school. Consequently, Moses and Susan Carver taught the two orphaned sons of their former bondswoman how to read and write and hired a tutor for them before sending the younger one to live with a Black couple in Neosho, which provided a school for its population of some four hundred African Americans. That precocious twelve-year-old, George Washington Carver, attended school for about a year before hitching a ride to Kansas with a family of exodusters. It was the beginning of a journey that would see him become one of the nation's most influential scientists and most famous members of his race. Just as incredible as a slave-born orphan's ascension to iconic status was the integrated Point Peter school deep in the Buffalo River wilderness of Arkansas. Living on Richland Creek in Searcy County, home to only sixteen Black residents in 1900, the children of African Americans Newton and Lucy Wyatt allegedly attended the local one-room school with white children in the 1890s and early 1900s.[9]

Relations between the white majority and tiny Black minority along Richland Creek were positive enough at the turn of the century that one of the Wyatts' neighbors penned a letter to a county weekly assuring readers that local African Americans were "all well thought of by the whites, which is proof that they are good people." What prompted the anonymous neighbor to put in a good word for the Wyatts was a recent string of incendiary, racist letters published in the *Marshall Mountain Wave* in 1899, including a local citizen's screed conjuring up the old psychosexual justification for lynching Black men. Identified only as "Scribe of Witts Spring," the writer warned readers that "no race has ever produced as large a percent of brutes who have a natural proclivity to assault unprotected females." As Scribe's letter revealed, the region's minuscule Black population did not magically preclude the existence of racism, nor did it prevent the incidences of violence and intimidation that propped up the Jim Crow order elsewhere in the South.[10]

Evidence suggests that some Ozarkers took steps to maintain their area's racial homogeneity. When the director of the State Fruit Experiment Station at Mountain Grove, Missouri, hired African Americans to dig a well, according to one account, locals schemed to tar and feather the Black laborers, forcing the director to sneak them out of town hidden beneath a load of hay. To the south in Douglas County, the plan to build the State Industrial Home for Negro Girls in a rural area ignited controversy in 1911. Gathering at the courthouse in Ava, angry citizens drafted a resolution of protest against the "young nigger-wench reform school" and made thinly veiled threats of arson, convincing state officials to relocate the institution. In fact, the absence of African Americans became a

point of pride and promotion for not a few locales in the region. A 1915 adver-
tisement for a realty business in the small town of Gentry, Arkansas, promised
newcomers "no saloons, no negroes." "We are pleased to announce that Shannon
County has no negroes," boasted an Eminence newspaper a half dozen years
later, "and we will no doubt be just as well off to continue without them."[11]

Exceptional breaches of the social order certainly existed, whether it be the
Point Peter integrated school or another Buffalo River community where a
Black man and his white wife raised their seven mixed-race children in seeming
harmony with their neighbors. But even in areas of the region with almost no
African Americans, the era's taboo against sexual contact between Black men
and white women was almost always rigidly enforced. In the 1890s a white
woman and a Black man were arrested in Crawford County, Missouri, after
the woman gave birth to a mixed-race child. When his wife gave birth to a
child by her African American lover, white Springfield policeman Jesse Brake
distributed pamphlets condemning Black men as lustful beasts and rapists. The
uproar eventually resulted in the conviction of the Black man in question, John
McCracken, on trumped-up charges of rape. Two attempts by angry mobs to
storm the jail convinced the sheriff to spirit McCracken away to safety.[12]

McCracken eventually had his sentence commuted upon the testimony of his
former lover, but similar episodes too often ended in tragedy for accused Black
men. The decades surrounding the turn of the twentieth century saw a rapid
uptick in lynchings and race-related violence across the nation. Over a dozen-
year period beginning in 1894, violence motivated by racial tensions erupted
with disturbing regularity in the Ozarks. Each one of these social infernos was
lit by the sparks most common to lynchings elsewhere in the country: the alleged rape of white women by Black men or killings of whites at the presumed
hands of African Americans. In some instances of white-on-Black violence, the
rapid modernization and demographic change introduced by the railroad had
brought young, semi-vagrant Black men into sudden proximity with suspicious
white communities. Such was the case with the 1903 Joplin lynching of Thomas
Gilyard, who was arrested for the murder of a white policeman, taken from the
jail by a battering-ram-wielding mob, and hanged from a telephone pole.[13]

In other cases, however, the Black victims of mob violence were not strangers
in their communities. In 1901 the grisly murder of Gisele Wild in the small town
of Pierce City, Missouri, led to the arrests of Will Godley and Eugene Barrett,
whose families had been among a colony of Black Kentuckians that settled in
town in the 1870s. That night a mob battered down the iron doors of the jail
and extracted Godley and Barrett. The horde hanged Godley, a man of poor
reputation who had previously served time in the state penitentiary for rape,
and went looking for another member of the town's small Black community
who had allegedly fired into the lynch mob. Wielding rifles taken from the

national guard armory, the mob killed Pete Hampton and his stepfather and then proceeded to rampage through the Black section of town. The result was the forced evacuation of practically the entire Black community in Pierce City.[14]

Pierce City would not be the last instance of racial cleansing in an Ozarks town. Two early twentieth-century eruptions of racist violence in Harrison, Arkansas, purged the railroad town of all but one of its Black residents. Events such as those in Pierce City and Harrison took the white reaction to alleged Black crime far beyond the typical lynching of the era, but it was an outcome not unique to the Ozarks and far too common in the border South and Midwest. While the catalysts for lynching and race-related violence emanated from psychosexual anxieties and cultural fears, the racial cleansings owed something to economics. "Blacks were not a critical component of the regional economy," notes historian Kimberly Harper. "Their forced departure did not threaten the labor needs of area industries."[15]

The site of the region's most notorious Black lynching was one of the few places in the Ozarks that did not fit this model. By the early twentieth century, Springfield's African American population was indeed critical to the city's economy and influential in its politics. But it was still a minority population that occupied a second-class position. As in other parts of the country, the years surrounding the turn of the twentieth century witnessed an increasingly volatile racial atmosphere in the Queen City. In early 1906 the murder of a homeless Union veteran, allegedly at the hands of two Black men, intensified white fears and anxieties. Two months later the play *The Clansmen* brought to Springfield its message condoning vigilante violence in the cause of maintaining white supremacy.[16]

On Good Friday, April 13, 1906, a young white woman informed local authorities that she had been robbed and raped by two Black men. An investigation led the next day to the arrest of two livery stable workers, Horace Duncan and Fred Coker. That night, less than ten hours before Easter sunrise, a mob broke into the jail and dragged the two prisoners to the city square. Both were hanged from a tower straddling a band platform, their bullet-riddled bodies dangling just below a ten-foot-high statue of the Goddess of Liberty. Their thirst for blood unquenched, members of the mob returned to the jail and seized another young Black man awaiting trial for murder, hanging William Allen from the tower before burning all three bodies.[17]

There was no fiery rampage through Black neighborhoods in the wee hours of Easter morning, but it didn't take one to convince many African Americans that Springfield was an unsafe place. Dozens, perhaps hundreds, boarded trains that Sunday and left town. Governor Joseph Folk dispatched national guardsmen to the city to prevent a replay of the targeted destruction of Pierce City, while civic leaders and churches denounced the mob's actions. A grand jury handed down twenty-two indictments to those believed to have been involved in the lynching and destruction of public property. Six weeks later a coroner's jury declared Duncan and Coker innocent of the charges of their discredited accuser. Ultimately, though, only one alleged mob leader faced a judge and jury, but Springfield prosecutors later dropped the charges against him. Springfield's Black community survived the ordeal but suffered serious demographic and political weakening. African Americans, who constituted less than 6 percent of the city's population by 1910, saw their once-prominent role in the local Republican Party shrivel away in the months and years after Easter 1906.[18]

As the white mob rampaged through the streets of Springfield in the darkness before Easter sunrise, some of the city's Black residents huddled in the basement of a brick building near the Frisco tracks at the foot of Washington Avenue. The building, Gibson Chapel, was a fitting refuge in a time of terror. Perhaps no institution better exemplified the African American quest for community autonomy and independence from white society than did the church. No facet of postwar Black life in the Ozarks provides a more valuable counter-narrative to the darkness of Jim Crow–era violence. In the years following the end of the war, freedmen and women exercised their newfound liberty by abandoning the congregations of former owners and founding institutions that would develop into social and spiritual anchors of Black life. The congregation that eventually became Gibson Chapel had been one of the region's first Black churches when freedman Peter Lair organized it as Springfield's Second Cumberland Presbyterian Church in 1865.[19]

Reflecting the religious demographics of the Ozarks in general, most freedmen and women in the region joined Methodist and Baptist churches. In Springfield Black congregations of these persuasions made early appearances. In fact, according to local tradition, a log building north of the town square had first been used by a group of enslaved Black Methodists in 1847. Arson claimed the building, Wilson's Creek Chapel, in 1865, but the congregation rebuilt and eventually changed its name to Pitts Chapel. In the 1870s a schism within this congregation resulted in the establishment of Springfield's first African Methodist Episcopal (AME) Church, later known as Benton Avenue AME. Initially established as a mission of the city's white First Baptist Church in 1867, Springfield's Black Second Baptist Church shared a meetinghouse with the Colored Cumberland Presbyterians until constructing its own building and forging its own identity as Washington Avenue Baptist Church.[20]

Baptist and AME churches emerged in practically every town and rural community with a critical mass of African Americans. In Neosho a population of a few hundred freedmen and women maintained Second Baptist Church and an AME congregation, where a young George Washington Carver professed religion in the 1870s. Carver's wasn't the only African American surname in postwar Neosho to gain fame in twentieth-century America. Under the careful watch of church clerk J. M. Clendenon—whose grandson, Donn, would earn World Series Most Valuable Player honors for New York's Miracle Mets in 1969— Second Baptist constructed a vernacular brick building with Late Gothic Revival flourishes in 1896. Second Baptist also hosted programs for the segregated Lincoln School and concerts by the Neosho Colored Band.[21]

That Old-Time Religion

The AME and Black Baptist churches of the Ozarks were symbolic of a more diverse religious landscape in the postwar era. The steady migration of upland Southerners into the Ozarks for more than sixty years before the Civil War had produced a homogenous, evangelical Protestant culture across most of the region. But the postwar expansion of rail lines into the Ozarks brought both foreign and domestic immigrants, and these immigrants brought "foreign" faiths and denominations. Newcomers to the region established small congregations of such groups as the Advent Christians, Society of Friends (Quakers), Reform and Orthodox Jews, and the Reorganized Church of Jesus Christ of Latter-Day Saints.[22]

German immigration into the interior Ozarks introduced Lutheranism, German Evangelicalism, and the Church of the Brethren to towns and farming communities heretofore unfamiliar with such strains of Protestantism. Almost two in three interior counties in the Missouri Ozarks contained at least one denomination of German Protestants by the early 1900s. Even more impressive was the spread of Roman Catholicism. At the outbreak of civil war, the Catholic Church had been virtually nonexistent beyond the region's fringes, but the church claimed a presence in almost three out of four counties in the interior Ozarks of Missouri in the early twentieth century. The interior's most substantial concentration of Catholics was in the Lead Belt, where immigrant miners and the descendants of French Creoles made Catholicism the majority faith in Washington County and the choice of more than one-third of churchgoers in St. Francois County. The railroad did its part to spread Catholicism. Springfield counted some five hundred Catholics in its parish by 1881. Ethnic and class divisions between the families of North Springfield's Irish railroad workers and Springfield's mostly German artisans and businessmen led to a split in the parish the following year.[23]

The Catholic Church's presence in both the Arkansas and Oklahoma Ozarks remained minimal, which no doubt pleased many Protestant inheritors of a long tradition of anti-Catholicism. Few in the region condemned "papists" more vehemently than did Arkansas newspaper editor Herb Lewis, a Minnesota native whose editorials in the *Gravette News Herald* grew increasingly vitriolic and paranoid after 1910. Lewis's adopted little railroad town became such a lightning rod for the movement that it hosted no fewer than four anti-Catholic newspapers for a time in 1914. But the unquestioned locus of such propaganda lay across the Springfield Plain in another railroad town. Aurora, Missouri, was home to *The Menace*, the country's largest circulating anti-Catholic publication. With its peripatetic Canadian founder and a nationwide subscription list that exceeded one and a half million in 1914, there was nothing particularly regional about *The Menace*. But few Ozarkers would have quarreled with its premise. The rise of a new incarnation of the Ku Klux Klan in the early 1920s owed as much or more to anti-Catholicism and nativism as to racism, especially in the rural and small-town interior Ozarks. Protestantism was an essential and implied element of the Klan's ideal of "One Hundred Percent Americanism." "People had a great fear and hatred of Catholics and especially the Pope," recalled Omer Brown of his boyhood in Ozark County, Missouri. "They didn't know a thing on earth about Catholics, but they didn't like them anyway."[24]

The most exotic brand of Christianity that Brown's home county could lay claim to was a modest gathering of Congregationalists. At the very least, the Greek library of longtime pastor Zenus Feemster must have struck the neighbors as more otherworldly than his name. The onset of the Civil War in the region found not a single congregation of this old Yankee church, but the postwar era witnessed a modest influx that located some twenty-five hundred Congregationalists in the interior of the Missouri Ozarks by the early 1900s. These descendants of Puritans left their largest footprint in Springfield, where they founded the city's first postwar college and where a group of ambitious parishioners played an outsize role in cultural and economic affairs.[25]

The arrival of Congregationalists and Catholics injected the interior Ozarks with a new ecclesiastical heterogeneity. Yet the primary story of religion in the postwar era remained a familiar one. A vast majority of people in the Ozarks would have been satisfied and familiar with the worship calendar in Melbourne, Arkansas, in the 1870s. In the tiny seat of Izard County, four denominations took time using the meeting house. The Baptists claimed the first Sunday of the month, followed by the Disciples of Christ on the second sabbath, the Methodists on the third, and the Cumberland Presbyterians on the fourth. It is unclear if the devil claimed the occasional fifth Sunday or if the churches drew straws. By 1906 these big four of evangelical Protestantism accounted for more than 83 percent of religious adherents in the interior counties of the Ozarks. In sixteen counties Baptists and Methodists alone made up more than three-quarters of all churchgoers.[26]

In general terms, the Ozarks was characterized by an evangelical Protestantism that emphasized an emotional, personal conversion experience; that relied on the King James Bible as the primary if not sole authority of God's mandates to mankind; that held fast to a set of fundamental beliefs (including the inerrancy

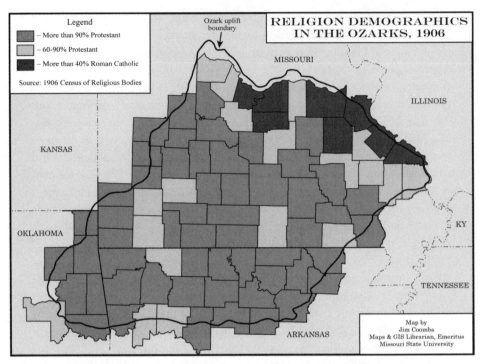

Religion Demographics in the Ozarks, 1906. Courtesy of Jim Coombs, Missouri State University, Springfield.

of the Bible and the imminent second coming of Christ); and that valued the emotional release triggered by the brush arbor revivals that carried on the camp meeting tradition in the post–Civil War era. As the nineteenth century turned into the twentieth—as higher criticism, cultural relativism, and the Social Gospel battered the hull of traditional Christianity—the vast majority of Christians in the Ozarks held fast to the old bulwark. Their conservatism hardly distinguished them from millions more in rural and small-town America.

From an outsider's perspective, the hegemony of evangelical Protestantism enervated every facet of social and cultural life, muting any distinctions among denominations. But denominational competition and antipathy were common elements of religious life in the Ozarks. Within American Protestantism the period between the Civil War and the Depression was a time of denominational splintering and the birth of new movements as theological, cultural, and economic differences drove wedges between cliques of believers. Ozarkers found themselves in the middle of these developments. The definitive history of religion in the Ozarks waits to be written. When that work comes to fruition, however, it is likely that it will reveal no *Ozarks religion*, no unique brand of religious practice incubated in the hills and hollers. Rather, it will reveal a story that, like Loyal Jones's study of religion in Appalachia, finds more similarities with the American mainstream than differences.[27]

The Ozarks may have been but a regional variation of a national story, but the most remote sections seemed to beckon to mainstream denominations "in search of destitute parts." The hills and hollers of the highlands of Middle America never attracted the legion of missionaries that reconnoitered Appalachia in the late nineteenth and early twentieth centuries, but a mixture of sectarian competition and paternalism pushed apostles into the Ozarks backcountry. The ultimate objective of what amounted to a "cultural invasion" was, according to historian William A. Link, "remaking mountain civilization in the image of Victorian American culture." Not surprisingly, it was the denominations based in the North that initially responded to this mission.[28]

In 1874 the Methodist Episcopal Church (or Northern Methodists) assigned J. S. Godbey to a sparsely populated circuit in southern Missouri. Godbey's denomination had distanced itself from its rather crude camp-meeting past, but the young minister discovered that his subjects in the Ozarks had not. "The habits of the people in most of this mountain region were quite primitive," he recalled. "They thought a meeting that did not raise a shout was a failure." For three years Godbey preached in dimly lit schoolhouses and tolerated the emotional outbursts that invariably erupted at mourners' benches. He paid a hunter to kill enough deer to feed fifty families at a camp meeting near Newburg and invited St. Louis ministers to "come and eat fish and venison and preach to the mountaineers—a people who believe they have souls." Godbey's condescending attitude toward backcountry dwellers and their beliefs was a product of the cultural superiority complex embodied by the educated leaders of his denomination. And that complex wasn't confined to northerners. By the early twentieth century, Southerners had begun dispatching missionaries into "the most destitute field" and to use similarly disparaging language to describe the state of religion in the rural Ozarks. A Southern Baptist minister in Arkansas fretted that the simple people of the hills would fall victim to every "heresy known to the human race," while a counterpart among the Southern Methodists feared that without his denomination's intervention, rural Ozarkers would be "left to the mercy of a sort of hobo gospel."[29]

Preconceived notions of regional backwardness and the rustic physical surroundings of a strange landscape obscured an often-vibrant religious life, even in the most unlikely of settings. A concern for spreading Christianity through mission work was one indicator of that vibrancy. Perhaps even more remote and rugged than Godbey's territory was Stone County, Arkansas, a place that took its name from its most prominent geologic feature. In this sparsely settled landscape—still unsullied by rail in 1889—the member congregations of the Blue

Mountain Association of Missionary Baptists declared Bickle's Cove "destitute of gospel preaching" and dispatched a minister to spread the word to this un-churched area. That same year the Disciples of Christ in southwestern Missouri's McDonald and Newton counties paid an evangelist forty dollars a month to "help the weak congregations and the destitute places in our counties." The missionary impulse of the Blue Mountain Baptists and McDonald County Disciples was almost certainly more about saving the wayward than civilizing the backward, but it contradicted the perception of Ozarks insularity nonetheless.[30]

For many Ozarkers missionary activity was valued not so much for spreading the faith to faraway places as for protecting home from undesirable alternatives. The Dallas County Baptist Association's decision to hire a missionary for its own "destitute places" in 1915 was motivated by a desire to "arrest the tide of evil that most surely is coming upon us from Romanism and Russellism."[31] The Catholic Church and Russellites (later Jehovah's Witnesses) were easy enemies of practi-cally all churchgoers in the heart of the Ozarks. But evangelical Protestants also leveled their sights on one another in the late nineteenth and early twentieth centuries. One result of this sectarian spirit became a staple of the rural and small-town entertainment calendar, the religious debate pitting ministers from differing denominations. No topic was more popular than baptism. Ozarkers debated both the method of the sacrament and baptism's essentialness to a soul's salvation. Commenting on an 1896 debate between a dunking Disciple and a sprinkling Cumberland Presbyterian in Ash Grove, Missouri, one critic observed that such a public argument "stirs up sectarian bigotry in the community and gets neighbors to hating one another."[32]

Hatred-inducing or not, few religious debates took place in the Ozarks with-out at least one Disciples of Christ voice. "Campbellites" (as Disciples were derisively labeled, after founder Alexander Campbell) became the great debat-ers of the American Protestant landscape. Not a few debates centered on the Disciples' claim to being the modern world's purest exemplar of the New Testa-ment church. Invariably the opponent was a Baptist preacher armed with D. B. Wray's sectarian diatribe warning the reader to "flee from Campbellism as he would from deadly poison, as from a moral pestilence which breeds death and ruin to the souls of men." Popularizing the "Landmark" Baptist claim on ancient authenticity, Wray bolstered confidence among his brethren with a convoluted genealogy tracing Baptist doctrine to the earliest followers of Christ, bypassing Rome in the process. An 1891 debate at Ash Grove between the Baptist elder James Bandy and the Disciple Dr. Lucas sought to settle, once and for all, the question of which of the two denominations is God's favorite. The verbal duel commenced on a Monday and continued for six straight days, two sessions each day, but the local paper declined to declare a victor.[33]

It was also an era of intradenominational disputes within most Protestant bodies, leading to an early twentieth-century landscape littered with fractured older denominations and hopeful new movements. Part of that fracturing was due to old schisms caused by quarrels over slavery and the Civil War, which left Baptists, Methodists, and Presbyterians divided into northern and southern branches in the postwar years. Class conflicts and a growing rural versus urban divide were but two of the wedge issues creating rifts among Disciples and Cumberland Presbyterians. Congregational and quarrelsome, Baptists sorted themselves according to theology, polity, and other sources of disagreement. The outcome was a confusing denominational directory consisting of Southern Baptists, Missionary Baptists, Primitive Baptists, Free Will Baptists, Black Baptists, German Baptists, Regular Baptists, and General Baptists, the latter flock long headquartered in Poplar Bluff, Missouri.

Yet nothing enlivened the religious landscape of the Ozarks in the years between the Civil War and the Depression more than movements within Methodism. The Wesleyan doctrine of holiness (or sanctification) exploded on the regional scene in the 1880s and 1890s. Before the dust settled, the Holiness movement spawned an even more powerful and popular offspring in the form of Pentecostalism. Both found thousands of willing converts in the Ozarks. Keying on an old teaching by Methodism's founder, John Wesley, believers in the Holiness doctrine stressed a second work of God's grace whereby the saved were sanctified, or granted a sinless state, through the anointing of the holy spirit. The fervent prayers and labors to reach such a state frequently broke into ecstatic physical and emotional displays at church services and camp meetings, resurrecting images of the Great Revival of the early 1800s. So wildly emotional and physical did their revivals become that Holiness devotees were labeled with the epithets "shoutin' Methodists" and "Holy Rollers." "There were several old ladies who shouted," recalled one woman of the revivals of her childhood in Arkansas, "and you better get out of their reach if you didn't want to get a pounding."[34]

Riding the rails across southern Missouri in the summer of 1884, young adventurer Charley Hershey encountered a string of Holiness tent meetings stretching from Springfield to Neosho. In zinc-mining country he discovered two tents on the outskirts of Webb City—one recently trampled by cattle and looted by herders, the other still going strong after a month and a half. It was no mere coincidence that a rail hopper like Hershey had such easy access to tent meetings. Though ambivalent over the railroad's potential for introducing people to unprecedented opportunities for sinfulness, Holiness (and later Pentecostal) evangelists were quick to take advantage of new technology to spread their message rapidly to the greatest concentrations of people. Despite "persistent images of the movements as rural and counter-modern," argues

historian Daniel Woods, the early Holiness and Pentecostal meetings almost
always featured two familiar sounds: "the thrilling shouts of victory and the
shrill blasts of a nearby train whistle."[35]

"Expect to take the morning train tomorrow to be in the battle for the Lord,"
confided Sadie Smith to her diary in the spring of 1895. In the middle of a nine-
month southwestern Missouri mission trip aiding Holiness evangelists, the
twenty-eight-year-old Smith prayed "for a special anointing and baptism of the
Holy Ghost on my soul." She also yearned "to become a successful soul winner,"
for Smith had found her way into the rare religious movement that allowed
women to deliver sermons from the pulpit. Smith exhorted alongside a "Sister
Sheets" and other women evangelists but soon gave up her budding ministry for
more traditional roles as wife and mother. Women preachers faced prejudice and
a life of inequality with male clergy. The Railroad Clergy Bureau, for instance,
refused to extend to women the discounted fares that male preachers received.
One of the Ozark region's earliest woman preachers was Amanda Coulson of
Boone County, Arkansas, who began her ministry in 1890. Disowned by her
father for disgracing the family, Coulson endured a rumor campaign in which
her enemies accused her of murdering her husband, deserting her children, and
"other stories too dark to be mentioned." During a revival at Bellefonte, a local
pastor encouraged his parishioners to drum Coulson out of the neighborhood
by pelting her with eggs. She persevered through the persecution, helped oversee
the building of a Holiness church house in Valley Springs, and eventually took
her ministry all the way to the West Coast.[36]

A new strain of the Holiness movement emerged at a tiny Bible college in
Topeka, Kansas, in early 1901. Believing that speaking in tongues was the initial
evidence of yet a third gift of grace to the redeemed and sanctified Christian,
Charles Fox Parham soon carried his message to the western edge of the Ozarks.
Invited by a convert to set up shop in the mining town of Galena, Kansas, just
across the state line from Joplin, Parham's massive crowds forced him to rent a
building to accommodate the hundreds "ripe for repentance." Parham would
eventually make Baxter Springs, Kansas, his permanent base of operations but
only after sparking a similar "Apostolic Faith" revival in the Houston, Texas, area
in 1905. It was there that Parham's teachings inspired a young African American
preacher named William J. Seymour. In 1906 Seymour and others in Parham's
circle took the Apostolic Faith movement to Los Angeles and launched the Azusa
Street Revival, an event that more than any other unleashed Pentecostalism as
the most significant Christian development of the twentieth century. With its
interracial services, women preachers, and class-leveling egalitarianism, the
Pentecostal movement was like the Holiness crusade on amphetamines.[37]

Pentecostalism soon boomeranged back into the heart of the Ozarks. In the
spring of 1907, Rachel and Joseph Sizelove, evangelists who had experienced

Union Evangelistic meeting inside temporary "tabernacle," Lebanon, Missouri, 1911. Courtesy of John F. Bradbury Jr. Collection, RA1652 (unprocessed at time of publication), State Historical Society of Missouri, Rolla.

the baptism of the Holy Ghost at Azusa Street almost a year earlier, rode the rails to Springfield, Missouri. There they converted to the cause Rachel's sister and brother-in-law, Lillie and James Corum. The Corums promptly left their Baptist church and gathered enough friends and neighbors to form a small congregation, which held its first tent revival that summer despite threats of vigilante action against this newest sect of "Holy Rollers." From Springfield the movement spread down the rails. Few places felt its impact more than a little Missouri border town. Upon the invitation of a Pentecostal convert who owned a hotel in Thayer, in the summer of 1909 a group of evangelists led by "Mother" Leonore Barnes of St. Louis converged on the small town just north of the Arkansas state line. Their two-month healing revival attracted the lame and languid (and plenty of gawkers) from miles around.[38]

Pentecostalism's spread refused to be limited by the country's rail network, however. An evangelist at Thayer recalled a farm woman who was converted at a tent meeting and immediately carried the message of "spirit baptism" deeper and deeper into the backcountry. Edgar E. Hulse remembered the Pentecostals' "perpetual revival" in the rugged White River Hills of southwestern Missouri during the World War I era: "When half a building of people turned loose at once . . . the place started rocking. Young people were ready to leave the dances and crowd into church services—'to see the show.'" Like revivalists before them, Pentecostals poured old oil into new vessels. "Hymns that other churchmen sang in an easy mountain drawl were stepped up to a sort of double time, giving old familiar hymns a new and vital meaning," noted Hulse. "The rhythm was so near dance time the youth were fascinated by it." The evangelist "preached with inspiration, racing back and forth before the jammed crowd, face flushed, eyes bright with zeal, blood vessels on his neck standing out." When the rural revival planted its seed, word invariably came of maiden territory somewhere beyond the next ridge. "New converts swarmed into old cars, trucks, wagons, or on horseback, and hit for it."[39]

Despite the movement's embrace of the railroad, Pentecostalism responded to the same streak of primitivism—the same desire to restore the New Testament church to its pristine origins—that motivated earlier American religious developments, from the Disciples of Christ to Latter-Day Saints. Pentecostals also shared with many other evangelical Christians a millenarian faith that the known world was nearing its end and that the last days demanded a torrid evangelizing effort. Pentecostalism had great appeal in the Ozarks—to the downtrodden of the mining districts and timber camps, to the poor and dispossessed drawn to the new movement's inviting message of equality and freedom from social judgment. Not surprisingly, such a decentralized movement refused neat classification and organization.

Once the movement started to take institutional shape, the Ozarks and its fringe areas played central roles. One of the earliest Pentecostal "interstate camp meetings" took place in the resort town of Eureka Springs, Arkansas, in 1911. There Ozarks native Howard A. Goss, a former miner who had found salvation at a Parham revival, made the acquaintance of E. N. Bell, a onetime Southern Baptist minister from Florida. Three years later Goss and his new wife, preacher Ethel Wright, collaborated with Bell to organize another Pentecostal conference in Hot Springs, Arkansas. There some three hundred clergy and lay leaders founded the Assemblies of God, a network of preachers and congregations decidedly less progressive in terms of race and the role of women than were the earliest Pentecostals. In 1918 the young denomination approved Bell's recommendation to relocate to "salubrious Springfield, right on the top of the Ozark Mountains." The Assemblies of God eventually built a large plant for its general offices and printing presses on the site of an old minor league baseball stadium. More than a century later, Springfield remains the nerve center for the largest Pentecostal denomination in the world.[40]

While they had once benefited from the same revivalistic fervor, the older, more-established churches of the Ozarks generally looked askance at the "Holy Rollers." Even in the rural Ozarks, traditional Methodists, Baptists, Disciples, and Presbyterians found the unbridled shouting and tongues speaking of the new Pentecostals unbecoming at best, downright un-Christian at worst. Perhaps no change in the rural evangelical church better reflected the old denominations' gradual climb up the Victorian socioeconomic ladder than their stance on the liquor issue. After the Civil War the temperance movement built momentum across the region as it transformed into a broad prohibition movement by the early twentieth century. The proliferation of saloons that accompanied the arrival of railroads and the growth of mining boomtowns spurred anti-liquor forces into action in the 1870s. Organizations such as the Temperance Alliance and the National Christian Temperance Union found eager converts in places like Springfield, Carthage, and Joplin. Traveling up and down the Frisco from his Springfield headquarters, American Sunday School Union missionary W. J. Hayden established more than fifty temperance lodges.[41]

The temperance crusade was not confined to towns along the rails, however. As early as 1874 the largely rural Freedom Baptist Association in Polk County, Missouri, resolved to "lift up her hand against the practice of selling intoxicating spirits" and to prevent "the granting of dram-shop licenses under any circumstances." The small town of Harrison, Arkansas, boasted a chapter of the Women's Christian Temperance Union (WCTU) a decade before it had rail service. The crusade spread into the rural country south and east of Harrison, prompting anti-liquor editorials in Yellville's *Mountain Echo* and spawning Marshall's *North Arkansas Temperance Voice* in 1897. Two years later a different Marshall newspaper denounced whiskey as "nothing more than a mind destroyer, character ruiner, [and] confidence killer . . . charged with the electricity of the devil."[42]

The small-town editor's beef with whiskey stemmed from the news that a recent Baptist meeting had been broken up by a group of drunken "boys." While national organizations like the WCTU brought rural Ozarkers into the crusade's orbit, just as many were motivated by developments at home—chief among them an increase in cases of disturbance of religious worship. At an 1883 protracted meeting in northwestern Arkansas, William Sherman watched as two inebriated "desperadoes" brandished pistols and shot it out inside the church house. More often the disturbers were unarmed young men who pelted the meeting house roof and walls with rocks or who came inside and stood at the back of the church jangling their spurs and stomping their boots. Exactly what was behind this rash of religious meeting disturbances is unclear. One Ozarker attributed the phenomenon not so much to an epidemic of bad behavior as to local ordinances that provided constables a fee for each arrest they made. Many churchgoers blamed the outbreak of meanness on liquor and determined to rid perpetrators of their fuel.[43]

Feds in the Hills

It is possible that more than a few of the disturbers of churches were moonshiners and bootleggers. By the late 1800s, many rural evangelicals had begun
to imbibe the middle-class message that illicit manufacturing of corn whiskey
lay at the root of societal problems. The Internal Revenue Act of 1862 required
even the smallest distiller to purchase a government license and pay a tax on
any beverages produced. In the postwar years ex-rebels resented the law and
the small army of federal agents as yet another manifestation of Yankee impe-
riousness. Many Unionist distillers likewise objected to the exorbitant tax of
two dollars per gallon. One such loyalist was J. E. Bunyard of Christian County,
Missouri, who "got in trubel with that old still" in 1869. "Tha com an tuck me a
prisoner," he wrote to a brother-in-law. Bunyard eventually reacquired his still
after it sold at a public auction and vowed to keep making wildcat whiskey. "If
thay will let me alone i will let them alone."[44]

Who exactly "thay" were is unclear. Bunyard may have run afoul of local officials, but most moonshine arrests were carried out by federal agents. Just two
years after Bunyard's scrape with authorities, in Bollinger County, Missouri,
twenty masked men attacked two federal deputy marshals escorting alleged
moonshiners to Cape Girardeau for trial. In 1876 a mini–civil war erupted in
Ripley County as local residents chose sides between deputy marshals from the
Bureau of Revenue and the wildcatters they targeted. As the twentieth century
neared, however, moonshiners and bootleggers increasingly found themselves
on an island. "Rural antiliquor sentiment . . . [rose] rather abruptly in Arkansas
during the last two decades of the nineteenth century," observes historian J.
Blake Perkins, "and became the most decisive factor in the state's march toward
statewide prohibition." The situation was little different in Missouri.[45]

The sensationalistic coverage of high-profile liquor raids and violence did little
to help the cause of wildcatters. By the time Confederate veteran and moonshiner Harve Bruce was apprehended for the killing of two federal marshals in
the Boston Mountains of Arkansas in 1897, many of his fellow rural Ozarkers had
sided with the urban newspapers that damned his kind for resisting authority out
of a stubborn connection to tradition. In actuality, argues Perkins, "the burdens
of an increasingly uneven rural political economy had much more to do with
. . . resistance than some timeless antigovernment culture." The expansion of
anti-moonshine fervor in rural areas reflected a growing chasm between those
like Bruce who turned to illegal distilling as a rational economic strategy and
the local elites who enjoyed ever-growing support for snuffing them out. The
marshals taken down by Bruce's bullets were, after all, Ozarkers themselves.[46]

Utilizing state local option laws, coalitions of anti-alcohol advocates declared
war on saloons and on wildcatters like Harve Bruce. Commenting on a vote

to ban liquor in Shannon County, Missouri, in 1906, a local editor chalked the victory up to an amalgam of preachers, women, and upwardly mobile young men, all of them motivated in part by the rowdy behavior of unruly timber workers. A growing wave of support for prohibition banned saloons and liquor sales across a wide swath of the Ozarks in the late 1800s and early 1900s. The WCTU, Anti-Saloon League, and other organizations made certain that Oklahoma entered the union as a dry state in 1907. By 1914 only the counties of the German fringe of the Ozark uplift held out against the teetotaling onslaught in Missouri. The following year saw the Arkansas legislature pass a dry law, four years before the Volstead Act mandated nationwide prohibition.[47]

The era of national prohibition, from 1920 until the repeal of the Eighteenth Amendment in 1933, continued to deliver sensational stories of moonshine busts and bootlegging. But the prohibition decade also saw a gradual shift in attitudes, with some writers even romanticizing speakeasies and moonshiners. None tried harder to rehabilitate the wildcatter's image than did Fayetteville native Charles Morrow Wilson. In articles published in national periodicals, Wilson worshipfully chronicled the "art of the hills" and its practitioners, intelligent and resourceful moonshiners motivated both by a need to make a living and a natural bent toward nonconformity. By the latter half of the 1920s, observes historian Bruce E. Stewart, many middle-class townspeople had "redefined Victorian standards of behavior and abandoned their previous support for prohibition." In towns across the Ozarks bootleggers and blind tigers supplied a growing demand for illicit alcohol from "respectable" people. Despite its being an otherwise "intolerant little town," recalled a native of Warsaw, Missouri, a customer of any of the burg's drugstores could get a shot of alcohol simply by asking for a Coke. In southwestern Missouri's Republican-controlled Christian County—for decades a bastion of prohibition sentiment—voters tired of a prosecuting attorney's rigid enforcement of liquor law and took the unprecedented step of replacing him with a Democrat.[48]

The arrival of revenuers in the postwar years marked the beginning of a more tangible government presence in the Ozarks. That presence expanded in the early twentieth century with the creation of the U.S. Forest Service (USFS) and implementation of the draft during World War I, both of which created rifts between federal employees and some Ozarkers. Setting aside more than 960,000 acres of public domain land in the Boston Mountains and White River Hills of Arkansas, in 1908 President Theodore Roosevelt created the Ozark National Forest (ONF). While not as polarizing as revenuers, employees of the USFS found few welcoming faces in the sparsely settled country they patrolled. Charged with enforcing the USFS's policy of complete fire suppression, rangers ran up against the long-standing practice of seasonal burns, a tradition that Ozarkers' ancestors had adopted generations earlier from Native Americans.

Encountering a "great deal of opposition to it by the settlers," the ONF erected a chain of sixty-five-foot-high observation towers manned by government "towermen" who alerted teams of rangers and local farmers-turned-firefighters to the presence of distant conflagrations. On occasion ONF employees cooperated with federal marshals to arrest "firebugs," though most received light sentences. Boonie Noe, for instance, was slapped with twenty-four days in jail and a stern lecture from the federal judge upon being convicted of starting fires in Newton County in 1915. In seasons of frequent infernos, federal employees weren't sure if the culprits were igniting blazes out of cussed traditionalism or as a way of generating wages for locals hired to fight fires.[49]

A source of even more widespread violence—one that revealed deep rifts between haves and have-nots in the Ozarks—was the draft. Inspired by religious beliefs and a suspicion that this poor man's fight was just another rich man's war, a small but determined minority in the backcountry defied the federal government's mandate of military service. In the summer of 1918, a firefight erupted when a sheriff's posse attempted to arrest draft resisters and deserters in Cleburne County, Arkansas. The death of a posseman sparked a weeklong national guard manhunt for a handful of Russellites (Jehovah's Witnesses). Especially attractive to the marginalized, "Russellism" promoted an end-of-times message that called for believers to disassociate themselves from the government and other institutions corrupted by Satan and sin. The Cleburne County draft board's refusal to grant local Russellites conscientious objector status put the dissenters on a collision course with their more orthodox neighbors. But Russellites held no monopoly on draft resistance in the Ozarks. Financial struggle and perhaps even socialist leanings may have contributed more to the defiance of a resister gunned down by a sheriff's posse in rural Searcy County, Arkansas, than did his Baptist religion. In Washington County, Arkansas, a "Holy Roller" preacher was arrested for denouncing the war and claiming that President Woodrow Wilson was the "beast" of end-times prophecy in the book of Revelation. Ultimately, the region's resisters pushed back not because of their isolation or ignorance but "because the draft violated their populist sense of justice, fairness, and morality and imposed unique burdens on their small farm families."[50]

The Well-to-Do

The objects of the poor man's resistance could be as distant and detached as the army, but more often they were the elites of their own communities. The image of a land of "ridge runners" and "hillbillies" obscured the same social and economic stratification that existed elsewhere in the nation. The era between Reconstruction and the Depression witnessed the rise of an affluent class in the Ozarks, and the emerging consumer culture beckoned to an even broader swath of Ozarkers. Houses, musical instruments, vehicles, and educational attainment became markers of material success and social standing. This was true even in rural areas. Settling on a farm in Dade County, Missouri, in the late 1800s, Taylor and Martha Hunt built an impressive I-house, the era's ubiquitous two-story symbol of agricultural prosperity. The Hunts installed acetylene-powered lights and furnished their stylish parlor with a piano and a writing desk with glass-enclosed bookcase. A barn near the house sheltered a fringe-topped surrey and, later, a brass-trimmed Ford automobile. Rarer in the most rugged reaches of the region, the I-house still lent its inhabitants an air of importance. "Those fine old homes were always painted white," recalled one Ozark County native of his boyhood in the early 1900s, "and the people living in them were the aristocrats of the community."[51]

The Hunts and other families swayed by the spread of middle-class virtues eagerly adopted the trappings of Victorian-era consumerism and status. Farmers in rural Howell County, Missouri, in the early 1900s, the Lilly family subscribed to national magazines and newspapers from St. Louis and Kansas City and stocked their home with an ice cream maker, a used organ, and a wind-up phonograph machine that played wax cylinder recordings. It was in the region's towns, however, that social stratification reached fruition. The elite of little Houston, Missouri—lawyers, doctors, merchants—clustered their houses in close proximity on Hawthorn Street, which locals referred to as "silk stocking row." No Ozark town boasted a more substantial "silk stocking row" than did Springfield. On Walnut Street and adjacent thoroughfares in the late 1800s and early 1900s, executives, professionals, and prosperous businessmen built showpiece Queen Anne and Foursquare houses and revival homes in the American Colonial and English Tudor styles. So extensive was the Walnut Street district that a mostly African American neighborhood of domestic workers and servants developed on its margins.[52]

Even the smallest of towns reflected the era's growing stratification. In the southeastern Missouri hamlet of Mine La Motte, the wife and daughter of a mine manager lived lives that would not have been foreign to most town-dwelling middle-class women of the time. Mary and Mabel Cogswell spent their days decorating the house; taking tea with the wives and daughters of a local doctor, merchant, and hotelier; riding horses and carriages; playing music; and attending lectures. Women like the Cogswells played a major role in the Victorianization of towns and cities in the Ozarks. Taking charge of their separate sphere in the home, and building on their experiences with the WCTU and similar societies, women took the lead in establishing civic and community organizations. A World War I–era magazine article praised the "well-dressed Neosho woman" as the kind of citizen who transformed the little town into the "cradle of culture, refinement, and character-stolidity." In the small northwestern Arkansas

John T. Woodruff's Ozarks—the Springfield, Missouri, square, 1927. Courtesy of
Domino Danzero Collection, Special Collections and Archives, Missouri State
University, Springfield.

railroad burg of Winslow, women organized the Suffrage Club, Ladies Aid, and
the Home Mission Society. No woman in Winslow had greater influence than
pharmacist Maud Duncan, whose weekly newspaper was a staunch opponent
of pool halls and whiskey. For two years in the 1920s, Mayor Duncan and her
all-woman city council championed band concerts, city parks, and civic pride,
gaining national media exposure for Winslow's "petticoat government."[53]

Even in rural areas and on Ozarks farms "hill women were not ignorant of the
bourgeois culture which dominated urban America," observes historian Janet
Allured of the late 1800s and early 1900s. Most women and girls in the more
rugged and infertile sections of the region worked alongside men and boys in
the fields and barns, but they knew from mail-order catalogs and magazines
the "changes underway in the definition of women's roles." Not surprisingly,
then, rural and small-town Ozarks society reflected characteristics of "the modern American companionate family," including a softening of old patriarchal
norms and a more affectionate relationship between husbands and wives. For
at least one farm woman in the turn-of-the-century Ozarks, those old patriarchal norms could not disappear quickly enough. In rural Cedar County,
Missouri, in the 1890s, feminist anarchist Kate Austin "wrote revolutionary
propaganda at her kitchen table in the evenings after chores." With family and
intellectual roots in the freethinker movements of the "Burned-over District"
of antebellum New York State, Austin championed sexual liberty, denounced
conventional marriage, and hosted visits and lectures by fellow anarchist Emma

Goldman—all while maintaining the unrelenting lifestyle of the farm wife and mother of a brood of children.[54]

A few miles to the north, in the small town of Osceola, another woman shared Austin's intellectual curiosity, if not her radical opinions. In 1903, just one year after tuberculosis prematurely silenced Austin's voice, Alice Johnson established the Twentieth Century Club, which for the next four decades sponsored presentations and discussions of English literature and other topics. Undoubtedly, one of those other topics would have been Greek philosophy, the favorite subject of Alice's husband. An attorney and sometime mayor of Osceola, Thomas Moore Johnson developed a deep interest in the Greek roots of theosophy and other esoteric philosophies, published a short-lived journal known as *The Platonist* in the 1880s, and amassed a library of books dating to the fifteenth century. The Johnsons passed on their inquisitiveness to their children. Son Franklin Plotinus Johnson earned a PhD at Johns Hopkins and spent a long career as an archaeology professor at the University of Chicago, while daughter Helen Moore Johnson followed up doctoral studies at the University of Wisconsin to become one of the West's foremost Sanskrit scholars and a pioneer in the study of Jainism, an ancient Indian religion.[55]

Readin', Writin', and Rescuin'

The Johnsons were obviously an anomalous case of scholarly curiosity, but the story of educational ambition was not an unusual one in the region. More than any other development of social and cultural life, the founding of schools and colleges reflected the modern ambitions of Ozarkers. The nineteenth-century American penchant for academy and college building may have made a belated appearance in the region, but educators and town boosters were eager to make up for lost time. Still, the region's evolving educational landscape reflected widening gulfs—between town and country, prosperous and poor, white and nonwhite. Ultimately, the crystallizing image of the Ozarks as an impoverished backwater played its part in the region's education story in the early twentieth century as religious denominations and missionary educators looked to rescue the children of hill folks.

Like most publicly funded endeavors in the last quarter of the nineteenth century, schools in the Ozarks fell victim to the tight-fisted policies of the "Redeemers." The conservative Democratic regimes that ended Reconstruction in Arkansas and Missouri in the mid-1870s rolled back the ambitious educational programs of their Radical Republican predecessors. In the retrenched and impoverished atmosphere of postwar Arkansas, miserly legislatures provided scant state funding. In many poor, remote districts, school funds were so limited that they would pay a teacher's modest salary for only three or four months a year. Arkansas historian Michael B. Dougan refers to this era, stretching from the end of Reconstruction into the early twentieth century, as "the dark age of public education."[56]

The little one-room schoolhouse with its potbellied wood-burning stove, belfry, and long chalkboards is a beloved symbol of a romantic American past. In the rural Ozarks, however, the one-room school too often reflected the life of limited opportunities into which the building's pupils had been born. One native of northwestern Arkansas recalled a tiny, rustic schoolhouse in the 1870s with split-log benches standing in for desks; the school's name, Stick-in-the-Mud, seemed a fitting moniker.[57] Most rural Ozarkers inherited a life of manual labor and gelded horizons, and the curriculum for one-room schools was geared toward basics—reading, handwriting, and arithmetic—supplemented with spelling, history, geography, and government. The quality of instruction varied widely, and it wasn't uncommon for teachers to be younger than some of their students. Harry Thaxton was only fifteen when he began teaching at a one-room school in Ripley County, Missouri, in 1897. Adept at Spencerian script, Thaxton at the very least made certain his charges ended the term with florid handwriting skills. In Taney County, Mary Elizabeth Prather was a ripe old seventeen when she taught a three-month term at the remote Turkey Creek School in 1894. Her measly twenty-dollar-per-month salary likely owed something to the district's impoverished conditions, but it was also common for women teachers to make less than their male counterparts.[58]

In the 1890s and early 1900s, lawmakers in Arkansas, Missouri, and Oklahoma passed a series of education bills instituting a variety of progressive reforms, such as statewide textbook adoptions, mandated teacher training, and rural consolidation, though underfunding continued as a major drawback. In the wake of Progressive Era advancements, schools in the early twentieth century reflected a mixture of the modern and the traditional. Taking over teaching duties at the Prairie Hollow School in Shannon County, Missouri, in the summer of 1911, nineteen-year-old William Aden French routinely hunted and trapped in the mornings, storing his rifle in a hollow log before the school day commenced. The little Prairie Hollow schoolhouse was "well-painted and well-built, having 6 windows, with screens and one door." Accoutered with two blackboards, a twenty-leaf wall chart, and a bookcase holding forty-seven books (many of them agricultural bulletins), the spartan furnishings of a dozen desks and one "teacher's box" were more than enough to accommodate the four or five students who showed up on a typical day. French's teaching notes—ranging from algebraic equations to Greek history—provide a glimpse into what most would consider a surprisingly rigorous level of elementary education for a young instructor in one of the region's poorest and most remote counties. It would be folly to consider the aspiring novelist French a typical teacher, but the modest strivings of these Shannon Countians were not isolated attempts at improvement.[59]

William Aden French did the best he could with the limited means available to a rural teacher. The most thorough and challenging classroom in this dark age of education was almost always found in the private sector. With public high schools practically nonexistent, young men of varying levels of education established academies in small towns across the Ozarks. Relying on the patronage of professionals, merchants, and prosperous farmers, academies lived hand-to-mouth existences sustained by modest tuition fees—never more than a tornado or fire away from closure. Most carried on the esteemed tradition of the classical curriculum in a region barely receptive to it, imparting the rudiments of Latin, Greek, higher mathematics, and other elements of a proper education to the offspring of the Ozarks "elite."

Some areas of the Ozarks became known for the proliferation of fine academies. The agriculturally productive Springfield Plain subregion—especially the northwestern corner of Arkansas—carried on a tradition of academic achievement begun in the antebellum era. Even in the less prosperous interior of the region, quality education became a hallmark for some places. The 1870s saw the founding of respected academies at Valley Springs, Rally Hill, and Bellefonte in southern Boone County, granting the area the local moniker "Athens of Arkansas." Teachers in the private academy business rarely made more than a bare living. Many preferred to measure their success through the achievements of former students and by the impact of those they had trained to become teachers. A few, like Isaac A. Clarke, became legendary figures in the Ozarks.[60]

A Confederate veteran who returned home to Berryville, Arkansas, Clarke operated his own academy for forty years after the Civil War. Persevering through a devastating fire, the loss of his young wife in a tragic accident, and the stress of tuition collection contingent on crop prices and the weather, Clarke built an eighteen-room brick schoolhouse at a time when Berryville was forty miles from the nearest railroad. Fluctuating enrollments and burdensome debt from his overly ambitious building plagued the respected educator until his death in 1907, forcing Clarke to offer multiple levels of schooling, from English-only primary and intermediate programs to a classical course centered on ancient languages. In the immediate postwar years, the student body of Clarke's Academy consisted primarily of the children of local families—including collateral ancestors of two future U.S. presidents, Lyndon B. Johnson and Barack Obama—but as free public schools gradually drew pupils away, Clarke came to rely on boarding students from families in more prosperous areas.[61]

The ultimate death knell for the private academy was the public high school. In 1890 the interior Ozarks of Missouri contained only about half a dozen high schools whose graduates met the requirements for full enrollment at the

University of Missouri. That number had barely doubled by 1907, translating into a mere 268 graduates qualified to advance to college work—and almost half of those came out of the region's two largest high schools in Springfield and Joplin. Still, the early twentieth century saw a proliferation of small-town public schools offering at least a couple of years of high school work. The fact that rural villages like Licking, Rocky Comfort, and Tuscumbia had high schools at all reflected the efforts of ambitious local leaders determined to keep pace with the latest educational reforms. When compared to its neighbor to the south, Missouri's high school system looked downright monumental. Only in 1911 did the Arkansas General Assembly provide state funding for high schools, reflecting an underfunded educational system in general. In 1919 60 percent of Arkansas districts with no school tax whatsoever were located in the Ozarks. Only three counties in the region exceeded the modest state average school term of 126 days (roughly six months in the classroom), and seven counties reported annual terms of fewer than one hundred days.[62]

The poor state of education in much of the Ozarks and the widespread lack of access to high schools spurred religious denominations to found mission schools in some rural communities. The oldest such institutions in the United States were those aimed at educating—and most often "civilizing"—Native Americans. In an effort to preserve autonomy and stave off assimilation, the Cherokees had established their own school system before the Civil War, including the comparatively rigorous Cherokee Male and Female Seminaries. Nevertheless, northeastern Oklahoma had its brushes with missionary-operated Indian schools, especially as Cherokees and other natives became minorities in their own region around the turn of the twentieth century. Among these were the Northern Presbyterians' Dwight Mission (later Indian Training School) in the Sequoyah County hamlet of Marble City, the Society of Friends' Seneca Indian School at Wyandotte in Ottawa County, and the Oaks Indian Mission and school operated by the United Danish Evangelical Lutheran Church in rural Delaware County.[63]

The Indian mission schools often leaned toward an "industrial training" model of education, which in the rural Ozarks usually meant a focus on agriculture for boys and home economics for girls. It was one of the commonalities between the Indian school and the "mountain mission school." The latter movement began in Appalachia in the 1880s as educators and social reformers (most often from outside the region) sought to save, civilize, and train poor mountain whites while sometimes also preserving their quaint folkways. In the Ozarks, between the 1880s and the Depression, eight different denominations founded mountain mission schools. Half were established by Southern Baptists or Southern Methodists. These denominations were more likely to emphasize the saving of souls, but their schools tended to provide a mostly traditional education for children in areas with no access to a public high school. Rarely did they teach vocational subjects or promote their mission in the hills by exaggerating the isolation of rural Ozarkers or by using the racialized catchphrases of the era—"Anglo-Saxon seedbed," "Elizabethan dialect," "One Hundred Percent American." Mission schools established by other Protestant denominations, however, frequently peddled regional stereotypes for the purposes of fund-raising and promotion.[64]

The earliest missionary schools in the Ozarks were affiliated with the Congregational Church. Founded in the raw railroad town of Rogers, Arkansas, in 1883, Rogers Academy developed into one of the state's most prestigious preparatory schools. Seven years later George Byron Smith and Mabel Smith, recent graduates of Knox College in Illinois, established Iberia Academy in the Miller County, Missouri, hamlet of the same name. Like Rogers Academy, Iberia Academy provided a classical college preparatory education for the handful of students who continued into its upper grades. But Iberia was in a rural territory ten miles from the nearest railroad, and thus the Smiths kept its doors open by instructing children of all ages and by developing alternative courses of study for students interested in becoming teachers.[65]

Fund-raising among affluent Congregationalists in St. Louis and New England was also key to the survival of the two schools. The Smiths at Iberia Academy and the various directors of Rogers Academy made use of popular perceptions of Arkansawyers and Ozarkers to convince would-be donors of the dire necessity of giving liberally to their missions. An 1893 report on Rogers Academy noted that the school had waged "warfare against ignorance and bigotry of all kinds" in a state that had "long been a synonym for backwoods and ignorance." Three years later a correspondent claimed that the efforts of the academy—once trapped in "ignorant and hostile surroundings"—had "actually transformed that whole region." It was a pronouncement that conveniently overlooked northwestern Arkansas's heritage of educational achievement stretching from antebellum days to the founding of the nearby University of Arkansas during Reconstruction. But no amount of context was likely to convince New Englanders and their midwestern progeny that Ozarkers were capable of anything more than a bare-bones education. This heroic Yankee narrative bore strong similarities to the white man's burden that drummed up support for Indian schools.[66]

As the social construct of the Ozarks solidified in the early twentieth century, this narrative of cultural salvation came into sharper focus. Nowhere was this more evident than in an *American Magazine* feature on George Byron Smith and his academy. In Bruce Barton's apocryphal retelling of Smith's arrival in Iberia, so life-altering was the presence of the virtuous hero of old Yankeedom in this backwater crossroads that he could have provided the inspiration for Harold Bell Wright's *The Shepherd of the Hills*. Barton painted the scene of the educators' first wagon ride into Iberia: "On the rude piazzas of bent and broken little one-room cabins, women reached steadying hands toward corn-cob pipes, lest their open-mouthed amazement at the arrival of the strangers should bring disaster." Smith managed to "[take] a boy or girl out of each one of those homes" and transform them. Playing to the Protestant establishment's prejudice against eastern and southern European immigration, Barton reminded readers that "'right here in these mountain counties are the purest-blooded Americans in America. . . . Rub your hand across them only half a dozen times and you are astounded at the ease with which they take on polish."[67]

The publication of "Smith of Iberia" in 1916—the very year that saw the release of Madison Grant's eugenics bible *The Passing of the Great Race*—reflected an ambivalence at the heart of the mountain mission school movement, a struggle between interventionists and preservationists. Northern Protestant reformers wrestled with competing impulses to alter the presumably backward ways of rural Appalachians and Ozarkers while at the same time preserving the traditions and bloodlines of a people believed to be the nation's purest descendants of the original "Anglo-Saxon" immigrants. The rhetoric of racism and nativism provided the starkest demarcation between the mountain mission schools of the Ozarks and denominational schools for Native Americans. Similar rhetoric infused the promotional efforts of other mountain mission schools, such as the Helen Dunlap School for Mountain Girls in Winslow, Arkansas, and the School of the Ozarks in Taney County, Missouri.[68]

The School of the Ozarks would prove to be the longest lasting of all the region's institutions founded as mountain mission schools. And a key to its survival was early leaders' use of stereotypical imagery to solicit donations from wealthy benefactors. Incorporated in 1906 by Southern Presbyterians inspired by settlement schools in Appalachia, the School of the Ozarks utilized the industrial-school model of education and followed the example of similar Appalachian institutions by requiring students to devote several hours each week to manual labor in a print shop, dairy, kitchen, or another campus enterprise. Though local leaders envisioned a preparatory academy for a community that had never had a high school, the institution's administrators gradually forged strong ties with metropolitan donors across the nation by appealing to the charitable impulse. Pamphlets stocked with photographs of forlorn cabin dwellers, featuring pathetic stories of the children of moonshiners and other ne'er-do-wells, tapped into images of Ozarks backwardness and destitution. More than those at any other institution of its kind, the directors and promoters of the School of the Ozarks "mastered the art of portraying the region's picturesque poverty to sympathetic patrons."[69]

The expansion of public high schools into rural areas in the post–World War I years brought an end to the mountain mission school movement, with the notable exception of the School of the Ozarks. The School of the Ozarks would

School of the Ozarks, Point Lookout, Missouri. Courtesy of Lynn Morrow Papers (R1000), folder 930, State Historical Society of Missouri, Rolla.

remain an academy with no college-level courses until the 1950s, but plenty of other institutions emerged in the years before the Great Depression with ambitions of becoming beacons of higher education. A few of them—the University of Arkansas, Springfield's Drury College, Rolla's Missouri School of Mines and Metallurgy, and Batesville's Arkansas College—survive to this day, but there were plenty of others whose brief lives left only a faint memory. Like other regions around the nation, the years between the Civil War and World War II saw the birth and demise of several long-forgotten institutions of higher education, colleges with names like Marionville and Morrisville, Quitman and Crescent. Three Missouri institutions joined the School of the Ozarks in adopting the increasingly popular regional label: Ozark Holiness College in Ava, Carthage's Ozark Wesleyan College, and plain old Ozark College in Greenfield.

Other than Arkansas College and Drury, the only success stories of the pre–Great Depression private colleges in the Ozarks were Bolivar, Missouri's Southwest Baptist College and John Brown University, both of which incorporated elements of the mountain mission philosophy. The latter may have been the most unique institution to spring from Ozarks soil in the era. At the very least, it boasted the most unique founder. A poor Iowa farm boy with a fifth-grade education who found spiritual conversion in a northwestern Arkansas Salvation Army mission, John E. Brown spent more than two decades traveling the nation and preaching in tents as "The Laughing Evangelist" before he decided to found an academy/college in Siloam Springs, Arkansas. Determined to provide a tuition-free education for poor rural students in a setting free of the city's vices, Brown opened his nondenominational institution in 1919. Uniformed students—striped overalls for young men and plain blue dresses for women— spent four hours a day engaged in manual labor on the college's farm or in its furniture factory, laundry, or cannery. Brown's extensive evangelistic outreach and his strong ties with the burgeoning fundamentalist movement resulted in an unusually high number of out-of-state students at what became "a rural, vocational version of the fundamentalist Bible school."[70]

Despite their penurious existences, schools like Southwest Baptist and John Brown provided a modest taste of refinement to their host towns and to the hinterlanders beyond. Most sponsored concerts and student recitals, plays, debates, and lectures. Still, in the late nineteenth and early twentieth centuries, the small college's most crucial role was the same role academies played in the nineteenth century: providing better-educated teachers for the region's expanding public school system. Institutions like Ozark Wesleyan College and Marble Hill's Will Mayfield College prided themselves on producing well-trained educators in the days before teaching required a four-year degree.[71]

The training of teachers, however, was increasingly the arena of state-supported institutions. Beginning in the 1870s, Southeast Missouri State Normal School in Cape Girardeau and Lincoln Institute in Jefferson City provided training for prospective teachers in the far eastern Ozarks and for African Americans, respectively. In Springfield in 1906, classes commenced at the Fourth District Normal School, which served the twenty-two counties of Missouri's fourth congressional district. Three years later the state of Oklahoma founded Northeastern State Normal School in Tahlequah on the grounds of the former Cherokee Female Seminary. The vast stretch of the Arkansas Ozarks between Fayetteville and Batesville remained a higher education wasteland in this era, but Ozarkers in the most southern reaches of the region enjoyed access to the Arkansas State Normal School, which opened its doors in Conway in 1908. By the 1920s all three schools—Southwest Missouri State Teacher's College, Northeastern State Teachers College, and Arkansas State Teachers College—had developed into four-year institutions offering bachelor's degrees in education as well as more traditional majors.[72]

The dawning of the Depression found more students enrolled in Ozarks colleges than ever before. But the financial hardships of the 1930s would take their toll. Only a handful of the region's private colleges survived the decade, and belt tightening limited growth at public colleges in the Ozarks. Significant higher education expansion awaited the G.I. Bill. Such a radical piece of legislation was almost unfathomable at the dawn of the Great Depression. For Ozarkers and other Americans in the late 1920s, the transformative decade and a half to come was truly beyond comprehension.

5 EXPOSING THE OZARKS

Like most Americans, Earl T. Sechler did not see this coming. In the late 1920s, only recently returned from New York's Union Theological Seminary, he enjoyed a solid annual salary as a roving caretaker for a dozen Disciples of Christ congregations in his native Dallas County, Missouri. By 1934, however, his income had been cut in half, forcing him to send his children and wife to live on her parents' Illinois farm while he hunkered down in a rented house in the hamlet of Red Top, a dozen miles up Route 66 from Springfield. He continued to preach, but he did so to gatherings of "people too poor to own cars" for as little as a dollar's worth of food. Behind on his rent, suffering from insomnia, and in fear that his well was about to run dry, literally, he occupied the growing chunks of downtime by reading voraciously. His eclectic tastes ranged from playwrights Henrik Ibsen and Oscar Wilde to philosopher Friedrich Nietzsche. No subscriber to the John T. Woodruff book-of-the-month club, he even found time to read Vance Randolph's *Ozark Mountain Folks* and *The Woods Colt* by Thames Williamson. As 1934 drew to a close, Sechler despaired of seeing so many front-page stories of suicide. Lamenting his own "strong sense of failure," he could do little more than pray that "a turn will come our way before many moons."[1]

Less likely to articulate their suffering but perhaps more representative of the Depression's impact on rural Ozarkers were the Acklins of Baxter County, Arkansas. About the time Sechler settled into his spartan existence in Red Top, Corgel and Chester Acklin welcomed their second child into the world in a remote community tucked in a bend of the White River. Son of an itinerant sawmiller, Chester Acklin walked a ten-mile roundtrip to shovel gravel onto boxcars for a dollar and a nickel per day. When worsening times brought an end to wage work, the Acklins moved even farther back into the hills and reverted to subsistence farming. At the end of their rope in 1937, they managed to obtain a 1926 Model T Ford and claimed an abandoned house amid a group of impoverished Arkansas expatriates in southern New Mexico. Living on "pinto beans, water gravy, and 'flap jacks,'" the tent-dwelling Acklins picked cotton and sought other seasonal jobs to scratch out an existence. In 1939 Corgel gave birth to her third child as a charity patient in a New Mexico hospital, and the shame and resentment over her poor treatment would remain with her for the rest of her life. When the newborn almost starved to death due to Corgel's own malnourishment, the Acklins received a letter from Chester's father containing twenty-five dollars, which they used to make a down payment on a '27 Dodge and headed for the Ozarks.[2]

But more hard times awaited back in Arkansas, and by the fall of 1940 their cupboards were bare of anything save black-eyed peas. Corgel boiled and baked peas into a bread substitute, which the family ate alongside more peas. In the summer of 1941, Chester Acklin got a job as an automobile mechanic in the little White River town of Norfork, providing the family rare material comforts. The town's light plant powered a few hours of electricity each day. Seven-year-old Emmit discovered Captain Marvel and other fantastic characters in the "funny books," and he and his older sister Normalea caught an occasional matinee at the Lyric Theater. When a car toppled off a jack and broke Chester's leg, however, the family sank back into destitution, moved into a drafty "slab house," and relied on kind neighbors and leftovers from the school cafeteria for survival. Ultimately, it was the war that brought the Acklins out of their years of struggle. Fully recovered, Chester was drafted into the army in the spring of 1944. With a regular paycheck for the first time in years, frugal Corgel saved twelve hundred dollars during Chester's twenty months in the military. It was enough to purchase twenty acres and set up a sawmill in the White River Hills in 1946.[3]

Years of poverty and struggle seared images of the Depression into the memories of millions of Americans. For Emmit Acklin, one stood out. He was barely beyond toddler age during the family's sojourn in New Mexico, but even as an old man he could picture Lonzo Coyle, a fellow impoverished "Arkie" migrant, driving a car with only three tires. Decades later Emmit could still hear gravel crunching beneath that bare rim, the sound of desperation.[4] That exposed rim encapsulated the era for Emmit Acklin, and exposure seems a fitting symbol for understanding the Ozarks in the age of the Great Depression and World War II. Plummeting agricultural prices and natural disasters exposed the region's unsustainable farming culture at the moment agribusiness began its ascension. The unprecedented intervention of government programs designed to address these crises exposed the physical scars and ecological repercussions of unregulated extractive industries and generations of destructive farming methods. New Deal agencies also exposed impoverished conditions, while the massive out-migrations of poor Ozarkers exposed people in far-flung parts of the nation to the migrant families who provided cheap labor. The experiences of these families and the tens of thousands of other Ozarkers who ventured out of the hills for survival in the fields of harvest, for uniforms and rifles, or for jobs in the booming factories of war exposed them to a wide world beyond the ridges and hollers. In short, the years of depression and world war opened the Ozarks to the world and opened the world to Ozarkers.

Down and Out

The economic struggles of Ozarkers were exacerbated by the systemic international downturn that emerged from the speculative bubble of the 1920s, but the roots of regional decline ran much deeper. With or without Wall Street's collapse, the Ozarks faced an uncertain future in the post–World War I era. The slow decline of rural stability produced a society poorly equipped to confront the challenges of the nation's worst economic disaster. Chronicling two decades of change in Hickory County, Missouri, from the vantage point of the late 1930s, James West (pseudonym of anthropologist Carl L. Withers) found a rampant increase in consumerist ideals among farm families and town dwellers alike: "Their minds were saturated . . . with the material and social values of the outside world, which reached them daily through talk, trips, movies, radio, newspapers, weekly picture magazines, 'comic books,' and so forth." For West, the conflict inherent in the clash of old ways and new undermined traditional community. "The leadership of old-style merchants failed, and lodges ceased functioning importantly. Neighborhoods and extended families lost much of their solidarity."[5]

While West's belief in an isolated Ozarks culture before World War I led him to overdramatize the starkness of culture clash, rural Ozarkers who lived through the era confirmed the broad outlines of his portrait of declension. Born in the hills of Lawrence County, Arkansas, in 1900, Marvin Lawson witnessed the decline of the thriving community of his youth. Between 1915 and 1930, half of the families in his neighborhood moved away, and the population decline decimated attendance at both the Hopewell Methodist Church and the two-room Post Oak School, both of which closed in the early years of the Depression. Explaining modernization's impact on his Boston Mountains family and community, Tate C. Page fell back on the rugged individualistic ethos so often associated with the rural Ozarks. "Old ways had been forgotten," Page lamented. "New skills were not acquired." In Page's estimation the coming of consumer culture had "eroded the moral fiber of the people and readied them for the collapse of their way of life."[6]

For Page, who worked his way through college and went on to a successful career far from home, the declension of his mountain community became an integral component of a triumphant personal narrative, while the more plebian life stories of relatives who stayed behind surely reflected a lack of character. It was a bootstraps mentality that may have served well his ancestors and that colored the region's image with its stoic individualism, but it proves inadequate as an explanation of the forces affecting the Ozarks and other rural areas of the nation in the generation between the world wars.

In the half century after the Civil War, large families—a product of exploding birthrates and declining mortality—became the norm, while thousands of new families found their way into the Ozarks. The result was the process of "rural infilling," whereby even the poorest parcels of land were subjected to agricultural development. By the second decade of the twentieth century, rural overpopulation had reduced average farm sizes to the extent that many were too small to provide a living. A survival strategy had been for marginal farmers and their sons to seek part-time and seasonal employment in extractive industries. But the timber boom had come to an end by the time world leaders converged on the Palace of Versailles for peace talks. A study of the Courtois Hills of Missouri found that lumber milling declined by more than half in the 1920s and by half again in the 1930s, costing more than two-thirds of sawmill jobs. The combination of rural overpopulation and denuded forests wiped out wildlife habitats, bringing whitetail deer, turkeys, and black bears to the brink of extirpation. The result of these factors was a growing dependency on store-bought and mail-order goods and the steady demise of safety-first farming and communal activities (hog killings, barn raisings) that had long enmeshed neighborhoods in reciprocal relationships. Falling agricultural prices of the 1920s, depleted soils, and the shortage of off-farm jobs contributed to rising farm tenancy rates. In many of the region's counties, more than one-third of all farms were worked by tenants or sharecroppers at the beginning of the Depression.[7]

The challenges facing the Ozarks in the long Depression era shared much in common with the obstacles confronting the vast rural stretches of the Midwest and South in general. Not least of those challenges were natural disasters. For some Ozarkers, the Depression began with the Great Flood of 1927, which forced the White River Division of the Missouri Pacific Railroad to shut down operations for ten days. More devastating and widespread was the destruction and suffering caused by drought. One of the worst on record descended on the heart of North America in the summer of 1930 and lingered into the following year. Triple-digit temperatures burned up crops and pastures that in some cases saw no rainfall for more than two months. The summers of 1934 and 1935 proved little better for many Ozarkers.[8]

Contrary to popular myth, however, the Ozarks was not part of the Depression-era Dust Bowl, a designation referring to the arid plains of the Oklahoma and Texas panhandles. At least part of the blame for this long-held misconception must be placed at the feet of one of the twentieth century's great writers. In his Pulitzer Prize–winning 1939 novel, John Steinbeck prefaced *The Grapes of Wrath* with a stirring description of the Dust Bowl before following the impoverished Joads as they escape Oklahoma for a new life in California. But the fictional "Okie" family hailed from the southwestern edge of the Ozarks in the vicinity of Sallisaw. Regardless of Steinbeck's perhaps unintentionally deceptive Oklahoma geography lesson, the Joads represented tens of thousands of real-life Ozarkers who hit the migrant-worker trails in the Depression.[9]

One by-product of the population boom and economic downturn in the rural Ozarks was a serious surplus of labor. Consequently, the Ozarks became one of the nation's chief suppliers of cheap migrant labor, a distinction the region would hold until well past the midpoint of the twentieth century. Even before 1900, young men were making annual treks to find seasonal work in the Great Plains wheat harvest. The same era found entire families in the southern Ozarks traveling by wagon to pick cotton in the vast bottoms of the Arkansas Valley. As the availability of automobile travel broadened the migrant's horizons, Ozarkers found their way to the cornfields of Iowa, the orchards of Michigan, the hops vineyards and hillsides of fruit in the Pacific Northwest.

Omer Brown and Edsel Holt of Ozark County, Missouri, hopped a train at Chadwick and found work for five dollars a day and board on a wheat farm in western Kansas. Satisfied with a job that paid better than his one-room teaching position back home, Brown made a couple more summer journeys to the plains before donning a uniform and heading off to World War I. Young single men like Brown and Holt dominated the early days of migrant labor, but in the years between the world wars the migrant family became a common phenomenon in the Ozarks. In the fall of 1922, the Humphreys family of Fulton County ventured eastward to the Arkansas Delta, where they harvested cotton on a farm owned by former neighbors in the hills. Living in a one-room house, Albert and Clara assigned each Humphreys child (even six-year-old Ruth) a daily quota of cotton to pick and allowed the children to keep any money earned from cotton that exceeded the quota. The surplus wasn't likely to amount to much—the going rate for pickers was one dollar for one hundred pounds of lint—but it was surer money than they'd left behind in the Ozarks.[10]

By the Depression years, the automobile had largely replaced the freight train as the mode of transportation for the Ozark region's surplus laborers. In the mid-1930s Ernest Webber and other young men rode two hundred miles in the back of a truck from Edgar Springs, Missouri, to the Mississippi River cotton fields south of Sikeston, bunking in a tenant house and coming back home with jingling pockets at Christmastime. Webber's journey from one part of Missouri to another was a leisurely jaunt compared with the cross-country treks that became commonplace for Ozarkers. In the spring of 1937, Dovie and

Arkansas migrant children, Berrien County, Michigan, 1940. Photographed for the Farm Security Administration by John Vachon. Courtesy of Library of Congress.

Edna Lee and their extended family of Arkansawyers converged on Hood River, Oregon. Working in apple orchards, canneries, and in other jobs, the Lees and their relatives made three to six dollars a day but were still too poor to afford Christmas presents for the children. Four years later the Lees loaded into a '29 Chevy and headed back to the Hood River for a bumper cherry crop, picking up relatives on the way through Oklahoma and arriving in the "Valley of Paradise" in late May.[11]

If there was a paradise out west, most Ozarkers expected to find it not in Oregon but in Steinbeck's California. In his study of Wheatland, Missouri, in the latter days of the Depression, James West found that practically every male in Hickory County could boast of at least one trip to the Golden State. In fact, quipped one source, "a boy's education ain't considered finished around here till he's been to Californy." Among females only married women were free to ride the migrant trails—and then only in the company of family. Leland Fox, a native of Cedar County, Missouri, remembered the year a local man installed benches in the back of a livestock truck and hauled nineteen passengers across the continent. When the truck driver informed an inspector at the California state line that the passengers were all family members, the incredulous trooper jumped off the truck, motioned them forward, and yelled "'Let 'em through, it's Brigham Young!'" Joining other Cedar Countians and Ozarkers in the expansive Central Valley, the truck riders went to work picking cotton, hoeing lettuce, and anything else that earned a few dimes. "Many made trips back and forth," noted Fox, "vowing at the end of every trip, 'this is the last one.'"[12]

Public Enemies

It took only one trip to convince some Ozarkers that any life was preferable to the migrant's life. Charley Floyd was a mere sixteen when he left his parents' farm in Oklahoma's Cookson Hills and hopped a freight at Sallisaw for the waving wheat fields on the plains in the summer of 1920. Years later his mother would claim that this premature journey into a workingman's life somehow changed young Charley. Maybe it was a few months rubbing elbows with bindlestiffs that transformed Charley Floyd, or maybe this Appalachian-born Ozarker just came into the world with a particularly wide ornery streak. Whatever it was that made him different from most folks, Charley Floyd—known to the world as "Pretty Boy"—became the U.S. Division of Investigation's public enemy number one in the heart of the Great Depression.[13]

The same post–World War I economic downturn that sent rural places like the Ozarks spiraling into a generation-long depression also made its contribution to one of the most colorful vignettes of the interwar years. Given the nation's fascination with midwestern criminals in the era of John Dillinger and "Baby Face" Nelson, it is surprising that the escapades of desperadoes played a rather insignificant role in shaping the popular imagination of the Ozarks. In the very age when images of Ozarks hillbillies and rustic mountaineers first came into sharp national focus, the region sprawled in the heart of country gangster territory. Moonshining and bootlegging were crucial to the region's full participation in the public enemy era, but there were other factors as well. Long before the days of Tommy guns, the challenge of law enforcement in the post–Civil War Indian Territory had created a haven for outlaws in places like the Cookson Hills, and the "wide-open" boomtown atmosphere of Joplin's Tri-State District attracted swindlers, thieves, and other shady characters. Practically every notable criminal of the interwar years claimed at least a passing familiarity with the "town that jack built."[14]

The public enemy era found some of the Depression's most wanted criminals lying low in rugged southern Missouri. In the summer of 1930, one of the Windy City's most wanted was apprehended in the heart of the Ozarks. Having already done time in six different states, Harry Lee Watson, the polite and profanity-free "Gentleman Bandit," admitted to a string of fifteen bank robberies after he was captured with his circus performer wife in Texas County. His arrest alerted authorities to the presence of another gangster on the lam in Missouri's hills. Unbeknownst to the citizens of Taney County, the disheveled chicken farmer and home brew peddler they knew as Walter Cook was actually murderer Jake Fleagle, a Kansas native known as the "Wolf of the West." Using handwriting samples to track his location to somewhere along the White River Line, a multiagency team of officers trapped and shot Fleagle aboard a passenger car at the Branson depot on October 13, 1930. He died in a Springfield hospital the following day.[15]

The small gang whose media coverage and legacy in the American conscious-ness probably best encapsulated the dark romanticism of the public enemy era found their way to the Ozarks multiple times. Texans Bonnie Parker and Clyde Barrow and their accomplices bungled a bank heist in the mining town of Oronogo and kidnapped a Springfield motorcycle cop on their first visit. It was their second tour of the Ozarks in 1933 that transformed them from small-time criminals to national celebrities in the sights of J. Edgar Hoover's Bureau of Investigation (later the FBI). Alerted to the odd comings and goings and lavish spending habits of a group of attractive youngsters, Joplin authorities mounted a raid on the Barrow apartment. Killing two of the five officers with blasts from a sawed-off shotgun, Clyde, his brother Buck, and another man received minor gunshot wounds but managed to escape with Bonnie and Buck's wife, Blanche, in a stolen car.[16]

Joplin police found in the abandoned apartment a roll of undeveloped camera film that contributed to the folklore and blossoming public interest surrounding these footloose bandits. Just two days after the raid, the *Joplin Globe* published a few of the prints, and they were quickly wired to other newspapers around the nation. One photograph featured waifish Bonnie playfully pointing a sawed-off shotgun at a smiling Clyde, while another pictured her chomping on a cigar and brashly wielding the pistol stolen from the Springfield motorcycle cop as she posed for the camera with one foot propped up on the front bumper of a swiped car. Within days almost every newspaper reader in the country had gotten an eyeful of Bonnie and Clyde. "The Joplin photos," observes Jeff Guinn, one of the duo's many biographers, "introduced new criminal superstars with the most titillating trademark of all—illicit sex."[17]

The Barrow Gang made a few more runs through the Ozarks during the desperate last months of their lives, but for Bonnie and Clyde the hills remained a place for passing through and hiding out. For one legendary gang, however, the Ozarks was home. Once again it was a woman that set this outfit apart from the other outlaw bands of the time. Like Bonnie Parker, Arizona "Arrie" Barker probably never squeezed a trigger on her way to becoming one of the country's most wanted villains. The comparison stopped there. The woman known to his-tory and legend as "Ma" Barker was no nubile femme fatale but a middle-aged, matronly looking Ozarker whose worst flaw was being an enabling mother who stayed by her law-breaking boys no matter the cost. Arrie raised her four sons—Herman, Lloyd, Arthur "Doc," and Fred—in Aurora and Webb City, Missouri. The Barker boys were already building rap sheets when the family left the Ozarks during World War I and relocated to Tulsa, where the sons fell in with members of that city's infamous Central Park Gang.[18]

It was the youngest brothers who would make up two-thirds of the core of the Barker-Karpis Gang, which came together in Joplin in 1931 when Fred and a fellow former inmate, Alvin Karpis, began a string of burglaries. Later that year Fred and Karpis, with Arrie in tow, moved their operation deep into the Ozarks. From a rented farm near Thayer, Missouri, Fred Barker and Karpis robbed a bank in nearby Mountain View, and Fred killed a night constable in Pocahontas, Arkansas. Their crime spree in the Ozarks came to an end a few days before Christmas, when the owner of a West Plains garage grew suspicious of two dapper dressers while fixing flats on their blue DeSoto. When the sheriff responded to the alert, Fred Barker killed him with four bullets at point-blank range. The trio escaped to Joplin, but the bulletins issued by the Howell County sheriff's office included a one-hundred-dollar reward for tips on the whereabouts of "Old Lady Arrie Barker," the first public mention of the woman now immortalized as "Ma." Paroled from a murder sentence a few months later, Doc Barker joined the gang in a rash of bank robberies, kidnappings, and murders before he was arrested in Chicago in early 1935. A week later Fred and Arrie Barker were gunned down inside a Florida lake cottage. Doc capped off the family's story in style when prison guards finished him off during an attempted escape from Alcatraz in 1939.[19]

More than a few G-men, deputies, and policemen fell victim in this desperate era. Though largely forgotten outside of southwestern Missouri today, the public enemy era's deadliest event for law enforcement officers took place just outside the Queen City of the Ozarks. Released from the federal prison in Leavenworth, Kansas, in late 1931, professional car thief Jennings Young reunited with his younger brother, Harry, another ex-con, who had been on the lam for killing a Republic, Missouri, night watchman. Resuming their favorite crime, the brothers showed up in stolen automobiles at their parents' Brookline farmhouse, just a couple of miles west of Springfield. When Springfield police arrested the Youngs' sisters for trying to fence the stolen cars on January 2, 1932, a posse of ten county and city officers, along with one civilian, converged on the Young farmhouse late that evening. Armed only with a Remington semiautomatic rifle and a Winchester shotgun, the brothers managed to kill or mortally wound six officers (including the county sheriff) before making a clean getaway. Trapped three days later in a Houston, Texas, boardinghouse, the Young brothers apparently killed one another in a suicide pact. When angry citizens in Greene County refused to allow the Young family to bury Jennings and Harry in a local graveyard, the bodies were transported sixty miles to the west and laid to rest in Joplin. Twenty-one months later, the burial of the Ozarks' most famous criminal, Pretty Boy Floyd, evoked a different reaction, as an estimated twenty thousand people flocked to the country cemetery in Akins, Oklahoma.[20]

Dealing with a New Deal

The banks terrorized by bandits like Pretty Boy Floyd were less stable institutions than the ones we patronize today, and not just because of an alarming rate of burglaries. In Floyd's Oklahoma, record numbers of farm foreclosures in the latter half of the 1920s put several banks out of business. With or without heists, the onset of the Great Depression proved cataclysmic for financial institutions and their patrons in the early 1930s. The trickling news of bank shutterings gradually grew into a torrent as depositors rushed to liquidate their accounts, instigating a vicious cycle with no end in sight. Missouri saw more than 300 banks close their doors in the darkest days of the Depression. In poor Arkansas the carnage was even more severe, comparatively speaking. By the spring of 1933, some 283 banks (more than two-thirds of Arkansas's institutions at the time of the 1929 stock market crash) were no longer open for business. The first order for Franklin D. Roosevelt upon taking office in early 1933 was a weeklong "bank holiday" to restore the nation's collective confidence.[21]

According to local historians, at least two small-town banks in the Ozarks didn't get the president's message. Bankers in Franklin, Arkansas, and Grandin, Missouri—so go the stories—opened as usual on Monday morning, the sixth of April, and remained in operation for an undetermined time afterward.[22] Whether apocryphal or factual, the stories of the banks that missed the holiday are tempting additions to the narrative portraying the rural Ozarks as isolated and unburdened by the forces affecting the rest of the United States. In the case of the Depression, it would make for a colorful story if common Ozarkers plodded through the 1930s blissfully unaware of the economic turmoil surrounding them. Many communities in the hills may have been on the margins of modern society, but the financial downturn did not pass them by.

In addition to the loss of banks and more than half the funds they once held, the early 1930s brought a 50 percent decline in retail sales and falling agricultural prices. Land values fell by more than 40 percent in Missouri, and in Oklahoma farm income decreased by almost two-thirds. By 1932 unemployment in both Arkansas and Missouri approached 40 percent. In the Lead Belt of southeastern Missouri, plummeting mineral prices culminated in mass layoffs in 1933, a year that saw the industry operating at one-quarter of its pre-Depression capacity. Companies provided unemployed miners free use of land for gardening, but a subsistence lifestyle was cold comfort for families accustomed to paychecks and weekly visits to the grocery store. A study of Pulaski County, Missouri, found that the average daily earnings of a tie hacker plunged from three dollars to a dollar, while a farm laborer who had received a dollar and a quarter in the late 1920s settled for fifty cents in 1933.[23]

In the earliest years of the Depression, the states encompassing the Ozark region shared a conservative leadership ideologically opposed to taking significant steps to address the fiscal emergency. State and local governments relied on the charity of the Red Cross as well as an underfunded relief program established in 1932 by the Hoover administration. Nationally known humorist and entertainer Will Rogers put on a series of benefit shows that raised one hundred thousand dollars for relief efforts in his native Oklahoma and another thirty-nine thousand for his wife's home state of Arkansas. But this was a mere drop in the bucket in the depths of the economic malaise. Even with Roosevelt's overwhelming victory in 1932, governors and legislatures in Arkansas, Missouri, and Oklahoma did not immediately embrace the deficit spending of the New Deal.[24]

Arkansas governor J. Marion Futrell cut expenditures by more than 50 percent and supported constitutional amendments that made it almost impossible to raise taxes. Only in the spring of 1935, when the U.S. government cut off federal aid to the bankrupt state, did Futrell and the general assembly take meaningful steps to boost revenues. Missouri's governor Guy B. Park was another champion of limited government with few progressive inclinations. But Park at the least cooperated with federal New Deal programs, which was more than could be said for Oklahoma's "Alfalfa Bill" Murray. More showman than statesman, Murray allowed a handful of homeless people to plant gardens on the lawn of the governor's mansion. But when it came to implementing federal relief programs, he wanted to call the shots, further alienating himself from New Dealers and limiting the flow of national dollars into Oklahoma.[25]

When former oilman and congressman Ernest W. Marland replaced Alfalfa Bill in 1935, Roosevelt finally had a loyal New Dealer in the governor's mansion. But the president had few other supporters in Oklahoma City, and Marland's grand vision of a "Little New Deal" ultimately led only to old-age pensions, aid for dependent children, and some money earmarked for public works. In Arkansas a similar story played out as the recalcitrant general assembly butted heads with loyal New Dealer Carl E. Bailey, who could accomplish little more than bringing the state into compliance with federal relief mandates. Of the three Ozarks states, only Missouri achieved something akin to a "Little New Deal." Working with a cooperative, Democrat-dominated state legislature, Governor Lloyd Stark supported bills addressing child welfare, unemployment insurance, old-age pensions, minimum wage, workers' compensation, and mine safety.[26]

Throughout the Ozarks it was the Roosevelt administration that came to the relief of the poor and jobless. New Dealers hit the ground in an all-out sprint in the spring of 1933, insinuating the national government into the lives of Ozarkers in unprecedented fashion. In addition to the bank holiday, the initial months of the Roosevelt administration churned out one agency after another. Programs such as the Federal Emergency Relief Administration and the Civilian Conservation Corps were concerned mainly with reducing unemployment and increasing the circulation of money. The Agricultural Adjustment Administration looked to improve farm incomes by addressing the country's imbalance between commodity supply and demand, while the Soil Erosion (later Conservation) Service tackled concerns about the environment and sustainability. Launched in 1935, the so-called Second New Deal added to this alphabet soup a helping of new agencies: the Rural Electrification Administration, the Resettlement Administration, the Social Security Administration, the Works Progress Administration, and the National Youth Administration. Collectively, these programs brought the federal government into closer and more constant contact with ordinary citizens. By the end of the decade, even the smallest county seats hosted several offices of federal agencies.

As far as thousands of destitute citizens were concerned, drastic government action could not come soon enough. "Our small children ask would Santa come," wrote an Izard County woman to Arkansas's governor in the trying winter of 1933. "I told them I guessed . . . maby he would bring us bread as that is what we need so bad . . . maby we wont starve." For other families in the Ozarks, it was turnips that sustained them through the winter, or rabbits caught in homemade gums. In southern Missouri the landless "woods people" marooned in the hollers after the collapse of the timber industry were the poorest of the poor. In Dallas County government workers found hundreds of such "squatter" families "living in one room cabins without floors, eking out a bare subsistence in the Ozark hills" by hunting, fishing, and gathering berries. In the Dallas County community of Windyville, Christian minister Earl T. Sechler estimated that three in four families were attempting to get on the relief rolls in early 1933. In the county seat of Buffalo, he witnessed a "near riot . . . over Relief Work."[27]

Aware of the stigma attached to those receiving handouts, the Roosevelt administration avoided direct relief when possible in the earliest days of the New Deal. Most efforts were directed toward putting people to work, even if some of the jobs were of dubious value and rigor. One of the era's most iconic federal programs grew out of this philosophy. The Civilian Conservation Corps (CCC) reflected both the president's dedication to environmental conservation and the nation's collective interest in getting tens of thousands of young men off the streets. Men between the ages of eighteen and twenty-five whose families qualified for relief rolls provided the primary workforce of the CCC. Camps of orderly tents or barracks directed by the War Department sprouted in forests and rural areas around the nation. Depending on the purpose of the camp, its projects were designed and administered by either the Interior Department (forestry) or the Department of Agriculture. Room and board during the six-month tour of duty came courtesy of Uncle Sam, and a typical worker received thirty dollars per month, most of which was sent directly back home to parents or dependents.[28]

During the agency's nine-year existence, approximately seventy different locations in the Ozarks hosted CCC camps. The majority focused on forestry work—planting seedlings, erecting and manning fire towers, building roads and hiking trails, and drafting topographical maps. Most of these camps were located in Arkansas's Ozark National Forest or on Missouri lands that in 1939 would be designated the Mark Twain and Clark national forests. The region also contained more than a dozen agricultural camps near towns such as Berryville and Heber Springs in Arkansas and Mount Vernon and Neosho in Missouri. Overseen by the Soil Conservation Service, workers in these camps terraced hillside farms, built stock ponds and dipping vats, and sowed nutrient-restoring cover crops such as kudzu and lespedeza.[29]

The camps that left the most visible and enduring legacy were those assigned to develop or enhance state parks. The Ozarks of Oklahoma and Arkansas contained not a single state park when the CCC came to life in 1933. Within a few years, however, workers built the picnic areas, trails, pavilions, and cabins of what would eventually become three new state parks: Spavinaw Hills, Devil's Den, and Buffalo Point. In Missouri, which could already claim a blossoming parks movement, the Depression "proved to be a golden age for the state park system." The state's first three CCC camps sprang up at state parks in the region: Sam A. Baker, Meramec, and Roaring River. Ultimately, thirteen Missouri state parks and future state parks benefited from CCC labor. A rare camp of World War I veterans left its mark on Montauk State Park on the Current River in southern Dent County. The vets not only built tourist cabins and other park structures but erected a dam and restored an old grist mill as well. An even rarer company of CCC workers (at least in the Ozarks) was the camp at Washington State Park, northeast of Potosi. The region's only long-running CCC outfit manned by African Americans built a dining lodge with a thunderbird motif and created a stone staircase known as the "1,000 Steps Trail." Almost all the lodges, cabins, and other structures built by the CCC on the grounds of state parks hewed to the rustic style of architecture previously developed by the National Park Service.[30]

The Federal Emergency Relief Administration (FERA) hired the unemployed to repair roads, maintain city parks, and take on other tasks often dismissed by critics as "make-work." In the fall of 1933, Roosevelt used an executive order to create the Civil Works Administration (CWA). A temporary agency designed to sustain millions of Americans through the winter, the CWA provided federal funds for road work, college work-study programs, and the construction of schools and other public buildings. The short-lived CWA left its architectural legacy in a few communities in the Ozarks. In Stockton, Missouri, more than five dozen local men built a community building and swimming pool. The native stone building continues to serve the Cedar County seat as a meeting place for the American Legion and as an exhibit hall during the annual Black Walnut Festival.[31]

Another early New Deal work program that had a much longer shelf life than the CWA was the Public Works Administration (PWA). Established in 1933 by the National Industrial Recovery Act, the PWA was technically not a "work relief" program, which meant that private construction companies oversaw its projects. Counties and municipalities around the Ozarks took advantage of PWA funds for a variety of undertakings, from a municipal waterworks in Ellington, Missouri, to the Hurricane Deck Bridge over the Lake of the Ozarks. The Madison County courthouse in Huntsville, Arkansas, a three-story structure made of glazed brick and limestone, remains a good example of the architectural style most commonly used by federal New Deal agencies, a style now known as PWA Moderne. But the budget of the little courthouse paled in comparison with the massive PWA-supported building boom on the University of Arkansas campus in Fayetteville between 1935 and 1940. Utilizing more than $2.2 million in grants and loans, the state's flagship university underwent a federally subsidized facelift with the construction of seven new buildings, including a library, student union, and fieldhouse.[32]

No New Deal agency was more iconic than the Works Progress Administration (WPA), created in 1935 to replace the FERA as the administrator of work relief programs. Through a panoply of projects ranging from roads and bridges to canning kitchens and art classes, the WPA touched practically every community and family in the country. A description of its projects in the Ozarks alone would fill volumes. Almost two-thirds of labor costs went toward road construction and repair, but the most visible legacy of the WPA—and its subordinate agency the National Youth Administration (NYA)—were the hundreds of buildings constructed across the region. WPA architecture ran the gamut from the rustic three-story lodge at Missouri's Roaring River State Park to the PWA Moderne courthouse in Jay, Oklahoma.[33]

Yet the agency's signature style was characterized by native-stone structures combining the vernacular with flourishes of modernity. On occasion this style showed up in public buildings—the Newton County courthouse in Jasper, Arkansas, for instance—but it was most often reflected in the dozens of schools and gymnasiums bequeathed to the Ozarks. The WPA/NYA's familiar native-stone schoolhouses went up in remote communities with names like Alco and Ozone, Gipsy and Wilderness. The employees of the work relief program completed a wide range of other building projects as well, including a University of Arkansas experiment station near Batesville, a fish hatchery in Neosho, and a stone building enclosing Sequoyah's cabin in the Cookson Hills of Oklahoma. In Joplin hundreds of relief workers altered the city's physical appearance in just a few years. In addition to paving roads, repairing sidewalks, and developing one-hundred-acre Landreth Park, the WPA and other federal agencies constructed a stadium, fire stations, schools, a viaduct, and an airport. One of the Ozark region's more unusual WPA projects was the completion of a dam and small lake on private property owned by a group of Black Kansas Citians. Nestled in the hills of an overwhelmingly white area of Morgan County, Lake Placid soon became the favored vacation destination for Kansas City's Black middle class. The Lake Placid project was a rare example of a New Deal undertaking that directly benefited African Americans in the Jim Crow Ozarks. Only a few other known examples survive, including a swimming pool and stone entry gates at Springfield's only park reserved for African Americans and the Lincoln Negro School that today houses the administrative offices of the Tahlequah Public Schools.[34]

The reach of the WPA extended well beyond construction projects. NYA boys and girls built benches, pauper coffins, and toys. A WPA handicraft shop in Rolla, Missouri, offered instruction in basket and rug weaving, woodworking, glass etching, embroidery, and crocheting. Some women found part-time employment in the region's earliest hot lunch programs at schools. Many more found work in sewing rooms making overalls, shirts, britches, and dresses for needy families. Perhaps the most common product of the New Deal sewing operations was the cotton mattress. Saless Hartley of Douglas County, Missouri, was among the hundreds of mattress makers. She and four other women received training from government representatives at a nearby schoolhouse, after which they went to work making two mattresses and coverlets a day with government supplies in a makeshift shop underneath a neighbor's shed. Public canning kitchens were also popular programs of the FERA and WPA. The kitchens made pressure cookers, jars, and cans available to relief clients who brought in their own vegetables, fruits, and meats. Local women were hired and trained to oversee the kitchens and instruct their neighbors in the art of pressure cooking and canning. Families using the kitchens were required to donate up to 25 percent of their food, which was then distributed to the destitute. Erma Humphreys recalled that her Fulton County, Arkansas, family left their neighborhood kitchen with so many cans of peaches, pumpkins, mustard greens, and other products that they dug a new cellar in which to store them.[35]

Not all WPA jobs were aimed at the unskilled poor. The WPA Writers' Project hired educated relief clients to conduct oral history interviews, inventory county records, and complete thick guidebooks on each state. The Missouri Writers' Project tapped perpetually penniless Vance Randolph to travel the

Farm woman with canned foods, Washington County, Missouri, 1939. Photographed for the Farm Security Administration by Arthur Rothstein. Courtesy of Library of Congress.

Ozarks collecting folklore for a volume to be published as the *Ozark Guide*. When the Springfield Chamber of Commerce got hold of a copy of the manuscript in late 1936, however, directors objected to Randolph's concentration on the region's earthier residents and promptly canceled their promised financial support for the book's publication; the project's leadership in St. Louis pulled the plug on the *Ozark Guide*. John T. Woodruff had not softened his views in the two years since the folk festival came and went in his city.[36]

The WPA also maintained a companion Federal Art Project, but the most notable artistic legacies of the New Deal were products of a different agency, the Treasury Department's Section of Fine Arts. Beginning in 1936 the Treasury Department funded the construction of more than twenty new post offices in the Ozarks, and almost all of them came adorned with commissioned artwork. Most of the works of art were murals or oil-on-canvas paintings rendered in the era's dominant stylistic combination of Regionalism and Social Realism. And no one was more crucial to the popularity of that movement than Ozarks native

Thomas Hart Benton, whose Depression-era output included a monumental, thirteen-panel mural at the state capitol in Jefferson City. In true Regionalist fashion, the postal artists focused on subject matter of local importance, from Olga Mohr's "Cherokee Indian Farming and Animal Husbandry" in Stilwell, Oklahoma, to James B. Turnbull's "The Lead Belt" in Fredericktown, Missouri. In Heber Springs, Arkansas, the new post office shone with an oil-on-canvas painting titled "From Timber to Agriculture." The work's creator, Missouri native H. Louis Freund, became the preeminent artist of the era in the Arkansas Ozarks, completing murals on buildings in Harrison, Rogers, and Eureka Springs. Freund fell in love with the latter town, married a fellow artist there, and established the Summer Art School of the Ozarks in a Victorian house once owned by prohibitionist Carry Nation.[37]

Another product of the Second New Deal took the place of FERA's direct relief program and laid the foundation for the modern welfare state. Created by Congress in the summer of 1935, the Social Security Administration coordinated old-age pensions, aid for dependent children and the disabled, unemployment insurance, and welfare payments. States were required to establish their own departments to oversee the new programs and distribute federal aid. Arkansas established its Department of Public Welfare only after the Roosevelt administration suspended federal payments to the recalcitrant state. Its paltry payouts—$8.00 per month for the blind and elderly and $6.67 for dependent children—were frayed safety nets at best. Relief clients also qualified for monthly rations of foodstuffs and other items from the Federal Surplus Commodities Corporation, and these were distributed by county welfare offices. Common commodities included butter, flour, cheese, lard, dried beans, potatoes, and occasionally more exotic fare. Missouri sharecroppers Ernest and Levista Webber signed up for commodities in the winter of 1936–1937 but had no idea how to cook the grapefruits and bouillon cubes they received from the Phelps County relief truck.[38]

The Webbers had survived the previous winter by eating rabbits and had spent the better part of a year cooking meals beneath a tent in the yard of their kitchen-less shack. Still, the young married couple were embarrassed to take the government's handouts. There was a stigma attached to people who accepted government money or commodities, especially when those people were able-bodied. The stigma even extended to "make-work" jobs in the early years of the Depression, but the sheer magnitude of the WPA gradually disarmed the opposition and concentrated resentment on direct relief programs. "I wouldn't have under any conditions, unless we were starving, taken help," declared one Hickory County woman some four decades after the Depression. Starvation wasn't even enough to convince the most stubborn to sign up for relief. Middle-aged Minnie

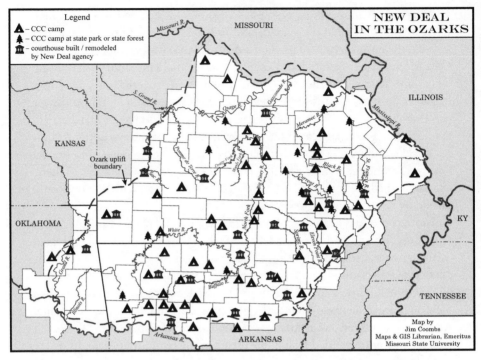

New Deal in the Ozarks. Courtesy of Jim Coombs, Missouri State University,
Springfield.

Atteberry ate infrequently in order to feed a son and two grandchildren on a
rocky hillside in Searcy County, Arkansas. Only a near-death bout with pellagra
convinced her to accept government commodities.[39]

The Raw Deal

The almost fatal reticence of people like Minnie Atteberry to receive government aid could have, as many suspected, represented the Ozarker's hidebound
independent streak. It may also have reflected opposition to the New Deal. Roosevelt's massive expansion of the federal government was certainly not without
its detractors. Many people, Republicans and Democrats alike, feared the loss of
local control as federal power expanded into the remotest communities. Others
decried what they viewed as reckless deficit spending and the cultural dangers
of placing millions on the government dole. The newspapers of Springfield were
early critics of the New Deal, as were other, smaller periodicals in southwestern
Missouri. Ozarkers were even among the notable national voices protesting the
New Deal. Rose Wilder Lane—now credited with helping lay the foundation

for the American Libertarian movement—was no fan. In magazine articles and a bestselling 1938 novel based on her father's homesteading experiences in the Dakota Territory, the daughter of children's book author Laura Ingalls Wilder championed hard work and self-reliance over government intervention.[40]

Perhaps no one in the nation played a more vocal role among the anti–New Dealers than did Ozarker Dewey Short, one of the most intriguing and accomplished characters ever produced by the region. Born into a well-to-do family in tiny Galena, Missouri, in 1898, Short completed theological training at Boston University and additional studies at Oxford, Heidelberg, Berlin, and Harvard Law. Following abbreviated stints as a college professor and Methodist minister, the staunch Republican gained election to Congress from a historically Democratic district in 1928, largely on the strength of his dazzling oratorical skills. His initial go-round in Washington produced little more than a bill raising the tariff on imported tomatoes—many constituents, including his father, were involved in canning and raising the crop—and he was booted out of office after a single term. Returned to Congress in 1935, the witty Short—the only Republican in Missouri's delegation—assumed the role as the president's nemesis in the Democrat-dominated House of Representatives.[41]

His first speech on the floor of the House in January was a blistering attack on the agencies of the "Raw Deal." Thornier than a honey locust tree, the young congressman warned that "Uncle Sam can't be a Santa Claus forever." Combining the theatrical sensibilities of a backcountry demagogue with the vocabulary of Winston Churchill, Short condemned the president's "Brain Trust" as "'theoretical intellectual, professorial nincompoops'" and dismissed his own colleagues as "the most supine, supercilious, superfluous, soporific, pusillanimous body of nit-wits ever gathered beneath the dome of the Capitol." Short's district would reelect him for ten consecutive terms, but his strident opposition to Roosevelt's policies did not go unchallenged. A union of WPA workers in labor-friendly Springfield hanged him in effigy, and on a visit to nearby Marshfield, where the local paper nicknamed Short the "Don Quixote from Galena," he had to be shielded from an angry crowd.[42]

Much of the opposition to the New Deal in the Ozarks emanated from the region's divided political loyalties. FDR's showing in the 1932 presidential election was the strongest ever for a post–Civil War Democrat, as he carried all but five counties in the Ozarks. So strong was the wave of anti-Republicanism in the depths of the Depression that the 1932 election swept into Congress longtime Springfield labor leader Reuben Wood on the Democratic ticket. A supporter of the more far-reaching Second New Deal, Wood served as a sort of regional counterbalance to Dewey Short throughout the remainder of the decade. Nevertheless, resentment toward the Republican Party gradually faded, paving the way for the reemergence of southwestern Missouri as a GOP stronghold. Roosevelt won the state in 1940, but his Republican opponent, Wendell Willkie, carried the Missouri Ozarks. The same election saw Buffalo newspaper publisher Phil Bennett trounce Wood to give southwestern Missouri two anti–New Deal Republicans in Washington.[43]

Despite the Republican resurgence, federal expansion had become ingrained in American life—even in the rural Ozarks—by 1940. Studying Hickory County, Missouri—a county so solidly Republican that it gave over 60 percent of its votes to Herbert Hoover in 1932—anthropologist James West found widespread acquiescence to the national government's large footprint. The Ozarker "saw the handwriting on the wall and realized that his way of life must go," claimed Ozarks promoter Otto Ernest Rayburn. "He decided to crush pride with the heel of necessity and accept government aid." Like other romanticizers of Ozarks life, Rayburn exaggerated the region's heritage of rugged individualism. Still, the crucible that was the Great Depression had burned away the old reality, and not even the resourceful dwellers of the back hills were immune to the new one.[44]

Plow-Ups, Power, and Peas

Few people experienced the revolutionary effects of federal expansion more than farmers, allegedly the most rugged individualists of the lot. The decade following the end of World War I produced a giant chasm between the lifestyles and purchasing power of urbanites and country folk, and the inability of farmers to fully participate in modern consumer society was a major contributor to the Depression. By 1933 the average American farm family made less than two-thirds the national median annual income of fifteen hundred dollars. In the Ozarks fewer than one in twenty farms had so much as an electric light bulb or an indoor toilet. The Roosevelt administration sought to restore some sort of equilibrium between the industrial sphere and the agricultural world with a series of bills that revolutionized American farming and eventually made "the agricultural sector a virtual ward of the state."[45]

One of the landmark pieces of legislation during the first one hundred days of the Roosevelt presidency was the creation of the Agricultural Adjustment Administration (AAA), designed to raise slumping commodity prices by addressing the imbalance between supply and demand. Adopting a domestic allotment plan, the AAA attempted to reduce the supply of corn, wheat, milk, and other commodities by paying farmers to voluntarily cut production. The responsibility for overseeing the program fell to the local agents of the Agricultural Extension Service (AES). Employees of a joint federal-state program managed by the nation's land-grant universities, extension agents organized local production-control committees that set acreage quotas, monitored compliance, and disbursed subsidy checks. The AAA's reliance on the AES also tied the agency's fortunes to the production-oriented vision shared by large producers and the conservative American Farm Bureau Federation. Though the infertile terrain across much of its expanse made the Ozarks a poor candidate for the large, specialized farms that would come to characterize post–World War II agriculture, the region reflected familiar socioeconomic divisions when it came to interaction between farmers and government representatives. In his study of Hickory County, Missouri, West found that "for the most part only upper-class men and women meet with the county agent to formulate plans involving agricultural reform."[46]

Poor and middling farmers may have held few meetings with extension agents, and their kids may have been noticeably absent from 4-H clubs, but even the lowliest agriculturist eventually experienced the new order. A drought of biblical proportions in 1934 landed most of the region on the federal emergency list, prompting the government to buy starving hogs and cattle through the AAA's Drought Relief Service. Receiving ten to fifteen dollars per head, thousands of farmers across the parched Ozarks gladly sold starving cows. In rare instances the drought cattle program brought back practices nearly forgotten even in the most remote sections of the Ozarks. More than a few motorists taking in the scenery along southern Missouri's U.S. 160 in the summer of 1934 came upon half a dozen young men driving a herd of drought cattle from Ozark County to West Plains. The fact that these Depression-era "cowboys" were on foot and their chuckwagon was a '28 Chevy truck may have dampened the romance, but none would forget the journey.[47]

For the most part, though, the New Deal nudged rural Americans into the modern era, no agency more so than the Rural Electrification Administration (REA). Created by executive order in 1935, the REA operated through locally organized cooperatives to extend the nation's power grid to the millions of American farmers who continued to live in the dark. In most places it was the budding land-grant-agribusiness nexus that took the lead in organizing cooperatives. AES personnel and their allies in local Farm Bureau chapters organized informational meetings in country schoolhouses and churches and completed the detailed surveys and maps required for REA applications. They traveled the backroads preaching the gospel of electrification to farmers, a message whose glory wasn't always as self-evident as we might think. Some old-timers failed to see how a couple of light bulbs were worth the bother. Others dismissed electricity as a fire hazard. The five-dollar membership fee was a deal breaker for the cash-strapped. But most welcomed electricity—members could even work off some of their expenses by helping clear rights-of-way and build lines—and the late 1930s and early 1940s saw cooperatives pop up across the region. Residents of little Ellsinore, Missouri, were certain a new day had arrived when the Ozark Border Electric Cooperative erected the first highline pole in town in 1938. Eager parishioners of the Disciples of Christ congregation of Summersville, Missouri, got the jump on Ellsinore when they wired their church house in 1937, but they would have to wait until 1940 before the Intercounty Electric Cooperative flipped its switch.[48]

On October 6, 1938, northwestern Arkansas's Carroll Electric Cooperative celebrated the energizing of its first fifty miles of power lines with a "Pageant of Light" in Berryville. Two of Carroll Electric's five board members were women, a testament to the central role played by AES-sponsored home demonstration clubs. Benton County farm woman Lillian Sears joined Carroll Electric's board in 1940 and in 1946 was named president—reportedly the first woman in the nation to hold that position in an REA cooperative. Carroll Electric served some twenty-seven hundred homes with one thousand miles of power lines by the time the war effort brought a temporary halt to expansion. For many in the Ozarks, the electric revolution would have to wait for the troops to come home. When it arrived, electricity had a truly transformative effect. Radios, refrigerators, washing machines, and other appliances eased the burdens of isolation and household chores. Rural electricity also paved the way for modernizing, profitable developments in dairy and poultry farming.[49]

The same land-grant-agribusiness partnership that promoted rural electrification agreed that it was time to address serious environmental issues such as soil erosion. The Soil Conservation Service (SCS) was the environmental yin to the AAA's price-boosting yang. The SCS promised government subsidies for those who permanently converted marginal lands to forests and nutrient-restoring cover crops. Favorites peddled by the agency included clovers and their grain legume cousins like soybeans, vetch, and field peas. The earthy whippoorwill still holds a hallowed place in the memories and gardens of twenty-first-century Ozarkers who swear the mottled little pea sustained Grandpa and Grandma through the Depression.[50]

Only in the years after World War II would the full impact of such government programs as rural electrification and soil conservation be felt across the Ozarks, but the seeds of a rural revolution had been planted. Yet there were unexpected consequences from the campaign of an army of progressive, scientific-agriculture advocates who did their jobs all too well. Bumper crops in 1937 contributed to the "Roosevelt Recession." With farm prices far below pre-Depression marks, the New Deal was on life support, having neither engineered economic recovery nor recalibrated the country's wealth imbalance. Thousands of families feared they were no closer to escaping the Depression than they had been in that hopeful spring of 1933. A few found wry humor in the era's unrelenting economic struggle. In 1939 the graduating class of Batesville's Arkansas College adopted a motto befitting the anxieties of a generation facing a bleak future: "Goodbye NYA, Hello WPA."[51]

The Depression may have been no respecter of education level, but there were segments of the population that were particularly unsuited to deal with the decade's privation. Farmers at least had the ability to grow food, even if it meant a winter of dining on "turnip sandwiches"—a turnip slice between two other slices of turnip. Residents of the region's small cities and larger towns often relied on increasingly tenuous industrial and service jobs, which could leave them at the mercy of relief agencies at a moment's notice. The largest concentrations of nonagricultural workers in the Ozarks were located in the region's two mining areas: the Lead Belt of southeastern Missouri and Joplin's Tri-State District. Depressed mineral prices sent both areas into financial tailspins, resulting in massive unemployment and tremendous pressure on relief programs. The efforts of the National Recovery Administration and its successors did little to bring real recovery to the mining sector, but legislation generated by the Roosevelt administration ushered in an unprecedented period of labor organizing among Ozarks miners.

The Depression placed tremendous stress on the notoriously anti-union "rural-industrial workers" of the Tri-State District. When the National Labor Relations Act guaranteed the right to unionize and strike, a radical union emerged under the umbrella of the Congress of Industrial Organizations. A National Labor Relations Board (NLRB) ruling against the district's dominant operator, Eagle-Picher, in 1938 opened the door for collective bargaining, but the area's long-standing distaste for organizing seems to have lingered. By 1943, after wartime demand revived the zinc industry, fewer than one in four miners in the Tri-State were unionized. Across the region in the old tiff fields of Washington County, Missouri, a local union received another favorable ruling from the NLRB. Years of labor disputes, however, simply prodded mine owners to mechanize, and the early days of World War II found strip mines where pick-and-shovel miners had labored for generations. Desperate miners paraded down Potosi's streets and barged into the office of the welfare supervisor demanding food, but no bureaucrat could bring back their lost jobs.[52]

It was the miners of the Tri-State District whose cause was taken up most creatively by the political left. In 1940 photographer and filmmaker Sheldon Dick, along with his wife, Lee, produced the strange but moving documentary *Men and Dust*, a leftist, avant-garde exposé lamenting the sickness and poverty plaguing the crumbling zinc-mining towns. To the Dicks and many others, the only hope for destitute miners was outside interference. The Ozarkers presented "an urgent problem" to those who sought to rehabilitate this land of "isolation, inbreeding, and ignorance," observed a former FERA social worker. "They cannot lift themselves by their own bootstraps." Dick's fellow Resettlement Administration photographers Arthur Rothstein and Ben Shahn shared this estimation. Snapping more than 120 pictures of rural hopelessness in the Arkansas Ozarks in

1935, both contributed to boss Roy Stryker's "goal of selling federal anti-poverty programs to the public." No image from the era better encapsulated that vision than Dorothea Lange's iconic "Migrant Mother." Florence Hill—the prematurely aged woman Lange discovered in a California migrant labor camp—was herself an Ozarker, born and raised in Cherokee County, Oklahoma.[53]

Year of the Ozarks

Yet the imagery of the Ozarks that dominated the region's public perception in the Depression bore little of the pathos pervading the era. Neither did it prefer the scenes of progressive prosperity promoted by the chamber of commerce. That image remained something more akin to Vance Randolph's vision than to Stryker's or John T. Woodruff's. It was the Depression years that brought the idea of the Ozarks most fully into focus, that introduced quaint Ozarkers to a mainstream American public with an appetite for a brand of exoticism tailor-made for the Jim Crow, jingoistic spirit of the age. The Ozarks took its place in the pantheon of American regions as a remote land of hills and hollers nestled in the middle of the forty-eight states, a smaller version of Appalachia inhabited by an Anglo-Saxon race who spoke a dialect essentially like that of the first English colonists and lived lives little different from those of their pioneer ancestors. Even as widespread poverty, an interventionist government, and technological breakthroughs laid the foundation for fundamental change, books, magazines, and movies portrayed the Ozarkers as quaint relics from a simpler and happier time. Symbolically, the Ozarkers could serve as escapist diversions in a depressing world or as examples of an alternate path. In the middle of the Depression decade, reliably romantic Charles Morrow Wilson introduced national readers to Hemmed-in-Holler. "There are no roads into the holler," marveled Wilson. "One usually enters it, afoot, fording the river from one to a dozen times, following a mountainside trail." In this remote hideaway in Newton County, Arkansas, spinning wheels outnumbered radios. The few families who made it their home lived in a time warp, true "contemporary ancestors." For Wilson, their isolation and lack of technology represented not bitter poverty but blissful primitivism. In the national consciousness the Ozarks was Hemmed-in-Holler writ large.[54]

The public's fascination with the region reached its crescendo in 1941. Until a certain history-altering event took place on a Pacific island chain, 1941 was the year of the Ozarks. Movie audiences around the nation watched a lean, fresh-faced John Wayne in the Technicolor rendition of Harold Bell Wright's classic novel, *The Shepherd of the Hills*. For those who found the accents decidedly non-Ozarkian, movie theaters provided more authentic fare in three pictures starring a troupe of southwestern Missouri vaudevillians known as the Weaver Brothers and Elviry. On radio 1941 saw the debut of *The Arkansas Traveler*, on which comedian Bob Burns spun windy stories of Uncle Fud, Aunt Doody, and other fictional relatives from the Crawford County foothills beyond the star's hometown of Van Buren. On stage *Maid in the Ozarks*, a lower-brow burlesque starring Robert Mitchum and Gloria Grahame, titillated Angelenos as it built momentum for a cross-country tour that would land it on Broadway. For readers a trio of nationally published nonfiction books—Marguerite Lyon's *Take to the Hills*, Catherine S. Barker's *Yesterday Today*, and Otto Ernest Rayburn's *Ozark Country*—hit shelves in 1941. Everyone, it seemed, had a story to tell about the region and its people.[55]

Nothing better represented the stubborn, romantic image of the Ozarks than the work of an obscure wanderer and artist from the Missouri Ozarks named Lennis Leonard Broadfoot, who was finishing his visual paean to his native hill folks in 1941. Boasting no formal training beyond a correspondence course from a diploma-mill art school, the middle-aged Broadfoot traipsed across rural southern Missouri, interviewing and sketching characters in hidden hamlets and on backwoods farms. His subjects were obscure, usually elderly folks—wood-cutters, farmers, hunters, housewives. They tended to exist on the margins of respectable society, securing a meager sustenance via some unique ability or unusual trade. There was Chester Piatt the root digger, Ellen Boxx the rug weaver, John Wilkins the bee hunter. Jess Thompson possessed an arm so accurate that a successful squirrel hunt required nothing more than a poke full of rocks.[56]

Eventually released as a book of charcoal character sketches accompanied by brief narratives in vernacular dialect, Broadfoot's *Pioneers of the Ozarks* celebrated a people and a way of life representing the fleeting remnants of the "good old days," old-timers living essentially nineteenth-century lives two-fifths of the way into the twentieth century. The romanticism and primitivism that motivated Broadfoot's sketches were very much in line with the spirit flowing through most other Ozarks works of the age and through the fascination with the region in general. His subjects were the "deliberately unprogressive" backwoodsmen who inspired Randolph's *The Ozarks: An American Survival of Primitive Society* a decade earlier. They were the anachronistic Ozarkers from "a world apart" who infused Rayburn's *Ozark Country* with color and mystique. For anyone disillusioned with the potential failure of America's brand of modernism, the Ozarks was a region upon which the hopes and desires of disenchanted observers could be projected.[57]

Broadfoot and Rayburn, native and newcomer, were kindred spirits. *Pioneers of the Ozarks* was in essence a visual rendering of Rayburn's *Ozark Country*. It was fitting that the latter, a sepia-toned love letter to "a modern Arcadia," would have the final word in the year of the Ozarks. It was this sentimental vision that held the upper hand in depictions of the region throughout the trying years of the Depression, and it was essentially this same nostalgic portrait that would reemerge in the aftermath of worldwide warfare. Six days after *Ozark Country*'s debut, Japanese planes at Pearl Harbor ended the year of the Ozarks and the precarious neutrality to which the nation clung.[58]

At War and at Home

The war accomplished in a matter of months what statesmen and bureaucrats had been unable to do in a dozen years. It brought a swift end to the Great Depression. Military service snatched millions of young men and tens of thousands of young women out of the domestic job market, and the unprecedented productivity of the industries of warfare provided work for anyone willing to wield a welding torch or tap a typewriter. But the relationship between the average citizen and the government had been altered permanently. At the onset of World War II, observes historian David M. Kennedy, "Americans assumed that the federal government had not merely a role, but a major responsibility, in ensuring the health of the economy and the welfare of citizens." For friend and foe, the vast relief and planning bureaucracy put in place by the Roosevelt administration was around to stay. The "drift is toward regimentation," opined Otto Ernest Rayburn in *Ozark Country*, "and all the king's horses and all the king's men cannot put the old freedom into the hills again."[59]

Thousands of Ozarkers left the hills to fight for some version of freedom. A few rose through the ranks to become decorated officers. Army brigadier general Paul McDonald Robinett, a native of Mountain Grove, Missouri, commanded an armored division in North Africa until a shattered leg sent him back to the States in 1943. Among the most notable Ozarkers in the navy was Edward Baxter Billingsley, great-grandson of Elisha Baxter, Arkansas's last Reconstruction governor. Commanding the destroyer USS *Emmons*, Billingsley helped escort President Roosevelt to the Tehran Conference in 1943 and took part in the bombardment of Omaha Beach during the invasion of Normandy. Ozarkers of much humbler rank received the military's highest decoration, the Medal of Honor. During General Douglas MacArthur's invasion of the Philippines, thirty-year-old army private Ova A. Kelley, from tiny Norwood, Missouri, single-handedly ousted a nest of Japanese machine gunners with a handful of grenades and a rifle recovered from one of his victims. Wounded by sniper fire, he died two days later. A bugler-turned-machine-gunner and former CCC worker from the Lead Belt, marine sergeant Darrell S. Cole took out three Japanese pillboxes using only a pistol and grenades but fell while trying to reach his squad. The USS *Cole*, a guided missile destroyer, commemorates his sacrifice, and the band hall at Quantico bears the name of the perpetual twenty-four-year-old from Esther High School.[60] Hundreds more died less-heralded deaths on islands and deserts, in mountains and fallow fields, memories of them now almost faded from the earth. Others came back home missing limbs, carrying shrapnel, and wearing permanent scars, visible and invisible.

Back on the home front there was peace and comparative prosperity. In rural Searcy County, Arkansas, Minnie Atteberry—just a few years removed from that near-death scrape with pellagra—and her two grandchildren experienced freedom from want for the first time in as long as they could remember. It was a painful ordeal to watch her son leave for the army—"He walked out of the yard & away. It made us sad & it was lonesome"—but the regular paychecks he sent home proved a godsend for the poor family. In Jasper County, Missouri, middle-aged farmers Lucy Campbell and her husband, Philip, found well-paying jobs at a TNT plant on the outskirts of Joplin. Lucy had never before worked off the farm or donned a pair of britches. Now she went to work each day in coveralls. Like thousands of others during the war, the Campbells "learned roles that changed their visions of the world."[61]

The war came to the Ozarks in the form of industry and military installations. But the region received only a tiny sliver of the nation's gargantuan spending on the war effort, a bill that expanded to more than 93 billion dollars in the last full year of the conflict. The military preferred to do business with large, well-established companies and funneled more than two-thirds of all contracts to one hundred of the nation's most powerful firms. That wasn't good news for a place like the Ozarks, especially the portion in Arkansas and Oklahoma. In the former state, wartime development took place almost completely outside of the Ozarks. Federal money flowed into Oklahoma after the election of Robert S. Kerr as governor in 1942, but the state's Ozark region experienced the impact only on its fringes, with a gunpowder plant near Pryor and military installations at Miami and Muskogee.[62]

In Missouri, St. Louis and Kansas City claimed more than four of every five dollars of war-generated spending. Nevertheless, federal money reached a handful of Ozarks communities. In southwestern Missouri war plants gobbled up the output of Southwest Lime Company, Missouri Chemical Company, and Atlas Powder Company. In southeastern Missouri the St. Joseph Lead Company's entire output went toward the war effort, requiring more than twenty-five hundred workers at peak production. On the far northern edge of the Ozark uplift, garment factories in the little town of California secured $7 million in contracts to produce cloth and uniforms. Springfield claimed a slice of the federal pie, including a new airport partially funded by government money. One factory received more than $2 million in contracts to produce parts for tanks, trucks, and aircraft gun turrets. Fifteen million dollars' worth of military patronage caused the Producers Produce Company to double its wartime labor force, and the building of O'Reilly General Army Hospital gave the Queen City a direct link with the war effort.[63]

Facility for constructing "demountable houses" for Fort Leonard Wood, Newburg, Missouri, 1941. Courtesy of Mary Alice Beemer Photograph Collection (R0496), State Historical Society of Missouri, Rolla.

By far the most transformative developments were the two U.S. Army installations that came to life in southern Missouri. The first and largest of these, Fort Leonard Wood, took shape in Pulaski County in a rugged stretch of hills and hollers flanked by the Big Piney River and Roubidoux Creek. Construction of the massive fort, which eventually grew to more than seventy thousand acres, began in January 1941. In a foretaste of the speed of the American war machine, in half a year's time more than thirty thousand workers built fifty-eight miles of roads, a twenty-mile spur from the Frisco Railroad, and 1,600 buildings, including 600 barracks, 205 mess halls, 9 infirmaries, and 5 theaters. At the peak of the frenzy in March 1941, work crews completed a new building every forty-five minutes. The Fort Leonard Wood workforce was reportedly the largest in the nation at the time, and each payday pumped well over one million dollars into the area's economy. Upon completion the fort housed up to forty-five thousand troops, most of them engineer replacement trainees. More than three hundred thousand soldiers received basic and specialized training at what they not so affectionately called Fort-Lost-in-the-Woods, Misery.[64]

At about the same time that Fort Leonard Wood's first trainees were leaving for field duty, some 170 miles to the southwest the dizzying process was repeating itself. In August 1941 work crews in Newton and McDonald counties began construction on the more than 350 buildings that would comprise Camp Crowder, a training site for signal corps replacement troops. In addition to teaching radio operation and repair, Camp Crowder hosted a band-training unit and the army's

pigeon breeding and training center. Though destined for a much shorter lifespan than Fort Leonard Wood, Camp Crowder left a larger footprint on American popular culture. The Camp Crowder experiences of Dick Van Dyke and Carl Reiner inspired an early episode of *The Dick Van Dyke Show*. Another G.I. who passed through Camp Crowder, Kansas Citian Mort Walker, used the place as inspiration for Camp Swampy in his long-running comic strip *Beetle Bailey*. And it was a collection of letters written by gay soldiers stationed at Camp Crowder that provided the foundation for Allan Bérubé's groundbreaking book, *Coming Out Under Fire*, and the award-winning documentary of the same name.[65]

Like other military bases, Fort Leonard Wood and Camp Crowder were segregated by race. African Americans generally received inferior living quarters and supplies, but there were limited efforts to accommodate Black troops who found themselves in the extremely white Ozarks. At Fort Leonard Wood the United Service Organizations arranged visits by boxer Joe Louis and Joplin-born poet Langston Hughes and staged a dance for Black G.I.s a few days before Christmas in 1942. Sports at Camp Crowder occasioned early signs of the integration that would come via President Harry S. Truman's executive order in 1948. In the final year of the war, the previously all-white post basketball team invited a former Harlem Globetrotter to join the squad. Later that year Camp Crowder's baseball team integrated when white player/coach Tommy Bridges, a former star pitcher for the Detroit Tigers, welcomed onto the team twenty-one-year-old African American Joe Black. A future National League

rookie of the year, the hard-throwing right-hander became the staff ace of a
Camp Crowder squad that won the Seventh Service Command championship
in 1945. Traveling to play other post teams, Black endured the indignities that
came with being an African American in Jim Crow society. But he also felt accepted by his white teammates and recalled the times when they stood by his
side in the face of prejudice, including one incident when the team wrecked a
diner after the owner proclaimed, "We don't serve niggers in here."[66]

Whether or not the arrival of military installations produced local racial
tension, they created antipathy aplenty of other kinds. Leading the charge of
the disgruntled were the hundreds of families who lost farms and homes in the
government's forced purchase of lands. According to one report, a combined
total of more than fourteen hundred farms were consumed in the creation of
the two massive installations. Army officials wasted little time in pushing con-
fused and reluctant families out of their homes with offers that frequently struck
recipients as below market. Many acquiesced out of a sense of patriotism, but
leaving behind houses and fields full of memories was a gut-wrenching ordeal
that left more than a few embittered. Whole communities disappeared almost
overnight. Bloodland—home to a high school, canning factory, roller mill, and
bank—was the most substantial of Pulaski County's lost villages, but the new fort
also erased from the map places named Tribune, Evening Shade, and Palace.[67]

Resistance to forced evacuation was most strident in southwestern Missouri,
where more than a few government officials "were met with hoes and shotguns."
"The controversy surrounding the creation of Camp Crowder," according to
historian Kimberly Harper, "led to an unexpected united front between local
businessmen and farmers born of a mutual antipathy toward outsiders and
unfair land valuations." In surrounding areas that weren't taken over by the
military, townspeople fretted over the vice and social disorder almost certain
to accompany a military post. Such fears, as well as concern over the plight of
displaced neighbors, prompted Neosho citizens to draft a resolution protesting the military's stingy appraisals. There was an ironic injustice to the whole
enterprise. Farm and homeowners received payments based on average appraisals from the late Depression era, a time when many in the Ozarks couldn't
give their farms away. But the moment construction began on Fort Leonard
Wood and Camp Crowder, area land valuations skyrocketed. What followed
was an economic boom built on the losses of hundreds of families who shared
the misfortune of being in the wrong place at the wrong time. The arrival of
thousands of soldiers shattered normality, but with this disruption came jobs
and economic stability. Men and women only recently on relief now commuted
dozens of miles to work on construction projects or in wood-frame buildings
that still smelled of paint. Traffic on Route 66 grew so heavy that a stretch of it
near Fort Leonard Wood was expanded to four lanes.[68]

Towns in the vicinity of the installations experienced unprecedented and stressful boom times. Neosho burgeoned on the outskirts of Camp Crowder. Near Fort Leonard Wood towns like Crocker and Rolla burst at the seams. In little Newburg, a San Francisco company employed 250 civilians. At the height of the construction boom, each day the workers built ten "pre-fabricated de-mountable houses," which were then trucked to the fort and assembled. The nearest town to the fort's front gates was Waynesville, a sleepy little county seat of four hundred people in 1940. The peak of the building frenzy swelled Waynesville's population to perhaps as many as twelve thousand. Such rapid growth pushed towns to the breaking point. The impact of the fort could be felt forty miles to the north at Dixon, where no fewer than two hundred newcomers taxed the local post office in January 1941. "Streets filled with cars, stores and cafes open late, rent has more than doubled, people begging for rooms," observed one local resident. "Can't get carpenter, plumber or electrician to work on our house. Firewood doubled in price." A year later the same chronicler noted the presence of a dozen prostitutes in the jail at Waynesville. Pulaski County would never be the same.[69]

The presence of the new military posts proved a boon to area businesses, some of whom secured lucrative government contracts. Pulaski and Newton counties in Missouri boasted more than $25 million in government contracts during the war. But in most counties the war years came and went without any noticeable influx of spending. As a result, one of the chief stories of the wartime Ozarks was out-migration. Factories in St. Louis and Kansas City drew thousands from farms and small towns. Ozarkers moved to Wichita and Tulsa in droves to take well-paying positions on aircraft assembly lines. Arkies and Missourians joined their Appalachian cousins in mass migrations to Detroit, Chicago, and other Great Lakes cities flush with government contracts. Massive plants and shipyards on the Pacific Coast quickened the stream of Ozarkers to the West. "There was all kinds of jobs in California, Indiana, Memphis, just everywhere," remembered an Arkansawyer. "All you had to do was just pack up and you'd get a job."[70]

In early 1944, after he received a medical discharge from the army, Guy Rhoads and his wife, Zela, moved from rural Fulton County, Arkansas, to St. Louis and immediately found jobs in war factories. Earning as much as $145 a week for their combined efforts, the Rhoadses "made more money than we'd ever made in our life." Living off one paycheck and squirrelling away the other, they saved enough to buy a farm back home. Another family of Arkansas Ozarkers had spent years on the margins of destitution until Dovie Lee and a grown son found shipyard work in Portland, Oregon, in 1942. A daughter recalled a grand Christmas that year, with Santa Claus leaving a new bicycle for her brother and bringing her a doll just like "rich girls get." Dovie's wife, Edna, was just as excited

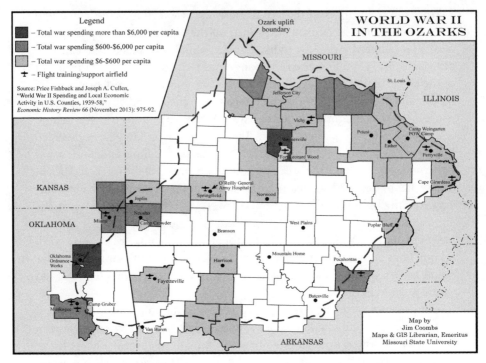

World War II in the Ozarks. Courtesy of Jim Coombs, Missouri State University, Springfield.

about the family's first washing machine, an electric Maytag with a ringer and two galvanized rinsing tubs.[71]

One result of the movement of job-hunting Ozarkers was a near-abandonment of some rural communities. "There wasn't anybody there," recalled one man of a rural neighborhood in Van Buren County, Arkansas. "All the people moved out of there, not a one left." It was perhaps the most tangible outcome of the dozen years spanning the New Deal and World War II. It is probable that the war's massive impact on the American economy would have precipitated an unprecedented exodus from farms even had there been no New Deal. But Roosevelt-era legislation designed to produce a commercial agriculture sector of fewer and larger producers had set the stage uniquely well for the rapid transformation that only an economy at full tilt could pull off. The New Deal and the nation's domestic war machine thus delivered a one-two punch to rural America. The Ozarks that emerged from the war was poised for a new era. Central to that new era were tourism and entertainment—and the regional images that fueled them.

6   PUTTING ON A SHOW

It was the tale of two cities—or one city and one village. In the White River valley, construction crews worked like beavers in the late winter and spring of 1960 to complete two tourist attractions that their developers hoped would appeal to the nation's nostalgic zeitgeist. The folk revival wafted across the land, inspiring in disconnected suburbanites an appreciation for the sounds and skills of old-timers. Viewers of screens big and small gorged on the western. Even in a post-Sputnik world of Levittowns and Naugahyde, Americans couldn't get enough of hitching posts and general stores, stagecoaches and bank robberies. Americans loved their pioneer history—or at least some whitewashed, romanticized version of it.

On the first day of May, just off twisting Missouri Highway 76 some ten miles west of Branson, Chicago native Mary Herschend and her sons, Jack and Peter, welcomed the first customers to Silver Dollar City. Four weeks later crowds descended on the little resort town of Bull Shoals, Arkansas, where attorney Roy Danuser's Mountain Village 1890 opened to local fanfare on Memorial Day weekend. Whether or not the Herschends and Danuser were aware of the similarities of their projects, the parallels were uncanny. Beneath the grounds of both venues were caves. In fact, it was the long lines of visitors waiting to tour Marvel Cave in the 1950s that convinced the Herschends to erect an elaborate diversion. That diversion, Silver Dollar City, consisted of a blacksmith shop, a general store, and three other frame buildings designed to evoke the spirit of a friendly, western yesteryear, alongside two reassembled structures plucked from the nearby countryside: a nineteenth-century log cabin and a rustic schoolhouse reimagined as the Wilderness Church. While Bull Shoals Caverns had opened to paying customers only the previous summer, Danuser attempted to make up for his late start by upping the ante to ten original buildings from the Ozarks in addition to an old iron jail cell and a moonshine still. Anchored by a general store and schoolhouse, Mountain Village 1890 also featured a railroad depot, church, and two-story log tavern, all of them taken from the surrounding region and reconstructed on site.[1]

Silver Dollar City and Mountain Village 1890 both took shape in tourism hot spots impacted by the Army Corps of Engineers' postwar dam-building frenzy. Few places in the Ozarks boasted a longer record of attracting visitors than did the "Shepherd of the Hills Country," but it was the corps' completion of nearby Table Rock Lake in 1958 that kick-started a new tourism era in Branson. Down the White River the blossoming "Twin Lakes" region was purely the work of the corps. The creation of Norfork and Bull Shoals reservoirs transformed the sleepy town of Mountain Home and its environs into a bustling destination for water recreationists. By the end of the 1950s, the Twin Lakes boasted more than 150 resorts, lodges, hotels, and restaurants. The town of Bull Shoals was just one of several that sprang to life to beckon vacationers and retirees.[2]

To say that Silver Dollar City and Mountain Village 1890 followed divergent paths in the years after 1960 is as much an understatement as saying evenings in Branson and Bangkok attract different crowds. Benefiting from the rich heritage of the Shepherd of the Hills Country, the Herschends used clever marketing (giving customers change in silver dollars) and a fortuitous brush with Hollywood (*The Beverly Hillbillies* filmed five episodes there in 1969) to grow their city into the region's most popular tourist attraction. Marvel Cave took a backseat to the city's shops, craftspeople, and street characters, and within a decade and a half the theme park welcomed annual crowds approaching one and a half million people. In the twenty-first century, Silver Dollar City remains the crown jewel of a far-flung Herschend Family Entertainment empire that includes aquariums, Dollywood, and the Harlem Globetrotters.

Mountain Village 1890 followed a different trajectory. More difficult to reach by automobile, the village functioned for several years as a poor region's Colonial Williamsburg, a living history museum entertaining summer lake visitors and school children on field trips. By the 1980s the farm animals were gone, as were the retirees in overalls and granny bonnets who milked the cows and plowed the garden. More than two decades into a new millennium, Mountain Village 1890 holds on, suspended in time, but not in the way Roy Danuser had in mind all those years ago. Touring what remains of the old village—amid rusting implements and sagging roofs—reminds the visitor not so much of an Ozarks settlement in 1890 as it does of a bygone era in American tourism. There's a palpable *Scooby Doo* abandoned-theme-park quality to Mountain Village 1890—so much so that what little publicity the place receives nowadays is generated by ghost hunters who can't resist the entombed quality of the old faux village.[3]

The Mabe brothers and Chick Allen (the Baldknobbers) performing at the grand opening of Silver Dollar City, 1960. Courtesy of Silver Dollar City.

The Ozarkers found themselves in the throes of an economic and cultural revolution at the moment Silver Dollar City and Mountain Village 1890 came to life. Even as old customs withered in the bright light of modernity in the years after World War II, the Ozarkers remained cloaked beneath an image of static backwardness, their region reduced to a repository of homespun authenticity, hillbilly humor, and old-timey music and crafts. In an era when the Ozarkers grew ever less "Ozarky," tourism became integral to the region's economy. It was downright essential to the well-being of some locales. When the old resort town of Noel was left off a new Missouri vacation map in 1961, McDonald Countians staged a tongue-in-cheek secession movement—complete with antique rifle–toting border patrolmen and "McDonald Territory" visas.[4] "Territorial" leaders, whose clever stunt generated national publicity and a convoy of curious tourists, appreciated the inextricability of the tourism industry and the region's backcountry image as surely as did the Herschends and Roy Danuser. The frantic growth and evolution of Silver Dollar City into a twenty-first-century theme park with a tenuous connection to its heritage tourism roots may better reflect the region's postwar experience, but it is Mountain Village 1890's stuck-in-amber immutability that best captures the nation's image of the Ozarks.

The Dammed Ozarks

In the spring of 1931, a St. Louis reporter described for readers of the *New York Times* his city's long-held view of the Ozarker. "The typical Ozarkian," wrote Louis La Coss, "was a man who went barefoot the year-around, supported his homespun garments with a single gallus, subsisted on corn pone and fat bacon and spent his days shooting squirrels and his nights chasing coons with a houn' dog." This archetypal hill dweller "chewed tobacco, smoked a corncob pipe, engaged in moonshining even before there was such a thing as prohibition and had never profaned his vision with the sight of a locomotive, much less an automobile."[5] The event that prompted La Coss's pontification was nothing less than the completion of one of the grand engineering feats of the era: Bagnell Dam and the Lake of the Ozarks. Visiting reporters covering this most modern of stories found the familiar narrative of deviancy too inviting to pass up. "Feuds raged for generations in the log-cabin settlements along the winding trails," marveled another St. Louis newspaperman chronicling the dam that would power his city's lights and juice its radios.[6]

Outsiders may have fixated on the region's reputation for primitivism, but nothing modernized and transformed entire districts in the twentieth-century Ozarks more than the creation of artificial reservoirs. The earliest dam-building projects in the Ozarks were comparatively minor undertakings: small hydroelectric dams near Joplin and Branson and on the Niangua and Elk rivers, as well as a reservoir for the city of Tulsa on Spavinaw Creek in northeastern Oklahoma. Bagnell Dam on the Osage River was a different matter. Completed in 1931 by St. Louis–based Union Electric Light and Power Company, the Lake of the Ozarks tattooed the map of central Missouri with a "great sprawling Chinese dragon" and launched the era of dam building in the process. The dam towered 148 feet above its bedrock base and spanned almost half a mile. Its powerhouse, stretching almost the length of five football fields, contained half a dozen 33,500-horsepower water wheels capable of supplying one-third of the electricity consumed by Union Electric's customers. The two-year project employed an average of three thousand workers per day. By the time the encroaching waters filled the basin, the Lake of the Ozarks sprawled as the largest man-made reservoir in the nation, stretching ninety-three miles up the serpentine Osage and creating more than eleven hundred miles of shoreline. The blue waters that inundated more than fifty-four thousand acres may have been the only thing transparent in the reservoir's birth, for bribery of public officials would eventually land Union Electric's president in prison.[7]

The lake permanently displaced hundreds of families, many of them farmers on the most fertile strips of soil the stony northern Ozarks had to offer. Local newspaper editor J. W. Vincent, whose town of Linn Creek was inundated, bitterly opposed the dam, though he later enthusiastically embraced the entrepreneurial opportunities it provided.[8] On rare occasions outside reporters joined the handwringing over displaced Ozarkers, but more often than not the massive building project and its cultural disturbance attracted chroniclers who delighted in the juxtaposition between Union Electric's ultramodern project and the locals whose somnolent society it roused. Birthed in an era of laissez-faire government, the Lake of the Ozarks was a reminder to rural Ozarkers that control over their marginal existences rested in faraway offices where men in three-piece suits trod marble hallways. Many would have to wait a decade or more to enjoy the electricity generated by the waters filling their hollers.

Even before the first spade of dirt was moved in the Bagnell Dam project, the foundation had been laid for a change in federal policy that would fundamentally alter the physical and cultural Ozarks. Until the 1930s levees were almost the sole means of flood control utilized by the Army Corps of Engineers. But the Great Flood of 1927 changed all that. Its physical and economic devastation brought about "a major shift in what Americans considered the proper role and obligations of the national government." Tasked by Congress to undertake a nationwide comprehensive analysis of streams, the corps produced a mountain of reports in the 1930s identifying potential sites for power-generating or flood-controlling dams. Most reports remained pessimistic about the ability of dams to significantly lessen the impact of flooding, but political pressure from members of Congress generated dam interest. Increasing demand for electricity and calls for public work projects ramped up support for reservoirs in the New Deal.[9] The result would be a four-decade era of dam building that altered the ecology on extensive stretches of streams and redefined broad swaths of the Ozarks.

The region's first large, publicly funded reservoir was the Grand Lake o' the Cherokees, completed in 1940. Formed by the Pensacola Dam on northeastern Oklahoma's Grand River, it was the first public dam equipped for electricity generation. Pensacola Dam was a project of a state agency, but it was the federal Army Corps of Engineers that did the lion's share of reservoir construction in the region. The Flood Control Acts of 1936, 1938, and subsequent years authorized the corps to construct a system of dams on streams across the nation. When the era of Ozarks damming finally came to an end in 1979, the region contained fourteen reservoirs built by public agencies. These lakes, combined with the Lake of the Ozarks and three reservoirs created to supply water to Tulsa and Springfield, covered almost 662 square miles. Flood control remained the stated objective throughout the era, but hydroelectricity generation and recreation played increasingly crucial roles in the postwar years. Neither of the latter concerns motivated construction of the region's first corps reservoir, Wappapello Dam, on the southeastern edge of the Missouri Ozarks in 1941.[10]

The corps' second Ozarks reservoir, Norfork Dam, on the White River's North Fork, was also originally envisioned as a flood-control facility only, but regional boosters expressed disappointment that plans did not call for power generation.

None did so more loudly than Tom Shiras, editor of the weekly *Baxter Bulletin* in Mountain Home. Without a hydroelectric dam, Shiras feared, Norfork would turn out to be "only a frog pond instead of a lake," and the editor arranged for delegations of local businessmen to travel to Washington, D.C., to lobby for a power plant. Before long one of his chief allies had an office in the capitol. No figure looms larger in the history of dam building and hydroelectricity generation in the Ozarks (and elsewhere) than Clyde T. Ellis, a northwestern Arkansas country-schoolteacher-turned-politician. Accusing third district congressman Claude Fuller of doing too little to bring electricity to farmers, Ellis unseated the long-serving incumbent and promptly announced his presence in the nation's capital in 1939 by proposing a White River Authority (WRA), a comprehensive planning agency modeled on the Tennessee Valley Authority. Winning a powerhouse for Norfork Dam and squeezing two more massive, hydroelectricity-generating White River reservoirs into the Flood Control Act of 1941, Ellis withdrew his WRA proposal and two years later was appointed the first general manager of the National Rural Electric Cooperative Association. Norfork's conversion into a hydroelectric dam set the stage for the years of corps activity that followed.[11]

The two White River dams that "Mr. Rural Electrification" helped secure proved to be the largest ever erected in the Ozarks. The first went up just a few miles south of the Arkansas-Missouri line. Using a seven-mile-long conveyor belt to transport aggregate from a quarry north of Yellville to the dam site, workers labored for four years on a reservoir covering more than forty-five thousand acres behind a 256-foot-high dam. Finished in 1951, Bull Shoals Lake stretched some eighty-seven miles upriver. Seven years later and a few miles upstream from Branson, construction crews completed Table Rock Dam and reservoir, only slightly smaller than Bull Shoals.[12]

Upon completion of Table Rock, many workers simply moved southward into the Arkansas Ozarks when the corps contracted the same company to construct Greers Ferry Dam on the Little Red River, a tributary of the White. Greers Ferry Dam had an immediate and remarkable economic impact on the nearest town, Heber Springs. Within less than two years of the beginning of construction, bank deposits in the Cleburne County seat jumped 57 percent, school enrollment doubled, and almost three hundred new houses went up. President John F. Kennedy himself made the trip to the Ozarks to formally dedicate the dam in October 1963, just as President Truman had done at Bull Shoals eleven years earlier. Kennedy's speech turned out to be the president's last major public appearance before his assassination in Dallas the following month.[13]

Both of the corps' dams in the Oklahoma Ozarks—Tenkiller Ferry on the Illinois River and Fort Gibson on the Grand—were equipped with powerhouses. The last of three corps dams in the Osage River watershed, Truman Dam on the main channel, came with a powerhouse in 1979 and remains to this day the final reservoir project undertaken in the region by the corps. Located on rolling prairie lands, Truman Lake inundated over fifty-five thousand acres and created almost one thousand miles of shoreline. Yet with shallower average depths and lacking the aesthetic appeal of the region's older reservoirs, Truman generated less electricity and attracted fewer visitors and residents to its marshy shores than promised. "We have no tourism," complained Osceola's embittered mayor seven years after the dam's completion, "because there is nothing to see except mud flats, debris, piles of driftwood, horse weeds and just plain unsightly landscape."[14]

The failure of Truman Lake to deliver on the promise of recreation and tourism is all the more stark because of expectations. By the 1950s, whether or not politicians and dam boosters owned up to it in public, flood control and hydroelectricity had taken backseats to economic development and recreation. Most areas around manmade reservoirs underwent significant economic growth. Arkansas's Twin Lakes area experienced the region's earliest reservoir-fueled development boom at the very moment that postwar American affluence began crowding the highways with vacationers. By the early 1970s, the tourist camps, hotels, and resorts in the Twin Lakes area could accommodate more than eighty-three hundred people on a nightly basis. Even more central to the Twin Lakes economy was retirement. In the 1970s and 1980s, the greater Mountain Home area emerged as one of the country's leading destinations for retirees as Midwesterners made their way southward to spend their golden years on the hillsides where stubborn Ozarkers had wrenched a living from rocky soils. Bringing pensions and savings unheard of by many of their native neighbors, the swarm of retirees inspired rapid expansion in the real estate and medical sectors of "Chicago's most remote suburb."[15]

The lake areas of the White River basin were central to one of the most crucial stories of post–World War II demographic change in the Ozarks. At the heart of the retirement story was a phenomenon that touched the Ozarks as much as any other place in the nation: the planned retirement community. Though housing developments from Florida to Arizona claim to be the blueprint for the planned retirement community, few if any trace their roots further back than does Cherokee Village, Arkansas. Like many affluent Memphis-area people, John A. Cooper Sr. grew up vacationing on the Spring River in the eastern Ozarks. Capitalizing on the bargain-basement, postwar land prices in the era of massive outmigration, Cooper bought up hundreds of acres in the hills along the South Fork of the Spring River west of Hardy. With the 1954 launch of his Cherokee Village Development Company, he targeted an expanding class of pensioners looking for an inexpensive retirement destination far from the crime and hassle of the city. Cooper and his platoon of salesmen and women peddled lots and homesites to thousands determined not to spend their golden years in the cold Midwest or the mosquito-infested Delta. The Ozarks, according to one reporter, had plenty to offer the prospective retiree: "fresh air, clean water, low taxes, and no crime," the latter word "being a delicate euphemism" for African Americans. Whatever motivated their relocation, by 1962 Cherokee Village boasted four hundred new houses and a variety of recreational and community amenities that made it a gleaming oasis in an otherwise poor and abandoned part of the region.[16]

The success of Cherokee Village spawned imitators. A few miles away in Izard County developers turned Cooper's blueprint into Horseshoe Bend, where a full-time sales staff of almost fifty people entertained tens of thousands of potential lot buyers in the late 1960s. Like Cherokee Village, Horseshoe Bend's clientele wasn't comprised of doctors and investment bankers. They were teachers and factory operatives, construction workers, electricians, and shopkeepers. The early years were not without cultural challenges, as newcomers often brought with them long-held stereotypes of Ozarkers, and the natives themselves resented the meddling ways and grating accents of those people "from off." Cooper would eventually achieve his greatest success in the Ozarks by converting the sleepy old resort town of Bella Vista, Arkansas, into an upscale version of his blueprint. Commissioning Arkansas architect E. Fay Jones to devise an environmentally conscious style that melded with the rolling, forested hills north of Bentonville, Cooper capitalized on the burgeoning prosperity in Sam Walton's neck of the Ozarks. The result was a destination that meshed the physical beauty and lower cost of living of the Ozarks with the superior amenities of northwestern Arkansas—a perfect combination to attract more affluent retirees.[17]

Still, it was the man-made lakes in the White River basin that attracted the greatest number of retirees. In the late 1950s new Army Corps of Engineers policies allowed more private ownership along reservoir shorelines. Kimberling City, Missouri, established in 1959 by Springfield developer John Q. Hammons, lured retirees and other newcomers to the banks of Table Rock Lake. Following Hammons's lead, planned communities sprang up at Diamond City on Bull Shoals Lake and on the upper reaches of Table Rock at Holiday Island, north of Eureka Springs. A Little Rock insurance magnate developed Eden Isle on a peninsular piece of property on the south side of Greers Ferry Lake. Across the reservoir another developer founded a more ambitious community, Fairfield Bay, which grew to be the second-largest town in Van Buren County. Beaver Lake attracted fewer retirement community developers than did Greers Ferry, but Lost Bridge Village became a favorite getaway for Sam Walton and his Walmart executives in the 1970s.[18]

The rapid development of the retirement industry in the southern Ozarks fundamentally altered the demographics of communities and counties. Taking place amid a massive exodus of rural Ozarkers, in some places the influx of retirees replaced the native born as the dominant population. A similar change took place in the ecosystem of the waters downstream from the new dams. The cold lake water that generated power turbines altered downstream ecology for miles, its temperature proving inhospitable to the stream's indigenous species. Trout, though not native to the Ozarks, thrive in these tailwaters. European brown trout reproduce in the White River, and on very rare occasions the rainbow trout replenishes its population in the Ozarks—the rainbows released in southwestern Missouri's Crane Creek in the late nineteenth century, for example. But most trout in the Ozarks are raised in hatcheries. The U.S. Fish and Wildlife Service established a trout hatchery in the shadow of Norfork Dam in 1957 and began stocking reservoir tailwaters. Hungry schools of this introduced fish brought a whole new breed of angler to the Ozarks, and a new nickname for the little town of Cotter just downstream from Bull Shoals: "Trout Capital, U.S.A."[19]

The extensive system of dams in the Ozarks quashed the region's once-popular float fishing industry, but it didn't spell the end of warmwater fishing in the region. In fact, the placid reservoir waters attracted even greater numbers of anglers. Fishermen from around the Southwest and Midwest trolled the lakes for elusive walleye—"jack" or "jack salmon" in the local parlance—and cast the coves for lunker largemouth bass. Stocked species such as muskies and striped bass provided added diversity to the region's game fish population. The lakes of the Ozarks even played their part in the emergence of professional sport fishing. Just one year after its completion, Beaver Lake hosted the All-American Invitational Bass Tournament. It was the first contest hosted by Ray Scott, founder of the Bass Anglers Sportsman Society (B.A.S.S.) Federation, the world's leading competitive bass-fishing organization.[20]

The twentieth-century phenomenon of the Ozarks as lake country created new opportunities in the region's business scene. Entrepreneurs in the Ozarks played leading roles in the expanding outdoor sports and recreation market. Just a few miles south of Bull Shoals Lake in the little town of Flippin, Arkansas, in 1968 Forrest L. Wood and his wife, Nina, founded a business that would eventually become the world's largest manufacturer of bass boats. A former fishing guide and sometime professional bass angler, Forrest L. Wood modified the Ozarks johnboat into the fiberglass craft he branded the Ranger Boat. By the time the Woods sold the company almost twenty years later, Ranger Boats had become synonymous with bass fishing on lakes around the nation. The only entrepreneur more associated than Wood with outdoor sports in the Ozarks is Johnny Morris, who purchased Ranger Boats in 2014.[21]

Morris's story is inextricably linked to the remaking of the Ozarks by the Army Corps of Engineers. "A lot of our favorite places on the river went away," noted Morris, who as a boy accompanied his grandfather to the official dedication of Table Rock Dam, "but it created a whole new fishery." Raised in Springfield, where his father owned the local Brown Derby chain of liquor stores, Johnny Morris found himself an easy drive from the White River reservoirs to the south and the Osage lakes to the north. In 1972 the twenty-four-year-old began selling lures, bait, and other fishing gear in the back of one of his father's stores. It was an inauspicious beginning for Bass Pro Shops, which opened its first stand-alone store just steps away from the Brown Derby nine years later. The Springfield entrepreneur contributed to the outdoor recreation and tourism boom as well. By the twenty-first century, Morris's Big Cedar Lodge on Table Rock Lake had expanded into one of the nation's leading resorts. In more recent years his Top of the Rock Ozarks Heritage Preserve (featuring a Jack Nicklaus–designed golf course) and Wonders of Wildlife National Museum and Aquarium have taken their place among the region's most popular attractions. The buyout of major rival Cabela's in 2017 made the Ozarks company the largest retailer of outdoor gear in the world.[22]

The prosperity reflected in gleaming pontoon boats and sprawling resorts tended to mask the cultural transformation wrought by the dams. Within a generation newcomers outnumbered natives in areas of reservoir development. In the Twin Lakes area—where pre-dam society was defined by evangelical Protestantism and Democratic political control—"exotic" in-migrants introduced Catholicism, Lutheranism, and Republicanism, among other unusual new practices. The nasal timbre of the Great Lakes accent began to drown out the twang of the hills. And newcomers and weekenders in the reservoir areas were more likely than natives to capitalize on the economic boom generated by dams. A study of the Greers Ferry Dam area found that nonresidents and recent settlers controlled a significant chunk of the wealth in Cleburne and Van Buren counties, while most jobs created by the boom tended to be low paying and seasonal.[23]

Perhaps the least-chronicled part of the dam saga was the plight of the thousands of families displaced by reservoirs. In the prescient 1938 movie *Down in Arkansaw*, the Weaver Brothers and Elviry depicted a family of Ozarkers under pressure to sell their farm to the government as part of a hydroelectric dam project. The hill folks at first resist but ultimately come around to the side of "progress," swayed by the modern comforts of an electrified demonstration home and the romance between their daughter and a dashing civil engineer. But reality was never as seamless as a Hollywood paean to the New Deal. Congressman Clyde T. Ellis crowed, "There is not a single person opposed to these projects that I know of." But it was only because he didn't read his mail.[24]

Objections to dams came from a variety of sectors. Ideological conservatives viewed them as "creeping socialism" by "huge government bureaus." Local politicians and community leaders fretted over the loss of valuable acreage for property tax purposes. The most vociferous complaints came from the residents

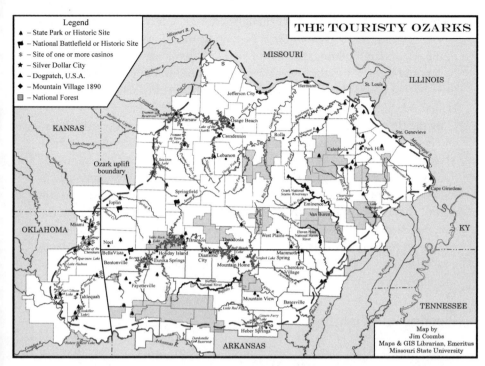

The Touristy Ozarks. Courtesy of Jim Coombs, Missouri State University, Springfield.

who stood to lose farms and homes to the reservoirs. Some made their peace with an unfortunate fate and moved on. Adlie and Cora Clinkingbeard, farmers in the flood basin of Norfork Lake, took what money the government men offered and relocated their family to Mountain Home, where Adlie found work as a night watchman. Others didn't go so willingly. Farther up the valley of the North Fork, teenager Sarah Stone watched as local authorities forcibly and physically removed her distraught octogenarian grandparents from their farm, the one on which her grandfather had been born before the Civil War.[25]

Landowners received the depressed prices characteristic of the poor Ozarks in the middle of the twentieth century, even though land values would experience a significant spike once the dam was completed. Only those with substantial financial means could afford to hire a lawyer to challenge the government's offer and wait months on a settlement. The corps' right to demand removal with thirty days' notice added insult to injury, especially when the federal bureaucracy could take more than twice that length of time to deliver payment checks. Leland Fox, whose Cedar County, Missouri, neighborhood was partly inundated by Stockton Lake in the late 1960s, watched the removal of longtime friends and neighbors. For those who "cultivated and grazed these acres for generations, there is a sense of bitterness that cannot be erased." A decade later Homer Ferguson lost his farm to Truman Dam. For Ferguson and many others displaced in the era of dam building, the loss of land and home was not quantifiable in dollars and cents. It was the loss of a sense of place. "I was born and raised right there in that goddam bend," Ferguson protested. "Went to school right there. Hell, it was home to me. You hate to give up home."[26]

By the time of the creation of Truman Lake, a new kind of opposition had emerged. Truman was the only one of the corps' completed reservoirs to survive a coordinated challenge by environmentalists. Arguing that the reservoir would flood valuable archaeological sites and destroy North America's premier spawning ground for the paddlefish, the Environmental Defense Fund brought suit against the corps in 1972. With Missouri's powerful senator Stuart Symington still on board, the corps saw the project to completion nonetheless. Scientists continued to decry the detrimental effects of the outsized turbines at Truman and Stockton dams, which they blamed for frequent flooding and fish kills of startling proportions.[27]

Floating and Fighting

In the end, though, it may have been the upper Osage's lack of scenic vistas that prevented opponents from killing Truman Dam. The aesthetic appeal of other streams in the Ozarks played a major role in saving them from impoundment. Even as the corps continued to lay rebar and pour concrete in the Ozarks in the 1960s and 1970s, canoeists and environmentalists organized to bring an end to the era of dam building. Before the 1960s the only corps plans to face formidable opposition in the Ozarks were those in the watershed of the Meramec River, a highland stream that originates in remote Dent County, Missouri, and meanders more than two hundred miles before meeting the Mississippi just downstream from St. Louis. The St. Louis District of the Army Corps of Engineers received support from small-town boosters envisioning tourism dollars, but just about everyone else who went on record—from state agencies to the St. Louis Chamber of Commerce—opposed the proposal to erect three dams in the watershed. When Gov. Forrest Smith announced his opposition to the project in December 1949, the corps' vision for the Meramec and its tributaries died—or, more accurately, slipped into a coma. Like the monster in a horror film franchise, the blueprints of the corps would prove difficult to kill.[28]

Governor Smith also expressed support for maintaining southeastern Missouri's Current and Eleven Point rivers as free-flowing streams. The idea of building dams on these rivers had gotten little traction to this point. But as streams in the White River watershed, the two rivers fell under the jurisdiction of the Little Rock District of the corps, which had identified no fewer than seven potential dam sites on the Current and three on the Eleven Point.[29] The battle over the fate of these two rivers fully introduced the modern environmentalist ethic into the discussion of the Ozarks outdoors for the first time. The struggle's echoes reverberated far beyond the hollers and steep ridges of the Courtois Hills.

In 1956 a joint state-federal study recommended a "national recreation area" along the Eleven Point and Current rivers and the Current's tributary, the Jacks Fork. The report sparked a turf war among federal agencies and between competing local interests. In late 1958 the U.S. Forest Service, which already controlled several thousand acres along the rivers, announced plans to establish special recreation areas on the Current and Eleven Point. When the Missouri state legislature passed a resolution supporting the concept of a national recreation area the following year, Congress authorized the National Park Service, not the USFS, to conduct a preliminary study. Released in 1960, the report proposed the creation of an "Ozark Rivers National Monument," which would be managed by the NPS.[30]

Within a year, Missouri congressmen presented competing bills to establish a "national monument" in the Courtois Hills. Suburban St. Louis Republican Thomas B. Curtis's bill called for USFS control of the monument, while the proposal from Democrat Richard Ichord, in whose district the monument would be located, favored NPS oversight. Valley property owners would have been tickled pink if the whole affair had just gone away, but most realized that was not the way these things worked. With the governor and the most powerful members of Missouri's Washington delegation on board, the idea of federal intervention in the region was a snowball rolling downhill. The only question was which agency's office it would roll into. Supporting the Curtis bill was the Current–Eleven Point Rivers Association, a group composed largely of landowners within the proposed monument boundaries. They preferred dealing with the USFS, which was less likely than the NPS to use eminent domain proceedings to obtain control of property. Favoring Ichord's legislation was the Ozark Rivers National Monument Association, whose leaders were mostly businessmen from small towns in the region who embraced the NPS's vision of a recreation zone that would generate an economic boost for one of the poorest areas in the country.[31]

The most influential leaders of the two camps were not Ozarkers but St. Louisans. Their prominent roles reflected the colonial nature of the saga. Leonard Hall was content to debate the fate of the Current and Eleven Point country without consulting the natives, more than a few of whom were afflicted with "ignorance, trachoma, mental illness, [and] the conviction that the world owes the area a livelihood through subsidies." Hall spent years writing outdoor columns for newspapers and became a convert to preservation after he and his wife left the city in 1945 to settle on a farm near the picturesque village of Caledonia.

His popular 1958 book, *Stars Upstream: Life along an Ozark River*, established him as an expert on all things pertaining to the Current. Hall initially disliked the idea of unleashing hordes of tourists on fragile river ecosystems, but the NPS's report convinced him that time was running out to preserve the region's semi-wilderness quality. His strident columns in the *St. Louis Globe-Democrat* bolstered public support for Ichord's NPS bill. Leo Drey lacked Hall's bully pulpit, but he almost made up for it with his wealth and influence. Inheriting a fortune from his St. Louis industrialist father, the World War II veteran amassed more than 140,000 acres in the rugged Courtois Hills. An innovative and conservation-minded timber entrepreneur, Drey owned some thirty-five miles of river frontage along the Current and Jacks Fork. With thousands of acres subject to NPS eminent domain, he was the founder and chief spokesperson of the Current–Eleven Point Rivers Association and the force behind Curtis's pro-USFS bill.[32]

Almost from the beginning, though, it was the supporters of Ichord and Hall who held the upper hand. In the fall of 1961, Ichord, Hall, and Missouri governor John M. Dalton scored a major coup when they hosted Secretary of the Interior Stewart Udall and NPS director George Hartzog on a whirlwind tour of the proposed national monument area. Despite numerous "MONUMENT NO" signs placed along the roadsides by the opposition, the visit convinced Udall to upgrade the proposal to national park status—a development that generated widespread publicity.[33]

The *Saturday Evening Post* provided the NPS proposal its most far-reaching positive coverage—but at a cost. Bernard Asbell's article "The Vanishing Hillbilly" was something of a cultural hatchet job. In an era when the media dwelled on Appalachian poverty and blight, the national press—when it chronicled the other highlands at all—still tended to portray the Ozarks as a bucolic landscape only slightly marred by a mostly harmless tribe of hill folks. Readers accustomed to such sepia-toned treatment must have recoiled at the sight of Ken Mooney. Wearing cuffed blue jeans and an unbuttoned shirt cinched at the waist, the lean, tattooed army veteran chomped an upturned cigarette while clutching a rifle and scowling at the camera like a shell-shocked composite of Popeye and Ernest T. Bass. The article never once mentioned the sinister-looking hillman, but it was Mooney's mug that welcomed readers to Asbell's Ozarks, where "extremists among the mountain folk were resuming their war against the Twentieth Century." Some thirty years after Bagnell Dam rustled recalcitrant Ozarkers out of cultural hibernation, the species was still ready to fight. "For over a century the proud Ozark mountaineer fiercely resisted change," proclaimed the second-page heading. "Now he's being modernized out of existence."[34]

The Ozarkers living on the Current River may have been carrying on the "tradition of the Nineteenth Century pioneer," but they were reading the twentieth century's magazines. A few weeks after the article's publication, the Shannon County chapter of the Current–Eleven Point Rivers Association issued "a call for all 'Vanishing Hillbillies'" to gather at the ballfield in Eminence to express their opposition when Ichord stopped by for a scheduled visit. The congressman was later hanged and funeralized in effigy on the court square. Of course, for the vast majority who opposed the idea of a national park, it was rational economics—not an irrational clinging to an outdated culture—that provided motivation. The opposition simply feared they would lose homes and farms. Resistance to the park bill was even more uniform and widespread down the Current River in Ripley County, where farming in the alluvial bottoms was more crucial to the local economy, and in the Eleven Point watershed of neighboring Oregon County.[35]

Fortunately for the park's detractors in Ripley and Oregon, their counties lay in a different congressional district. By the time President Lyndon B. Johnson signed the bill creating the Ozark National Scenic Riverways (ONSR) in 1964, Rep. Paul C. Jones had extricated his constituents from the park proposal. Consisting of some eighty thousand acres along the Current and Jacks Fork, the first "national river" system in the United States extended southward only as far as the Carter-Ripley county line. The NPS waived its standard policy against hunting and fishing on its lands. The bill also attempted to strike a sort of middle ground with some landowners. Instead of requiring outright, fee-simple ownership of parkland, as had been agency practice, the bill floated the possibility of "life estates," whereby some owners could remain on their property until death. The new proposal also included usage of the still-novel practice of scenic easements, which allowed some residents to retain ownership of their lands with stipulated restrictions on its use.[36]

Nevertheless, the NPS retained the right of eminent domain, and any hiccup in negotiations between landowners and the ONSR could result in condemnation proceedings. The NPS "did indeed condemn a great deal of ONSR lands," notes historian Will Sarvis, and the often-underqualified, government-contracted real estate appraisers offered buyout prices that were "ridiculously low." The federal courts in eastern Missouri routinely awarded the owners of condemned lands at least twice as much as the government offered. Still, the miserly appraisals and "bullying tactics" during the stressful years of land acquisition engendered "a significant degree of ill will among landowners and area residents who might justifiably have perceived the NPS as dishonest."[37]

The influx of tourists wasn't quite as large as the NPS predicted, but the more than three hundred thousand annual canoeists by the early 1980s prompted one writer's wistful longing for "the solitude that once enhanced a river experience." Leonard Hall himself lived long enough to take issue with the NPS's commitment to outdoor recreation for the masses, a principle he once embraced. In the twenty-first century, the Current and Jacks Fork remain two of the most popular float streams in the nation, attracting upward of a million and a half visitors each year. But the local legacy of the ONSR is a complex one. The economic recovery promised by politicians and boosters never happened. The seasonal service jobs of a tourist economy proved no match for the remoteness at the heart of the poverty that seemed to be the birthright of the Courtois Hills. Shannon, Carter, and neighboring counties remain among the poorest in the region, their names written in ink on Missouri's list of "persistently low-income counties." In statistics released by the U.S. Census Bureau fifty years after the creation of the ONSR, Shannon County—home of the "vanishing hillbillies" who fought the park bill—ranked dead last in Missouri in median household income and first in childhood poverty.[38]

A legacy of bitterness toward the NPS and the government in general lingered long after the divisiveness of the 1960s. It was a legacy that contributed to the growing right-wing property rights movement and continued to complicate the jobs of succeeding generations of NPS personnel. In the 1970s the NPS sponsored a series of "living history" programs that salved wounds by hiring locals to give public demonstrations of sorghum making, johnboat building, and moonshine distilling. But these popular initiatives soon disappeared, replaced by local animosity over a short-lived federal ban on trapping in the ONSR in 1986 and a prolonged scrum over the NPS's attempt to remove feral horses in the 1990s. The wild horse controversy owed less to animal rights activism and more to resentment toward the government agency that had become the symbol for condescending outsider power. In a study focusing on the ONSR in the early 2000s, anthropologist Kelly Fish-Greenlee found "considerable stress and animosity" between natives and newcomers, an insider-versus-outsider mind-set that often played into the stereotypes of rural Ozarkers.[39]

Just four years after President Johnson signed the ONSR into existence, he inked his name on the even more ambitious Wild and Scenic Rivers Act. A stretch of just over forty-four miles of the Eleven Point River was among the eight streams designated for national protection. Following a blueprint more akin to Leo Drey's vision, the Eleven Point fell under USFS jurisdiction, and private landowners maintained their lands in exchange for scenic easements on riverfront property. With Missouri having become ground zero for the public protection of streams, in the late 1960s and early 1970s bureaucrats, canoeists, and environmentalists pushed for a statewide system of scenic rivers. But the fresh wounds of eminent domain in the ONSR and the property rights movement stirred intense landowner opposition, prompting one suburban St. Louisan's fear "of an open-range war and bloodshed in the Ozark region." The campaign for public protection petered out in the mid-1970s, leaving the Current, Jacks Fork, and Eleven Point the only designated "scenic" rivers in Missouri to this day.[40]

Segments of half a dozen small streams in the Arkansas Ozarks would be added to the National Wild and Scenic Rivers System in 1992, but all were located in the Ozark National Forest and required no transfer of land ownership. Included in this group was the uppermost 16-mile section of the Buffalo River, a tributary of the White that originated in the Boston Mountains and descended 150 miles through some of the most inaccessible and stunning terrain in the Ozarks. The remainder of the Buffalo had been designated a "national river" by federal law twenty years earlier. The fight for the Buffalo shared much in common with the overlapping struggle on the Current in Missouri, but they weren't carbon copies. The damming of the Current was never a serious prospect, leaving the NPS, the USFS, and their respective supporters to contend for the prize. The impoundment of the Buffalo was a much more serious possibility. By the 1950s the Army Corps of Engineers had drawn up blueprints for as many as five dams on this small stream.[41] And the political support was in place to get at least one of them built. Despite a strong heritage of Jeffersonian democracy, Arkansas politicians eagerly supported public funding (when it was federal funding) for river impoundment.

The struggle for control of the Buffalo began in the late 1950s, when Congress passed a bill authorizing construction of two dams on the river. President Dwight D. Eisenhower vetoed the dams, pointing toward the corps' own study questioning their cost-benefit ratio, but the return of Democrats to the White House in 1961 saw the reintroduction of Buffalo-damming legislation. Meanwhile, at Sen. J. William Fulbright's request, the NPS conducted a study of the Buffalo Valley, a rosy report predicting that a tourism and economic boom would follow creation of a national recreation area. Dam boosters in Marshall—hopeful that their town would be transformed in the same way Norfork and Bull Shoals dams had remade Mountain Home—organized the Buffalo River Improvement Association (BRIA), pledging support for the efforts of Congressman James Trimble and the corps. In response canoeists and other nonlocal dam opponents created the Ozark Society. The almost simultaneous establishment of the Buffalo River Landowners' Association—a group that wanted no part of a dam or a national park—complicated the imbroglio.[42]

By mid-decade there was still no resolution but plenty of tension. On Memorial Day weekend in 1965, pro-dammers felled trees across the Buffalo to impede a float trip organized by Kansas City's Ozark Wilderness Waterways Club and reportedly fired at canoeists from wooded banks. Later that year a melee between pro- and anti-dam men at a high school basketball game resulted in four arrests. When Trimble's 1965 dam bill received endorsement from the three other Arkansas members of the House, optimistic supporters feted their congressman at a celebration in Marshall. But the bill failed to make it out of committee, and in December 1965 an unlikely environmental champion stepped forth. Gov. Orval Faubus made public a long and eloquent letter imploring the chief of the corps to leave the Buffalo alone. Opposition from a sitting governor was tantamount to a death penalty for such projects, and within a few months the corps shelved plans for damming the stream. Republican John Paul Hammerschmidt's surprise upset of Trimble in the election of 1966 drove the final nail in the coffin. Hammerschmidt promptly filed a bill for a national recreation area in 1967. It would take five more years and a good deal of political wrangling in both Little Rock and Washington, but on March 1, 1972, President Richard Nixon signed the bill creating the 95,000-acre, 135-mile-long Buffalo National River (BNR).[43]

Residents in three small areas of the park designated private use zones were guaranteed options (such as scenic easements) that would allow them to remain in their homes. Yet these zones made up only about 10 percent of all privately owned acreage in the national river's boundaries, and anyone living outside of them had no choice but to vacate their property. In the end many Buffalo Valley residents—"as violently opposed to a park or recreational area as they [were] a dam"—found themselves trapped between warring factions that had little concern for the people on the land over which they fought. Natives of the valley remained conspicuously silent and scarce in press coverage leading up to the nationalization of the river. The most visible native was Orphea Duty, an articulate nineteenth-century-born Boxley storekeeper who accompanied members of the Ozark Society on a trip to speak before a Senate subcommittee. "Most of the people in the valley 'heired' their land and their roots are deep," she told the senators. "Like all proud farmers they wish to retain their land to pass on to their children. If you can bring a park that will not disrupt the citizens, . . . a park that will allow reasonable use of the land, then we see eye to eye." But even this conditional vote of support for the park proposal placed Duty in the minority among her neighbors. Most reacted to the idea of a nationalized river with the puzzled exasperation of St. Joe resident Lunce Cash. "If they are not going to get those dams, why don't we just draw off and leave the Buffalo alone?"[44]

The creation of national rivers in the Missouri and Arkansas Ozarks caused plenty of hard feelings, and both developments reflected a federal agency much better at dealing with the natural world than with cultural heritage. The hardball tactics of the NPS's land acquisition staff, who often pressured owners to sell their property outright, resulted in three-quarters of the lands in the Buffalo River's private use zones being vacated. A decade into the life of the BNR found only forty "unsettled, even embittered" residents remaining in the park. For a national river designed to maintain "the rural community and its pastoral landscape," this was alarming. What the NPS so often overlooked was the appeal of the rivers as "human" environments, not just natural environments. For many who floated the streams and followed the winding highways into these remote places, the people and their farms were just as interesting as the weathered bluffs and clear waters. Neil Compton, who as founder and president of the Ozark Society played a leading role in saving the Buffalo from the corps, recalled his first trip by car into the Boxley Valley in 1946. It wasn't the memory of the rushing river that stayed with him for forty years. It was the homes, barns, and voices "of the self-sufficient yeoman farmers whose ancestors had settled here over one hundred years before." In the mid-1980s officials with the BNR launched a public relations initiative designed to establish at least a modicum of goodwill between the park service and valley residents while returning some properties to former owners.[45]

Old Ozarkers Still

Boxley Valley remains the most visited place in the BNR. Its frozen-in-time physical appearance was meant to inspire admiration for the sturdy Ozarkers of a romantic past. Just a few years after the creation of the Buffalo National River, Kansas City journalist C. W. Gusewelle cautioned that "a region and its people cannot be kept as a living museum." But it was a warning that most chroniclers of the postwar Ozarks ignored. The intensity of interest in the region never regained its 1941 peak. Nevertheless, plenty of postwar publications peddled depictions of the Ozarks and Appalachia as sleepy, innocent refuges from the anxiety of the Cold War. So unaffected was the social construct of the region that a Californian looking to relocate in the 1950s could inquire after a "small *one-horse village* in [the] Ozarks . . . [with] old-fashion folks who live in cabins, drive model-T's, take corn to grist mill, etc." For almost two decades the *New York Times* ran annual features that betrayed no confidence in the Ozarkers' ability or willingness to modernize. "Their life is much the same as that of the pioneers who first settled here," intoned a 1948 entry otherwise enamored with the building of Bull Shoals Dam. A dozen years later it was the "taciturn mountaineers" of the booming Shepherd of the Hills Country who "still depend for subsistence on a scrawny patch of corn and 'taters and black-eyed peas, a few hogs and an infallible trigger finger."[46]

Alongside the travel writing accounts of the Ozarks, folklore constituted the primary currency in the public's exchange of information about the region. Vance Randolph's prodigious postwar output reinforced the perception of his adopted region as a last bastion of white exotics with at least one foot planted squarely in the nineteenth century. The old-timers who inspired a youthful Randolph to construct an anachronistic image of the Ozarks in the 1920s and 1930s were mostly gone by mid-century. In the postwar years the folklorist abandoned his earlier pseudo-anthropological ruminations on Ozarkers. Instead,

Randolph issued a steady stream of books chronicling the relics of a lost world that had so enchanted him in the 1920s—superstitions, dialect, and tall tales, as well as his monumental four-volume *Ozark Folk Songs*. Capturing Ozarkers in a sort of pre-Depression gilded fog, Randolph and his vision of the region carried the day in the postwar years. After the death of John T. Woodruff, even the "rubophobic" Springfield Chamber of Commerce took to bestowing upon the city's visiting dignitaries the title "Honorary Ozark Hillbilly," though "Mr. Ozark" never received one of the medallions that marked the occasion.[47]

Randolph's friend Otto Ernest Rayburn never ceased banging the drum of romanticism. Determined to make Eureka Springs the "folklore capital of the world," Rayburn settled in the old resort town in 1946 and promptly helped found the annual Ozark Folk Festival and the Arkansas Folklore Society. A hopeless romantic, he continued to promote the Ozarks as a rural idyll and tourist's dream in the pages of his widely circulated magazine, *Rayburn's Ozark Guide*. By the time the guide ceased publication upon Rayburn's death in 1960, a new periodical had emerged to carry the torch. The *Ozarks Mountaineer*, founded in 1952 as a hybrid between a regional news source and promotional publication, blossomed into a popular tribute to an enduringly romantic Ozarks under the capable watch of editor Clay Anderson. Until the magazine's demise in the twenty-first century, nothing did more to perpetuate the nostalgic Ozarks.[48]

Even before Clay Anderson converted the *Ozarks Mountaineer* into a glossy magazine in 1966, however, the national narrative of Appalachia diverged sharply from that of the Ozarks. Responding to the pleas of regional activists and to the John F. Kennedy campaign's focus on Appalachian poverty, hand-wringing journalists and idealistic student volunteers altered the public discourse on Appalachia. In the 1960s and 1970s national magazines carried more than fifty features on Appalachian poverty and government efforts to combat it, along with another twenty stories on strip mining and beleaguered coal miners. The same two decades produced only one magazine piece on Ozarks poverty, as writers focused instead on river canoeing and vacation getaways. *Life*'s treatments of Appalachia and the Ozarks in 1964 encapsulated the contrast: "The Valley of Poverty" and "Wonders of a Cave Find." "While Appalachia draws the headlines and massive doses of federal aid," observed a *Wall Street Journal* reporter in 1965, the Ozarkers were "in greater economic distress." But depictions of the Ozarks remained remarkably consistent, the Ozarker seemingly immutable in the face of historical progression.[49]

If the era's immutable Ozarker had a face, it looked a whole lot like Junior Cobb's. Nephew of hard-luck Depression survivors Chester and Corgel Acklin, Cobb grew up on the White River in Baxter County, Arkansas, where he received almost no formal schooling but early on discovered a talent for wood carving. Even as the Army Corps of Engineers transformed the countryside around him into the touristy Twin Lakes region, he hunted and trapped and explored the woods, fields, and streams. The early 1960s found Cobb in the Three Brothers community a few miles from Bull Shoals Lake, and it was here that he was discovered by Silver Dollar City woodcarver Peter Engler, whose parents owned a craft shop in the shadow of the dam. At the theme park Engler began marketing Cobb's creations through the Ozark Mountain Woodcarvers Guild. The Ozarker's forte was lifelike animals, but he could also produce stunning human studies. Unlike the "insensitive stereotype of the hillbilly carved by the hundreds in the Ozarks," noted scholar Donald Van Horn, Cobb's subjects were "depicted with sensitivity and a keen awareness of their pride." Before the end of the decade, his work would be on display at the Smithsonian Institution, he would visit the White House as the guest of Arkansas governor Winthrop Rockefeller, and a Rockefeller-commissioned bust of Glen Campbell would bring him national attention when it was revealed on the Arkansas-born singer's musical variety television show.[50]

In a 1969 cover story for the *Ozarks Mountaineer*, Clay Anderson suggested that Junior Cobb was "possibly the greatest Ozarkian artist of his time." But it wasn't Cobb's obvious talent that stimulated Anderson's fascination with the "unbelievable" twenty-eight-year-old. It was his unapologetic and seemingly unaffected backwoods lifestyle and the authentic, salt-of-the-earth hillbilly demeanor that inspired it. "His is not the iconoclasm or eccentricity of practiced non-conformity so often associated with those in the field of fine arts," Anderson marveled. "His home and his home life are as rustic as his carvings are refined."[51] Cobb was the personification of the region in the national consciousness—a friendly, plain-talking hillbilly who lived off the land and was oddly immune to the materialism of modern American society. "I mostly do what I wanna do," he informed Van Horn. "If I git up and don't feel like carvin' that day, well, I take off and go huntin' arrerheads or go cave explorin' or somethin' like that." In a country plagued by warfare and cultural upheaval, in a place enduring unrelenting technological change and the ever-present cloud of nuclear annihilation, Junior Cobb was a refreshing and romantic symbol of simplicity and unconscious nonconformity—the perfect totem of the nation's image of the Ozarker.

But the carver's existence wasn't quite as idyllic as it may have seemed. By the time Van Horn visited his ramshackle workshop in 1977, Cobb lived on the margins of poverty with his wife and five children, the sales of carvings his only income. Aside from a local patron or two, his clientele were the tourists who descended on the Twin Lakes each summer. They had no interest in his "good carvings," the masterpieces into which he put heart and soul, the ones that evoked the fullness of his fellow rural Ozarkers. The visitors wanted a representation of the stereotypical Ozarks, the kind of knickknack one found at a roadside tourist trap and took back home as a conversation piece. Thus, an obliging Junior Cobb found himself carving on "both sides of the fence," devoting more and more time to caricature, to things like spirit faces etched in driftwood or the heads of walking sticks. "I really don't even call them much of a carving," he told Van Horn. "Just a little ol' hillbilly's face on 'em . . ., just something to sell to the tourist when somebody wants something real fast."[52]

The Lake

The commodification and exploitation of culture was nowhere more evident than in Junior Cobb's Twin Lakes and other places "grown big and busy with tourism." In the first postwar decades, no place in the region grew bigger and busier with tourism than the Lake of the Ozarks. Befitting a watering hole built by an electric company, the lake was the Ozark region's neon bug light in an era of blue-collar pensioners, V-8 land barges, and faux-coonskin-cap Americana. Decades before the popular Netflix show *Ozark* introduced the world to a shockingly violent but fictional mélange of hillbilly heroin makers, Mexican drug lords, and ethically challenged city folk, this once-isolated backwater flashed with an overdose of kitsch. Nothing shouted Ozarks garishness louder than Dogpatch Village. "Something of a theme park all its own," recalled humorist Bill Geist of his days as a summer worker in the 1960s, the souvenir store featured a reptile garden and caged lion in addition to "Old Bob's Cabin, a hillbilly jail, an animated graveyard with protruding, wiggling toes, and an outhouse occupied by a seated mechanical man who yelled when someone opened the door." But the Lake of the Ozarks did more than hillbilly tawdriness. Unlike Branson, the lake country developed a penchant for ignoring regional culture and history, except when lampooning it for financial gain.[53]

The first lake enterprise to signal a clear break with local custom may have been Musser's Ozark Tavern and Resort. While most early lake destinations were bare-bones businesses providing amenities for fishermen and boaters, Musser's was an elaborate travel complex featuring a golf driving range, tennis courts, swimming pool, and cocktail lounge. In the big band era the resort's Crystal Ballroom hosted late-night dances to orchestras and jazz ensembles featuring young saxophonist Charlie Parker and other Black musicians. Despite the surrounding area's almost lily-white population, the lake region's strong connection to urban Kansas City and St. Louis led to its hosting at least three resorts catering to an African American clientele.[54]

But the tourism industry remained in a state of infancy until after World War II, when the Securities and Exchange Commission forced Union Electric to sell any property extraneous to power production. Acquiring forty thousand acres for the bargain price of $320,000, St. Louis developer Cyrus Crane Willmore built roads, hired salesmen to peddle real estate, and promoted the lake in

Kansas City, St. Louis, and Chicago with headline-grabbing events like speedboat races and waterskiing contests. Salesmen targeted affluent city dwellers looking to buy lots for a summer home or weekend getaway. Weekenders saw an increasingly eclectic variety of businesses and activities in the 1950s. Rare was the station wagon that didn't make at least one stop at the Ozark Deer Farm, the "mystery house" at Phantom Acres, Max Allen's Reptile Gardens, and the Aquarama, a knockoff of Florida's Weeki Wachee "mermaid" show. The lake region maintained at least a tenuous link with a rural past drawn more from popular American culture than from actual Ozarks history. The lake became a hotbed of square dancing—if it's permissible to use those four words in that order—and the annual J Bar H Rodeo in Camdenton attracted one hundred thousand onlookers a year during the heyday of the television western.[55]

In the 1960s St. Louis entrepreneurs introduced an element of overt elegance and Rat Pack/Palm Springs hipness never before seen in the Ozarks with the opening of the posh East Asian–themed Tan-Tar-A resort, the ritzy Lodge of the Four Seasons, and the exotic, tiki-themed Mai Tai resort. Top-notch golf courses, spas, professional chefs, strolling violinists, and waiters in tuxedoes were just a few of the amenities signaling the "beginning of the end of the 'old lake' era." Looking to distinguish the Lake of the Ozarks from a more backwoodsy, blue-collar boom taking place in Branson, from the 1980s into the early twenty-first century developers concentrated on filling high-rise condominiums with affluent escapees from the metropolitan world, the kind attracted to the shopping, fine dining, yachting, and party-cove atmosphere of the modern lake.[56]

But there was one Lake of the Ozarks institution that smacked of Branson: Lee Mace's Ozark Opry. Founded by native Ozarkers Lee Mace and his wife, Joyce, in the lakeside town of Osage Beach in 1953, the Ozark Opry predated Branson's original live music show by seven years. A former jig dancer on the *Grand Ole Opry* television show, Lee played the upright bass and bucked and stomped like a manic marionette as the leader of the Ozark Opry's band. From the very first performance, the Maces were wise to their audience. "Folks were coming from Chicago and the first thing they wanted to see was the Dam, the next thing was a hillbilly," recalled Lee of those early shows. The result was a sort of hillbilly minstrel show—real Ozarkers masquerading as regional caricatures. In the early years the Maces played up the standard stereotypes—checked shirts and gingham dresses, comedians with blacked-out teeth and baggy britches. The truth was, though, that the Ozark Opry's playlist wasn't quite as old-timey as the suburbanites believed. The still comparatively new bluegrass style—a jazz-tinged mountain music in overdrive—was the band's chief influence, the records of Earl Scruggs and Bill Monroe its mentors. The Ozark Opry eventually perfected the formula that would come to define the first generation of live performances in Branson: over-the-top hillbilly hijinks scattered throughout

a playlist of contemporary country and high-lonesome bluegrass, with an occasional hymn and patriotic number mixed in for God and country.[57]

Ozarkers on the Airwaves

Starting in 1956 a Jefferson City station broadcast a weekly Ozark Opry television show.[58] But the Ozark Opry wasn't the first program to bring the region's
music to the small screen. That was the *Ozark Jubilee*, a show broadcast far
beyond the confines of the Ozarks, a groundbreaking production that put the
region squarely on the nation's entertainment map. With the *Ozark Jubilee* as
its primary weapon, for a few years Springfield battled Nashville for supremacy
in the world of country music and became Middle America's most significant
generator of nationally broadcast television content.

No element of Ozarks culture has been more central to its image than music—
but not just any old kind of music. It was the ballads and fiddle tunes carried
across the Mississippi River in the nineteenth century by upland southern settlers that became "Ozarks music." Twentieth-century seekers of a slipping past
discovered ancient songs and many more in comparatively isolated American
places like the Ozarks and Appalachia. Armed with portable tape recorders,
Mary Celestia Parler, John Quincy Wolf Jr., and other collectors traveled the
dirt roads and sat on vine-trellised porches to document a region's musical
heritage. The sounds of white mountain music came to define the Ozarks in
the reductionist universe of the folk festival.[59]

Yet the musical score of the Ozarks offers variations on this theme. In the
early twentieth century Springfield became a serious regional nexus of parlor
song sheet music, as well as the home of one of the country's largest Boy Scout
marching bands. Phonograph cylinders and radio shows exposed Ozarkers to
modern sounds and emerging genres. Before the Depression came to an end,
the big band movement was in full swing in towns up and down Route 66. By
mid-century the region's musical scene was diverse enough that small towns in
southwestern Missouri could produce one of the world's greatest tuba players
and Walt Disney's most prolific composer. Of course, the true regional celebrities
who could pack a rural high school gymnasium still delivered sounds rooted
in the soil of the countryside. They were people like Arkansawyer Elton Britt,
whose country crooning made a hit out of "There's a Star Spangled Banner
Waving Somewhere" during World War II, and Missourian Ferlin Husky, who
not only recorded hit country tunes but also performed as his hillbilly alter ego,
Simon Crum. They wrote and sang songs like "Why Don't You Haul Off and
Love Me" and "Company's Comin'," not scores for *Winnie the Pooh* movies.[60]

The *Ozark Jubilee* represented its creators' desire to make Springfield the
"Crossroads of Country Music." The Queen City of the Ozarks had been building

the foundation for years. With the financial backing of businessman Lester E. Cox, Springfield transplant Ralph Foster became the region's modern media kingpin, signing on the air with his KWTO (for Keep Watching the Ozarks) on Christmas Day in 1933. The radio station quickly created regional stars. None rivaled the career longevity and popularity of Clyde "Slim" Wilson, a grinning farm boy from nearby Christian County who became a fixture on Springfield radio and television for half a century. For years Wilson was the busiest man on KWTO, leading the western-themed Prairie Playboys (Springfield's answer to the Sons of the Pioneers), joining the cast of the daily "Ozark Farm and Home Gang," and playing in the Goodwill Family alongside his sister and nephew. Another popular local act was the Haden Family, whose little "Cowboy Charlie" would grow up to be virtuosic jazz double bassist Charlie Haden.[61]

By the war years KWTO was a staple in homes around the Ozarks, but Ralph Foster had his sights set on something bigger. In 1943 he launched his own weekly barn dance program to compete with entrenched shows like the *Grand Ole Opry* and Chicago's *National Barn Dance*. Two years later the Mutual Broadcasting Company picked up *Korns-A-Krackin* for national distribution, airing the show live from Springfield's Shrine Mosque at nine o'clock on Saturday nights. On air Slim Wilson's Prairie Ramblers were joined by the Ozarks Famous Four Fiddlers, the Sagebrush Serenaders, and the comedy duo of Flash and Whistler, former vaudevillians who had toured with the Weaver Brothers and Elviry. *Korns-A-Krackin* featured no breakout star, which likely contributed to its cancellation in 1949, but one half of its Matthews Brothers gospel quartet created a new foursome shortly after the show went off the air and achieved fame as the Jordanaires.[62]

Before they left Springfield, however, the Jordanaires participated in KWTO's latest endeavor, the transcription show. As the proliferation of small-town radio stations in the region cut into KWTO's audience, Foster's young right-hand man, Springfield native Ely "Si" Siman Jr., established RadiOzark Enterprises, which specialized in producing fifteen-minute shows that could be leased to other stations. An early version of syndication, the transcribed shows of the late 1940s and early 1950s brought some of country music's biggest acts into the KWTO studios, including Tennessee Ernie Ford and the Carter Sisters. The last artist to record transcripted shows for RadiOzark was the biggest name of all, Clyde "Red" Foley. Red's move to Springfield signaled Foster and Siman's most ambitious undertaking yet.[63]

The steady stream of talent passing through the doors of KWTO convinced Foster and Siman to up the ante on their challenge to Nashville. Working for Crossroads Productions, the new television production company founded by Foster and Lester E. Cox, Siman initially brought the *Ozark Jubilee* to life as a local Saturday night show, first broadcast on Springfield's KYTV on December

The *Ozark Jubilee*, from a souvenir "album," 1955. Courtesy of John Richardson, Springfield, Missouri.

26, 1953. Siman's vision for the program began to take shape when he traveled to Nashville to convince one of country music's heavyweights to serve as star of the new show. Longtime emcee of radio's *Grand Ole Opry*, Kentuckian Red Foley was in the middle of a reputation crisis generated by personal peccadillos and jumped at Siman's offer of a fresh start. Foley gave Foster and Siman the national star they never had on *Korns-A-Krackin*, convincing ABC executives to make *Ozark Jubilee* the first regularly scheduled country music show broadcast on network television.[64]

The *Ozark Jubilee* aired for the first time on national television on January 22, 1955. Broadcasting from the stage of Springfield's Jewell Theatre, the cast of the *Ozark Jubilee* included several KWTO regulars and veterans of *Korns-A-Krackin*: Slim Wilson, the Foggy River Boys quartet, and instrumentalists Speedy Haworth, Jimmy Gateley, and Harold Morrison. Among the legendary guest performers to take the stage during the *Ozark Jubilee*'s five-and-a-half-year run were Roy Acuff, Gene Autry, Johnny Cash, Jimmy Dean, and Minnie Pearl. The rotating cast of semi-regular stars featured singers from across the nation and from a variety of styles of the day: West Virginian Hawkshaw Hawkins, crossover hit–maker Sonny James from Alabama, and rockabilly Oklahoman Wanda Jackson.[65]

It wasn't unusual for the *Ozark Jubilee* to veer even farther away from stereotypes of Ozarks music, with guests performing anything from ragtime piano to
hits from the big band era. The Philharmonics, a Springfield African American
ensemble, made frequent appearances on the show singing popular standards
and spirituals. The variety of musical acts owed more to KWTO's tradition of
crossing genres than it did to a conscious network attempt to de-hillbillyize the
Jubilee. But there is some evidence that the show's producers were sensitive to
criticism within an infant television industry that still frowned on low-brow
programming. In fact, recalled one of the *Jubilee's* writers, the wives of ABC
executives disliked the idea of a show with no "class." Despite good ratings and
the increasing popularity of country music television shows in the late 1950s,
ABC looked to de-regionalize the program in the summer of 1957 when the
Ozark Jubilee became the *Country Music Jubilee*. When Oklahoman Norma Jean
joined the cast, she was prohibited from accompanying herself on the guitar.
"They thought it looked too 'country'—too 'hillbilly,'" she remembered. "Seemed
like even back then . . . they always want[ed] to upgrade us a little bit."[66]

The show's two breakout stars reflected its mixture of hillbilly and country
pop sounds. The first was a gangly, toothy, blond grocery-store stock boy from
West Plains, Missouri. Best remembered for his rhinestone Nudie suits and for
introducing the world to Dolly Parton, Porter Wagoner became a bona fide ce-
lebrity when his rendition of "A Satisfied Mind" went to the top of the country
songs chart in 1955. He remained with the program until heading to Nashville
in early 1957, where his hall-of-fame career was highlighted by more than two
decades as star of his own syndicated television show. By the time he left the
Ozark Jubilee, however, Wagoner was playing second fiddle to the show's pint-
sized sensation. Eleven-year-old Georgian Brenda Mae Tarpley made her first
appearance on the program in March 1956 as "Brenda Lee." When "One Step at a
Time" (written by Ozarker Hugh Ashley) became a crossover hit for Lee in 1957,
she left the *Jubilee* cast that summer. After a succession of country and rockabilly
hits in the late 1950s, Lee embarked on a successful pop career with the iconic
"I'm Sorry" and several other charting songs written by Ozarker Ronnie Self.[67]

In addition to singers and musicians, each episode of the *Jubilee* offered
comedy acts and square dancing. Infusing their square-dance sets with the
raucous spirit of country jig dancing, the Promenaders became the nation's
most famous practitioners of a craze sweeping the suburbs and schools in the
1950s. Seamlessly transitioning from rockabilly guitars to square-dance callers
was the person who made the whole thing click, Red Foley. The affable singer
was the key to the *Jubilee's* success, but his personal demons eventually came
back to haunt the production. Plagued by alcoholism and marital problems,
the emcee grew increasingly undependable until he was arrested on federal tax
evasion charges in late 1959. The show continued with guest hosts Eddy Arnold

and Jim Reeves until ABC pulled the plug in September 1960. Ralph Foster's Crossroads Productions gave it one more shot in 1961 with *Five Star Jubilee*, the first color television show created outside the nation's big three metropolises, but this final national program broadcast from the Ozarks got the hook after only six months on the air.[68]

The death of Springfield's entertainment dreams marked the end of the Ozarks as a producer of national television shows, but it didn't signal the end of the Ozarks as the inspiration for them. Just one year after *Five Star Jubilee* left the airwaves, CBS introduced audiences to the Clampetts, a fictional clan of Ozarkers who strike oil on their hardscrabble farm and move to a palatial estate in Southern California. Utilizing a comedic trope as old as civilization itself—the fish out of water—*The Beverly Hillbillies* took the nation by storm. The show's 39.1 Nielsen rating for the 1963–1964 season remains the highest for any television program in the post-Eisenhower era. It would remain in the top twenty of the annual rankings until its final season, 1970–1971. Viewing audiences couldn't get enough, but a little dab of cornpone schtick went a long way for critics, who roundly denounced *The Beverly Hillbillies* as one of the low points in the history of television.[69]

The creator of *The Beverly Hillbillies* was Paul Henning, a veteran writer of radio and television sitcoms who had grown up in Harry S. Truman's hometown of Independence, Missouri. As a youngster Henning had accompanied his Boy Scout troop on a camping trip to the Elk River in far southwestern Missouri, the same area that instilled in young Vance Randolph a lifelong fascination with the Ozarks. Drawing on a similar appreciation for the rustic dignity of rural Ozarkers, Henning became one of Hollywood's best interpreters of the comic interplay between uppity city folk and country bumpkins. The success of *The Beverly Hillbillies* left CBS executives hankering for more of Henning's brand of homestyle hilarity, resulting in the premier of *Petticoat Junction* in September 1963. Based on his wife Ruth's childhood visits to her grandmother's small hotel in Eldon, Missouri ("Gateway to the Lake of the Ozarks"), *Petticoat Junction* was set in the fictional Missouri hamlet of Hooterville. Two years later *Green Acres*, a CBS sitcom on which Henning served as producer, turned the tables on the *Beverly Hillbillies* formula by having a cultured couple from New York City settle amid Hooterville's rustics. With all three shows performing well in the ratings throughout the 1960s, Henning reigned as one of the princes of Hollywood and his fictional Ozarks as a haven for escapism in troubled times.[70]

A Redneck Hong Kong of a Town

Henning appreciated that even a "real hillbilly" understood the comedic gold in the Clampetts' story. "I reckon the more farther a person gets from home," observed backcountry woodcarver Junior Cobb, "the funnier he looks to other people." Cobb's "review" of *The Beverly Hillbillies* appeared in a two-page spread in *TV Guide* in the summer of '63. Though written by Silver Dollar City publicity director Don Richardson as a sly bit of advertising, the final article contained not a single mention of the upstart theme park. But the PR man may have been playing the long game. Cobb's endorsement of the popular sitcom—"They's got a good, funny pergr'm"—and Richardson's persistence eventually brought *The Beverly Hillbillies* to Silver Dollar City in 1969. The convergence of America's most famous fictional Ozarkers and the region's busiest tourism district benefited the Branson area more than it did the aging television show, which would fall victim to CBS's infamous "rural purge" less than two years later. At the time of Hollywood's visit, Branson was still in the early stages of its transformation into a live music town. Its makeover from a place dependent on float fishing expeditions and *Shepherd of the Hills* fans to a clean-cut, Middle American Vegas owed debts to a lot of the developments chronicled earlier, from Lee Mace's Ozark Opry to the creation of Table Rock Lake.[71]

The Branson that Paul Henning found in the summer of the moon landing had not completely forsaken the old charms. The year that the Herschends launched Silver Dollar City, 1960, also marked the first full season of the Old Mill Theatre nearby. The Old Mill featured a nighttime amphitheater production of a dramatic play based on *The Shepherd of the Hills*, which would become the nation's most popular outdoor drama in the 1970s. The Old Mill Theatre and Silver Dollar City signaled a new era in regional tourism and maintained a synergistic relationship. One thing the two venues shared was a musical act. The Mabe brothers (Bob, Lyle, Jim, and Bill) and Bob's father-in-law, Chick Allen, provided musical entertainment at Silver Dollar City's opening day. That summer they had bit parts in the Shepherd of the Hills outdoor drama and played for the audience during intermission.[72]

The most monumental thing the busy Mabes and Allen did in 1960, however, was open a live music show in Branson's community building. It turned out to be the first in a long line of shows that rebranded the little town. Taking their name from the vigilante band that first put Taney County, Missouri, on the national map seventy-five years earlier, the Baldknobbers performed two nights a week at their Hillbilly Jamboree Stage Show. The Mabe brothers, raised on a farm about halfway between Branson and Springfield, made an even greater effort than Lee Mace's Ozark Opry to flash the stereotypical Ozarks image for their out-of-town customers. After all, Chick Allen, former proprietor of a local tourist trap called the Wash Gibbs Free Museum and Ghost Town, was a seasoned hillbilly huckster. Adopting cornpone stage names and coaxing rhythm out of "instruments" like a jawbone (the "jackassaphone"), a washtub, and a washboard, the Baldknobbers featured not one but two band members as hick

Silver Dollar City founder Mary Herschend (third from left) and Paul Henning (middle in dark suit) surrounded by the cast of the *Beverly Hillbillies*, 1969. Courtesy of Silver Dollar City.

comedians in patched overalls, rope belts, and black felt hats. Growing crowds throughout the 1960s forced the show to relocate three times before the band opened their own theater west of town on the highway connecting downtown Branson to Silver Dollar City in 1969.[73]

By the time the Baldknobbers Hillbilly Jamboree opened for business on Missouri Highway 76, it was the second live music theater on "the strip." Two years earlier the Mountain Music Theatre had opened nearby in a small metal building with a concrete floor and 363 secondhand folding chairs. The Mountain Music Theatre was the creation of the Presley family. Patriarch and Ozarks native Lloyd Presley, a former produce deliveryman and fishing guide, was, like the Mabes, a veteran performer, and his son, Gary, provided the requisite blackened-teeth, straw-hat comedy as the hillbilly character Herkimer. The Presleys and Mabes reflected the intricate connections between the country music scene in Springfield and the live shows of Branson. In September 1959, KWTO's decision to abandon its twenty-six-year history of studio acts in favor of record-spinning disc jockeys opened the gates on a stable of performers look-ing for work. Many found their way to Branson. Bob Mabe and Lloyd Presley were both former KWTO musicians, and Presley had appeared on the *Ozark Jubilee* as a member of the Ozark Playboys. Presley and *Jubilee* stalwarts Slim Wilson and Speedy Haworth also took the stage at Herman Mead's Underground Theater near Silver Dollar City in the early 1960s. The Herschends hired *Jubilee* set designer Andy Miller as Silver Dollar City's art director; *Jubilee* writer Don Richardson oversaw the park's publicity for years.[74]

With the foundation laid by the Mabes and Presleys, the Branson strip began to take form after 1970. Throughout the next decade most new music shows followed the proven formula of the established theaters—Ozarks natives singing a mixture of country, bluegrass, and gospel, highlighted by at least one rube comic. The Plummer family from Knob Lick in the eastern Missouri Ozarks began an eighteen-season run in 1973. One year later the re-formed Foggy River Boys opened their own theater on the strip. Led by original Jordanaire Bob Hubbard, the suit-wearing Foggys brought their tight harmonies to a wide range of music, from gospel to pop. Even in the 1970s, a decade that witnessed a broader societal embrace of the sexual revolution, Branson's theaters held to an old fashioned, G-rated standard that seemed not the least bit off-putting to the tens of thousands who sought entertainment in the buckle of the Bible Belt. Whether a legacy of Harold Bell Wright's underlying spiritual message or the product of a more recent conscious Christian conservatism, clean-cut shows leavened with nonsectarian evangelicalism and served with an ample side of overt patriotism became the recipe for the Branson strip.[75]

The Wilkinson Brothers established the last of the original "native" shows in 1981, giving Highway 76 almost a dozen hillbilly jamborees. That same year brought the strip its first outsider production, the Hee Haw Theatre, affiliated with the popular syndicated comic country television show. From this point forward, the growth of the Branson music scene would be dominated by new-comers. In 1983 *Hee Haw* star Roy Clark opened his own theater at a convention center called the Lodge of the Ozarks. It was a watershed moment—the first musical venue launched by a performer whose notoriety extended well beyond the confines of the Ozarks. Before the decade came to a close, half a dozen new music shows had been added to a strip now jammed with "miniature golf courses, go-cart tracks, animal shows, old-timey trains, water slides, . . . and motels built to stand gaudily for five years." This "redneck Hong Kong of a Town" was tailor-made for a joint like the Boxcar Willie Theatre, starring a middle-aged imitation hobo. Less typical was the show headlined by Shoji Tabuchi, a virtuoso Japanese fiddler who had fallen in love with old-time American music after hearing Roy Acuff in concert in Osaka.[76]

By the early 1990s a stampede of past-their-prime country legends threatened to remake Branson in old Nashville's image. Mel Tillis traded the tour bus for a lake house, opening his first Branson show in 1990 and building his own theater two years later. The cavalcade of graying stars who followed him onto the strip included Ray Stevens, Mickey Gilley, Jim Stafford, and Loretta Lynn. Country outlaws Willie Nelson and Merle Haggard shared the Ozark Theatre for a time, and the "man in black" began construction on Cash Country. The jostling of so many stars in such a tiny space created reverberations felt as far away as New York City, prompting the television news program *60 Minutes* to dispatch a crew to southwestern Missouri to see what all the fuss was about. Enamored with the new star wattage in Branson, the December 1991 broadcast gave short shrift to Silver Dollar City and *The Shepherd of the Hills*. But the national exposure for a place already bursting at the seams sparked a frenzy of interest among both tourists and performers. In the first half of 1992, Branson's chamber of commerce received an average of three thousand calls per day, and tourist traffic increased by 50 percent in the next two summer seasons.[77]

Mel Tillis's coy insinuations of the millions to be made on the strip piqued the interest of declining stars from around the country—and not just country stars. After all, it was pop crooner Andy Williams's decision to build his Moon River Theatre in Branson in 1991 that likely caught the attention of *60 Minutes* producers in the first place. In short order a platoon of decidedly non-country performers joined Williams on the strip: Bobby Vinton, Wayne Newton, Yakov Smirnoff, Tony Orlando, and the Rockettes. Even Bob Hope dropped into the Ozarks to try a few one-liners on the aging "Greatest Generation" whose oversized cars clogged the strip. So optimistic were the Herschends that they partnered with Kenny Rogers to build the massive Grand Palace, which brought in a steady stream of headliners from Garth Brooks to Bill Cosby. When Branson and the Moon River Theatre became the butt of jokes on an episode of *The Simpsons* in March 1996, it was a clear sign that the little buttoned-down Vegas in the Shepherd of the Hills Country was now a recognized member of the American pop cultural universe.[78]

Ironically, though, the town's hopes of joining Vegas and Orlando as national tourist destinations had already ebbed by the time Nelson Muntz choked up over an Andy Williams encore. The Branson blitz plateaued in the mid-1990s. Cash Country never got built, Tony Orlando and Wayne Newton barely stayed long enough for the paint to dry on their theaters, and the cavernous Grand Palace couldn't sell enough tickets to keep the doors open. The ten million annual visitors expected by the end of the millennium leveled out into a robust but hardly Orlando-worthy crowd of about half that size. Over the years most of the marquee names left, retired, or died and were replaced by lesser-known talents. The neon skyline in modern Branson no longer advertises the giants who roamed the strip in the early 1990s. Branson remains essentially what it was before Andy Williams and *60 Minutes*: a popular regional destination for Middle Americans within a day's drive—only now without the homegrown musical acts. By 2021 only Presleys' Country Jubilee maintained a direct link to the origins of the Highway 76 strip.[79]

The Many Faces of Ozarks Tourism

While Branson celebrated an antimodernist sensibility that appealed to a wide swath of the populace in the 1960s and 1970s, up the White River valley an old resort town underwent a makeover that revived its financial fortunes and made for strange bedfellows. With its narrow, twisting streets and bungalows perched on steep hillsides, Eureka Springs had never been a typical backwoods burg. A retreat for artists, poets, and others who rejected convention, Eureka Springs at the dawn of the space age awaited its next dreamer with a plan for remaking the town. In stepped Gerald L. K. Smith, an aging, anti-Semitic publisher from California who purchased a Victorian mansion and set about building a little Christian-themed tourist empire. After commissioning the building of a seventy-foot-tall concrete Jesus on Magnetic Mountain, Smith embarked on his most ambitious undertaking: the creation of an outdoor amphitheater production of the last days of Christ. The Great Passion Play featured more than two hundred professional and amateur actors when it premiered in 1968. By the mid-1970s Smith's Sacred Arts Complex boasted a Bible museum, the Christ Only Art Gallery, and a tram tour of biblical landmark replicas called the New Holy Land.[80]

The 1970s also saw an influx of a different variety in Eureka Springs as denizens of the counterculture flocked to the old spa town and to rural retreats across the Ozarks. Smith may not have seen eye to eye with them, but his reinvention of Eureka Springs undoubtedly paid off for local officials and entrepreneurs. In less than a decade after his arrival, Eureka Springs became the number-one destination of tourists in the Arkansas Ozarks.[81] But Eureka Springs didn't feature what many tourists came to the Ozarks in search of. "They want to see real hillbillies who pick the guitar, play the fiddle, and sing the old traditional ballads," concluded Otto Ernest Rayburn. "We have killed the goose that laid the golden egg." The mountaineer image was a crucial element of heritage tourism in the Ozarks, even if the frenetic modernization of the postwar era was thinning the ranks of backwoods Ozarkers. The folk revival inspired wistful ruminations on the remnants of a seemingly ancient world, books filled with hauntingly nostalgic photographs—maudlin epitaphs like *Ozark Log Cabin Folks: The Way They Were* and *Ozark Mountain Folk: These Were the Last*. The revival's siren song lured disenchanted and idealistic Baby Boomers back to the land, where many of them formed unlikely bonds with the last of the mountain folk. The same primitivist lament invigorated the era's tourism industry, spawning two new attractions in the very year that Gerald L. K. Smith unveiled his Great Passion Play.[82]

In the little town of Hardy, the Arkansaw Traveller Folk Theatre featured actual Ozarks natives picking the guitar and playing the fiddle while recreating a mythical encounter between an urbane adventurer and a backcountry squatter, all for the entertainment of midwestern tourists and retirees. The show's most unforgettable performer was Neal Crow, a coon hunter, cattle rancher, and root digger by choice and janitor by necessity who brought the squatter to life three nights a week every summer. "Where's this road go?" asked the spiffily dressed straight man. "I been here pert near twenty year," the squatter retorted, "and it ain't never went nowhere that I could tell." In the heyday of the national play in the late 1800s, urban audiences usually saw the traveler emerge victorious from the verbal sparring match, but on Ozarks soil in the late twentieth century it was Crow's squatter who always carried the day. Across the Arkansas hills a more ambitious undertaking embraced hillbilly caricature.[83]

Since the 1930s cartoonist Al Capp had entertained the nation with his hillbilly comic strip *Li'l Abner*. Hoping to emulate the success of Silver Dollar City, a team of investors in Harrison, Arkansas, convinced Capp to license the use of his fictional characters to a new theme park built alongside a winding two-lane highway ten miles south of town. While Dogpatch, U.S.A. featured a kiddie train, roller coaster, and other carnival rides typical of theme parks, its most distinctive characteristic was the troupe of costumed actors portraying the residents of Dogpatch. Estimates of the park's economic impact were overblown, and the decision to build a real-life snow skiing lodge next door proved both farcical and financially unwise. Dogpatch, U.S.A.'s remote location may have lent it an air of authenticity, but it proved a drag on attendance, especially after the artist and his comic strip bid farewell to the public in 1977. By the time Dogpatch, U.S.A. shuttered for good in the early 1990s, Abner Yokum, Daisy Mae Scragg, and the rest of Capp's creations were but dim memories in American popular culture.[84]

Al Capp had frequently used *Lil' Abner* to poke fun at the pretensions and vapidity of the greedy upper class—not unlike Paul Henning's satirical use of the Clampetts. But social commentary wasn't the order of the day for the theme park. Visitors at the Arkansaw Traveller Folk Theatre went back home with fond memories of rural Ozarker Neal Crow. If Dogpatch, U.S.A. claimed a most influential employee, it was probably woodcarver Harold Enlow, whose lanky, floppy-hatted figurines inspired how-to books and earned him recognition as the world's foremost hillbilly caricaturist. What the two tourist enterprises shared in common, however, was an antimodern portrayal of an imagined past that is more authentic and desirable than the present. This conceit of the folk revival fueled most all the region's touristic undertakings in the 1960s and 1970s, or at least the ones taking shape somewhere away from a lakeshore. The same nostalgic spirit infused a rekindling of the folk festival. In the Ozarks no place became more intimately connected with the revival of the festival than Stone County, Arkansas, and its quaint seat, Mountain View.[85]

Among the poorest, least populated, and hilliest places in the region, Stone County may also have been the favorite destination of folk song collectors in the post–World War II years—from John Quincy Wolf Jr. and other regionalists to national figures like Alan Lomax. Impoverished Stone County had one major asset in the heart of the folk revival. Born James Morris on a farm in 1907, Jimmy Driftwood was a longtime teacher and administrator at the public school in the tiny hamlet of Timbo. He was also an inveterate songwriter and aspiring performer who at the age of fifty made his way to a Nashville tryout in front of producer and native Ozarker Don Warden and his partner, former KWTO musician Chet Atkins. Specializing in songs that put new lyrics to age-old folk melodies, Driftwood's timing could not have been better. The Arkansawyer's first album of "newly discovered American folk songs" was released in 1958. In another era Driftwood's lack of polish might have banished his music to obscurity, but the runaway popularity of the Kingston Trio's "Tom Dooley" that year launched the folk revival. Johnny Horton's rendition of Driftwood's "Battle of New Orleans"—set to the melody of an old fiddle tune called "The Eighth of January"—became the most-played record in North America in 1959 and won Driftwood a Grammy Award for Song of the Year. No one-hit wonder, Driftwood's folky songs—"The Wilderness Road," "Tennessee Stud," "Billy Yank and Johnny Reb"—became hit recordings for other country artists. At the height of his success, in September 1959, the Ozarker was credited with half a dozen songs on *Billboard*'s country Top 40. With gigs at the Grand Ole Opry and Carnegie Hall, Driftwood rode the folk revival to stardom.[86]

By 1963, his moment in the spotlight seemingly over, Driftwood had returned home to Timbo. It was at this moment that organizers of a local craft fair solicited his help for a music show, confident that Driftwood's Nashville connections could bring a headliner to Mountain View. Driftwood instead gathered a crew of "timber cutters, farmers, [and] housewives" for the first annual Arkansas Folk Festival, in April 1963, which attracted folk enthusiasts from as far away as Chicago. Among the "plain people of the hills" who stood behind the microphone at that first festival were "granny singers" Ollie Gilbert and Almeda Riddle, both of whom became minor celebrities on the national folk circuit. With her oaken voice and mastery of dozens of songs, Riddle came to rival Driftwood as the regional bearer of a cherished but endangered sound. In the years that followed, the Arkansas Folk Festival mushroomed into one of the nation's most popular old-time-music celebrations, attracting crowds of more than one hundred thousand visitors in the halcyon days of the early 1970s.[87]

The throngs are a distant memory now, but the festival continues to draw people to Stone County at about the time the dogwoods bloom each spring. The frenetic strains of the more "modern" sound of bluegrass fill the air on the courthouse square in Mountain View these days, but one mile to the north the tunes and styles of the old-timers remain the order of the day at an institution that emerged from the rip-roaring success of the Arkansas Folk Festival. After years of lobbying and political maneuvering, a three-million-dollar grant from the federal Economic Development Administration funded a Mountain View center that would train younger generations of hill folks to preserve their disappearing music and crafts. By the time the Ozark Folk Center came to fruition in 1973, however, financial setbacks and political compromises had transformed the institution into a state-operated living history museum and music show geared toward the tourism market.[88] A popular draw in the 1970s and 1980s, the Ozark Folk Center State Park, along with nearby Blanchard Springs Caverns, helped turn remote little Mountain View into one of the premier tourist destinations in the southern Ozarks. But the park faced obstacles to its long-term health and growth. As aging local artisans and musicians retired or died, they were most often replaced not by other native Ozarkers but by newcomers to the region typically attracted to the area by a countercultural fascination with the old ways of the hills. It was the newcomers who mostly kept the old ways from dying, but the loss of regional authenticity embodied in the callused hands, sun-faded bonnets, and backwoods drawls of the Ozarkers who had lived the days of one-room schools and mule-drawn plows proved a blow to the spirit of the center.

Whatever magic elixir the park and its old-timers once possessed was largely gone by the twenty-first century. It must have seemed as if the modern world had finally wrung the neck of Rayburn's goose. But modernity had made its appearance long before the new millennium, even in a place like Stone County. At the moment the Ozark Folk Center opened its doors in 1973, the shiny metallic chicken house had replaced the creek-side corn patch as the local symbol of farm life. It wasn't handicrafts like quilting and white oak basketmaking that put money in the hands of Stone Countians. The typical worker spent a long shift operating a sewing machine at the Blanchard Shirt Factory or turning out assembly-line salad bowls on a lathe at the Ozark Woodworking Company.[89] Beyond the quaint court square and the consciously anachronistic confines of the Ozark Folk Center, a new era had dawned.

7   FARM TO FACTORY

Visitors to the remote farm of Slay and Mabel Holliday may have wondered why the couple had decided to abandon civilization. Slay and Mabel were young migrants from the rural Ozarks when they met at the Pontiac Motor Company in Michigan in the 1920s. Before the Depression had time to claim their jobs, they "moved back some twenty years or more to live the agrarian life," swapping a slick '28 Pontiac Roadster for forty acres and a house more than a dozen miles southeast of Branson. In the rugged White River Hills with no automobile, no electricity, and no running water, the Hollidays did little more than survive the Depression. But the years on the other side brought rapid change and allowed the Hollidays to reclaim some of the amenities and opportunities they had given up a decade earlier when they decided to return to familiar, if isolated, surroundings.[1]

During the war years, high agricultural prices finally produced dividends on the farm. The Hollidays grew tomatoes for a local canning factory and milked a small herd of dairy cows, selling the cream and using the leftover blue john (skim milk) to fatten hogs. Slay received a tobacco allotment of almost two acres and funneled his newfound profits into the purchase of Hereford cattle and additional land. A used Chevy pickup rendered the community of Pine Top less remote and isolated. By the time a rural electric cooperative ran power lines to the house in 1948, the Holliday farm was generating almost three thousand dollars in annual sales. But rejoining the modern world came at a price for rural families. There were things to buy: refrigerators, ranges, washing machines, milk coolers, and, in a few years, televisions and air conditioners. The immediate postwar years promised a bright future for rural Ozarkers like the Hollidays, but declining commodity prices and increased consumer spending spelled the end of the general family farm, that romantic icon of Americana that flourishes more endearingly in collective memory than it ever did in real life.[2]

They may have lived in the orbit of the Shepherd of the Hills Country, but it wasn't the tourism industry to which the Hollidays turned for sustenance. To supplement stagnant agricultural earnings, in 1953 Slay took a job at a cheese factory in Branson, working six days a week during the heavy season from April to November. Mabel joined him in the manufacturing labor force a couple of years later when she hired on at a new garment factory. In the 1950s their teenage children followed the wheat harvests from Oklahoma to the Dakotas, picked apples in the Pacific Northwest, and tried their hands as assembly line workers in Wichita aircraft factories. Even nearby Hollister High School seemed to know the score. The little school's curriculum didn't prepare students to stay—it pushed them away. The Holliday children joined the first generation of rural Ozarkers of modest means to go to college. None came back to rural Pine Top, and in 1968 Slay and Mabel sold the farm and moved into town.[3]

The New Deal and World War II laid the foundation for an economic transformation that took shape in rapid fashion after 1945. A region long characterized by independent farm families was swept up in the nation's emerging agribusiness economy. Rural Ozarkers were pragmatists, and they experimented with new farming trends as the region groped for its position in a national marketplace shaped by the dictates of integration. Row crops, grains, and orchards gave way to pastures and hayfields, livestock, and poultry. General diversified farmers like the Hollidays ceded ground to fewer and larger specialized operators. The shrinking farm population produced a massive pool of surplus labor, unleashing an unprecedented exodus from the region and attracting cost-cutting manufacturers who found a new frontier filled with hardworking, underemployed country folks. Images of backcountry rustics continued to define the Ozarks in the national discourse, but the stories of farm flight and factories were more central to everyday life in the region than the stories of fiddlers and foxhunters.

Down on the Farm

The quarter century following World War II witnessed nothing short of a revolution in the American countryside, a transformation characterized by the rise of agribusiness and the government policies that cultivated it. The face of this new reality was the Agricultural Extension Service's county agent, who encouraged productivity, efficiency, and profitability. Extension agents were simply the vanguard of a drastically increased federal presence in rural America. The Farmers Home Administration lent money for rural houses and farm expansion, and the Agricultural Stabilization and Conservation Service continued to pay farmers to take marginal land out of production. For a decade and a half after the war, the federal government also operated the Veterans' Agricultural Training Program (VATP). A creation of the Servicemen's Readjustment Act of 1944 (the "G.I. Bill of Rights"), the VATP provided monthly payments and weekly classes to farm-dwelling veterans. Once they used up their VATP eligibility, most joined the exodus from the farm.[4]

One G.I. who stuck it out was Walter Severs, a young navy veteran who returned home to Stone County, Arkansas. The one hundred dollars he received each month from the VATP subsidized a hand-to-mouth existence on the small farm he and his brother bought in the White River Hills. Severs made use of the vocational education shop at the local high school to build and repair farm equipment and learned the benefits of commercial fertilizer from his instructor. When Severs married Dorothy Davis in 1948, the newlyweds used his VATP checks to set up house with a new refrigerator and gas range. By the time his three and a half years in the program came to an end, he had formed a partnership with his father-in-law, the two of them purchasing a stock truck for hauling hogs and cattle to market and a new International Farmall M tractor with a turning plow, disc, and cultivator. Walter Severs would remain on the land into the twenty-first century.[5]

Tractors, automobiles, and household appliances cost money. Acquisitiveness was no novel concept in the region, but even on the backroads of the most rugged and remote areas of the Ozarks, consumer spending ramped up in the years following World War II. The nation's unprecedented affluence in the 1950s and 1960s assumed a somewhat muted form in most of the hill country, but it was obvious to any observer that there was more money in circulation than ever before. Contrasting rural Hickory County, Missouri, of the mid-1950s with its Depression-era version, sociologist Art Gallaher Jr. observed that farm families had "developed expectations of a constantly expanding standard of living" and dismissed as "archaic" the conditions of the late 1930s. Farm families gradually abandoned generations-old efforts to grow and butcher almost everything they consumed. Old-timers with the Depression burned into their memories continued to raise massive gardens, but by the 1960s hog killings and sorghum makings had become sources of curiosity and nostalgia, not integral signs of the seasons. Widespread specialization and commercialization were also new developments in the Ozarks. When the U.S. Census Bureau classified farms into types in 1940, well over half of them in the Ozarks were semi-subsistence farms in which the bulk of production was consumed by the household. On the cusp of the rise of agribusiness, most rural Ozarkers were ill-equipped to compete and survive in the coming age of commercial farming and consumerism.[6]

Between 1940 and 1969 the number of farms in the United States, and in the Ozarks, decreased by more than half. A major reason was that agricultural payments failed to keep pace with wages and prices in other segments of the economy. In the Ozarks there were other factors at work as well. Wide swaths of the region's most rugged lands were simply poorly suited for anything other than scratch farming. In the interior Ozarks more than one-fifth of all farmland in 1940 was no longer used for agricultural purposes thirty years later. In effect, then, the war years and the quarter century that followed purged the Ozarks of its poor, semi-subsistence farming populace, the very class that came to define the region in the national consciousness. The Hollidays and other marginal families who stayed on the land did so by following the migrant labor trails for a time before finding off-farm jobs in manufacturing or tourism in a reinvented postwar Ozarks.[7]

The challenging terrain and infertile soils of much of the Ozarks produced a diversified, if not always profitable, farming populace in the era before World War II. The story in the postwar Ozarks, however, centered on increasing homogenization as the region found its niche in the national marketplace. The two decades following the war completed the demise of the row cropper and truck farmer in the hills. With only a few localized exceptions, commercial production of tomatoes, apples, and grapes declined to insignificance by the 1960s. Even in Adair County, the "Strawberry Capital of Oklahoma," farmers left the ground fruit business within a few years. Northwestern Arkansas canneries like Springdale's Steele Canning Company—with its Popeye brand spinach and Wagon Master Western Beans (sponsor of the Beatles' first American tour)— kept some farmers growing vegetables until it sold out in the 1970s. Steele's competitor, Allens Inc. of Siloam Springs, survived almost two decades into the twenty-first century but imported its vegetables from places well outside the Ozarks.[8]

The ubiquitous cornfield, once a common site from the creek bottoms of the Boston Mountains to the prairies of the Springfield Plain, gradually receded into memory as well. Government programs paid farmers to take corn out of cultivation, and the tractor's steady replacement of mules and horses eliminated the need for grain as livestock feed. The trip to the mill with a "turn of corn" was a thing of the past for most Ozarkers even by the onset of the Depression. Water-powered Dillard Mill on Huzzah Creek in Crawford County, Missouri, was an anachronistic oddity when it closed its doors in 1956. Cotton experienced an even quicker and more thorough demise. Almost 90 percent of the Ozarks cotton crop disappeared during the 1950s, and federal legislation allowing farmers to sell or lease their cotton acreage allotments to tillers elsewhere in the same state finished off the crop in the 1960s. The shuttering of the region's last cotton gin, in Quitman, Arkansas, in 1969, provided an epitaph for the hill country's contribution to Deep South agriculture.[9] The future of farming in the Ozarks was in livestock, dairy, and poultry. Some of the region's earliest nineteenth-century explorers had predicted that the salvation of the Ozarks lay not in plows but cows. Ozarkers are a stubborn lot. It took a century and a half to heed the advice.

The Switzerland of America

As the postwar era dawned in the Ozarks, no frontier in farming seemed quite so promising as milking cows. Before the widespread availability of electrical refrigeration, dairy operations were small, local, and farm-based. In the early twentieth century Springfield's Henry LeCompte milked a small herd of cows twice daily and then took to the streets in his two-horse wagon, ringing a bell to announce his arrival and pouring warm milk into the customer's own container. Up the Wire Road near Marshfield, a Massachusetts native named Edmund Hosmer developed Missouri's largest farm-based butter operation. Hiring half a dozen men to hand milk a herd of some eighty Jerseys, the Hosmer family made use of a mechanical cream separator and marketed butter along the Frisco Railroad. Dairy profits put two daughters through Vassar College and a son through the University of Michigan.[10]

The Hosmers eventually closed the butter business and began selling cream to a local butter-making factory called a creamery, an important initial step into a regional dairy industry. The establishment of the Ozark region's first permanent creamery in Springfield, in 1910, provided a market for farmers as far away as northern Arkansas. The University of Missouri College of Agriculture also promoted dairy farming through farmers' institutes and its experiment station at Mountain Grove. In 1911 the Frisco Railroad made the scene and hired its first dairy agent, Marshfield attorney and farmer A. J. McDowell. Praised years later as "the man who began commercial dairying in the Ozarks," McDowell traveled the rails in a special demonstration car, giving instructional lectures and helping dairymen procure Holsteins and Guernseys from Wisconsin. Within a few years Frisco cars brimmed with shiny five- and ten-gallon cans collected from hundreds of cream stations across the region and destined for butter manufacturers in "the most highly developed dairy section of any place in the southern United States."[11]

But southwestern Missouri was still a far cry from living up to the moniker bestowed by a hopeful state dairy commissioner: "the Switzerland of America." (The *Frisco Employees' Magazine* later tried the label "Denmark of the World," but it didn't stick, either, maybe because the world already had a Denmark.) After World War I, however, the region began to churn with dairy activity. Nothing better signaled southwestern Missouri's arrival as a serious player on the American dairy stage than the day in the summer of 1923 when some eight hundred automobiles clogged the court square in Mount Vernon for a public meeting with representatives from the Carnation Milk Products Company. Within a year 750 farmers supplied Carnation's new condensing plant with more than forty tons of milk per day. The Pet Milk Company built its own condensery in Neosho in 1927. But it was the building of Producers Creamery Company's plant in Springfield the next year that prepared the industry for its explosive growth in the 1940s and 1950s. A cooperative operation affiliated with the Missouri Farmers Association, the factory was the largest and most diversified in the region to date, with the capacity to market milk directly to the public and manufacture cheese, butter, condensed milk, and powdered milk.[12]

Escalating wartime demand prompted a boom in dairy production that built momentum for a decade following the end of World War II. The 1940s alone brought twelve new dairy plants to southwestern Missouri, and the region's emergence as a new dairy hot spot attracted interest from outside investors. The Illinois-based Milnot Company built an evaporated and condensed milk factory in the little Missouri-Oklahoma border town of Seneca in 1948, and two years later Wisconsin's L. D. Schreiber Cheese Company opened a factory in Carthage. Nationally known corporations Kraft and Armour also expanded their footprints in the region. The value of dairy products produced on Ozarks farms almost quadrupled between 1939 and 1949. An examination of the dairy industry in southwestern Missouri in the late 1950s found thirteen Grade A distributors of bottled milk and twenty-nine manufacturing plants, most of them producing American or processed cheese. By the mid-1950s milk money accounted for more than one-third of all agricultural sales in southwestern Missouri.[13]

The rise of dairy also stimulated allied industries. No single firm benefited from the boom more than the Paul Mueller Company of Springfield. Established in 1940 as a sheet metal fabricator, the business began catering to the dairy industry in 1946 by crafting vats, tanks, and other stainless-steel equipment for cheese factories and farms. Former Mueller employees launched their own fabricating businesses, making Springfield "Tank Town U.S.A." But the rapid adoption of new technologies like cooling tanks and electric milking machines (some thirteen thousand in the Ozarks by the end of the 1950s) pressured dairy farmers to invest heavily or get out of the business. Those who could swing a loan built modern milking barns of concrete block and masonry—"the heights of progress" in the 1950s. Those unable or unwilling to scale the heights either exited the dairy business or continued to sell less-lucrative manufacturing (Grade C) milk to cheese plants and other dairy factories.[14]

By 1963 slightly more than half of the roughly twenty thousand dairy farms in the interior Ozarks had made the jump to Grade A status. The typical Grade A dairy farmer milked cows in a three-stanchion barn built from a blueprint provided by the extension service and equipped with an automated pipeline system that pumped milk into a cooling tank, where it remained until a tanker driver arrived to pick it up and deliver it to the plant or a receiving station. Dairy manufacturing had already begun to consolidate, but 1963 found a still-vibrant industry. The eighteen regional cheese factories were comprised of small-town, independent plants in places like Greenfield and Koshkonong, Missouri, as well

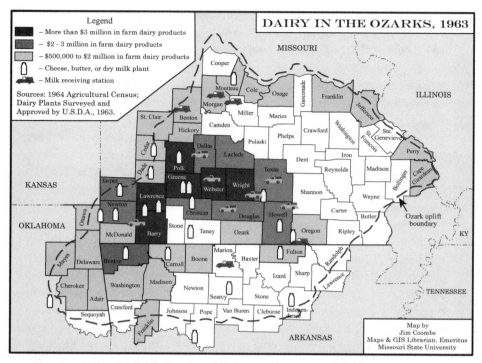

Dairy in the Ozarks, 1963. Courtesy of Jim Coombs, Missouri State University, Springfield.

as corporate giants like Kraft Foods, which maintained eleven receiving stations scattered from Versailles, Missouri, to Yellville, Arkansas, and cheese plants in Springfield and in Bentonville and Berryville, Arkansas.[15]

In an age when farms were disappearing at an alarming rate, the success of the dairy industry prompted celebration in the Ozarks. The chamber of commerce of Monett launched its first dairy show and carnival in 1949. Three years later Mansfield—where Laura and Almanzo Wilder had been early supporters of dairy—celebrated its inaugural Butter Day. By the mid-1950s Missouri had cracked the top ten among milk-producing states and had ascended to number two on the list of manufacturers of American cheese. But this marked a pinnacle in rankings in relation to older and more-established dairy states like Wisconsin and Minnesota. The number of dairy farms in the Ozarks fell by more than half in the 1960s, and dairy would never recover its briefly prominent place in the region's agricultural hierarchy. By 1978 dairies accounted for only one in fifteen farms across the region.[16]

The Ozarks made great strides but never rivaled older dairy regions with stronger infrastructures. It could be that the small farms of the region were simply unable to keep pace with an industry built on rapid change and expansion, or that the drive toward national marketplace efficiency was just too much to overcome. Still, Ozarks farmers held their own into the late twentieth century, selling more than $300 million worth of milk in 1986 (14 percent of the region's agricultural output) before a rapid fall in the early twenty-first century. Today the dairy industry has become little more than an afterthought in the Ozarks. The 2017 census found only 645 dairies in the entire region, barely more than 1 percent of all farms. The decline in dairy manufacturing has been just as precipitous.[17]

Like dairy farming, hog raising exercises only the faintest impact on the region's agricultural ledger today. It has been a drastic loss of status for the animal that served as a staple of the typical Ozarker's diet into the mid-twentieth century, the beast whose feral cousin provided the Ozark region's largest university its mascot. In 1939 the money generated by hog sales in the Ozarks ($9.3 million) compared favorably with receipts from cattle sales ($14.1 million) and dairy ($12.1 million). In the postwar years, however, the Corn Belt came to dominate the industry in the middle of the continent. The extension service's promotion of feeder pig farming in the 1960s and 1970s produced a minor resurgence in swine production, but few farmers in the Ozarks followed the industry's adoption of concentrated animal feeding operations—raising pigs in the kinds of large metal buildings that became common practice years earlier in the poultry industry.[18]

Big Chicken

The poultry industry provided the vertically integrated blueprint that the pork industry would eventually emulate. In the process it made a rapid climb to the top of the ladder as the region's top money-producing commodity, but it did so at the expense of the independence of the hundreds of farmers whose livelihoods depend on caretaking the genetically engineered birds so crucial to the fortunes of some of the most powerful companies in the Ozarks. Big poultry's social, economic, and demographic impacts have proven even more revolutionary than the industry's business model. Almost every crucial development of the past half century—from the rise of Walmart to the ascendance of corporatist conservatism, from the Hispanic population explosion to the emergence of the modern trucking industry—traces at least a few of its roots back to the meat-producing empire brought about through the efforts of Tyson Foods and other corporations birthed in the region.

At the turn of the twentieth century, hobbyists debated the relative merits of Barred Plymouth Rocks and Rhode Island Reds, but poultry remained the domain of women—a favorite subject of Laura Ingalls Wilder's *Missouri*

Ruralist columns—and thus well outside the zone of "serious" agriculture. Baby steps toward a mature poultry industry took place in 1911 when the University of Missouri established its State Poultry Experiment Station just outside the Frisco town of Mountain Grove, and Arkansas followed suit three years later in Fayetteville. Springfield emerged as the "center of the poultry industry in the Ozarks" after World War I, with Frisco headquarters processing more than thirty-six hundred carloads of eggs and live and dressed poultry in 1926. Yet, by the time the United States entered World War II, the heart of the industry had shifted to northwestern Arkansas.[19]

Edith Glover's successful return on a batch of mail-order White Wyandottes prompted her father to build what may have been Arkansas's first stand-alone broiler house on his Cave Springs farm in the early 1920s. One of several orchardists who followed the Glovers into poultry raising would become the "Father of the Broiler Industry" in the Ozark region. Using a kerosene-fueled incubator to hatch his own chicks and coal-fired stoves to warm them on his small farm outside of Springdale, Jeff D. Brown began supplying chicks to neighbors, mixing his own feeds, and experimenting with improved breeds. By 1929 Brown's business was promising enough that a local banker loaned him the down payment on a ten-thousand-egg electric incubator, the centerpiece for his Depression-defying hatchery and feed mill. He eventually expanded his reach into southwestern Missouri, and by the 1960s Brown's Ledbrest breed was the most common chicken grown to be slaughtered (broiler) in the United States.[20]

Most birds raised in the Ozarks were shipped live to distant markets until mid-century, making northwestern Arkansas a premier center for interstate haulers such as Jones Truck Lines and Willis Shaw Express and leading to an outsize role for truckers in the region's industry. Charles L. George, founder of the processor today known as George's Inc., established his first hatchery in 1930 to supply chicks to the farmers whose birds he'd been hauling to St. Louis. Even the Ozark region's most recognizable name in trucking initially catered to the poultry business. Native Ozarker Johnnie Bryan (J. B.) Hunt was working as a truck driver when, in 1961, he invented a machine that bagged the rice hulls that poultry farmers used to cover the floors of their broiler houses. Hauling truckloads of this "chicken litter" from the rice fields of eastern Arkansas to the state's poultry districts, he eventually headquartered his trucking company midway between Springdale and Rogers. By 1990 the J. B. Hunt Company was the largest trucking outfit in the nation.[21]

No trucker's name became more synonymous with the poultry industry around the world than John Tyson. The native Kansan moved his wife, Mildred, and young son, Don, to Springdale in 1931 to find work as a chicken hauler. For several years Tyson was just one of dozens of wildcat truckers who bought birds from local farmers, trusting he would find a buyer in a distant city. On a

Don Tyson (second from right) and employees at Tyson's Feed & Hatchery, Springdale, Arkansas, 1957. Courtesy Shiloh Museum of Ozark History/Tyson Foods, Inc. Collection (S-86-109-78).

1936 trip to Chicago—a journey that has become part of the company's lore—Tyson turned a profit of almost fifty cents a bird on five hundred chickens. Keeping fifteen dollars for the return trip, he wired the remainder back home to Mildred with instructions to have another load waiting on him when he arrived in Arkansas. The wide-open, Wild West world of the poultry industry was made for people like John Tyson, gamblers with little to lose and the world to gain. Not long after, Tyson joined the growing ranks of hatchery owners in northwestern Arkansas.[22]

The early days of the chicken business broke just as many gamblers as it rewarded, but the good fortunes generated by World War II were more than a wildcatter like John Tyson could have hoped for. Federal rationing did not extend to poultry, and the average American's consumption of chicken almost doubled during the war years. Northwestern Arkansas became a leading supplier for Chicago, St. Louis, and other midwestern markets, while skyrocketing chicken numbers attracted national processors to the Ozarks. By the mid-1940s

Swanson, Armour, Swift, and Campbell Soup operated plants in Springdale, capital of the Ozarks poultry industry. The end of that decade found Arkansas ranked fourth among the states in the production of broilers, and the northwestern counties of Benton and Washington ranked third and fourth, respectively, among the country's producers.[23]

The system of vertical integration had been in development on the Delmarva Peninsula since the 1920s, but only after 1950 did it take shape in the Ozarks. In less than two decades, firms like Tyson's would gain control over every stage in the process, from the hens that laid the eggs for hatcheries to the trucks that transported frozen meats to supermarkets. They would do so amid a volatile market that bred cutthroat competition among companies and reduced farmers to little more than bird caretakers. Behind the phenomenal growth of Tyson Foods (as the company has been known since 1971) and other major processors in the Ozarks, northwestern Arkansas became the nerve center for the nation's fastest-growing agricultural enterprise.

Several factors played into the growth of the industry in the Ozarks: the postwar spread of electricity; the synergy of university researchers, extension agents, and industry leaders; and advances in genetics. Perhaps most importantly, northwestern Arkansas was home to a group of savvy entrepreneurs who understood the importance of marketing and the power of political connections. First among them was Roy Ritter, a hatchery owner who opened the region's first specialty fried chicken restaurant in 1947, a business that beat Kentucky Fried Chicken to the franchise punch. The AQ Chicken House survives today only at its original Springdale location, but Ritter influenced the trajectory of the industry in more lasting ways. He spearheaded the creation of the Arkansas Poultry Federation as a lobbying agency and demonstrated the possibilities of political action when he chaired Orval Faubus's successful 1954 gubernatorial campaign. Faubus remained a steadfast supporter of the industry throughout his dozen years in office. On the national level, Fayetteville's J. William Fulbright, whose father was an early poultry investor, ran interference for the industry from his seat on the U.S. Senate's agriculture committee.[24]

The late 1940s and 1950s saw a significant increase in poultry plants in the region as entrepreneurs capitalized on growing bird production and a plentiful supply of cheap labor. Facilities for butchering chickens or turkeys became symbols of progress for small towns across the Ozarks in this golden age for independent processors and farmers. In 1957, the year that John Tyson began constructing his first processing plant in Springdale, Congress passed a bill mandating federal inspection of all processing facilities. The increased costs associated with inspections drove many small operators out of the industry, but more than anything it was poultry's volatile market that tightened profit margins and spurred consolidation.[25]

In the two decades after 1940, the number of chickens marketed in the Ozarks increased by 1,500 percent. The poultry market's wild price swings could bank-rupt a firm and a farmer in a matter of weeks. Conservative corporations like Armour and Campbell Soup exited the industry, creating a vacuum filled by the most aggressive "integrators," or fully vertically integrated firms. The most effective way to expand—and perhaps the only way to survive—was to buy out other companies. Acquiring several competitors as well as a lucrative chicken nuggets contract from McDonald's, Tyson Foods scratched its way into the *Fortune* 500 in the early 1980s. The Springdale-based company had already become the country's top producer by 1989 when its takeover of North Carolina's Holly Farms gave it more than a quarter of the U.S. poultry market. Tyson's buyout of Iowa Beef Processors in 2000 made it the world's largest meat producer. In 2017 Tyson's one hundred plants and 114,000 employees generated $41.3 billion in sales, 22 percent more than its nearest competitor. George's Inc., Simmons Foods, and OK Foods—headquartered in Springdale, Siloam Springs, and Fort Smith, respectively—all ranked among the country's top forty meat producers.[26]

The poultry producing behemoth has been criticized and sued over the years for any number of transgressions, from environmental degradation to allegations of bribing high-ranking government officials. And Tyson Foods and other integrators have never been hesitant to throw their weight around to stem the tide of unionization. The low rate of union membership among modern processing plant workers owes as much to demographic change as it does to anti-organizing efforts. No impact of the modern poultry industry is more visible around the country than the transformation of its labor force to a largely Hispanic one. On the heels of a round of anti-union campaigns by Tyson and other processors, President Ronald Reagan signed into law the Immigra-tion Reform and Control Act (IRCA) of 1986. Though initially conceived as a bill prohibiting businesses from hiring undocumented immigrants, the IRCA would, ironically, open the floodgates to the employment of both documented and undocumented workers.[27]

For corporations like Tyson Foods, historian Brent E. Riffel observes, the IRCA proved a godsend, "giving it a revolving supply of workers, most of whom . . . were reluctant to join a union and unwilling to complain about tough work-ing conditions or company violations." Attracted to northwestern Arkansas by plentiful jobs, cheap rent, and personnel offices that rarely checked immigration papers, Latinas/os from California, Mexico, and Central America began pouring into the region in the early 1990s, an immigration wave that catapulted Arkansas to first place among all states in Hispanic growth in the decade. Within a few years Latinas/os composed as much as 70 percent of the workforce at process-ing plants in a region that had long been among the nation's least racially and ethnically diverse.[28]

From the farmers' angle, however, the most revolutionary outcome of the rise of the modern poultry industry has been a loss of independence due to vertical integration. Modern contract farming—whereby a fully integrated processing company supplies a farmer with chicks or poults (young turkeys) and then pays the farmer a predetermined price for the grown birds—was a product of poultry's volatile market. It was a risky proposition to purchase a house full of chicks, feed them on grain propped up by federal price supports, and then face the prospect of selling them in the unregulated marketplace. On the other side, integrators required a steady supply of birds for their plants. Though they assumed more risk with contracts, integrators were freed from the necessity of growing their own birds on corporate farms and received greater profits during market upswings. In essence, according to Riffel, "farmers traded independence . . . for less income but greater certainty."[29]

By the 1960s most poultry farmers were under contract to an integrated producer. Growers provided shelter and water for birds and paid to heat and cool their buildings, while the integrator supplied chicks or poults, feed, and medicines. A union's characterization of contract farming as a "modern form of indentured servitude" may be on the hyperbolic side, but it is no stretch to compare modern poultry farmers to landowning sharecroppers—bird caretakers who are in effect employees of the integrators but without access to insurance and workers' compensation. In the early 1960s farmers in northwestern Arkansas organized and attempted to negotiate more favorable contracts. Tyson and Arkansas Valley Industries of Dardanelle pushed back with such questionable tactics that the federal Packers and Stockyards Administration (PSA) launched an investigation culminating in a 1965 federal trial charging the integrated firms with discriminating against and harassing growers. A PSA report referring to the growers as "nothing more than poorly-paid employees" verified that processing companies blacklisted and cancelled the contracts of those who spearheaded the union's efforts. Nonetheless, Tyson and Arkansas Valley emerged from the fracas victorious, having silenced the grower protests and cemented corporate control of the contract system.[30]

The trend in the twenty-first century has been toward fewer and larger growers. Between 2002 and 2017 the number of farms in the Ozarks classified as poultry operations declined by 22 percent while poultry sales more than doubled to $3.5 billion. This steep drop-off may reflect a winnowing of the industry's more marginal growers in favor of larger operations, but it is a rare family indeed who makes ends meet solely from income generated on the farm. In the twenty-first century—and much of the twentieth—the part-time farmer was the rule in the Ozarks, not the exception. As early as 1959, more than half the income for a typical farming household in the region came from off the farm. Poultry integrators claimed that contract grow-out operations actually

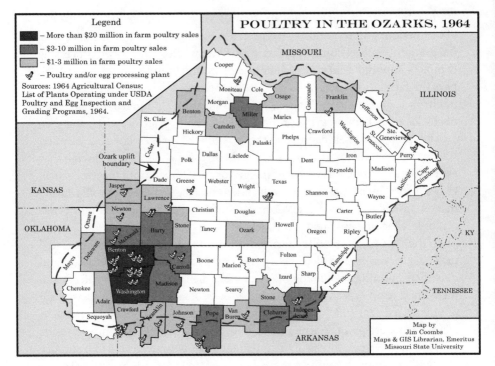

Poultry in the Ozarks, 1964. Courtesy of Jim Coombs, Missouri State University, Springfield.

saved family farming by allowing those who desired to stay on the land to do so. While a poultry operation may be the surest bet for sustaining a full-time farming livelihood, the vast majority of modern part-time farmers in the Ozarks carry on their families' rural traditions by raising beef cattle, an activity that provides far more flexibility than dairy farming and restores the independence denied poultry growers. Though poultry sales account for almost two-thirds of the region's agricultural income, it is the herd of beef cattle that best represents farming in the Ozarks in the early twenty-first century. Of the more than fifty-four thousand Ozarks farms in 2017, over 63 percent derived their principal agricultural income from the sale of cattle.[31]

Cattle Country

Modern beef cattle farming only took shape in the decades after World War II, but its foundation was laid in the interwar years. With the cattle tick quarantine a thing of the past, Union Stockyards opened for business in western Springfield in 1928. Sprawling across three city blocks, the stockyard housed several commission dealers and attracted cattle traders from around the region to its weekly auction. Not to be outdone, businessmen and the chamber of commerce in "the town that jack built" established Joplin Stockyards Inc. two years later. With two full blocks of corrals and a rail switch, Joplin Stockyards was even larger than Springfield's Union Stockyards. Its heavy traffic required an expansion to more than twice its original size in 1950.[32]

Other factors spurred the development of the modern cattle industry in the Ozarks. In 1950 Arkansas voters approved an initiative closing the range statewide. Cattle and hogs continued to roam free in the sparsely settled Courtois Hills of southeastern Missouri until the U.S. Forest Service banned free animal foraging within its boundaries in 1965. The state legislature closed all remaining no-fence zones four years later. For years the raising of Hereford, Black Angus, and other varieties of highbred animals had been the exclusive domain of wealthy hobbyists and a few of the region's most affluent ranchers. In the 1930s extension agents coordinated the purchase of purebred bulls, and county and regional breed associations sprang up to sponsor sales and promote progressive cattle farming. In the environs of the old lumber town of Leslie in Searcy County, Arkansas, Ed Mays built the largest Hereford herd in the state, some 450 head by the start of World War II. An operation of that magnitude was an anomaly, but it foreshadowed an almost regionwide effort to jump on the beef bandwagon.[33]

The quick shift away from plowed fields also altered the region's physical appearance. Taking advantage of federal subsidies, farmers converted landscapes of grain into hayfields and pastures of clovers, orchard grass, and fescue. The latter, developed by researchers at a Kentucky experiment station, became the most popular forage crop in the Ozarks. A hardy grass that emerges early in the spring and thrives late into the fall, fescue underwent extensive studies at the University of Missouri's Southwest Research Center near Mount Vernon, which developed three new strains specifically adapted to the Springfield Plain. In Arkansas, researchers at the Livestock and Forestry Branch Station, founded near Batesville in 1937, conducted some of the earliest forage tests on less-fertile soils in a section of the region once devoted to hillside cotton. Fifteen years later the university established its new beef cattle experimental farm west of Fayetteville.[34]

Farmers responded to extension agents and other promoters with a generation of phenomenal growth of cattle numbers in the Ozarks. In the 1960s alone the number of cattle on Ozarks farms more than doubled, surpassing the two million mark for the first time, and the 1970s saw an additional increase of 25 percent.[35] The cattle industry in the Ozarks was not prodded by local processing plants, as had been the case with dairy and poultry farming. As the postwar industry evolved, massive feed lots emerged in Kansas, Nebraska, and other Corn Belt

Ash Flat Livestock Auction, Ash Flat, Arkansas, c. 1960s. Courtesy of Brien Nix Hall, Ash Flat, Arkansas.

states. Farmers in the Ozarks came to specialize in herds of brood cows that raise their offspring until the calves reach a weight of about five hundred pounds, at which point the calves are typically sold at auction and transported northward or westward to be fattened on grain in a confined feed lot.

Today cattle outnumber people in the Ozarks. In 2017 the bovine population in the interior counties approached three million head, while the number in the entire Ozark uplift was above three and a half million, giving the region one of the densest concentrations of cattle in the nation. Large herds of cattle present their own environmental challenges, but the twenty-first-century landscape of hayfields and pastures has at the very least hidden most of the scars left on the land by generations of row crops. The acreage needed to sustain the grazing and hay requirements of a cow-calf herd large enough to supply a living income was far greater than the region's average 223-acre farm in 2017. The hay-mowing, bush-hogging, part-time cattle farmer remains the region's typical agriculturist and contributes more to the maintenance of the diverse landscape of forests and fields than anyone else in the region. As long as the lack of regulation in the cattle market makes it the last bastion of the small operator, the cattle farmer will carry on the agrarian traditions of a place poorly suited to agriculture but long dependent on it nonetheless.[36]

Surplus Ozarkers

Despite the thousands of cattle farms that dominate the landscape of much of the Ozarks today, the region's farm population—like that of the nation as a whole—is minuscule. Most of this exodus of farmers from the land occurred within the twenty years or so following American entry into World War II. People not only left farms in the 1940s and 1950s in wave after wave; they abandoned the region altogether in record numbers. For the only time in the story of the Ozarks as a part of the United States, the region watched its population shrink in those two decades.[37]

But regionwide statistics tell only part of the tale of outmigration. It was rural areas that hemorrhaged residents in these years. Between 1940 and 1960, twenty-three counties in the region lost at least one quarter of their population. Especially hard hit were the old cotton-raising areas and places that had been dependent on the timber industry. Arkansas's Izard and Newton headlined a list of half a dozen counties that saw their populations plummet by more than 40 percent. Kennard Billingsley, an Izard County native who graduated high school six months before Pearl Harbor, recalled that for his peers and the generation that followed there was no "choice except to leave. Over the years, there wouldn't be one young person out of ten . . . that stayed." The 1950s were particularly unkind to rural counties. Izard and Newton lost almost one-third of their residents during that decade alone, and eleven additional counties experienced declines of greater than one-fifth. Tremendous growth in cities like Springfield and Fayetteville and in the counties boosted by the recommissioning of the army's Fort Leonard Wood cancelled out most of the countryside's prodigious losses. Excluding the four counties that provided almost all the growth between 1940 and 1960, population in the remainder of the region fell by nearly 17 percent.[38]

The steady exodus of rural Ozarkers from their homes in the postwar years was entwined with another of the region's phenomena: the comings and goings of thousands of people as migrant laborers. In places like the Ozarks and Appalachia, an unusually large percentage of the population seemed reluctant to completely sever ties with home communities, and this reluctance bred an era of neighborhood instability as families and young men traveled the highways in search of the paying jobs so hard to come by in the hills and hollers. Earning enough to carry them through another winter, most migrants saw their journeys as temporary, and they headed back to the hills when the harvest ended

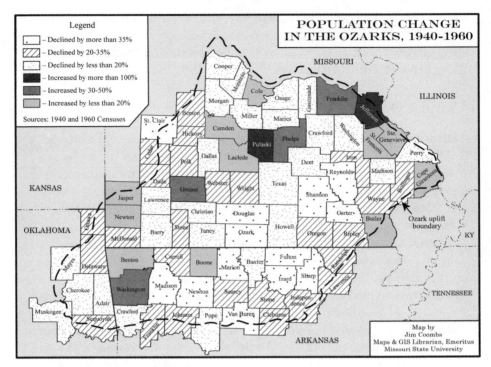

Population Change in the Ozarks, 1940–1960. Courtesy of Jim Coombs, Missouri State University, Springfield.

or when the assembly line grew too monotonous. For many, however, the lure of steady work and the deepening hardships of life in the hardscrabble Ozarks led to permanent relocation.[39] By the 1940s migrant labor trails snaked out of the Ozarks in every direction. Ozarkers found their way to the apple orchards of southwestern Michigan, the cotton fields of Arizona, the logging woods of Oregon, even the orange groves of Florida. Others sought work in the Michigan automobile industry, in Wichita aircraft factories, or on assembly lines in the plants of Indianapolis and Peoria.

The most commonly traveled trails barely made it out of the hills. Geneva King was only thirteen in the spring of 1948 when she left her Sharp County, Arkansas, home in the dark each morning for the hour-plus ride in the back of a tarp-covered cattle truck to the strawberry fields at Bald Knob, where she and hundreds of other pickers worked until mid-afternoon, earning three to five cents per quart. In later harvests her grandmother attempted to allay any anxieties an older Geneva had over her blackish purple, strawberry-stained hands. It "shows who the working girls are," Grandma reassured her, and everyone knows "the boys want the working girls for their wives." Come fall, Geneva had money to buy books and pay her typewriter rental fee at the local high school.[40]

Ellis and Junia King allowed their daughter to keep her earnings from the strawberry harvest, but the same couldn't be said when it came to cotton picking. In a phenomenon memorialized by the stereotypical Spruills of John Grisham's *A Painted House*, the Kings and countless other families in the Ozarks traveled each fall into the Arkansas lowlands to tramp the rows of yawning white bolls that stretched as far as the eye could see. During harvest season cotton farmers in the "bottoms" routinely dispatched trucks into the hills to recruit pickers and haul them back to the flat country. Subsisting on a farm in rugged Stone County, Arkansas, the Thomases piled into the back of one of these trucks many Octobers for the slow ride to the Delta town of Osceola. There, almost in sight of the Mississippi, they slept on piles of straw in a shotgun house, lived on potatoes and canned vegetables they'd brought from home, and spent their days pulling long, heavy cotton sacks up and down endless rows. On Saturday afternoons in Osceola, the Thomases socialized with other migrant hill people and gawked at unfamiliar sights, not least of whom were the African Americans who made up most of the local population and the Mexican braceros imported by the government to supplement the dwindling domestic labor force. Pooling their earnings to buy shoes and fabrics that Opal Thomas turned into dresses for her daughters, after a few weeks the family made the trip back to the Ozarks in the crisp autumn air. "Seeing those mountains did more to warm us than all the sun could do," recalled Jack Thomas.[41]

The Thomases could attest to one thing: the annual trip to the cotton patch was no vacation. Ellis King pushed his family (he, Junia, Geneva, and her two younger sisters) to harvest a bale a day—roughly thirteen hundred pounds of raw, un-ginned cotton in the sack—and "rared" at the girls when they picked their rows too carefully and cleanly, a process that veteran pickers dismissed as "ginnin' it." Living in a tent on a farm in the Missouri Bootheel for up to two months and working Monday through Saturday, the seven members of the Hastings clan could earn $125 in a good week, five times as much as Joe Hastings made back home in Ripley County, Missouri, hacking ties and working in a sawmill. "It wasn't an adventure you looked forward to," recalled Ray Joe Hastings, who was barely a teenager at the time. "Sore fingers from them cotton bolls sticking in and bent over all day picking cotton. That wasn't my idea of an adventure." Yet, he conceded, "it taught us how to work, how to be on our own, how to make a living."[42]

The single young men who had always provided a crucial labor source at harvest time continued to find their way to far-flung fields and forests. Growing up in Taney County, Missouri, Leon Combs longed to follow relatives on their journeys to Washington and Idaho and envied schoolmates who returned each fall with stories of mountains and deserts beyond the western horizon. He finally got his chance as a seventeen-year-old in 1952, when he and two high school buddies lit out for Washington's Yakima Valley. Embarking on a Greyhound bus from Springfield, he encountered his first television in the Kansas City terminal, straining to see a boxing match on a snowy screen. From Yakima, Combs made his way southward to the manic harvest at Milton-Freewater, Oregon, where he worked the twelve-hour night shift at a pea-packing plant. Enamored of the freedom and adventure he found on this first trip, Combs returned to the Pacific Northwest the following two summers. Working in the wheat harvest near Walla Walla, Washington, he received room and board and fifteen dollars a day. Combs's migrant labor career ultimately came to an ignominious end when he lost his last summer's earnings in a poker game, a hand that led to his dropping out of college and joining the U.S. Marines. But the cocky teenager on the wrong side of the ante was a product of the totality of the migrant experience, and that confidence and fearlessness would serve him well as a salesman and entrepreneur.[43]

Like so many whose migrant days were confined to young adulthood, Leon Combs summoned positive memories from those summers far from home. "Those were exciting days," he declared. "It was to me one of the . . . more enjoyable parts of my life . . ., seeing the world when everything is fresh." Traveling to the Yakima Valley with four friends from Ozark County, Missouri, a decade before Leon Combs made the trip, Leslie Turner spent long, backbreaking days cutting asparagus, topping sugar beets, and picking fruit. But "we had a lot of fun, too," he reminisced, hearkening back to nights on the town in Sunnyside and Saturday night square dances with other migrants in the "Little Missourah" neighborhood of Zillah.[44]

As automobiles became a common sight in the Ozarks, so did the migrant family. Siblings Don Keeth and Verna Keeth Pemberton, whose family made multiple trips to the Yakima Valley between the 1930s and 1950s, remembered big picnics with fellow Missourians and ice skating on frozen ponds. But their parents, Eather and Malone Keeth, endured more stress than did the youngsters. The Miller Countians represented a new breed of migrants in the postwar years. They were farm owners, not the displaced, landless transients of the Depression. The Keeths were simply caught in the purgatory created by the decline of the family farm. Unable to make a decent living on the land in the Ozarks, they nonetheless had a place pulling them back to native ground. In times when Eather found no local off-farm work, the Keeths made their way to Wapato, Washington, working on hop farms and in the fruit harvest. By the age of thirteen, Don Keeth was doing a man's work in the orchards, but it was easier, and more remunerative, than the endless list of chores on the farm back home.[45]

Eather and Malone Keeth ultimately abandoned the migrant trail for the familiarity of home in the Ozarks. The prudent financial move would probably have been to join Eather's brothers as permanent settlers in Washington. But "they wouldn't have been better off mentally, because they liked Missouri better," observed their daughter almost sixty years after the family's final migrant journey. "This is home. That's it." A strong sense of place led more than a few Ozarkers to forgo the superior material comforts and paychecks far from home for the very real prospect of a marginal existence back in the hills. Ray Joe Hastings, who dropped out of high school in the 1950s to support his family by taking a job in a St. Louis automobile factory, moved back and forth between rural Ripley County and the metropolis during hard times for years afterward. "When I got everything paid off, boy I was back down here, because I love this country."[46]

One factor that made home seem so appealing was the chilly reception that awaited many migrant workers. "In those days it was almost like *The Grapes of Wrath*," recalled Leon Combs of his experiences on the trail in the early 1950s. "Okies and Arkies and Missourians were kind of the bottom of the heap." "An Arkansawyer was dirt under their feet," observed an Izard County native who found work in the Washington apple orchards. After more than half a century, there remained an immediacy to the condescension Dub Rush experienced as an East Wenatchee orchard worker. "These people out here wanna think that people from Arkansas are poor, beaten down, dirt floors and all this," Rush complained. "But they didn't know a damn thing about us." Perhaps no migrants faced more hostility than did children, who found themselves enrolled in strange new schools among unwelcoming peers. "They thought we were hillbillies and didn't know anything and wasn't smart enough," recounted Verna Keeth Pemberton of her days in a Yakima Valley school. Arnie Clark endured bullies at schools in Wenatchee and East Wenatchee. "We were the dumb-ass Arkies and Okies, you know . . . lots of getting picked on." Another former migrant child declared, only partially in jest, "You don't have to whip 'em but once and then the rest of 'em was all nice to ya."[47]

In places where the migrant population was substantial, newcomers from the Ozarks displayed a tendency to associate almost exclusively with fellow migrants. "Little Oklahomas" and "Little Missourahs" sprang up in the lowest-rent districts of agricultural towns. Home folks held picnics and shindigs featuring down-home cooking and old-timey fiddling. Perhaps no institution better reflected the migrants' self-segregation and the transmission of Ozarks culture than the church. Migrant Ozarkers couldn't avoid patronizing schools where their children became cultural and economic minorities. They couldn't escape basic interactions with condescending locals. But many of them could and did join congregations that were composed of people who talked and believed like they did. "The people who moved west clung to their church because it was the last symbol of their original culture," observed Cecil Sims, one of the first ordained Southern Baptist ministers dispatched to the Pacific Northwest.[48]

By the 1980s the presence of Southern Baptist churches was one of the most notable legacies of the migrants from the Ozarks and the South. The popularity of country music was another, as was the rise of conservative politics.[49] Proof of the latter was former migrant Clyde Ballard, once chided as a "dirty Arkie" by a classmate but by the Reagan era well on his way to becoming perhaps the most powerful Republican in Washington State government. Though migrant workers and their children may have harbored resentment toward those who discriminated against them, their whiteness ultimately provided an avenue to assimilation into the mainstream. Those inclined to take that road could doff the bib overalls or flour sack dress, effect a less Ozarky-sounding accent, or, like nineteen-year-old Leon Combs did upon joining the Marines, claim to be from Oregon instead of Missouri. In a nation where whiteness was the standard, the fact that the next wave of lowly migrant workers couldn't blend in with generic accents and a J. C. Penney wardrobe only served to hasten the Ozarkers' rise toward respectability. In the 1960s seasonal workers from the Hispanic Southwest, Mexico, and Central America mostly replaced white migrants from the Ozarks. The wave of migrant workers from the Ozarks crested in the mid-1950s, when an estimated 13 percent of all working-age adults in much of the Arkansas Ozarks were professional transient laborers. By 1970 the days of the white harvest migrant had effectively come to an end.[50]

We Sell for Less

New opportunities in the Ozarks provided exit ramps off the migrant trail. Some former migrants found low-paying but steady employment in an expanding retail sector with strong ties to the region. Native Ozarker H. R. Gibson was a pioneer in the discount department store industry, opening the first Gibson's Discount Center in Texas in 1958. By 1970 Gibson's trailed only K-Mart as it strove for the top of the discount chain heap. But it was a transplant in the Ozarks who would perfect Gibson's techniques on his way to building the nation's largest private employer and most powerful retail empire. Oklahoma-born Sam Walton was a thirty-two-year-old former J. C. Penney management trainee in 1950 when he and his wife, Helen, settled down to run a Ben Franklin franchise in Bentonville, Arkansas, a bustling little oasis of poultry and cattle profits on the Springfield Plain. With capital supplied by local banks and Helen's wealthy father, Sam and his brother, James "Bud" Walton, acquired fifteen more franchises over the next dozen years. The Waltons proved there was money to be made off the common folks of the Ozarks, but to big-money investors and corporate retailers "small towns and their rural trade areas looked distinctly unpromising."[51]

When Butler Brothers of Chicago rebuffed Sam's vision of a chain of small-town discount retail stores, in 1962 he and Helen used her family land and trust as collateral to borrow money for the construction of the first Wal-Mart Discount City a few miles away in Rogers, a town of about six thousand people. By the time the newly incorporated Wal-Mart Stores finished its first distribution warehouse in Bentonville in 1970, Sam Walton had opened eighteen Wal-Marts, mostly in small Ozarks towns ignored by larger discounters like K-Mart, Target, and Woolco—all of which also launched their first stores in 1962. Torrid growth in the 1970s and 1980s broadened the company's geographic reach well beyond the Ozarks. The introduction of wholesale Sam's Clubs in the early 1980s and expansion into the grocery market with Wal-Mart (now Walmart) Supercenters later in the decade catapulted Walton's empire to the top of the American retail hierarchy by 1990. At the time of Sam Walton's death two years later, the company boasted more than nineteen hundred stores and a workforce of some 371,000 "associates"—the whole enterprise orchestrated from an Ozarks town with a population smaller than the enrollment of the nearby University of Arkansas. Neither the founder's demise nor the humble confines of Bentonville did anything to curb the corporate behemoth's appetite. Under the direction of chief executive officers David Glass (an Ozarker from rural south-central Missouri) and Lee Scott Jr. (a native of Baxter Springs on the Kansas periphery of the Ozark uplift), Walmart continued to mushroom into the twenty-first century, topping the *Fortune* 500 list of U.S. companies for the first time in 2002.[52]

Perhaps American history's most unlikely tale of business triumph, the Walmart saga is obviously one of the most defining and transforming stories of the modern Ozarks—a complex one that at turns defies and reaffirms long-held assumptions about life in the region. Birthed and nurtured in a place that wore its egalitarianism like a badge of honor, Walmart bore the marks of a regional population that may have resented the high-collared, moneyed crowd of the Northeast but shared their spirit of acquisitiveness and competition. The result, writes historian Bethany Moreton, was the creation of a "new corporate populism, a distinctly Ozarks version of capitalism with broad appeal across the Sun Belt." Sam Walton's legendary regular-guy persona, best exemplified by his plain red and white '79 Ford pickup and his beloved bird dog Ol' Roy, was gold for the brand, but the founder's aw-shucks image also served as a down-home smoke screen obscuring the company's cutting-edge innovations. From the installation of an early computer system linking each store's sales and inventory with the home office to the launching of the world's largest privately owned satellite network, Walton's innovations reflected a rapid adaptability that few in the business world associated with the laid-back Ozarks.[53]

Still, the image of the humble billionaire was no mere marketing gimmick. It was part and parcel of Walmart's corporate culture, at least during the three decades that a live Sam was part of that culture. In its formative years Walmart didn't just depend on the patronage and loyalty of customers from the farms and small towns of the Ozarks. The company, suggests Moreton, imbibed the culture of those customers (and associates) right down to the traditional family-values, evangelical mind-set that encouraged Christian servanthood among employees and inspired a patriarchal structure that effectively eliminated women from the managerial ranks. When a 2004 class action lawsuit charged Walmart with discriminatory promotion policies toward women, it was an ironic, if not surprising, development. Walmart's early success had depended heavily on a multitude of hardworking, nonunion, rural Ozarks moms—the very associates who infused corporate culture with their "ethos of service," according to Moreton. The lawsuit was just one of several public relations torpedoes launched at the corporation in the years after Walton's death. As Walmart grew, so did the target on its stern. By the early twenty-first century, critics accused Walmart of everything from the annihilation of downtown shopping districts to environmental desecration.[54]

Doug McMillon was a point guard on Bentonville High School's basketball team when he began unloading trucks at a Walmart distribution center as a teenager. When he took the reins as CEO of the country's largest retailer in 2014, it was a sign that some part of that populist, home folks spirit survived in a modern corporate giant with more than eleven thousand stores and 2.3 million associates. But McMillon's previous position at the company reflected just how much had changed since the old days when Sam Walton sacked goods on personal visits to his Ozarks stores. As head of Walmart's international division, McMillon saw the company's global reach extend to more than two dozen foreign nations, from Japan to Brazil and from South Africa to the United Kingdom. Pivoting from Walton's "Buy American" campaign in the heart of the Reagan '80s to an open embrace of globalism in the early 1990s (capped by intense public lobbying for the North American Free Trade Agreement of 1993), Walmart was one of several major companies in the Clinton years to draw criticism for propping up Asian sweatshops and for hastening the departure of American factory jobs. It was an abrupt about-face that many of their customers in the rural and small-town Ozarks felt acutely.[55]

Old Scars and New

Sam Walton's retail odyssey coincided with the rise of postwar manufacturing in the Ozarks. In fact, for years the bottom line at the old Discount City likely depended on blue-collar spending bolstered by factory jobs. In the post–family farm economy of the mid-twentieth century, small towns and government agencies across the heartland of America took up "smokestack chasing" to stem the tide of outmigration. It was a trip into unfamiliar territory for most of the Ozarks. Before World War II, manufacturing was a minor player in the region's economy, and it was almost always tied to agricultural products, mining, or timber. These older industries continued to provide jobs after the war, but only in a few locations did they drive the economy. The Department of Defense's stockpiling of critical minerals in the early years of the Cold War temporarily spurred localized mining booms in places like Howell and Oregon counties in Missouri (iron); Independence County, Arkansas (manganese); and Madison County, Missouri (cobalt and nickel). Still, mining remained a rare form of employment in the region, especially when compared to Appalachia, where workers were more than four times as likely as those in the Ozarks to earn a living below the surface.[56]

Production of lead in Missouri had just about petered out after more than two centuries of mining. The heart of the Tri-State District had long ago migrated from Missouri into northeastern Oklahoma. On the other side of the Show-Me State, miners in St. Francois County were entering the home stretch in the "Old" Lead Belt when in 1955 drillers for the St. Joseph Lead Company discovered a narrow band of ore stretching some forty-five miles across parts of six counties. Mining in this Viburnum Trend, roughly fifty miles west of the Old Lead Belt, commenced in 1960. By the time the last of the Old Lead Belt's mines was shuttered in 1972, milling operations in the New Lead Belt maintained Missouri's position as the nation's leading lead-producing state. In the process, mining employment in southeastern Missouri shifted westward. In Reynolds County, home to the country's largest lead mining and milling facility, 22.5 percent of all workers labored in the mining industry by 1980. In the twenty-first century, modern technology has severely reduced the need for human labor in the mines, and the mining town of old is but a memory, even in the remote, wooded hollers concealing the Viburnum Trend. Chances are pretty good, though, that the lead in your automobile battery came from this last great complex of mineral extraction in the Ozarks.[57]

The New Lead Belt is part of the mixed legacy of an industry that was the lifeblood of large swaths of the Ozarks for a quarter of a millennium. Descendants of the employees of St. Joe and other lead and zinc companies look back with justifiable pride at the thousands of people who helped put the region on the world's industrial map. But the twenty-first century's inheritance from the boom days at the mines is a familiar story. Once they plundered the ancient riches of the earth, the companies moved on, depriving former mining towns of both corporate paternalism and contributions to public coffers. More often than not the long-term result was abandoned business districts, crumbling infrastructure, and a physical environment pocked and poisoned by decades of callous or clueless exploitation.

By the time the Environmental Protection Agency (EPA) began sniffing around the lead districts in the 1980s, generations of families had lived with contaminated water, soil, and air. Abandoned slime ponds contained toxic cocktails of finely ground metals mixed with synthetic chemicals. Yards, driveways, and gravel roads were littered with the contaminated tailings from the mills. And most of this chat remained in mountainous piles that were part of the local landscape— noxious, man-made hills that became favored spots for campers and off-road motorists. When the EPA began cleanup operations in the 1990s, the old mining districts of the Ozarks were home to no fewer than a dozen Superfund sites on the agency's National Priorities List. Studies of school children in the Tri-State District and the Old Lead Belt revealed elevated blood lead levels, prompting soil replacements at thousands of residences since the late 1990s. Even more extreme were the EPA's actions in the old Tri-State towns just beyond the western edge of the Ozark uplift. When the EPA deemed the towns too contaminated for human habitation in 2009, Congress appropriated funds for a buyout and relocation of all the residents of Picher, Oklahoma, and Treece, Kansas.[58]

Another regional industry that once contributed to serious environmental damage occupied a more prominent place in the industrial output of the post– World War II Ozarks. In 1960 one in seven manufacturing jobs in the region involved the processing or finishing of wood. Despite decades of corporate cutting, enough timber had grown back to support localized specialties: walnut gun stocks in Benton County, Missouri; pallets in Missouri's Bollinger and Wayne counties; barrels in Lebanon, Missouri; and hardwood flooring in Izard County, Arkansas. When the "boys of summer" still played pepper, a West Plains factory crafted baseball bats endorsed by Ted Williams, the legend who tried to steal the region's thunder back in the year of the Ozarks. Hammons Products relied on the nuts that litter the ground each autumn—not the wood of the tree—to put little Stockton, Missouri, on the map as the world's leading supplier of black walnut food products. Dozens of laborers at the I. C. Sutton Handle Factory in the remote Boston Mountains village of Lurton (and later in Harrison, Arkansas) turned hickory into handles for axes, picks, mauls, and hammers.[59]

The Ozark region's plentiful supply of hickories also provided much of the wood for another forest product: charcoal. The modern industry in the Ozarks came to focus not on the charcoal once used in lead and iron smelting but on the briquettes used in outdoor cooking grills. The briquette industry would eventually spread into the Courtois Hills and White River Hills, but it got its start in the old German communities of the northern Ozarks, where farmers in places like Freeburg, Argyle, and Meta built and operated kilns on their own property. Vienna farmer Victor Wulff designed the popular "Missouri Charcoal Kiln," which could produce up to twenty-five tons from one fifty-cord batch of wood. In 1963 half a dozen briquette plants in the Missouri Ozarks purchased raw charcoal from more than eighty producers. One of those plants, Keeter Charcoal of Branson, rose to national prominence under the brand name Royal Oak. At the end of the twentieth century, Missouri—the only state in the nation with no regulations on kiln smoke—controlled three-quarters of the country's briquette charcoal production, and almost all of it took place in the Ozarks. But amendments to the federal Clean Air Act brought an end to the state's advantage in the early 2000s, by which time the expense of installing environmentally friendly "afterburners" on kilns had driven almost everyone besides Royal Oak and Kingsford out of business.[60]

The charcoal industry wasn't the only threat worrying environmentalists in the Ozarks. The early 1970s saw a dramatic increase in clear-cutting the region's forests, as experts at land-grant universities and in the U.S. Forest Service advocated "even-aged management" to allow for quicker regrowth. Rising opposition to clearcutting on federal lands in southern Missouri sparked the creation of the activist Mark Twain Forest Watchers. In 1989 the Watchers won a crucial appeal to the USFS that dramatically decreased clearcutting on public lands. The emergence of a new counter-philosophy in the 1990s promised an alternative to clearcutting, and it was a vision that had taken shape in the Ozarks—specifically across the sprawling hills of St. Louis entrepreneur Leo Drey's Pioneer Forest. Drey and his professional foresters instituted an uneven-aged, single-tree selection system that proved both profitable and ecologically responsible. (Ironically, though, it was Drey's profits from exploitative lead mining and his penurious policies with local governments that allowed him to weather the lean years before the Pioneer Forest plan matured.) Swayed by the evidence of Drey's work, other foresters began to champion uneven-aged management in the 1990s, about the same time that they rejected a longtime USFS prohibition against controlled burns. The vast majority of timberlands in the Ozarks remains in the hands of private owners, and the region's Jeffersonian traditions ensure that environmental regulations on loggers and landowners will likely stay the stuff of environmentalists' dreams for the foreseeable future.[61]

The lack of strict governmental oversight and regulation in the states of the Ozarks has long appealed to would-be industrialists. The same political and cultural sentiments helped create a region unfriendly to unions, while the rapid disappearance of small, marginal farms generated a vast pool of cheap labor. In the post–World War II era the future of industry in the Ozarks lay not in mining or timber but in a new frontier: the factory.

Smokestacks and Shirt Factories

Before World War II a few larger towns such as Springfield and Joplin developed small manufacturing districts. Likewise, the St. Louis and Kansas City garment industries spread into the Ozarks on occasion, leaving a lasting imprint in at least one case. Relocated to Carthage in 1916, Smith Brothers secured a contract to make coats for doughboys headed off to war. By the late 1930s some 350 women labored in the Carthage plant, hundreds more in Smith Brothers's factories in Neosho and Webb City. Though the company made a wide variety of clothing, it was the Big Smith brand of overalls that reached iconic status. The gallused workers' attire symbolized a region of farmers, miners, and timber workers. The overall plant at Carthage closed its doors in 2000, but Big Smith lived on in Ozarks culture as the name of a unique, Springfield-based band blending traditional mountain music with bluegrass and rock-and-roll.[62]

Smith Brothers remained a rarity in the Ozarks in the 1920s and 1930s, but in the postwar years towns and counties across the region looked to the manufacturing sector to provide jobs and save declining communities. Despite such challenges as a poor transportation network and schools that lagged behind the national norm, the Ozark region was attractive to industrialists. Surplus labor and the lack of unionization kept wages far below those of heavily industrialized areas like the Northeast and the Great Lakes region. In the late 1950s the Daisy Manufacturing Company (maker of the iconic Red Ryder BB gun) abandoned its longtime headquarters and factory in suburban Detroit for the cheaper and less union-friendly confines of Rogers, Arkansas. The one hundred families who made the move from Michigan provided an injection of Republicanism and Catholicism when both creeds were still rare in Benton County, and the new plant generated more than four hundred additional jobs for locals. The southward creep of low-skill manufacturing was often dictated by industry in the two metropolitan areas nearest the Ozarks, St. Louis and Kansas City, where average factory wages more than doubled those in rural counties downstate. In the towns of the far northern Ozark uplift and along Route 66 (now Interstate 44), auto parts factories sprang up to service the massive vehicle assembly plants of Missouri's two largest cities. And nothing better exemplified St. Louis's impact on postwar manufacturing in the Ozarks than the spread of shoe factories into rural southern Missouri.[63]

The postwar industrialization of the Ozarks tended to advance in waves from the North, creating a time-lag effect that brought factories and punch clocks to rural southern Missouri a decade or more before they crossed the line into Arkansas. Not surprisingly, then, it was desperate Arkansas that developed the region's earliest strategy for attracting industry. Using Mississippi's Balance Agriculture with Industry program as a blueprint, in the postwar years poor, farming states enacted law after law to create a manufacturer-friendly environment. In Arkansas, one of the nation's least industrialized states, voters passed one of the country's first "right-to-work" amendments. The Resources and Development Commission worked hand in hand with the state chamber of commerce for the next decade, laying the groundwork for a series of acts and amendments passed by the legislature or by statewide referendum between 1955 and 1960. The first of these acts established the Arkansas Industrial Development Commission (AIDC) at the behest of new governor Orval Faubus. To run the AIDC, Faubus tapped Winthrop Rockefeller, New York–raised grandson of the late oil magnate John D. Rockefeller and recent immigrant to Arkansas. Subsequent legislation paved the way for community financing of factory construction through a variety of bonds issued by towns, counties, and local industrial development corporations. Missouri joined Arkansas in legalizing municipal industrial bonds in the early 1960s.[64]

These bond issues allowed counties and towns and their taxpayers to foot a big chunk of the bill for building industrial parks and factory plants, always in the optimistic faith that corporate jobs would stem the population outflow. Spreading the word was a cadre of boosterish missionaries. "In contrast to quaint stereotypes," writes historian Keith Orejel in his study of manufacturing in post–World War II north-central Arkansas, "small-town business leaders were modernizers who frequently reconfigured the physical landscape and . . . environment to facilitate industrialization." Chambers of commerce, civic clubs, and local editors in the Ozarks preached a gospel of "low business taxes, cheap labor, weak unions, and infrastructural upgrades." It was a gospel that echoed from the pulpits of promotion across the rural South and Midwest. By the late 1960s a multitude of federal programs subsidized and supported rural industrialism. John F. Kennedy's Area Redevelopment (later Economic Development) Administration and Lyndon B. Johnson's Ozarks Regional Commission worked alongside older agencies like the Small Business Administration to provide grants and loans for new and expanding industries. Vocational education programs used state and federal tax dollars to provide employee training at no cost to corporations. The Hill-Burton Act provided federal finances that spurred the building of hospitals in small towns across the Ozarks. "Government largesse provided the crucial ingredient for enabling rural industrialization," observes Orejel, and "small-town business leaders pursued [it] with alacrity."[65]

In the late 1960s and 1970s, federal policy makers looked to redistribute manufacturing jobs from urban areas to rural places and small towns. National alarm over the postwar migration of poor Southerners to northern cities spurred calls to action. "By generating a kind of 'urban crush,' they create a problem in the cities to which they go," lamented one report. "By depopulating the countryside, they create a problem in the rural areas from which they come." President Johnson's National Advisory Commission on Rural Poverty recommended federal spending and incentives to coax corporations into relocating factories from cities to places like the Ozarks. And it happened. In the 1960s factory jobs in nonmetropolitan areas expanded more than five times faster than those in metropolitan places. It was the age of the great manufacturing boom in the Ozarks. Between 1965 and 1973 the Missouri Ozarks reported more than 100 new and expanding industries annually, reaching an all-time high of 165 in the latter year, before the oil crisis drained the boom of its fuel.[66]

The eager if halting transformation from rural farming village to factory town played out in little burgs across the Ozarks in the years after World War II. Ava, Missouri, emerged from the war era as the only town providing employment and services for a large rural region amid a dairy-farming boom. Like so many small Ozarks towns, Ava's limited industry was almost wholly dependent on natural resources and agricultural goods. Despite the rise in milk production, the two decades between 1940 and 1960 saw more than half of the county's agricultural jobs disappear. Throughout the early 1950s, the Ava Chamber of Commerce struck out time and time again as it tried to attract industries. One of the chief drawbacks for Ava's industrial quest was the area's poor transportation network, with curvy, hilly state Highway 5—the county's primary artery—turning away at least one major employer.[67]

But things began to look up for Ava in mid-decade. In 1955 a group of chamber members formed an industrial development corporation and soon after purchased a thirty-five-acre lot as an industrial site. In 1957 the state began massive upgrades that would make Highway 5 one of southern Missouri's premiere two-lane roads by the end of the decade. Both developments contributed to Ava's first minor victory in 1958 when a wood-treating company agreed to locate a modest plant at the industrial site. But Ava's real introduction to the new postwar order came a year later. In the summer of 1959, the St. Louis–based Rawlings Sporting Goods Company announced plans to establish a factory that would provide up to three hundred new jobs. As with most agreements between big industry and desperate small towns, the jobs came at a price. Rawlings insisted that the Ava Industrial Development Corporation construct a factory building, which the company would then lease at a bargain rate. So eager were the citizens of Ava to raise the quarter of a million dollars required for the building that merchants closed their doors on the day before Halloween to canvass the county selling stock in the industrial development corporation, a campaign that attracted some fourteen hundred local investors. To meet the company's demands for water, waste treatment, and fire protection, Ava citizens almost unanimously approved a bond issue of $225,000. Subsequent physical expansion at Rawlings's request required the industrial development corporation to seek loans from banks and the federal Area Redevelopment Administration.[68]

With the addition of a golf bag factory owned by another midwestern sporting goods company, Spalding, Ava's industrial park hosted three plants and 315 jobs by the mid-1960s—at a cost of some twenty-five thousand dollars per worker in public and private funds. Additional ancillary costs (and benefits) of the town's promotion and recruitment included the construction of a new high school, the building of a modern nursing home, the creation of the county's first country club, and expensive improvements to local telephone and electric utility systems. Out-migration did, in fact, slow; bank deposits rose rapidly; property values escalated; and the increased flow of tax monies funded county services and padded school budgets. In the early 1970s, the Ozarks Regional Commission helped fund additional infrastructural improvements in the industrial park, and the closing of the Spalding plant made way for an even larger tenant: a motor-making factory established by another St. Louis corporation, Emerson Electric. In 1981 Ava boasted more than one thousand manufacturing jobs, over 90 percent of them at one of three facilities: Emerson, Rawlings, and a garment factory owned by regionally based Hagale Industries.[69]

Plants owned by Rawlings, Hagale, and other manufacturers shared something in common with Walmart: a largely female workforce. It was a new reality in the small-town, industrializing Ozarks. Douglas and similar poor, rural counties in the region tended to attract low-wage, low-skill factories providing "sewing machine jobs" typically held by women. So prominent were women in the postwar manufacturing workforce that it became something of a regional pastime to poke fun at a new symbol of modern manhood in the rural Ozarks, the "go-getter" who dropped his wife off at the factory door in the morning and had to "go get her" when the shift ended that evening. Nowhere was this more evident than in two of the region's leading employment sectors: garment factories and shoe plants. More than three in four jobs in such industries were held by women, and it wasn't uncommon for females to compose over 90 percent of the workforce in garment factories. Given the era's gendered pay scales, it is not surprising that garment factory workers were the lowest-paid hourly employees in the region in the 1970s. The average wage of these workers was less than half of that earned in the male-dominated automobile, aircraft, and steel industries, all of which were rare in the Ozarks.[70]

In the heyday of late twentieth-century manufacturing, no industry employed more Ozarkers than did apparel production. Primarily making garments but also turning out hats, caps, and gloves, the industry spread throughout the region after mid-century. The number of apparel factories doubled between 1947 and 1981, while jobs in the industry almost doubled in the 1970s alone. More than three hundred workers in Houston, Missouri, produced a steady supply of Lee's women's jeans; just up the highway in Licking, an even larger workforce sewed athletic clothing and uniforms for Rawlings. St. Louis–based Angelica Uniform Company maintained factories in the small Missouri towns of Eminence, Marquand, Mountain View, and Summersville. Key Industries cranked out overalls, coveralls, and jackets at small factories in Hermitage, Buffalo, and Stockton. While garment factory jobs were almost nonexistent in Springfield's

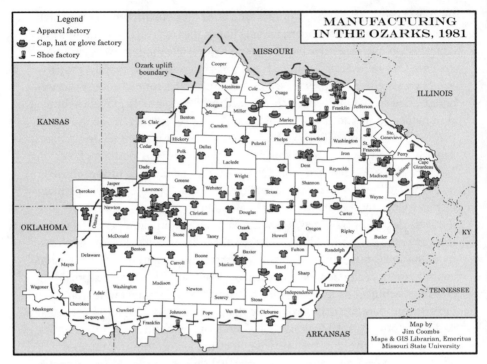

Manufacturing in the Ozarks, 1981. Courtesy of Jim Coombs, Missouri State
University, Springfield.

prosperous Greene County, some of the region's poorest counties depended
heavily on apparel plants. More than four in five manufacturing employees in
Missouri's rural Dade County made men's sport coats in Greenfield or caps in
Lockwood, and such jobs accounted for at least two-thirds of factory employment in the poor counties of Dallas, Hickory, St. Clair, Stone, and Taney. Despite
the low pay for sewing machine jobs, more than three thousand women applied
at the new Mar-Bax Shirt Factory in Gassville, Arkansas, in the early 1960s. The
surrounding area bent over backward to satisfy the New York corporation's
directors, throwing in tax breaks, bond issues, and land donations to sweeten
a pot that already included substantial federal funding.[71]

Beyond the ubiquitous garment factory, the region also saw specialized industries develop in certain areas or towns: mobile homes in McDonald County,
Missouri, boats in Lebanon and Richland, caskets in Crane and Marshfield.
Tourism even fueled the development of unique subregional specialties. Two-
thirds of the 120 manufacturing workers in little Stover, Missouri, made their
livings in the quilting industry, while small wooden novelty factories dotted
the landscape of such tourism-dependent places as Branson and the Lake of

the Ozarks country. And then there were the enterprises that flew in the face of bumpkin figurines and hillbilly salt shakers. No facility in the region challenged the image of Ozarks backwardness more than California-based Rocketdyne's plant just outside of Neosho, Missouri, in the late 1950s and 1960s. There, on the decommissioned army training site once known as Camp Crowder, more than one thousand employees built and tested rockets for Atlas and Thor missiles, as well as components for other rocket engines, including the one that powered Apollo 11 to the moon in 1969. "These guys were a bunch of hillbillies," recalled a former Rocketdyne engineer half a century later, "but they were able to build and put the thing together that went more than 200,000 miles to the moon and back."[72]

Though their products might not have been as crucial to the nation's role in the Cold War, a number of towns across the Ozarks boasted large and diversified manufacturing bases by the 1970s. Laborers in Fayetteville, Arkansas, made anything from tractor parts to electronic organs, from fishing reels to electric fuses. But one city reigned as the unquestioned manufacturing leader in the postwar Ozarks. Springfield had emerged in the nineteenth century as the region's economic and cultural hub—the Queen City of the Ozarks. The crown became a perfect fit during the 1950s and 1960s, when the city's population almost doubled to 120,000. By 1970 almost one in five jobs in the Queen City was in manufacturing, attracting a steady stream of Ozarkers from the depressed hinterland. They came to Springfield to make potato chips and cheese, cattle feed and boys' pants, furniture and pharmaceuticals, writing tablets and Sunday School books.[73]

The Lily-Tulip Cup Corporation signaled the beginning of an era of mushrooming factory growth in 1952 when it opened a plant on what was then the northeastern edge of town. By the end of the 1960s, some nineteen hundred Springfieldians and commuters received a steady paycheck and benefits from Lily-Tulip. The year 1959 brought two massive additions to the city's industrial sector: a Royal McBee plant that was reportedly the world's largest portable typewriter factory and an automotive belt plant opened by Dayton Rubber Company, both of which provided more than eleven hundred jobs by the end of their first decade in town. The 1960s saw the establishment of new factories turning out circuit boards, brake drums, industrial adhesives, and chain saws, among other products.[74]

Even the Queen City's largest factories paled in comparison to the plant that opened in 1967. Engulfing more than forty acres under a single roof, the gargantuan Zenith factory "had a greater impact on the local economy and on the lives of Ozarks workers than any other manufacturing operation ever located in the area." The television maker was attracted to Springfield by familiar amenities: cheap land, subsidized services, and the promise of municipal bonds to fund

Inspecting the products at Lily-Tulip, Springfield, Missouri, c. 1982.
Photo by *Springfield News-Leader*, used by permission.

expansion. Even Springfield's strong tradition of labor organizing didn't deter
Zenith, for wages in the Queen City were still significantly lower than those in the
corporation's Chicago backyard. At the peak of Zenith's production in the 1970s,
almost fifty-five hundred employees in Springfield made over half the company's
color televisions. The region's largest factory spawned and supported ancillary
industries as well, including a plant that built wooden television cabinets.[75]

From Goods to Services

By the time Zenith made its first television set in the Ozarks, the region had
yet another federal program designed to bolster economic development. The
Ozarks Regional Commission (ORC), created in 1966 and modeled after the

Appalachian Regional Commission (ARC), joined the growing chorus of agencies promoting factory growth as a substitute for the dying small farm economy. More than two-thirds of ORC grants went directly to industrial parks and the infrastructure that supported them. The ORC lacked the ARC's substantial budget and publicity, but both federal agencies followed a blueprint that privileged larger regional trading and employment hubs. "Although the federal government's regional program had been initially justified by underscoring the severe poverty of rural communities," observes historian J. Blake Perkins, "the growth-center strategy ensured that most projects ignored those areas that needed assistance the most." Ultimately, though, it was Ozarkers in general who received short shrift. By 1974 the ORC's geographic range had been expanded to include all of Missouri, Arkansas, and Oklahoma, as well as Louisiana and Kansas. Of the eighty grants awarded in fiscal year 1976, only seven went to towns actually located in the Ozarks. The ORC had few ardent supporters by the end of the decade, and its death in Ronald Reagan's domestic budget–slashing crusade of 1981 elicited little protest.[76]

The most enduring and positive legacies of the ORC in the twenty-first century are the community colleges and vocational schools that benefited from the agency's grants and that continue to offer a gateway into careers and higher education for thousands of rural and small-town Ozarkers. At the end of World War II, the interior Ozarks was home to only five institutions offering a four-year bachelor's degree and only one, the University of Arkansas, providing graduate education. Residents of a vast swath of the region's interior lived nowhere near a college or trade school.

Widespread consolidation of rural districts made a high school education available to almost all Ozarkers by the 1950s. Most rural graduates of the era caught the first ride out of town to find work, but an increasing number made their way to colleges in a first step toward realization of an American dream that seemed more within reach than ever before. In the decades after the war, junior colleges became four-year institutions (Joplin's Missouri Southern State College, Bolivar's Southwest Baptist College, and Point Lookout's School of the Ozarks), and four-year institutions developed into graduate-level universities (Southwest Missouri State University in Springfield and Northeastern State University in Tahlequah). The rapid expansion of manufacturing in the region spurred its own brand of postsecondary education geared toward industrial promotion. In the wake of the 1963 Vocational Education Act, federal grant money triggered the creation of vocational-technical schools across the Ozarks, while towns like Flat River, Harrison, and Neosho created community colleges. Today community colleges in Springfield and Bentonville each enroll more students than did all the higher education institutions in the Ozarks combined at the time of Pearl Harbor.[77]

Springfield's Ozarks Technical Community College was still a tiny upstart institution when it suddenly faced the prospect of retraining hundreds of displaced workers. In October 1991 Zenith announced plans to shutter its Springfield plant—the last American-owned television factory on American soil. The company in recent years had begun shifting production to cheaper facilities in Mexico, where laborers earned less than 15 percent of the average wage at the Springfield factory. By the time a skeleton crew closed the plant's doors for the final time, Zenith's demise had become an apt symbol for the economic and employment transformation under way in the Ozarks—and in the nation.[78] While they didn't receive the level of publicity generated by the largest layoff in the region's history, the closings of dozens of factories large and small in the 1990s and early 2000s sent tens of thousands of jobs to cities from Latin America to southeastern Asia. The era of manufacturing in the Ozarks had come to an end. No one in the domestic labor market worked harder and for less money than the Ozarkers. They had taken jobs from other American regions and cities in the postwar years, and only desperate workers in developing nations provided cheaper alternatives.

The shutdown at Zenith and other plants caused "serious short-term economic hardships" and most likely a permanently lower standard of living for most factory operatives, as jobs with pensions and first-rate health-care plans grew scarce in the post-manufacturing economy. But the transformation of the last generation has been felt most acutely not in a place like Springfield but in rural areas and small towns, where factories provided a much greater percentage of full-time jobs and where the service economy could not replace those jobs. The demise of the manufacturing economy hastened the growing gulf between haves and have-nots. In the Ozarks poverty has most often been a rural phenomenon, and physical remoteness from the region's few growth centers of commerce and investment continues to be the surest predictor of low per capita income and low educational attainment. In other words, the farther Ozarkers live from Springfield, northwestern Arkansas, and a few other regional hubs, the more likely they are to depend on government transfer payments, the less likely they are to enjoy the financial and material benefits of modern American life, and the less likely they are to be motivated to pursue those benefits.[79]

Despite the hard times faced by many displaced workers, the region's larger towns emerged from the transformation no worse for wear. By 2011, when another of Springfield's golden age factories (Solo Cup, formerly Lily-Tulip) closed its doors after almost sixty years, the Queen City of the Ozarks had reinvented itself. A paltry 6 percent of jobs in the region's largest city were in manufacturing, while almost two in five people worked in either education or health care, with retail and government employment ranking close behind. Only two behemoth hospitals, Mercy and Cox, provided more jobs than the retail giant

Walmart. As for the massive plant that produced the last American-made televisions, it was converted into the sprawling headquarters of a rapidly expanding, homegrown business: Bass Pro Shops. Beginning life as a humble Springfield bait shop, Bass Pro is today every bit the corporate titan that Zenith was in its heyday. Like Walmart and Tyson Foods, Bass Pro represents a thoroughly modern and American Ozarks, one crafted by the efforts of the marketplace, federal agencies, and other forces of the post–World War II world. They all represent a twenty-first-century Ozarks that has undergone a massive transformation but maintains strong ties to a rural past and rugged landscape.[80]

Conclusion

John Moody was not the first young man to look for a fresh start in the Ozarks, but he was definitely a pioneer. Abandoning a native ground that was short on opportunity and long on poverty, he journeyed to northwestern Arkansas, where he found steady work, married a local woman, and settled down. On visits back home he described the place he had found as a land of hope and promise. Like the chain migrations that drew thousands of nineteenth-century Tennesseans, Kentuckians, and Carolinians to the hearths of kinfolk in a new hill country, Moody's relatives and old neighbors gradually followed him through the "door of opportunity." In a few years a trickle became a migratory flood.[1]

The quest for a better, more secure life tied John Moody and his people to the tens of thousands of settlers who preceded him to the Ozarks, but there was little else in Moody's story that reminded observers of the generations of Ozarkers who came before. At the moment he arrived in Springdale in the 1980s, he may have been the first person ever to make this particular migration. John Moody was born and raised some six thousand miles southwest of the Ozarks in the Marshall Islands, a sparsely populated Pacific nation occupied by the U.S. military during World War II and used for nuclear bomb target practice for years afterward. A 1986 agreement with the island nation allowed the Marshallese to travel and settle at will in the United States. Moody was in the vanguard of a diaspora that deposited perhaps as many as fifteen thousand islanders in and near Springdale, Arkansas, a Marshallese population greater than anywhere else on the North American continent. By 2018 Springdale was home to about twenty Marshallese churches, a Marshallese-language radio station, Marshallese stores, and a Marshallese consulate.[2]

More than five hundred miles from the nearest coast, the Ozarks was an unusual landing place for a people raised within earshot of the Pacific's rhythmic

Taquería Don Güero, Springdale, Arkansas, 2020. Courtesy Shiloh Museum of Ozark History.

waves. But it was perhaps no more unlikely a destination than the region had been for the descendants of Ulster tenant farmers or artisans from the Rhine Gorge. After all, life back home—whether in eighteenth-century Europe or the twentieth-century Pacific islands—shared little in common with human society in the heart of North America before the great migrations commenced more than five hundred years ago. As with the newcomers who preceded them to the Ozarks, it was the "door of opportunity" that beckoned. For the Marshall Islanders, it was Tyson Foods that opened the door. Almost all the Marshallese, including John Moody, found their first Ozarks job inside a Tyson processing plant. Their arrival coincided with the poultry industry's aggressive push toward a low-wage workforce unlikely to organize. Processing plants recruited even larger numbers of Latinas/os as well as smaller populations of Somalis, Sudanese, Hmong, and Laotians.[3]

Twenty-first-century northwestern Arkansas epitomized the "Nuevo South," according to scholar Perla M. Guerrero, where "immigrants provided the inexpensive labor necessary for the poultry industry to grow quickly and profitably as a new plantation regime." But the rapid transformation to the Nuevo South has not been a smooth or uniform one. The burdens of such a sudden demographic shift—language barriers, cultural misunderstandings, lack of documentation— tended to fall on the shoulders of institutions like schools, law enforcement, and hospitals.

While Rogers mayor John Sampier spearheaded efforts to help Hispanic families adjust to their new communities, not everyone was so welcoming to immigrants. In 1997 Dan Morris, himself a recent transplant from New Mexico, founded Americans for an Immigration Moratorium, an organization that helped unseat Sampier the following year. Before long, complaints of racial profiling led the Mexican American Legal Defense Fund to file a class-action suit against the Rogers Police Department. The department adopted anti-profiling policies, but in 2007 the continued presence of thousands of Latinas/os—broadly painted as illegals—and blooming fears of gang violence swayed officials to enroll in a federal program authorizing local involvement in matters pertaining to the U.S. Immigration and Customs Enforcement agency. The police in neighboring Bentonville and Springdale followed suit, sparking accusations of intimidation and racism.[4]

The Hispanic population and other communities of immigrants remain confined primarily to towns with poultry processing plants and to the area dominated by corporate Walmart and its "Vendorville," but in these places the impact of newcomers has been substantial. Attracting "a variety of well-educated urban types of all ethnicities and religions, often with MBAs or advanced engineering degrees," Walmart and its vendors have pulled off a demographic makeover unfathomable thirty years ago. The multi-campus megachurch known as Cross Church and its Baptist brethren continue to define mainstream spirituality in northwestern Arkansas, but Islamic mosques, Jewish synagogues, Buddhist retreats, and Hindu temples reflect a burgeoning cosmopolitanism that shows no sign of abating. In a cluster of four counties in the heart of the processing district (Benton, Carroll, and Washington in Arkansas and McDonald in Missouri), more than one in four residents in 2019 was nonwhite or Hispanic—and this in an area that was 98 percent white in 1990. Latinas/os alone made up 16.7 percent of the population. In southwestern Missouri in 2020, Hispanic children comprised more than one-third of the enrollment in the public schools of Carthage, Monett, and Aurora. Down in Arkansas white students were in the minority in the classrooms of Decatur, Green Forest, Rogers, and Springdale. In the latter city the proportion of nonwhite students ballooned from 4 percent in 1989 to 68 percent in 2020. Multilingualism thrived amid a scene of Spanish-language radio stations and taquerias. More than anywhere else in the Ozarks, these areas challenge ingrained regional constructs and the very notion of who Ozarkers are and who they will be.[5]

The Ozarks—or at least the parts inhabited by Tyson Foods and other processors—is more racially and ethnically diverse now than at any point since the earliest days of European and American immigration. But the changes in the modern Ozarks go deeper than demographics. Nothing better symbolized the transformation under way in the Springfield Plain than the festivities in Bentonville, Arkansas, on November 11, 2011. It was on that day that Alice Walton's Crystal Bridges Museum of American Art opened to the public. A short walk from the cozy town square where Alice's father, Sam, once stocked the shelves of his five-and-dime, Crystal Bridges boasted the greatest collection of American-created artwork ever assembled in one location. In a region where "vernacular" had been an all-encompassing term for art, this was a monumental departure from the norm. Alice Walton applied her dad's old "Buy American" slogan to her passion, spending tens of millions of dollars to pluck works of iconic artists from the walls of venerable galleries on the coasts: John Single-ton Copley, Thomas Eakins, Winslow Homer, Thomas Hart Benton, Georgia O'Keeffe, Jackson Pollock, Andy Warhol. And it didn't go unnoticed. A trans-formed, affluent corner of the Ozarks might have been ready for one of the world's greatest art museums, but the world of art and sophistication wasn't quite ready to embrace the Ozarks and its Molly Brown.[6]

The arbiters of culture and sophistication leveled their sights on Alice Walton and the retail behemoth that enriched her. Skewering the heiress's buying spree and her plans for Crystal Bridges in *The Nation*, writer Rebecca Solnit accused Walton and Walmart of "turning hallowed American art into a fig leaf to paste over naked greed and raw exploitation." A writer in *The Guardian* charged her with collecting "art with the same disregard for fair practices and competition that Wal-Mart shows in the retail sector." Critics in the Big Apple grew apoplectic when Walton paid the New York Public Library $35 million for Asher B. Du-rand's *Kindred Spirits*, one columnist condemning the transaction as "the most egregious act of self-desecration since the demolition of Pennsylvania Station." The cultural elites may have feared a Walmartization of high culture, but as art historian and curator Theodore Stebbins Jr. observed, "Art always goes where the money goes."[7]

Even the loudest tantrum throwers repeated the hollow mantra that people everywhere deserved access to fine art, but it was clear that no one was prepared for that art to go where Walmart money went. Alice Walton was no neophyte and no shrinking violet. Spending an estimated $1.2 billion from her own fortune and from the Walton Family Foundation, she commissioned Israeli-born architect Moshe Safdie to design a gallery that blended with its natural surroundings. To run the joint Walton hired Brooklyn, New York–born Don Bacigalupi, who brought his husband and son to the town made by a company built on the backs of an army of hardworking, evangelical farm-women-turned-retail-associates. By the time Crystal Bridges greeted the public, coastal outrage had given way to a sanguine reappraisal of "one of the most cosmopolitan small cities in America."[8]

Rebranding the Ozarks

Crystal Bridges Museum was simply the most newsworthy sign of the makeover of northwestern Arkansas. With Walmart, Tyson Foods, J. B. Hunt, and the university leading the way, this corner of Arkansas blossomed in the 1990s, its per capita income leaping by 50 percent and its population increasing by almost as much. A new airport in 1998 (another initiative spearheaded by Alice Walton) provided direct flights to New York, Chicago, San Francisco, and other major destinations. Walmart pressured its stable of national and international vendors to build satellite offices in booming "Northwest Arkansas City." Not only did this contribute to the unprecedented demographic transformation already under way, but it helped turn this nook of the Ozarks into one of Middle America's most well-to-do places. By the early twenty-first century, the northwestern Arkansas metropolitan area sat atop the Milken Institute's Best Performing Cities index, and *Forbes* ranked the district among the top twenty-five metro areas for business and careers. It was a leading market for golf courses, mansions, and luxury cars. Bentonville was a "small town on steroids." According to an article in the *New Yorker*, it had become "an odd hybrid—a diminutive country town with suburbs on a scale befitting Dallas." It was enough to inspire boosters to concoct false rags-to-riches narratives. "Fifty years ago we were the poorest area of [the] state," intoned a chamber of commerce director, ignoring the fact that northwestern Arkansas had long been an oasis of comparative prosperity in the state and in the Ozarks. But his second observation was dead on. The "idea that the world would beat a path to do business in those hills" would have been a ludicrous thought a few decades earlier.[9]

Today vendors from around the world do in fact find their way to the Ozarks to do business with the country's largest retail corporation, and art lovers and afficionados beat a path to Crystal Bridges. The one-two punch of affluence and demographic shift—at least in northwestern Arkansas and Springfield, Missouri—have planted the seeds of an image transformation. In the years since the opening of Crystal Bridges, the Ozarks has been the subject of several pieces in national publications. A clear trend has emerged, a sort of rebranding campaign fueled by Walton money and hipster ostentation. Most of the attention has been focused on Bentonville and its convergence of big incomes and high art. Thanks to the Walton Family Foundation, Walmart's town and its environs boast some of the nation's most extensive biking trails, a modern symbol of affluence and upward mobility. The days of Sam Walton's legendary displays of modesty seem safely in the past. The small farms and narrow backroads that Sam once navigated in his '79 Ford pickup have been replaced by million-dollar subdivisions and even pricier gated communities. Like the agents of gentrification everywhere, the transformers of northwestern Arkansas have grown adept at co-opting and paying feint tribute to elements of the culture they've erased. The result is a sort of upmarket caricaturing of a romanticized Ozarks past. The little houses of the Black Apple pocket community sport reclaimed wood siding, sliding barn doors, and steel chimneys as elements of their "modern agrarian" style. The area's dining scene developed its own signature cuisine, "High South," a hybrid that uses locally sourced foods to produce a "refined country" menu of down-home cooking with gourmet touches.[10]

Even in its early stages the metamorphosis has attracted attention from the most unlikely quarters, suggesting that John T. Woodruff's Depression-era vision of a prosperous, modernized Ozarks may yet carry the day. At the very least, the promoters of Vance Randolph's counter-vision of a traditional and deliberately unprogressive Ozarks must have gone into damage-control mode when *Vogue* explained "Why You Should Plan a Road Trip through the Ozark Mountains." It was an approach that flew in the face of a century of travel writing. Gone were the overall-clad farmers, float trips, and fiddlers that *Life*, *National Geographic*, and other magazines trafficked throughout the twentieth century. In their place were art galleries, bistros, and spas. Destinations like Crystal Bridges and the nearby 21C Museum Hotel were no-brainers. Springfield's boutique Hotel Vandivort, "abuzz with iPhone-toting locals come cocktail hour," promised visitors a unisex bathroom that had "become a hotbed for the perfect selfie." A local French pastry shop was "tailor-made for Instagram," while the Mediterranean dishes at a trendy tearoom provided "a nice respite from this biscuit-and-gravy-loving town." Even the Shepherd of the Hills Country—that old tourist trap specializing in economy motels and chicken-fried steak the size of a hammered dulcimer—showed signs of rehabilitation for the *Vogue* set. "Working to move away from its reputation as a kitschy country music hub with top-billed golf courses and the Branson Landing," the river valley where Jim Owen's guides had once told campfire tales of the legendary gowrow was now home to places like the Chateau on the Lake Resort and Spa. Lest the name suggest a rusticity more genuine than faux, the magazine assured readers that Johnny Morris's Big Cedar Lodge reflected an "upscale cabin-chic vibe that's done right."[11]

This wasn't Randolph's Ozarks anymore. Then again, life for most people in the region had never conformed to the boiled-down images of Randolph's Ozarkers. By the time *Vogue* discovered the Ozarks, the region and its image had coexisted for more than a century, the strands of each entwining until it was difficult to tell where fact ended and legend began. The Ozarks of Vance Randolph's romantic and contrarian vision may no longer exist, but it is safe to say that the Ozarks of Alice Walton is in no danger of overtaking the plateau anytime soon—perhaps not even in her own hometown. Less than a year after the grand opening of Crystal Bridges, another Bentonville resident launched his

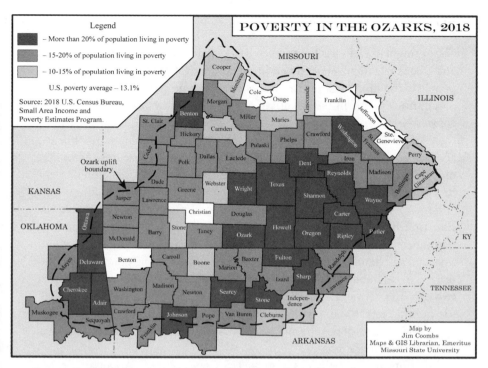

Poverty in the Ozarks, 2018. Courtesy of Jim Coombs, Missouri State University, Springfield.

own equilibrium-restoring headline grabber—the first annual World Championship Squirrel Cook Off. Not everyone was thrilled with this kind of old-school publicity. And that was just fine for cook-off founder Joe Wilson, who envisioned the annual event as a way "to stave off big-city airs and remind locals that they still live in the Ozarks."[12]

A few miles beyond the city limits of places like Bentonville and Springfield there was no need to remind people where they lived—and plenty of rural areas where folks ate squirrel unironically. The region still contains vast stretches of countryside. More than 75 percent of the counties in the interior Ozarks have no city with at least ten thousand residents, and more than one-third lack a town of even twenty-five hundred people. It remains the region's most enduring trait, but even the Ozarks isn't as rural as it once was. Between 1990 and 2019 the number of Ozarkers living in metropolitan areas more than doubled. By the latter date, two in five resided in either "Northwest Arkansas City" or Springfield.[13] Almost all the kinds of economic and cultural development highlighted by *Vogue* was confined to these two places.

Evolving and Enduring

The Springfield Plain has long served as a counterbalance to the more modest and frequently impoverished conditions in the rest of the Ozarks. It was the people living in the rest of the Ozarks who became the Ozarkers in the eyes of a curious public in the twentieth century. In the twenty-first century the contrasts between these two versions of the Ozarks are starker than ever. Northwest Arkansas City and Springfield are home to large universities, *Fortune* 500 companies, manicured professional baseball fields, and museums. Across the old "cultural fault line" in the Oklahoma portion of the Springfield Plain, the proliferation of casinos following a 2004 state referendum provided revenues and services undreamed of by the thousands of members of the Cherokee Nation, United Keetoowah Band, Eastern Shawnee, and other federally recognized native peoples.[14] As these oases capture ever-increasing portions of the region's financial and human capital, Ozarkers in large swaths of the poorer, older hinterland find remoteness even more of a challenge than it was a generation or two ago. The very seclusion that makes such places so highly valued for their scenic and recreational possibilities subjects residents to the economic and cultural challenges of poverty and isolation, conditions unalleviated by seasonal tourism and service jobs.

According to 2018 estimates from the U.S. Census Bureau, Arkansas's Benton County, home to Walmart and Crystal Bridges, boasted a median household income almost nineteen percent greater than the next-richest county in the interior Ozarks. By contrast, eight rural counties in the rugged hills reported median household incomes less than half of Benton's. Poverty rates exceeded 20 percent in one out of three counties, creating a block of persistent poverty that rendered the Ozarks (alongside pockets of Appalachia) one of the nation's bastions of poor whites. Childhood poverty rates routinely swelled to more than 30 percent in the rural interior, where children were 61 percent more likely to live in poverty than were kids in the region's metropolitan areas.[15]

Chronic underemployment dogged well over half the counties in the interior Ozarks. It was just one factor accounting for extremely high rates of dependence on government transfer payments, a measurement that skyrocketed in the early twenty-first century. Nothing more starkly delineated Alice Walton's sanctuary from the downward spiraling, rural interior. Whereas government transfer payments (social security, welfare, disability) accounted for only 7.5 percent of income in Benton County in 2018, they constituted more than 40 percent in fourteen rural counties.[16] In the first two decades of the twenty-first century, rural economic decline, methamphetamine sales, and opioid addiction defined a forlorn subculture of the Ozarks. An epidemic of drug-related crimes so plagued southern Missouri that the region's 417 area code became a slang term for crystal meth. Incessant media coverage of the war on narcotics inspired novelist Daniel Woodrell to pen the haunting tale of a teenage heroine trying to overcome family dysfunction and rural drug culture to save her kin and their land. Director Debra Granik's award-winning cinematic version of *Winter's Bone* in 2010 blossomed into the region's biggest pop-cultural touchstone in decades, its visual realism and powerful performances convincing more than a few coastal reviewers and cinephiles that the film was equal parts dramatic fiction and cinema verité. The fact that the movie *Winter's Bone* dominated national perceptions of the Ozarks during the year and a half preceding the opening of Crystal Bridges made the museum's premiere that much more jarring and its impact on the region's image that much more transformative.[17]

The birth of Crystal Bridges in 2011 did not magically erase powerful visions of meth-addled Ozarkers, nor did it stamp out generations of stereotypical Ozarks imagery. Similarly, the arrival of tens of thousands of Latinas/os, Marshallese, East Asians, and Africans has not yet expunged the nation's engrained portrait of a lily-white region. But the twenty-first century has certainly sparked a reimagining of the Ozarks and Ozarkers. It was inevitable that at some point the reality of life in the Ozarks would stray so far from the region's stubborn image that the dissonance would be impossible to ignore.

Even if High South cuisine and other self-conscious symbols of an alternative Ozarks aren't destined to rebrand a regional population, they nonetheless reflect the tremendous changes to a place long mislabeled as unchanging. Each summer more than one hundred thousand Vietnamese American Roman Catholics make the pilgrimage to the Marian Days celebration held at Carthage, Missouri's Congregation of the Mother of the Redeemer. The crowds attracted to this event on the former campus of Our Lady of the Ozarks College dwarf those at the Arkansas Folk Festival, the War Eagle Fair, and other once-massive celebrations of traditional Ozarks culture. Gatherings like yoga festivals and LGBTQ pride parades also reflect changes in the modern Ozarks. Pockets of progressivism thrive in places like Eureka Springs and Fayetteville, Arkansas, both of which were ahead of the curve on ordinances liberalizing marijuana use and prohibiting discrimination based on sexual orientation and gender identity. Eureka Springs, where "not even our streets are straight," has carved out a special niche as a year-round safe haven and vacation spot for the LGBTQ community. With its rainbow parades and biker bars, its busloads of evangelical Christians, its new age boutiques and haunted hotel tours, Eureka Springs is the most unusual and unexpected place in the Ozarks.[18]

Just fifty miles away from Eureka Springs, however, the College of the Ozarks stands as one of the nation's most aggressively conservative institutions of higher education, topping the *Princeton Review*'s 2021 list of colleges most unfriendly to LGBTQ students and regularly grabbing headlines with its defiantly rightist stances on hot-button issues. The institution's hyper-patriotism exceeds that of nearby Branson, and a "biblical worldview" infuses every facet of the curriculum at the college's high school–level academy. The profile of the College of the Ozarks comes nearer to representing the rank-and-file Ozarker than does the image projected by Eureka Springs.[19]

Going well beyond the merely "unfriendly," in the latter decades of the twentieth century the region's overwhelmingly white demographic profile and stretches of rural remoteness attracted several groups harboring racist and anti-Semitic beliefs. Thom Robb, an Arizona-raised Christian Identity pastor who settled in Boone County, Arkansas, in the 1970s and later made it the headquarters of the Knights of the Ku Klux Klan (KKK), is only the most notable of the genre's leaders. Texas preacher James Ellison—leader of the Covenant, the Sword, and the Arm of the Lord—found his way to the remote Ozarks around the same time, eventually establishing a militaristic compound near Bull Shoals Lake in northern Arkansas. The hills of the Ozarks are also home to a number of documented cells affiliated with other incarnations of the KKK and the League of the South. In 2010 more than a few Missouri listeners were shocked to hear the blatantly racist and anti-Semitic radio campaign ads of U.S. Senate candidate Frazier Glenn Miller, an army veteran from North Carolina who settled in Aurora, Missouri, a few years earlier. Founder of the White Patriot Party, Miller murdered two people in a shooting spree outside a suburban Kansas City Jewish community center four years later.[20]

The same era that witnessed increasing demographic diversity as well as a larger footprint for hate groups in the Ozarks has also signaled the development of an unprecedented political homogeneity. This red monolith is of recent origin. The Ozarks entered the second half of the twentieth century with its Civil War–generated political divisions intact. But a variety of factors chipped away at party solidarity in the region's longtime "yellow dog" Democrat districts. Some factors were the same ones threatening Democrat control across the South: the national party's continuing leftward drift away from its Jeffersonian origins and especially its increasing embrace of the cause of civil rights for African Americans. Others were more local in nature. Beginning in the 1950s the steady influx of retirees and other Midwesterners padded the rolls of the Grand Old Party. Furthermore, as historian J. Blake Perkins has demonstrated, the failure of many federal programs to address fundamental regional economic problems left many onetime New Dealers disillusioned with Democrats and with big government in general. While local and state elections maintained traditional blue-red divisions into the twenty-first century, presidential elections flashed glimpses of the region's political future. Dwight D. Eisenhower made significant inroads into Democrat territory, carrying more than two-thirds of interior counties in 1956. Four years later only the yellowest of dogs in the Protestant interior stayed true to the Democratic candidate as Richard Nixon blew the doors off Roman Catholic John F. Kennedy's campaign in the Ozarks.[21]

Yet 1960 wasn't to be the watershed moment in Ozarks politics. Democrats with a drawl continued to poll well throughout the remainder of the century. Lyndon B. Johnson's Texas Hill Country twang was familiar enough to carry more than two-thirds of the region's interior counties in 1964, and Southerners Jimmy Carter and Bill Clinton did almost as well in the Ozarks in their first go-rounds. But any Democratic hopeful lacking the common touch and saddled with a hint of elitism had no shot in the populist hill country. George McGovern fell victim to Richard Nixon's clean sweep of the Ozarks in 1972, and Walter Mondale and Michael Dukakis fared little better in the 1980s. By the twenty-first century, the last generation of "yellow dogs" had mostly passed from the scene, leading to a quick and complete Republican triumph in the region. No Ozarker has been represented in Congress by a Democrat since 2011. A Democratic presidential candidate last carried an Ozarks county in 2008, and Donald J. Trump's sweep of the region in 2016 was the most thorough in history, as nine out of every ten interior counties returned more than 70 percent of the vote for the Republican. Counties whose local offices had been in the firm control of Democrats since Reconstruction have turned dependably Republican amid the culture wars and the Barack Obama/Hillary Clinton backlash, rendering the Ozarks effectively a one-party region. Had J. D. Vance's *Hillbilly Elegy* not focused the nation's gaze so intently on Appalachia, the Trump-supporting Ozarks might have attracted the lion's share of publicity following the 2016 election.[22]

Given the reddening of the regional political map, it seems clear that liberal sensibilities thrive only in those few pockets of progressivism—that the Ozarks mirrors the national trend toward spatial segregation when it comes to political and cultural viewpoints. Still, paradoxes remain a part of the region's fabric. For generations cheap land and relative isolation have attracted to the Ozarks a variety of escapists from other parts of the country. Bunkering bigots have certainly been among them, but they've elbowed for space with religious sects convinced the final days are nigh, idealistic back-to-the-landers, communal counterculturists, retirees, Old Order Amish farmers, and doomsday preppers. The hill country dictum "kill your own snakes" bred a willingness among Ozarkers to mind their own business. Maybe that helps explain rural Douglas County, Missouri. To be sure, Douglas featured flyover-country stripes like major declines in manufacturing jobs and a 2016 election in which more than 82 percent of voters cast ballots for Trump. But this lily-white evangelical county was also home to lesbian communes, a remote abbey of Trappist monks, a "clothing optional" campground for gay men, and a rural mercantile whose Martin Luther King Jr.–quoting owner specialized in tie-dye, bikers' leather, and Grateful Dead memorabilia.[23] Still, like so much of Middle America, the Ozarks continues to elicit sweeping generalizations from observers whose knowledge of the region comes courtesy of political maps and tired stereotypes that cling to the region like beggar's lice in the fall.

Visiting a town in the touristy Ozarks in the late 1990s, a writer for *National Geographic* marveled that "nearly everyone I met was from somewhere else."[24] Frantic in-migration over the past quarter century has further reduced the percentage of Ozarkers with family trees populated by nineteenth-century settlers from the upcountry of Tennessee, Kentucky, Virginia, and the Carolinas. These were the people who planted their culture in the hills and hollers and whose descendants inspired stereotypes forged of equal parts admiration and disdain. These were the people whose authenticity and anachronism charmed the romantic and repulsed the impatient. Their descendants, the "native" Ozarkers, have watched their hold on the demographics and culture of the region slip. In many parts of the Ozarks today, natives and newcomers alike share the reaction of that *National Geographic* writer. The physical place we call the Ozarks has undergone noticeable change in the places of greatest growth. Yet much of the Ozark uplift remains essentially unaltered. More than anything it is the Ozarkers themselves who have changed and are changing. Whether immigrant poultry workers, back-to-the-land baby boomers, boomtown executives and vendors in Bentonville, or retirees in search of a mild climate and a lower cost of living, "the Ozarkers" no longer means what it once did.

For more than a century, stereotypes have defined the Ozarkers in the nation's consciousness. This popular idea of the Ozarks was born in an age of Jim Crow and jingoism, of romanticism for the rural and recalcitrant. Race and racism played key roles in concocting both the positive and negative aspects of the hillbilly/mountaineer image and in applying those stereotypes to Ozarkers. But Ozarkers have never been chained to the images that have reduced their society to simple caricature. They have been otherwise occupied—living their lives, defining themselves by their own reckoning. An increasing number of them follow the path championed by John T. Woodruff, an existence barely distinguishable if at all from other upwardly mobile Americans. The hollers and ridges are still home to some whose deep rural heritage or conscious contrarianism continue to fascinate romantics and modern-day primitivists drawn to people and places on the margins. The old images cling to these Ozarkers, the ones to which a twenty-first-century Vance Randolph would gravitate. Demographic shifts since the 1990s have rendered the regional construct of the poor, white hillbilly/mountaineer less representative of Ozarkers than ever before. It is a regional image that belongs to the twentieth century. In a modern nation where six out of seven people live in a metropolitan county and where non-Hispanic whites will soon constitute a minority of the population, the Ozarkers' backwoods brand of exoticism may have finally outlived its usefulness.

Wrestling with these final thoughts on my native region, it occurs to me that it was almost exactly five years ago when I wrote the first words of this trilogy. It is fall again. Daylight recedes. In the ditch across the dirt road from my house, towering, winged stalks of white crown-beard (or frostweed) jostle with pokeweed, sumac, and foxtails straining for the sun's weakening rays. The first freeze will come soon. Then the cold morning air will work its magic on the groundwater seeping from the dead stems of frostweed. The time of rabbit ice nears. I'm reminded how brief has been our intersection with this eroded mound we call the Ozarks. The mountains that once were here disappeared millennia ago, their jagged edges and looming cliffs dissolved into the sea by rains and winds across what seems an eternity of days. All that remains is the Ozarks, a place whose hollers, worn ridges, and prairies shaped the Ozarkers. I'm reminded that *The Old Ozarks* and *The Conflicted Ozarks* were but fleeting eras. And so it is with the age of *The Ozarkers*, a people with an image and identity as weathered and tired as the ancient plateau they call home. This beautiful but unforgiving land still demarcates places of poverty from pockets of prosperity. Its inhabitants continue to evolve with a changing nation and world. As for that impermanent rabbit ice, there is no predicting what form tomorrow morning's will take. All we know for certain is that those shimmering labyrinths of frozen crystals won't be the same as yesterday's or today's—and neither will the Ozarkers.

Notes

Introduction

1. "Writers Called Ignorant of the Genuine Ozarks," *Springfield Leader and Press*, April 17, 1934; Robert Cochran, *Vance Randolph: An Ozark Life* (Urbana: University of Illinois Press, 1985), 133–36.
2. "'Freak Show' Will Not Get C.C. Support," *Springfield Leader and Press*, March 19, 1934; "Deny C. of C. Turning Back upon Festival," *Springfield Leader and Press*, March 20, 1934.
3. Thomas A. Peters, *John T. Woodruff of Springfield, Missouri, in the Ozarks: An Encyclopedic Biography* (Springfield, MO: Pie Supper Press, 2016), 4.

4. Ibid; Vance Randolph, "Sees Good 'Ad' in 'Hill-billies,'" *Springfield Leader and Press*, April 18, 1934.
5. Robert Cochran, "Vance Randolph," *EOA*, accessed November 28, 2018; Cochran, *Vance Randolph*, 13, 125.
6. Peters, *John T. Woodruff*, 2–4, 69, 81, 160, 197–203.
7. Vance Randolph, *The Ozarks: An American Survival of Primitive Society*, ed. Robert Cochran (Fayetteville: University of Arkansas Press, 2017), 6, 9.
8. Peters, *John T. Woodruff*, 227; John Thomas Woodruff, *Reminiscences of an Ozarkian and Early Tourism Developments*, ed. Steve Illum (Springfield, MO: Office of Leisure Research, Southwest Missouri State University, 1994), 11, 23–31; "Writers Called Ignorant."
9. "A History of the Springfield Symphony: 1934–Present," https://www.springfieldmo symphony.org/history, accessed August 4, 2020.
10. Randolph, "Sees Good 'Ad.'"
11. Randolph, *The Ozarks*, 20.

Chapter 1. Change and Continuity

1. Harold Bell Wright, *The Shepherd of the Hills* (New York: Grosset and Dunlap, 1907), 346.
2. Lynn Morrow and Linda Myers-Phinney, *Shepherd of the Hills Country: Tourism Transforms the Ozarks, 1880s–1930s* (Fayetteville: University of Arkansas Press, 1999), 26–31.
3. Ibid., 6, 49; Walter M. Adams, *The White River Railway: Being a History of the White River Division of the Missouri Pacific Railroad Company, 1901–1951* (Branson, MO: The Ozarks Mountaineer, 1991), 49–60; Brooks Blevins, *Arkansas/Arkansaw: How Bear Hunters, Hillbillies, and Good Ol' Boys Defined a State* (Fayetteville: University of Arkansas Press, 2009), 62.
4. Ronald D. Eller, *Miners, Millhands, and Mountaineers: The Modernization of the Appalachian South, 1880–1930* (Knoxville: University of Tennessee Press, 1982), xix; Richard H. Brodhead, *Cultures of Letters: Scenes of Reading and Writing in Nineteenth-Century America* (Chicago: University of Chicago Press, 1993), 119.
5. Brodhead, *Cultures of Letters*, 132–33.
6. Adams, *White River Railway*, 11; James R. Fair Jr., *The North Arkansas Line: The Story of the Missouri & North Arkansas Railroad* (Berkeley, CA: Howell-North Books, 1969), 5, 22–54, 61–83.
7. Fair, *North Arkansas Line*, 90–108; Lawrence R. Handley, "Settlement across Northern Arkansas as Influenced by the Missouri & North Arkansas Railroad," *AHQ* 33 (Winter 1974): 277–84; Theodore Catton, *Life, Leisure, and Hardship along the Buffalo*, Historic Resources Study, Buffalo National River (Omaha, NE: Midwest Region, National Park Service, 2008), 165–66; Ralph R. Rea, *Boone County and Its People* (Van Buren, AR: Press-Argus, 1955), 139, 151.
8. Adams, *White River Railway*, 13–37, 43–59.
9. Ibid., 48, 67–68, 99.

10. Fair, *North Arkansas Line*, 87, 63, 133–36, 229, 253–60; Rea, *Boone County and Its People*, 168–72.

11. H. Roger Grant, "The Ozark Short Line Railroad: A Failed Dream," in *The Ozarks in Missouri History: Discoveries in an American Region,* ed. Lynn Morrow (Columbia: University of Missouri Press, 2013), 123; Arrell M. Gibson, *Wilderness Bonanza: The Tri-State District of Missouri, Kansas, and Oklahoma* (Norman: University of Oklahoma Press, 1972), 83; Robert Sidney Douglass, *History of Southeast Missouri: A Narrative Account of Its Historical Progress, Its People, and Its Principal Interests* (1912; Cape Girardeau, MO: Rimfire Press, 1961), 384–85; *Douglas County (MO) Herald,* September 9, 1909, quoted in Grant, "Ozark Short Line Railroad," 124; J. E. Curry, *A Reminiscent History of Douglas County, Missouri, 1857–1957* (Ava, MO: Douglas County Herald, 1957), 29–38.

12. Grant, "Ozark Short Line Railroad," 124–38.

13. Blevins, *Arkansas/Arkansaw*, 24–33.

14. Will Wallace Harney, "A Strange Land and a Peculiar People," *Lippincott's Magazine,* October 1873, 429–38; George Ward Nichols, "Wild Bill," *Harper's New Monthly Magazine,* February 1867, 274; "Ku-Klux," *St. Louis Globe-Democrat,* September 7, 1877, 7; New York *Evening World,* May 22, 1888, Three O'Clock Edition, 3; Brooks Blevins, *A History of the Ozarks,* vol. 2, *The Conflicted Ozarks* (Urbana: University of Illinois Press, 2019), 239–41.

15. Brodhead, *Cultures of Letters*, 115–16.

16. John Monteith, *Parson Brooks: A Plumb Powerful Hard Shell, A Story of Humble Southern Life* (St. Louis: O.H.P. Applegate, 1884), 14, 7.

17. Ibid., 21.

18. Mary Stewart, *Unspotted from the World* (New York: Robert Lewis Weed Company, 1897), 14.

19. Ibid., 20–21.

20. Rose Emmet Young, *Sally of Missouri* (New York: McClure, Phillips and Co., 1903), 14.

21. Grover Clay, *Hester of the Hills: A Romance of the Ozark Mountains* (Boston: L. C. Page and Company, 1907.)

22. Wright, *Shepherd of the Hills*, 17.

23. Ibid., 5, 220, 11, 125.

24. Clifton Johnson, "Life in the Ozarks," *Outing,* January 1906, 435.

25. Johnson, "Life in the Ozarks," 435–42.

26. Victor H. Schoffelmayer, "White River Trails," *New Age Magazine,* March 1913, 203–208.

27. Lawrence F. Abbott, "An Arkansas Traveler," *The Outlook,* June 1, 1927, 148; Charles Phelps Cushing, "The Ozarks: The Highlands of the Middle West," *Mentor,* July 1927, 27.

28. Charles Morrow Wilson, "Moonshiners," *Outlook and Independent,* December 19, 1928, 1,350; Cushing, "The Ozarks," 24–28; F. M. Van Natter, "Highlands of the Ozarks," *National Republic,* June 1930, 6.

29. William R. Draper, "The Ozarks Go Native," *Outlook,* September 10, 1930, 60–61; W. R. Draper, "Motoring into the Ozarks," *New York Times,* July 20, 1930, XX7.

30. *New York Times*, May 24, 1931, E1.

31. Brooks Blevins, *Hill Folks: A History of Arkansas Ozarkers and Their Image* (Chapel Hill: University of North Carolina Press, 2002), 134–43.

32. Ibid., 143.

33. Ellen Compton, "Charles Morrow Wilson," *EOA*, accessed July 19, 2016; Wilson, "Moonshiners," 1, 350–52; Charles Morrow Wilson, "Backwoods Morality," *Outlook and Independent*, January 9, 1929, 65–67; Charles Morrow Wilson, "Elizabethan America," *Atlantic Monthly*, August 1929, 238–40.

34. Vance Randolph, *The Ozarks: An American Survival of Primitive Society* (New York: Vanguard Press, 1931), v.

35. See James Agee and Walker Evans, *Let Us Now Praise Famous Men* (New York: Houghton Mifflin, 1941).

36. Randolph, *The Ozarks*, 21–22.

Chapter 2. Living off the Land

1. Stephen W. Hines, ed., *Laura Ingalls Wilder, Farm Journalist: Writings from the Ozarks* (Columbia: University of Missouri Press, 2007), 2.

2. John E. Miller, *Becoming Laura Ingalls Wilder: The Woman behind the Legend* (Columbia: University of Missouri Press, 1998), 13–16, 44, 70, 86–95; Hines, *Laura Ingalls Wilder*, 17.

3. Miller, *Becoming Laura Ingalls Wilder*, 96–97.

4. Ibid., 102–109, 171; Milton Rafferty, "The Ozarks as a Region: A Geographer's Description," *OzarksWatch* 1 (Spring 1988): 2; Hines, *Laura Ingalls Wilder*, 18–19.

5. James M. Wilson to Brother and Sister, February 25, 1873, folder 1, box 1, Wilson Family Papers, Shiloh Museum of Ozark History, Springdale, Arkansas.

6. B. Franklin Kimmins to J. E. Kimmins, June 16, 1867, Joseph E. Kimmins Papers, #4306-z, Southern Historical Collection, Wilson Library, University of North Carolina, Chapel Hill; Peter B. Engels to Nephew, January 26, 1868, folder 1, box 1, Engels-Kinnibrugh Family Papers, MC 554, UASC.

7. *Arkansas Gazette*, June 25, 1872, 4; 1880 Agri census, cotton, Office of the Census, *Tenth Census of the United States, 1880: Agriculture* (GPO, 1883), 214, 232; Theodore Catton, *Life, Leisure, and Hardship along the Buffalo*, Historic Resources Study, Buffalo National River (Omaha, NE: Midwest Region, National Park Service, 2008), 123–27.

8. Douglas Mahnkey, *Bright Glowed My Hills* (Point Lookout, MO: School of the Ozarks Press, 1968), 26; Elmo Ingenthron, *The Land of Taney: A History of an Ozark Commonwealth* (Point Lookout, MO: School of the Ozarks Press, 1974), 317–23; Oliver E. Baker, "Agricultural Regions of North America, Part II—The South," *Economic Geography* 3 (January 1927): 65.

9. Marvin Lawson, *By Gum, I Made It! An Ozark Arkie's Hillbilly Boyhood* (Branson, MO: The Ozarks Mountaineer, 1977), 71; Larry Stroud, ed., *Old Time Preacher Man: The Life Story of Herman A. Lewis* (n.p. ., n.d.), 7–9.

10. CB, *Fourteenth Census of the United States, 1920: Agriculture* (GPO, 1922), 575–81;

CB, *Census of Agriculture, 1935: Reports for States, with Statistics by Counties*, vol. 1, part 2 (GPO, 1936), 670–76, 685–91.

11. Office of the Census, *Ninth Census of the United States, 1870: Wealth and Industry* (GPO, 1872), 100–103, 188–95; James W. Parins, *Elias Cornelius Boudinot: A Life on the Cherokee Border* (Lincoln: University of Nebraska Press, 2006), 87–102; Mary Jane Warde, *When the Wolf Came: The Civil War and the Indian Territory* (Fayetteville: University of Arkansas Press, 2013), 301.

12. J. Dickson Black, *History of Benton County* (n.p., 1975), 79–80, 280; *Tenth Census . . . Agriculture*, 254; *A Reminiscent History of the Ozark Region* (Chicago: Goodspeed Brothers, 1894), 555; Walter M. Adams, *The White River Railway: Being a History of the White River Division of the Missouri Pacific Railroad Company, 1901–1951* (Branson, MO: The Ozarks Mountaineer, 1991), 104–105.

13. Oliver E. Baker, "Agricultural Regions of North America, Part III—The Middle Country Where South and North Meet," *Economic Geography* 3 (July 1927): 309.

14. Erma Humphreys, *Down on the Farm* (Fort Dodge, KS: self-pub., 1976), 76; J. E. Curry, *A Reminiscent History of Douglas County, Missouri, 1857–1957* (Ava, MO: Douglas County Herald, 1957), 164; Ella Lilly Horak, *Good Old Days on the Farm* (n.p., 1968), 14–15.

15. Unknown to H. E. Woodruff, January 1, 1880, folder 6, box 1, Engels-Kinnibrugh Family Papers; Catton, *Life, Leisure, and Hardship*, 129.

16. Lawson, *By Gum, I Made It!*, 80; Curry, *Reminiscent History*, 164; Nell Sutton Jordan, *The Doctor's Daughters* (San Antonio, TX: Naylor Company, 1972), 81.

17. *Ninth Census . . . Wealth and Industry*, 100–103, 188–95; *Tenth Census . . . Agriculture*, 179, 195–97; Office of the Census, *Twelfth Census of the United States, 1900: Agriculture* (GPO, 1903), 154–55, 162, 171–73; John K. Hulston, *An Ozarks Boy's Story, 1915–1945* (Point Lookout, MO: School of the Ozarks Press, 1971), 24.

18. Joel T. Livingston, *A History of Jasper County, Missouri and Its People*, vol. 1 (Chicago: Lewis Publishing Company, 1912), 122; Jonathan Fairbanks and Clyde Edwin Tuck, *Past and Present of Greene County, Missouri*, vol. 1 (Indianapolis: A. W. Bowen & Company, 1915), 668–71.

19. Livingston, *History of Jasper County*, 256–57; *Reminiscent History of the Ozark Region*, 283, 383; Fairbanks and Tuck, *Past and Present*, 1:675–76; Fairbanks and Tuck, *Past and Present*, 2:1816–17.

20. *Marshall Mountain Wave*, December 2, 1898, 2.

21. CB, *Thirteenth Census of the United States, 1910*, vol. 6, *Agriculture* (GPO, 1913), 120–26, 928–38; CB, *Thirteenth Census of the United States, 1910*, vol. 7, *Agriculture* (GPO, 1913), 380–87; CB, *Fourteenth Census of the United States, 1920*, vol. 6, part 1, *Agriculture* (GPO, 1922), 600–610; CB, *Fourteenth Census of the United States, 1920*, vol. 6, part 2, *Agriculture* (GPO, 1922), 575–81, 643–49; CB, *Fifteenth Census of the United States: 1930, Agriculture*, vol. 2, part 1 (GPO, 1932), 1014–1023; CB, *Fifteenth Census of the United States: 1930, Agriculture*, vol. 2, part 2, (GPO, 1932), 1168–73, 1316–21; Steven D. Smith, *Made in the Timber: A Settlement History of the Fort Leonard Wood Region* (Fort Leonard Wood, MO: Maneuver Support Center; Engineer Research and Development Center/Construction Engineering Research Laboratory

Special Report 03–5, July 2003), 133; *Springfield Leader and Press*, December 4, 1951, thelibrary.org/blogs/article.cfm?aid=2517, accessed July 5, 2017.

22. Rose Fulton Cramer, *Wayne County, Missouri* (Cape Girardeau, MO: Ramfire Press, 1972), 346.

23. Lawson, *By Gum, I Made It!*, 38–39; Janet Florence and Ronnie Hough, "Sorghum Molasses," *Bittersweet* 1 (Spring 1974), 19–29; Humphreys, *Down on the Farm*, 88; Horak, *Good Old Days*, 17; Catton, *Life, Leisure, and Hardship*, 130.

24. Livingston, *History of Jasper County*, 37; Wiley Britton, *Pioneer Life in Southwest Missouri* (Kansas City, MO: Smith-Grieves Co., 1929), 79–80; Jesse Lewis Russell, *Behind These Ozark Hills* (New York: Hobson Book Press, 1947), 60; Jordan, *Doctor's Daughters*, 21.

25. John J. Sitton Diary, vol. 2, October 23, 1869, John James Sitton Collection, R1286, SHSMR.

26. Office of the Census, *Eleventh Census of the United States, 1890: Agriculture* (GPO, 1895), 357, 373–74; *Thirteenth Census . . . Agriculture*, 120–26, 380–87, 928–38.

27. Carl O. Sauer, *The Geography of the Ozark Highland of Missouri* (1920; New York: Greenwood Press, 1968), 192; Bill Stiritz, ed., *Beecher Moss's Turn of the Century Coming of Age Memoir* (St. Louis, MO: n.p., 1999), 16.

28. *Tenth Census . . . Agriculture*, 143, 160–161; Lawson, *By Gum, I Made It!*, 35–36; Horak, *Good Old Days*, 17–18; Cora Pinkley Call, *Within My Ozark Valley* (Eureka Springs, AR: Times-Echo, 1956), 59–60; Humphreys, *Down on the Farm*, 83–85; Omer E. Brown, *Son of Pioneers: Recollections of an Ozarks Lawyer* (Point Lookout, MO: School of the Ozarks Press, 1973), 81; Betty R. Manuel, *Opal Pense, Winfrey Valley Girl: Stories of a Child of the 1920s Ozarks* (Republic, MO: The Ozarks Mountaineer, 1994), 30–31; V. R. "Jack" Thomas, *Life in the Heart of the Ozarks* (Kearney, NE: Morris Publishing, 2007), 53, 81–82.

29. "Hog Drovers," as sung by Ollie Gilbert, Mountain View, Arkansas, October 28, 1969, Max Hunter Folk Song Collection, https://maxhunter.missouristate.edu/song information.aspx?ID-1043, accessed July 7, 2017; John Thomas Woodruff, *Reminiscences of an Ozarkian and Early Tourism Developments*, ed. Steve Illum (Springfield, MO: Office of Leisure Research, Southwest Missouri State University, 1994), 18; Evalena Berry, *Time and the River: A History of Cleburne County* (Little Rock: Rose Publishing, 1982), 293; Kirby, *Drummer Boy of the Ozarks*, 85.

30. Wayne Martin, *Pettigrew, Arkansas: The Hardwood Capital of the World* (Springdale, AR: Shiloh Museum of Ozark History, 2010), 67–68; *Marshall Mountain Wave*, November 19, 1897, 1.

31. *Tenth Census . . . Agriculture*, 143, 160–61; *Fourteenth Census . . .* vol. 6, part 1, 589–99; *Fourteenth Census . . .* vol. 6, part 2, 568–74, 636–42.

32. *Ninth Census . . . Wealth and Industry*, 100–103, 188–95; *Eleventh Census . . . Agriculture*, 238, 255–56; *Twelfth Census . . . Agriculture*, 419–21, 454–57; *Thirteenth Census . . .* vol. 6, *Agriculture*, 104–111, 906–916; *Thirteenth Census . . .* vol. 7, *Agriculture*, 364–71; James Lee Murphy, "A History of the Southeastern Ozark Region of Missouri" (PhD diss., Saint Louis University, 1982), 247; Tate C. Page, *Voices of Moccasin Creek* (Point Lookout, MO: School of the Ozarks Press, 1972), 68.

33. *Thirteenth Census* . . . vol. 6, *Agriculture*, 104–111, 906–16; *Thirteenth Census* . . . vol. 7, *Agriculture*, 364–71; *Fourteenth Census* . . . vol. 6, part 1, 589–99; *Fourteenth Census* . . . vol. 6, part 2, 568–74, 636–42.

34. *Ninth Census* . . . *Wealth and Industry*, 100–103, 188–95; *Eleventh Census* . . . *Agriculture*, 277–78, 295–96; *Fourteenth Census* . . . vol. 6, part 1, 589–99; *Fourteenth Census* . . . vol. 6, part 2, 568–74, 636–42; Kirby, *Drummer Boy of the Ozarks*, 96.

35. Mrs. J. N. Bromley, *Biography of John W. Morris* (Marshall, AR: n.p., 1916), 80–81; James Wilson to William Wilson, May 19, 1875; James Wilson to William Wilson, March 24, 1876, folder 1, box 1, Wilson Family Papers; Hugh Tan Harlin, *The Harlins of Ozark County*, 2nd ed. (n.p., 1999), 43, 51.

36. Robert Flanders, "Alley, an Ozarks Mill Hamlet, 1890–1925: Society, Economy, Landscape," unpublished report for the Ozark National Scenic Riverways (Springfield, MO: Center for Ozarks Studies, Southwest Missouri State University, 1985), 9, 18; Christian County History Committee, *Christian County*, 29.

37. "Potomac" letter to *Arkansas Gazette*, reprinted in *Marshall Mountain Wave*, October 7, 1898, 1, 4; Thelma S. McManus, *That's the Way It Was: Interviews of Ozark Folk Born in the 1800s* (Morley, MO: Acclaim Press, 2008), 130; Page, *Voices of Moccasin Creek*, 40.

38. Craig R. Heidemann, "Fencing Laws in Missouri: Confusion, Conflict, Ambiguity and a Need for Change," *Missouri Law Review* 63 (Spring 1998): 543; Russell, *Behind These Ozark Hills*, 36; *Carthage (MO) Press*, August 22, 1901, cited in Charles and Neva Chrisman, *Memories of Bowers Mill* (Verona, MO: Johnson's Valley Printers, 1987), 38; Curry, *Reminiscent History*, 48, 105.

39. J. Blake Perkins, "Dynamics of Defiance: Government Power and Rural Resistance in the Arkansas Ozarks" (PhD diss., West Virginia University, 2014), 165–69; Brooks Blevins, *Hill Folks: A History of Arkansas Ozarkers and Their Image* (Chapel Hill: University of North Carolina Press, 2002), 95; *Yellville Mountain Echo*, November 27, 1896, 1; February 26, 1897, 1.

40. Perkins, "Dynamics of Defiance," 165, 171–72; Blevins, *Hill Folks*, 95.

41. Perkins, "Dynamics of Defiance," 167–68.

42. Blevins, *Hill Folks*, 42–43.

43. Robert Gilmore, "The Missouri State Fruit Experiment Station," *OzarksWatch* 3 (Winter 1990), 11; Marilyn Odneal, "Centennial of the State Fruit Experiment Station," https://ag.missouristate.edu/statefruit/history/centennial-fes.htm, accessed July 11, 2017.

44. John J. Sitton Diary, vol. 2, July–December 1870, October–November 1871; Julia West Parker, *Nan of Tennessee and the Girl Who Was Me* (Springfield, MO: Empire Printing, 1974), 51–53; Russell, *Behind These Ozark Hills*, 5–6; Walter F. Lackey, *History of Newton County, Arkansas* (Independence, MO, n.d.), 408.

45. Charles Draper Ledger, folder 38, Draper-McClurg Family Papers, State Historical Society of Missouri, Columbia; Robert Flanders, "Haseltine Orchards Historic Area Survey," 1994, https://dnr.mo.gov/shpo/survey/GRAS005-R.pdf, accessed July 12, 2017, 14–15.

46. Finding aid to Nelson Family Collection, 1879–1973, R 252, SHSMR, shsmo.org/

manuscripts/rolla/r0252.pdf, accessed July 12, 2017; Jim Hinckley, *The Route 66 En-cyclopedia* (McGregor, MN: Voyageur Press, 2012), 186; *35th Annual Report of the State Horticultural Society of the State of Missouri, 1892* (Jefferson City: Tribune Printing Company, 1893), 249.

47. *Among the Ozarks*, 22; *Transactions of the Kansas State Horticultural Society*, vol. 31 (Topeka, KS: State Printing Office, 1912), 197; *Better Fruit* (Hood River, OR), March 1920, 34; *Our Horticultural Visitor* (Kinmundy, IL), April 1905, 9; *National Nursery-man* (Rochester, NY), November 1905, 174; *The Southwest* (Springfield, MO), January 20, 1900, 5; Mansfield Area Historical Society, *Around Mansfield* (Charleston, SC: Arcadia Publishing, 2013), 77; *Fruit Trade Journal and Produce Record*, December 24, 1921, 19; *Cornell (NY) Daily Sun*, March 6, 1914, 7.

48. *Among the Ozarks*, 15; *Koshkonong: The History, The Heritage 1840–1987* (Koshko-nong, MO: Koshkonong Active Involvement Committee, 1987), 2–6; *Frisco System Magazine*, September 1904, 38–39, https://thelibrary.org/lochist/frisco/magazines/fsm_1904_09/fsm_1904_09_41.pdf, accessed July 13, 2017; Cora Ann Pottenger, "Place Names of Five Southern Border Counties of Missouri" (MA thesis, University of Missouri–Columbia, 1945), shsmo.org/manuscripts/ramsay/ramsay_howell.html, accessed July 13, 2017; Debra Bates-Lamborn, "First City History: A Woman's Un-usual Decision to Return Family Members to Leavenworth," *Leavenworth (KS) Times*, June 30, 2014, www.leavenworthtimes.com/article/20140630/NEWS/140639962, accessed July 13, 2017; *Fruit Trade Journal and Produce Record*, July 17, 1915, 14; Fruitville Farm Pamphlet c. 1910, R 9, SHSMR; *Koshkonong*, 21.

49. *Among the Ozarks*, 13; *37th Annual Report of the State Horticultural Society of Mis-souri*, 351.

50. Susan E. Dollar, "Viney Grove Methodist Church: A View into the Frontier Minis-try of Western Washington County, Arkansas," *Ozark Historical Review* 29 (Spring 2000): 7; A. M. Wilson to William Wilson, October 16, 1875, in *The William Wilson Records*, ed. W. J. Lemke (Fayetteville, AR: Washington County Historical Society, 1960), 96.

51. Blevins, *Hill Folks*, 42–43; Hugh D. Britt, "Personal Memoirs," unpublished typescript, Hugh D. Britt Papers, UASC.

52. *Benton County, Arkansas* (Kansas City, MO: Kansas City Southern Railway Com-pany Industrial Department, n.d.), 10, 15; *Thirteenth Census . . .* vol. 6, *Agriculture*, 104–111, 906–916; *Thirteenth Census . . .* vol. 7, *Agriculture*, 364–71.

53. *Eleventh Census . . . Agriculture*, 501–502, 518–19, 638–39; Charles Y. Alison, *A Brief History of Fayetteville, Arkansas* (Charleston, SC: The History Press, 2017), 78–80; Black, *History of Benton County*, 58–59.

54. *Twelfth Census . . . Agriculture*, 622–24, 656–60; *Thirteenth Census . . .* vol. 6, *Agri-culture*, 120–26, 928–58; *Thirteenth Census . . .* vol. 7, *Agriculture*, 380–87; *Fourteenth Census . . .* vol. 6, part 1, 600–610; *Fourteenth Census . . .* vol. 6, part 2, 575–81, 643–49; Black, *History of Benton County*, 87, 206; "Fruit and Truck Growing along the K.C.S. Ry.," *Current Events*, September 1914, 336; "The Fruit Crop of 1915," *Current Events*, July 1915, 149.

55. H. P. Gould and W. F. Fletcher, *Apples and Peaches in the Ozark Region*, Bulletin No.

275, Bureau of Plant Industry, USDA (Washington, DC: Government Printing Office, 1913), 8–9; *Koshkonong*, 23; Lewis A. W. Simpson, *Oregon County's Three Flags, Six County Seats via the Horse & Buggy*, 2nd ed. (Thayer, MO: Thayer News, 1980), 62; "Fruit Crop of 1915," 149.

56. Marilyn Collins, *Rogers: The Town the Frisco Built*, Making of America Series (Charleston, SC: Arcadia Publishing, 2002), 85; Black, *History of Benton County*, 206.

57. Gould and Fletcher, *Apples and Peaches*, 29; "Where Our Apples Are Grown," *Country Gentleman*, June 29, 1918, 13.

58. Tom Dicke, "Red Gold of the Ozarks: The Rise and Decline of Tomato Canning, 1885–1955," *Agricultural History* 79 (Winter 2005): 6–9, 14; "Dairying and Trucking in the Ozark Region," *Port Arthur Route Agricultural and Industrial Bulletin*, June 1926, 7; Sybil Shipley Jobe, *A History of Newton County, Missouri* (Cassville, MO: Newton County Historical Society, 1998), 171; Robert McGill, "Red Gold Ozark Tomatoes," *OzarksWatch* 9 (1996), 23.

59. Dicke, "Red Gold," 9–13; McGill, "Red Gold Ozark Tomatoes," 25; Paul W. Johns, *Unto These Hills: True Tales from the Ozarks* (n.p.: Bilyeu-Johns Enterprises, 1980), 86–88.

60. Dicke, "Red Gold," 12; "Dairying and Trucking," 7; Adams, *White River Railway*, 104–108.

61. Dicke, "Red Gold," 12, 17; McGill, "Red Gold Ozark Tomatoes," 24; Curry, *Reminiscent History*, 147.

62. Mark Parker, "Legend of Hermann Jaeger," *Missouri Ruralist*, April 2009, 34; *The Southwest* (Springfield, MO), May 20, 1900, 1; "Carl Starck—The Ozarks Pioneer Grape Grower," *OM*, September 1956, 13.

63. Leslie Hewes, "Tontitown: Ozark Vineyard Center," *Economic Geography* 29 (April 1953): 135–36; Susan Young, *"So Big This Little Place": The Founding of Tontitown, Arkansas, 1898–1917* (Tontitown, AR: Tontitown Historical Museum, 2009), 15, 21; Joseph R. Castelli, "Grape Growers of Central Missouri," *Rocky Mountain Social Science Journal* 1 (April 1964): 113–15.

64. Brent E. Riffel, "Prohibition," *EOA*, accessed July 18, 2017; Hewes, "Tontitown," 133–42.

65. *The Southwest*, April 20, 1900, 1; Blevins, *Hill Folks*, 99.

66. *The National Newspaper Directory and Gazetteer* (Boston: Pettingill and Co., 1899), 386; *The History of Jasper County, Missouri* (Des Moines, IA: Mills & Company, 1883), 667–68; Malcolm G. McGregor, *The Biographical Record of Jasper County, Missouri* (Chicago: Lewis Publishing Co., 1901), 91–92; Stevenson Whitcomb Fletcher, *The Strawberry in North America: History, Origin, Botany, and Breeding* (New York: Macmillan Company, 1917), 74; *40th Annual Report of the State Horticultural Society of Missouri* (Jefferson City: Tribune Printing Company, 1898), 225–27.

67. "The Fruit Crop of 1915," 148; *The Southwest*, February 20, 1900, 1; Chrisman, *Memories of Bowers Mill*, 58; Jobe, *History of Newton County*, 166–69.

68. *Fourteenth Census . . .* vol. 6, part 1, 600–610; *Fourteenth Census . . .* vol. 6, part 2, 575–81, 643–49.

69. C. M. Morrison, "Fighting the Middleman," *Technical World Magazine*, December

1912, 402–405; "Selling Ozark Strawberries," *Country Gentleman*, March 16, 1918, 14, 25.

70. Leslie Hewes, "The Oklahoma Ozarks as the Land of the Cherokees," *Geographical Review* 32 (April 1942): 280–81; Leslie Hewes, "Cultural Fault Line in the Cherokee Country," *Economic Geography* 19 (April 1943): 138–40.

71. Lackey, *History of Newton County*, 431; Tom Shiras, "'Green Gold' of the Ozarks Attracts Many Prospectors," unidentified newspaper clipping in Ozarko Scrapbook, Ozarks Scrapbooks c. 1927–1944, Southeast Missouri State University Special Collections and Archives, Cape Girardeau; Mahnkey, *Bright Glowed My Hills*, 24.

72. Julia Parker, *Out of the Past* (Springfield, MO: Empire Printing, 1968), 17, 58–60.

Chapter 3. Industry and Image

1. B. C. Forbes, "A Barefooted Boy in the Ozarks: James L. Dalton," *Hearst's Magazine*, October 1920, 26.

2. Ibid.

3. Ibid.

4. Ibid., 26, 53; Peggy Aldrich Kidwell, "Calculating Machine," in *Instruments of Science: An Historical Encyclopedia,* ed. Robert Bud and Deborah Jean Warner (New York: The Science Museum and the National Museum of American History, Smithsonian Institution, 1998), 77; "Big Industry," *The Cincinnatian*, June 1914, 1.

5. "Neosho, Newton County, Missouri," *Current Events*, October 1915, 202.

6. Emily Lenhausen and Rachel Nugent, "The Rice-Stix Building," NR, 2019, 8–13, https://dnr.mo.gov/shpo/docs/council-copy-Rice-StixBuilding.pdf, accessed September 17, 2020; Steven Lee Stepp, "'The Old Reliable': The History of the Springfield Wagon Company, 1872–1952" (MA thesis, Southwest Missouri State College, 1972), 72–132; "Wagons Roll Frank Fellows into Circus, Carnival Field," *Billboard*, June 30, 1951, 90; Omer E. Brown, *Son of Pioneers: Recollections of an Ozarks Lawyer* (Point Lookout, MO: School of the Ozarks Press, 1973), 71.

7. James Lee Murphy, "A History of the Southeastern Ozark Region of Missouri" (PhD diss., Saint Louis University, 1982), 153–56, 174, 198; Donald L. Stevens Jr., *A Homeland and a Hinterland: The Current and Jacks Fork Riverways* (Omaha, NE: National Park Service Midwest Region, 1991), 75–88; Steve Kohler and Oliver Schuchard, *Two Ozark Rivers: The Current and the Jacks Fork* (Columbia: University of Missouri Press, 1984), 87–89; Gene Oakley, *The History of Carter County* (Van Buren, MO: J-G Publications, 1970), 95–115; Mary Lee Douthit, et al., *Overview of Cultural Resources in the Mark Twain National Forest, Missouri*, vol. 1, CAR-94 (Springfield, MO: Center for Archaeological Research, Southwest Missouri State University, 1979), 227–30.

8. Oakley, *History of Carter County*, 100–20; Kohler and Schuchard, *Two Ozark Rivers*, 89; Robert J. Cunningham and Carl Hauser, "The Decline of the Missouri Ozark Forest between 1880 and 1920," in *Proceedings of Pine-Hardwood Mixtures: A Symposium on Management and Ecology of the Type*, General Technical Report SE-58, ed. Thomas A. Waldrop (Asheville, NC: U.S. Department of Agriculture, Forest Service, Southeastern Forest Experiment Station, 1989), 35.

9. Stevens, *Homeland and a Hinterland*, 76; Murphy, "History of the Southeastern Ozark Region," 199–200; Kohler and Schuchard, *Two Ozark Rivers*, 91; Judy Ferguson, *The Boom Town of West Eminence and Its Lumbering Days* (Rolla, MO: Rolla Printing Company, 1969), 10–12.

10. Historical Committee, *Leaves of Birch Tree* (n.p.: Birch Tree Bicentennial Project, 1976), 16; Murphy, "History of the Southeastern Ozark Region," 158, 202, 175–76; Douthit et al., *Overview of Cultural Resources*, 231–34, 267; *American Lumbermen: The Personal History and Public and Business Achievements of One Hundred Eminent Lumbermen of the United States* (Chicago: American Lumberman, 1905), 363–66.

11. Jerry Presley, "The Missouri Ozarks: Once a Timber Empire," *Missouri Log* 11 (1958): 23; Murphy, "History of the Southeastern Ozark Region," 177; *American Lumbermen*, 363–66; David Benac, *Conflict in the Ozarks: Hill Folk, Industrialists, and Government in Missouri's Courtois Hills* (Kirksville, MO: Truman State University Press, 2010), 26–27.

12. Murphy, "History of the Southeastern Ozark Region," 203–205, 152, 170; Rose Fulton Cramer, *Wayne County, Missouri* (Cape Girardeau, MO: Ramfire Press, 1972), 297–301.

13. *Eleventh Annual Report of the Bureau of Labor Statistics of the State of Missouri* (Jefferson City: Tribune Printing Company, 1890), 56–66, 415–17; Thelma S. McManus, *That's the Way It Was: Interviews of Ozark Folk Born in the 1800s* (Morley, MO: Acclaim Press, 2008), 121, 49; Benac, *Conflict in the Ozarks*, 83; Murphy, "History of the Southeastern Ozark Region," 185.

14. Benac, *Conflict in the Ozarks*, 33–47.

15. Ibid., 58–85.

16. Office of the Census, *Statistics of the Population of the United States at the Tenth Census* (GPO, 1883), 381, 399; Office of the Census, *Twelfth Census of the United States, 1900: Population, Part 1* (GPO, 1901), 10–11, 27–28, 47.

17. *Twelfth Annual Report of the Bureau of Labor Statistics of the State of Missouri* (Jefferson City: Tribune Printing Company, 1891), 15–18.

18. John F. Bradbury Jr., "Tie-Hackers, Tie-Rafting, and the Railroad Crosstie Industry at Arlington and Jerome," *Old Settlers Gazette* (2005), 4–5; Murphy, "History of the Southeastern Ozark Region," 206–207.

19. Murphy, "History of the Southeastern Ozark Region," 208–209; Bradbury, "Tie-Hackers," 7–12; George Clinton Arthur, *Backwoodsmen: Daring Men of the Ozarks* (Boston: Christopher Publishing House, 1940), 51–53.

20. Joel P. Rhodes, *A Missouri Railroad Pioneer: The Life of Louis Houck* (Columbia: University of Missouri Press, 2008), 101–103; Cletis R. Ellinghouse, *Mingo: Southeast Missouri's Ancient Swamp and the Countryside Surrounding It* (Philadelphia: Xlibris, 2008), 151–56; Ferguson, *Boom Town*, 10; Murphy, "History of the Southeastern Ozark Region," 202.

21. Murphy, "History of the Southeastern Ozark Region," 212–32; Cramer, *Wayne County*, 383; Stevens, *Homeland and a Hinterland*, 91; James R. Fair Jr., *The North Arkansas Line: The Story of the Missouri & North Arkansas Railroad* (Berkeley, CA: Howell-North Books, 1969), 53; Historical Committee, *Leaves of Birch Tree*, 132;

Robert Sidney Douglass, *History of Southeast Missouri: A Narrative Account of Its Historical Progress, Its People, and Its Principal Interests* (1912; Cape Girardeau, MO: Rimfire Press, 1961), 751.

22. Brooks Blevins, *Hill Folks: A History of Arkansas Ozarkers and Their Image* (Chapel Hill: University of North Carolina Press, 2002), 72–73; Wayne Martin, *Pettigrew, Arkansas: The Hardwood Capital of the World* (Springdale, AR: Shiloh Museum of Ozark History, 2010), 4–30, 116; Charles Y. Alison, *A Brief History of Fayetteville, Arkansas* (Charleston, SC: History Press, 2017), 77–78.

23. Elmo Ingenthron, *The Land of Taney: A History of an Ozark Commonwealth* (Point Lookout, MO: School of the Ozarks Press, 1974), 191–94; Blevins, *Hill Folks*, 72–82; "Ships Golf Sticks," *Baxter Bulletin*, July 28, 1922, 1.

24. Blevins, *Hill Folks*, 75–76; Guy Lancaster, "Leslie," *EOA*, accessed August 7, 2017; Theodore Catton, *Life, Leisure, and Hardship along the Buffalo*, Historic Resources Study, Buffalo National River (Omaha, NE: Midwest Region, National Park Service, 2008), 152.

25. Fair, *North Arkansas Line*, 144; Douthit et al., *Overview of Cultural Resources*, 277.

26. Cunningham and Hauser, "Decline of the Missouri Ozark Forest," 34–36; James M. Guldin, "A History of Forest Management in the Ozark Mountains," in *Pioneer Forest: A Half Century of Sustainable Uneven-Aged Forest Management in the Missouri Ozarks*, USDA Forest Service General Technical Report SRS-108, ed. James M. Guldin, Greg F. Iffrig, and Susan L. Flader (Asheville, NC: Southern Research Station, 2008), 5–6; Carl O. Sauer, *The Geography of the Ozark Highland of Missouri* (1920; New York: Greenwood Press, 1968), 181; David Ware, "Official State Mammal, aka: White-tailed Deer," *EOA*, accessed August 7, 2017; Catton, *Life, Leisure, and Hardship*, 153.

27. Tate C. Page, *Voices of Moccasin Creek* (Point Lookout, MO: School of the Ozarks Press, 1972), 103–109.

28. J. B. White to Alex Johnston, January 18, 1910, folder 753, MLM Records, SHSMR; J. B. White to Alexander Johnston, February 5, 1910, folder 755, MLM Records; Benac, *Conflict in the Hills*, 85.

29. J. B. White to J. E. Defenbaugh, May 27, 1898, folder 1a, MLM Records; Benac, *Conflict in the Hills*, 52–53; Murphy, "History of the Southeastern Ozark Region," 244–48.

30. Eric Hedburg, "The Missouri and Arkansas Zinc-Mines at the Close of 1900," *Transactions of the American Institute of Mining Engineers* 31 (1901): 397; Howard L. Conard, *Encyclopedia of the History of Missouri*, vol. 3 (New York: Southern History Company, 1901), 268–69; Steven Teske, "Boxley," *EOA*, accessed August 9, 2017.

31. Arrell M. Gibson, *Wilderness Bonanza: The Tri-State District of Missouri, Kansas, and Oklahoma* (Norman: University Oklahoma Press, 1972), 6; Jonathan Fairbanks and Clyde Edwin Tuck, *Past and Present of Greene County, Missouri*, vol. 1 (Indianapolis: A. W. Bowen & Company, 1915), 777; John K. Hulston, *An Ozarks Boy's Story, 1915–1945* (Point Lookout, MO: School of the Ozarks Press, 1971), 87; Joel T. Livingston, *A History of Jasper County, Missouri and Its People*, vol. 1 (Chicago: Lewis Publishing Company, 1912), 235; "Carthage Marble," www.stone.poplarheightsfarm.org/carthage_marble.htm, accessed August 9, 2017.

32. Sauer, *Geography of the Ozark Highland*, 214; *Nineteenth Annual Report of the Bureau of Labor Statistics and Inspection of the State of Missouri* (Jefferson City: Tribune Printing Company, 1897), 147; Walter M. Adams, *The White River Railway: Being a History of the White River Division of the Missouri Pacific Railroad Company, 1901–1951* (Branson, MO: The Ozarks Mountaineer, 1991), 98–99; Fair, *North Arkansas Line*, 191; O. E. Berninghaus and Allen W. Clark, *The Story of Barytes: Where and How It Is Found and Its Importance in the World's Industries* (St. Louis: De Lore Baryta Company and J. C. Finck Mineral Milling Company, 1920), unpaginated.

33. E. R. Buckley and H. A. Buehler, *The Quarrying Industry of Missouri*, Missouri Bureau of Geology and Mines, vol. 2, 2nd series (Jefferson City: Tribune Printing Company, 1904), 62–84.

34. Henry C. Thompson, *Our Lead Belt Heritage* (1955; n.p.: Walsworth Publishing, 1992), 145, 172; Robert M. Blackwell, *Bonne Terre: The First Hundred Years* (Bonne Terre, MO: Bonne Terre Centennial Corporation, 1964), 15–16; "The History of St. Joe Lead Company," *St. Joe Headframe*, newsletter of St. Joe Minerals Corp., Fall 1970, www.rootsweb.ancestry.com/~mostfran/mine_history/stjoe_history.htm, accessed August 10, 2017; Sauer, *Geography of the Ozark Highland*, 212; Stevens, *Homeland and a Hinterland*, 91; *Fortieth and Forty-First Annual Report of the Bureau of Labor Statistics, State of Missouri* (Jefferson City: Missouri Bureau of Labor Statistics, 1920), 79, 90.

35. *Fortieth and Forty-First Annual Report*, 79; Gibson, *Wilderness Bonanza*, 8, 72; Dolph Shaner, *The Story of Joplin* (New York: Stratford House, 1948), 78–84.

36. Shaner, *Story of Joplin*, 84; CB, *Thirteenth Census of the United States, 1910*, vol. 2, *Population* (GPO, 1913), 1077; Gibson, *Wilderness Bonanza*, 80–83.

37. Gibson, *Wilderness Bonanza*, 41, 80–106; James D. Norris, *AZn: A History of the American Zinc Company* (Madison: State Historical Society of Wisconsin, 1968), 19–28.

38. Gibson, *Wilderness Bonanza*, 122, 147; Norris, *AZn*, 5–31.

39. Norris, *AZn*, 58–77; Gibson, *Wilderness Bonanza*, 40; Shaner, *Story of Joplin*, 92; "The Zinc and Lead Mining Industry," *Current Events*, July 1915, 150.

40. Yellville *Mountain Echo*, January 1, 1897, 1; Catton, *Life, Leisure, and Hardship*, 142; Ingenthron, *Land of Taney*, 207; Bill Stiritz, ed., *Beecher Moss's Turn of the Century Coming of Age Memoir* (St. Louis, MO: n.p., 1999), 40.

41. "Zinc and Lead Mining Industry," 150; Fair, *North Arkansas Line*, 117–33; Yellville *Mountain Echo*, January 1, 1897, 1; Catton, *Life, Leisure, and Hardship*, 142–46; Bill Dwayne Blevins, "Rush [Ghost-town]," *EOA*, accessed August 12, 2017.

42. Gibson, *Wilderness Bonanza*, 171–79, 266; Norris, *AZn*, 73–77.

43. Norris, *AZn*, 201; Gibson, *Wilderness Bonanza*, 80; H. Dwight Weaver, *Lake of the Ozarks: The Early Years* (Charleston, SC: Arcadia Publishing, 2000), 7.

44. Gibson, *Wilderness Bonanza*, 104–108; Blackwell, *Bonne Terre*, 27; Mike McGraw, "Fear of Losing Jobs to Immigrants May Have Led to Riots of 1917," *St. Louis Post-Dispatch*, July 12, 2017, https://www.stltoday.com/business/local/fear-of-losing-jobs-to-immigrants-may-have-led-to-riots-of-1917/article_7bee9061-efbe-5f80-a83c-37c1802b29b9.html, accessed August 12, 2017.

45. Blackwell, *Bonne Terre*, 27; Bob Faust, "Lead in the Water: Power, Progressivism, and Resource Control in a Missouri Mining Community," *Agricultural History* 76 (Spring 2002): 406–417.
46. Ethel Strainchamps, *Don't Never Say Cain't* (New York: Doubleday, 1965), 58.
47. R. Alton Lee, *From Snake Oil to Medicine: Pioneering Public Health* (Westport, CT: Praeger, 2007), 86–88; A. J. Lanza and Edwin Higgins, *Pulmonary Disease among Miners in the Joplin District: A Preliminary Report*, Bureau of Mines Technical Paper 105 (Washington, DC: GPO, 1915), 7–11; A. J. Lanza, Edwin Higgins, E. B. Laney, and George R. Rice, *Siliceous Dust in Relation to Pulmonary Disease among Miners in the Joplin District, Missouri*, Bureau of Mines Bulletin 132 (Washington, DC: GPO, 1917), 65–68; Lanza and Higgins, *Pulmonary Disease*, 13–40.
48. Lanza and Higgins, *Pulmonary Disease*, 39; *Bonne Terre Register*, April 28, 1905; *Bonne Terre Star*, September 12, 1913; typescripts of both articles at www.rootsweb.ancestry.com/~mostfran/mine_history_index.htm, accessed August 15, 2017.
49. Lanza and Higgins, *Pulmonary Disease*, 8; Jarod Roll, "Sympathy for the Devil: The Notorious Career of Missouri's Strikebreaking Metal Miners, 1896–1910," *Labor: Studies in Working-Class History of the Americas* 11 (Winter 2014): 12–15, 36; Gibson, *Wilderness Bonanza*, 199–210, 227–29; Norris, *AZn*, 65.
50. McGraw, "Fear of Losing Jobs"; Michael Roark, "The Effect of Lead and Iron Mining on the Cultural Development of Eastern Missouri, 1860–1880," *Pioneer America Society Transactions* 11 (1988): 15; Lanza and Higgins, *Pulmonary Disease*, 8; Jarod Roll, *Poor Man's Fortune: White Working-Class Conservatism in American Metal Mining, 1850–1950* (Chapel Hill: University of North Carolina Press, 2020), 10, 3.
51. Herbert Asbury, *Up from Methodism* (New York: Alfred A. Knopf, 1926), 25; Ted Chamberlain, "'Gangs of New York': Fact vs. Fiction," *National Geographic News*, March 24, 2003, news.nationalgeographic.com/news/2003/03/0320_030320_oscars_gangs.html, accessed August 15, 2017.
52. *Bonne Terre Register*, April 28, 1905; V. L. Lawson, *The Lead Belt Mining Riot of 1917* (n.p.: n.p., 1976), 13–14; McGraw, "Fear of Losing Jobs."
53. Mark D. Hughes, "Capitol Perspectives: Social Unrest Spans Nearly a Century: Missouri Mining Riots of 1917," *Missouri Digital News*, www.mdn.org/mpacol/COL27.htm, accessed August 15, 2017; Thompson, *Our Lead Belt Heritage*, 166; Lawson, *Lead Belt Mining Riot*, 18–46; McGraw, "Fear of Losing Jobs."
54. Lawson, *Lead Belt Mining Riot*, 46–68; McGraw, "Fear of Losing Jobs"; Christina V. Pacosz, "Leadwood," *Légèreté*, Issue No. 4 (Fall 1985): 56–61.
55. Christopher C. Gibbs, *The Great Silent Majority: Missouri's Resistance to World War I* (Columbia: University of Missouri Press, 1988), 151–55.
56. Fair, *North Arkansas Line*, 136–54; Stephen L. McIntyre, "'Considerable Bad Feeling in this City': Cross-Class Solidarity and Federal Power in the 1922 Springfield Frisco Shopmen's Strike," in *Springfield's Urban Histories: Essays on the Queen City of the Missouri Ozarks*, ed. Stephen L. McIntyre (Springfield, MO: Moon City Press, 2012), 172, 192–96; McIntyre, introduction to *Springfield's Urban Histories*, 2–3.
57. Donald R. Deskins Jr., Hanes Walton Jr., and Sherman C. Puckett, *Presidential Elections, 1789–2008: County, State, and National Mapping of Election Data* (Ann Arbor: University of Michigan Press, 2010), 215–352.

58. *N. W. Ayer & Son's American Newspaper Annual* (Philadelphia: N. W. Ayer and Son, 1889), 24–30, 276–99, 609–615; "Hazeltine, Ira Sherwin," *Biographical Directory of the United States Congress*, https://bioguide.congress.gov/search/bio/H000417, accessed August 26, 2017.

59. Berton E. Henningson Jr., "Northwest Arkansas and the Brothers of Freedom: The Roots of a Farmer Movement," *AHQ* 34 (Winter 1975): 308–322; Berton E. Henningson Jr., "Root Hog or Die: The Brothers of Freedom and the 1884 Arkansas Election," *AHQ* 45 (Autumn 1986): 209–213; Matthew Hild, "Isaac McCracken," *EOA*, accessed August 25, 2017; Edward J. Chess, "Agricultural Wheel," *EOA*, accessed August 25, 2017; Matthew Hild, "Labor, Third-Party Politics, and New South Democracy in Arkansas, 1884–1896," *AHQ* 63 (Spring 2004): 27, 38; Jason McCollom, "The Agricultural Wheel, the Union Labor Party, and the 1889 Arkansas Legislature," *AHQ* (Summer 2009): 162–63, 172–75; Deskins, *Presidential Elections, 1789–2008*, 244.

60. "The Ozarks' Only Real Presidential Candidate," *OM*, September 1956, 4; "Bland, Richard Parks," *Biographical Directory of the United States Congress*, https://bioguide.congress.gov/search/bio/B000544, accessed August 26, 2017.

61. Blevins, *Hill Folks*, 125; Gaye Bland, "'Coin' Harvey," *EOA*, accessed August 27, 2017; Lynn Morrow and Linda Myers-Phinney, *Shepherd of the Hills Country: Tourism Transforms the Ozarks, 1880s–1930s* (Fayetteville: University of Arkansas Press, 1999), 63–64.

62. Blevins, *Hill Folks*, 125–26; Bland, "'Coin' Harvey"; Allyn Lord, "Monte Ne," *EOA*, accessed August 27, 2017.

63. Ralph R. Rea, *Boone County and Its People* (Van Buren, AR: Press-Argus, 1955), 114; Ben F. Greer, *Greer Family Reminiscences* (Fayetteville, AR: Washington County Historical Society, 1956), 16.

64. Fullbright to Thompson, June 9, no year, folder 3, Elizabeth Remay Dabbs Thompson Papers, R671, SHSMR; A. G. Unklesbay and Jerry D. Vineyard, *Missouri Geology: Three Billion Years of Volcanoes, Seas, Sediments, and Erosion* (Columbia: University of Missouri Press, 1992), 66; Paul W. Johns, *Unto These Hills: True Tales from the Ozarks* (n.p.: Bilyeu-Johns Enterprises, 1980), 67–69; William Neville Collier, *Ozark and Vicinity in the Nineteenth Century* (Long Beach, CA: n.p., 1945), reprinted in *WRVHQ* 2 (Winter 1966–67): 15; Floyd C. Shoemaker, "Cedar County: Land of Mineral Springs and Flowing Streams, Ozark Highland and Rolling Prairies," *MHR* 53 (July 1959): 333–34; Marilyn Collins, *Rogers: The Town the Frisco Built* (Charleston, SC: Arcadia Publishing, 2002), 51.

65. Blevins, *Hill Folks*, 123; Fair, *North Arkansas Line*, 1–5; Bethany May, "Eureka Springs," *EOA*, accessed September 4, 2017.

66. Ed to Fatty, July 29, 1885, folder 1, Bannister Family Collection, Missouri Historical Museum and Archives, St. Louis.

67. Blevins, *Hill Folks*, 123; Fair, *North Arkansas Line*, 14–20; John W. Kearney, *The Summit of the Ozarks* (n.p: Bryan Snyder, 1903), 47.

68. Jennifer Crets, "Landscape and Vacation Culture in the Missouri Ozarks, 1900–1940" (MA thesis, University of Missouri, St. Louis, 1995), 17; Larry Wood, "Lebanon's Magnetic Water," *Ozarks History*, Ozarks-history.blogspot.com/, accessed September

4, 2017; *Benton County, Arkansas* (Kansas City, MO: Kansas City Southern Railway Company Industrial Department, n.d.), 5–13.

69. May, "Eureka Springs"; Milton D. Rafferty, *The Ozarks, Land and Life* (Norman: University of Oklahoma Press, 1980), 199.

70. James F. Keefe and Lynn Morrow, eds., *A Connecticut Yankee in the Frontier Ozarks: The Writings of Theodore Pease Russell* (Columbia: University of Missouri Press, 1988), 114, 189n9; Lynn Morrow, "John Wesley Emerson," unpublished article manuscript, November 1993, copy in possession of author, 1–18; Stevens, *Homeland and a Hinterland*, 151.

71. Morrow and Myers-Phinney, *Shepherd of the Hills Country*, 116–18; Lynn Morrow, "Before Bass Pro: St. Louis Sporting Clubs on the Gasconade River," in *The Ozarks in Missouri History: Discoveries in an American Region*, ed. Lynn Morrow (Columbia: University of Missouri Press, 2013), 147–49; Lynn Morrow, "What's in a Name, Like *Johnboat*," *WRVHQ* 37 (Winter 1998): 12; John Bradbury and Terry Primas, *Old Pulaski in Pictures: Rivers, Rails, Roads, and Recreation, Pulaski County, Missouri* (Duke, MO: Big Piney Productions, 2012), 123–25; Terry Primas, "Cave Lodge on the Gasconade," *Old Settlers Gazette*, July 27, 2013, 30.

72. Morrow, "Before Bass Pro," 142–46; Bradbury and Primas, *Old Pulaski in Pictures*, 123–24; Primas, "Cave Lodge on the Gasconade," 30; Morrow, "What's in a Name," 11; Vance Randolph, *Wild Stories from the Ozarks* (Girard, KS: Haldeman-Julius, 1943), 3; Morrow and Myers-Phinney, *Shepherd of the Hills Country*, 121.

73. Morrow and Myers-Phinney, *Shepherd of the Hills Country*, 14, 121–32; Morrow, "What's in a Name," 12–15; Charles Phelps Cushing, "Floating through the Ozarks," *Outing* 58 (August 1911), 537–46.

74. Morrow, "What's in a Name," 13–20; Catton, *Life, Leisure, and Hardship*, 159–60; Morrow and Myers-Phinney, *Shepherd of the Hills Country*, 132–42, 206; Dana Everts-Boehm, "The Ozark Johnboat: Its History, Form, and Functions," pamphlet published as part of "The Masters & Their Traditional Arts" Series (Columbia, MO: Cultural Heritage Center, University of Missouri, 1991), 3.

75. Morrow and Myers-Phinney, *Shepherd of the Hills Country*, 44–55; Thomas E. Morrissey, "Cityscapes and Ozark Views: The Art of Frank B. Nuderscher," *Gateway Heritage* 11 (Winter 1990–91): 70–74.

76. Morrow and Myers-Phinney, *Shepherd of the Hills Country*, 25–50.

77. Ibid., 180, 164–66, 194, 138–39; Crets, "Landscape and Vacation Culture," 55.

78. Morrow and Myers-Phinney, *Shepherd of the Hills Country*, 156–61; Aaron Ketchell, *Holy Hills of the Ozarks: Religion and Tourism in Branson, Missouri* (Baltimore: Johns Hopkins University Press, 2007), xvii.

79. Ibid., 153–55, 183–96, 32–34.

80. *St. Paul (AR) Republican*, August 26, 1887, 1; "The Ozark Trails and Other Trails," *Current Events*, July 1915, 141–42; Nan Marie Lawler, "The Ozark Trails Association" (MA thesis, University of Arkansas, Fayetteville, 1991), 7–14.

81. Lawler, "Ozark Trails Association," 30–46, 68; Thomas A. Peters, *John T. Woodruff of Springfield, Missouri, in the Ozarks: An Encyclopedic Biography* (Springfield, MO: Pie Supper Press, 2016), 147–57; Vearl Rowe, *Sketches of Wright County*, vol. 1 (Hartville, MO: Wright County Historical Society, n.d.), 25.

82. Richard S. Kirkendall, *A History of Missouri*, vol. 5, *1919–1953* (Columbia: University of Missouri Press, 1986), 36–37; Jeannie M. Whayne, Thomas A. DeBlack, George Sabo III, and Morris S. Arnold, *Arkansas: A Narrative History* (Fayetteville: University of Arkansas Press, 2002), 317–18; Dianna Everett, "Highways," *EOHC*, accessed March 26, 2020; Catton, *Life, Leisure, and Hardship*, 167–68; Peters, *John T. Woodruff*, 171–79.

83. Bradbury and Primas, *Old Pulaski in Pictures*, 74–81; Elbert I. Childers, "Basketville: Roadside Community on Route 66," *Phelps County Historical Society Newsletter*, New Series no. 13 (April 1996), 3–14.

84. Keith A. Sculle, "'Our Company Feels That the Ozarks Are a Good Investment': The Pierce Pennant Tavern System," in Morrow, *Ozarks in Missouri History*, 209–19; *Neosho (MO) Daily News*, June 28, 1928, 4.

85. Crets, "Landscape and Vacation Culture," 83–84; Robert Flanders, "Alley, an Ozarks Mill Hamlet, 1890–1925: Society, Economy, Landscape," unpublished report for the Ozark National Scenic Riverways (Springfield, MO: Center for Ozarks Studies, Southwest Missouri State University, 1985), 72; Stevens, *Homeland and a Hinterland*, 177–80; Lynn Morrow, "Keith McCanse: Missouri's First Professional Conservationist," *WRVHQ* 31 (Winter 1992): 3–9.

86. Flanders, "Alley," 73; Stevens, *Homeland and a Hinterland*, 181–82; Morrow, "Keith McCanse," 9; Crets, "Landscape and Vacation Culture," 98–100.

Chapter 4. Ozarks Society

1. B. F. Adams to John Quincy Wolf Sr., January 13, 1936; February 8, 1936; and August 5, 1936, John Quincy Wolf Collection, Lyon College Special Collections, Batesville, Arkansas.

2. Leslie Hewes, "The Oklahoma Ozarks as the Land of the Cherokees," *Geographical Review* 32 (April 1942): 277–80.

3. Joseph C. G. Kennedy, *Population of the United States in 1860; Compiled from the Original Returns of the Eighth Census* (GPO, 1864), 12–16, 274–87; Office of the Census, *Report on Population of the United States at the Eleventh Census, 1890: Part 1* (GPO, 1895), 403, 418–19; CB, *Fourteenth Census of the United States, 1920*, vol. 3, *Population* (GPO, 1922), 91–97, 551–61, 817–23.

4. Katherine Lederer, *Many Thousand Gone: Springfield's Lost Black History* (n.p.: Missouri Committee for the Humanities and the Gannett Foundation, 1986), 19–20; Steven Teske, "Clinton," *EOA*, accessed October 5, 2018.

5. Jamie C. Brandon and James M. Davidson, "The Landscape of Van Winkle's Mill: Identity, Myth, and Modernity in the Ozark Upland South," *Historical Archaeology* 39 (2005): 125; Lederer, *Many Thousand Gone*, 15.

6. Lederer, *Many Thousand Gone*, 11–13; Richard L. Schur, "Memories of Walter Majors: Searching for African American History in Springfield," in *Springfield's Urban Histories: Essays on the Queen City of the Missouri Ozarks*, ed. Stephen L. McIntyre (Springfield, MO: Moon City Press, 2012), 119–25.

7. Lederer, *Many Thousand Gone*, 7–44.

8. *Twelfth Census . . . Population*, 10–11, 27–28, 47.

9. Gary R. Kremer, *George Washington Carver: A Biography* (Santa Barbara, CA: Greenwood Press, 2011), 9–13; Mark D. Hersey, *My Work Is That of Conservation: An Environmental Biography of George Washington Carver* (Athens: University of Georgia Press, 2011), 13; James J. Johnston, *Shootin's, Obituaries, Politics; Emigratin', Socializin', Commercializin', and the Press: News Items from and about Searcy County, Arkansas, 1866–1901* (Fayetteville, AR: James J. Johnston, 1991), 167; Theodore Catton, *Life, Leisure, and Hardship along the Buffalo*, Historic Resources Study, Buffalo National River (Omaha, NE: Midwest Region, National Park Service, 2008), 199.

10. *Marshall (AR) Mountain Wave*, August 26, 1899, 2; September 9, 1899, 1; November 18, 1899, 4.

11. Vearl Rowe, *Sketches of Wright County*, vol. 1 (Hartville, MO: Wright County Historical Society, n.d.), 75; J. E. Curry, *A Reminiscent History of Douglas County, Missouri, 1857–1957* (Ava, MO: Douglas County Herald, 1957), 122; "Don't Like Niggers," *Wright County Republican*, September 2, 1911, quoted in Leroy M. Rowe, "A Grave Injustice: Institutional Terror at the State Industrial Home for Negro Girls and the Paradox of Juvenile Delinquent Reform in Missouri, 1888–1960" (MA thesis, University of Missouri, Columbia, 2006), 48; *Current Events*, May 1915, 305; *Eminence (MO) Current Wave*, October 27, 1921, 4.

12. Walter F. Lackey, *History of Newton County, Arkansas* (Independence, MO, n.d.), 61; John Thomas Woodruff, *Reminiscences of an Ozarkian and Early Tourism Developments*, ed. Steve Illum (Springfield, MO: Office of Leisure Research, Southwest Missouri State University, 1994), 64; Ralph R. Rea, *Boone County and Its People* (Van Buren, AR: Press-Argus, 1955), 141; Jacqueline Froelich and David Zimmermann, "Total Eclipse: The Destruction of the African American Community of Harrison, Arkansas, in 1905 and 1909," *Arkansas Historical Quarterly* 58 (Summer 1999), 140–41; Kimberly Harper, *White Man's Heaven: The Lynching and Expulsion of Blacks in the Southern Ozarks, 1894–1909* (Fayetteville: University of Arkansas Press, 2010), 131–33.

13. Harper, *White Man's Heaven*, xix, xxiii, 73–79.

14. Ibid., 22–30.

15. Ibid., 21, xxv; Guy Lancaster, "Harrison Race Riots," *EOA*, accessed August 20, 2018.

16. Harper, *White Man's Heaven*, 124–34, 140.

17. Ibid., 144–60.

18. Ibid., 162–71, 188–98, 216–33.

19. Lederer, *Many Thousand Gone*, 17–21; *Minutes of the Thirty-Seventh General Assembly of the Colored Cumberland Presbyterian Church Held at Nacogdoches, Texas, May, 1911*, www.cumberland.org/hfcpc/cpca/cpcaga1911.htm, accessed July 31, 2018.

20. Richard Lee Burton, "Benton Avenue A.M.E. Church," NR, 2001, https://dnr.mo.gov.shpo/nps-nr/, accessed July 31, 2018.

21. Mary Jean Barker, "Second Baptist Church," NR, 1995, https://dnr.mo.gov.shpo/nps-nr/, accessed August 1, 2018; Lori Peterson, *A Study of African-American Culture in Southwest Missouri in Relation to the George Washington Carver National Monument* (Lincoln, NE: National Park Service Midwest Archeological Center, 1995), 10.

22. CB, Department of Commerce and Labor, *Religious Bodies: 1906*, part 1, *Summary*

and General Tables (GPO, 1910), 296–98, 331–34, 348–49; Mara W. Cohen Ioannides and M. Rachel Gholson, *Jews of Springfield in the Ozarks* (Charleston, SC: Arcadia Publishing, 2013), 8.

23. CB, *Religious Bodies: 1906*, 331–34; Charles K. Piehl, "The Race of Improvement: Springfield Society, 1865–1881," in *The Ozarks in Missouri History: Discoveries in an American Region,* ed. Lynn Morrow (Columbia: University of Missouri Press, 2013), 90–92.

24. CB, *Religious Bodies: 1906*, 296–98, 331–34, 348–49; Omer E. Brown, *Son of Pioneers: Recollections of an Ozarks Lawyer* (Point Lookout, MO: School of the Ozarks Press, 1973), 50; Carl O. Sauer, *The Geography of the Ozark Highland of Missouri* (1920; New York: Greenwood Press, 1968), 147; Kenneth C. Barnes, *Anti-Catholicism in Arkansas: How Politicians, the Press, the Klan, and Religious Leaders Imagined an Enemy, 1910–1960* (Fayetteville: University of Arkansas Press, 2016), 9–11, 53, 92; Justin Nordstrom, *Danger on the Doorstep: Anti-Catholicism and Print Culture in the Progressive Era* (Notre Dame, IN: University of Notre Dame Press, 2006), 64–65.

25. CB, *Religious Bodies: 1906*, 296–98, 331–34, 348–49; *A Reminiscent History of the Ozark Region* (Chicago: Goodspeed Brothers, 1894), 743.

26. *Melbourne Clipper*, June 30, 1877, 3; CB, *Religious Bodies: 1906*, 296–98, 331–34, 348–49.

27. Loyal Jones, "Mountain Religion: An Overview," in *Christianity in Appalachia: Profiles in Regional Pluralism,* ed. Bill J. Leonard (Knoxville: University of Tennessee Press, 1999), 100. See also Loyal Jones, *Faith & Meaning in the Southern Uplands* (Urbana: University of Illinois Press, 1999).

28. William A. Link, *The Paradox of Southern Progressivism, 1880–1930* (Chapel Hill: University of North Carolina Press, 1992), 90, 83; Brooks Blevins, "Mountain Mission Schools in Arkansas," *AHQ* 70 (Winter 2011): 413.

29. J. S. Godbey, *Lights and Shadows of Seventy Years* (St. Louis, MO: St. Louis ChristianAdvocate, 1913), 103–130; *Proceedings of the Arkansas Baptist State Convention, Sixty-Seventh Annual Session, December 8–10, 1919* (n.p.: Arkansas Baptist State Convention, c. 1919), 42; *Baptist Advance* (Little Rock), October 5, 1916, 1; James A. Anderson, *Centennial History of Arkansas Methodism: A History of the Methodist Episcopal Church, South, in the State of Arkansas, 1815–1935* (Benton, AR: L. B. White Printing Co., 1935), 510.

30. Brooks Blevins, *A History of the Ozarks*, vol. 1, *The Old Ozarks* (Urbana: University of Illinois Press, 2018), 202; Blue Mountain Association of Missionary Baptists, *Minutes of the Proceedings of the 15th Annual Session of the Blue Mountain Association of Missionary Baptists* (n.p., 1889), 5; Earl T. Sechler, *Our Religious Heritage: Church History of the Ozarks (1806–1906)* (Springfield, MO: Westport Press, 1961), 71.

31. Sechler, *Our Religious Heritage*, 70–73.

32. Ibid., 70–73; *Ash Grove Commonwealth*, December 3, 1896, quoted in Robert K. Gilmore, *Ozark Baptizings, Hangings, and Other Diversions: Theatrical Folkways of Rural Missouri, 1885–1910* (Norman: University of Oklahoma Press, 1984), 88.

33. Sechler, *Our Religious Heritage*, 84; Gilmore, *Ozark Baptizings*, 88; D. B. Wray, *Textbook on Campbellism* (Nashville: South-western Publishing House, 1867).

34. Erma Humphreys, *Down on the Farm* (Fort Dodge, KS: self-pub., 1976), 16; Maude Kendrick Coffin, "Pioneer Days," unpublished manuscript, 24, folder 3, box 2, Maude K. Coffin and Fairy Coffin Lynd Papers, MC 915, UASC.

35. Charley Hershey, "The Turible Times in the Swamps and the Narrow Escapes from the Swamp Devils," ed. Lynn Morrow, *WRVHQ* 35 (Spring 1995): 20; Daniel Woods, "'Spiritual Railroading': Trains as Metaphor and Reality in the Holiness and Pentecostal Movements, c. 1880 to c. 1920," unpublished paper presented at Ferrum College, February 3, 2015, copy in possession of author, 12–13.

36. "Miss Sadie Smith's Diary," transcribed by Dorothy Ann Steele Fostar, West Plains (MO) Public Library; Charles Brougher Jernigan, *Pioneer Days of the Holiness Movement in the Southwest*, digital ed. (1919; n.p.: Holiness Data Ministry, 1997), 24–25; Woods, "'Spiritual Railroading,'" 13.

37. James R. Goff Jr., *Fields White unto Harvest: Charles F. Parham and the Missionary Origins of Pentecostalism* (Fayetteville: University of Arkansas Press, 1988), 67, 88–94, 107–111; Edith L. Blumhofer, *Restoring the Faith: The Assemblies of God, Pentecostalism, and American Culture* (Urbana: University of Illinois Press, 1993), 51–55.

38. Glenn W. Gohr and Darrin J. Rodgers, "The Sparkling Fountain: Early Pentecostalism in Springfield, Missouri," *Assemblies of God Heritage, Annual Edition* 37/38 (2017–2018): 5–7; Harry E. Bowley, "The Great Ozark Mountains Revival," *Assemblies of God Heritage* 2 (Summer 1982): 1–3.

39. Bowley, "Great Ozark Mountains Revival," 3; Woods, "'Spiritual Railroading,'" 6; Edgar E. Hulse, *The Ozarks: Past and Present* (Springfield, MO: Irwin Printing, 1977), 85–91.

40. Ethel E. Goss, *The Winds of God: The Story of the Early Pentecostal Movement (1901–1914) in the Life of Howard A. Goss* (1958; Hazelwood, MO: Word Aflame Press, 1977), 221, 280; Richard A. Lewis, "E. N. Bell—A Voice of Restraint in an Era of Controversy," *Enrichment Journal*, enrichmentjournal.ag.org/199904/048_enbell.cfm, accessed August 13, 2018.

41. Piehl, "Race of Improvement," 93; Dolph Shaner, *The Story of Joplin* (New York: Stratford House, 1948), 59–62.

42. J. W. Haines, *The History of the Polk County Baptist Association* (Bolivar, MO: Bolivar Herald, 1897), 28, 49; *Reminiscent History of the Ozark Region*, 311; Yellville *Mountain Echo*, February 12, 1897, 1; *Marshall Republican*, May 19, 1899, 4.

43. *Marshall Republican*, May 19, 1899, 4; William Sherman, *A Brief Account of the Life of William Sherman: An Autobiography* (Fayetteville, AR: Washington County Historical Society, 1955), 20; Brown, *Son of Pioneers*, 49; Estella Wright Szegedin, *As I Remember Piney* (n.p., n.d.), 69.

44. Bruce E. Stewart, *Moonshiners and Prohibitionists: The Battle over Alcohol in Southern Appalachia* (Lexington: University Press of Kentucky, 2011), 64, 77–78; J. Blake Perkins, *Hillbilly Hellraisers: Federal Power and Populist Defiance in the Ozarks* (Urbana: University of Illinois Press, 2017), 37; J. E. Bunyard and Eav Bunyard to Jacob Roller, May 31, 1869, Roller Family Papers, 1866–1871, R310, SHSMR.

45. Blevins, *History of the Ozarks*, 1:216; "The Nightriders in Missouri," *MHR* 37 (July

1943): 445; Brooks Blevins, *A History of the Ozarks*, vol. 2, *The Conflicted Ozarks* (Urbana: University of Illinois Press, 2019), 174–76; Perkins, *Hillbilly Hellraisers*, 38.
46. Perkins, *Hillbilly Hellraisers*, 35–36, 63.
47. *Eminence (MO) Current Wave*, June 21, 1906, 8; Jeannie M. Whayne, Thomas A. DeBlack, George Sabo III, and Morris S. Arnold, *Arkansas: A Narrative History* (Fayetteville: University of Arkansas Press, 2002), 286–87; Lawrence O. Christensen and Gary R. Kremer, *A History of Missouri*, vol. 4, *1875 to 1919* (Columbia: University of Missouri Press, 1997), 21, 200; Linda D. Wilson, "Billups Law," *EOHC*, accessed September 13, 2020.
48. Johnson, *John Barleycorn Must Die*, 66; Kathleen Drowne, *Spirits of Defiance: National Prohibition and Jazz Age Literature, 1920–1933* (Columbus: Ohio State University Press, 2005), 4; Charles Morrow Wilson, "Moonshiners," *Outlook and Independent*, December 19, 1928, 1351; Charles Morrow Wilson, "Moonshining Booms as Spring Arrives," *New York Times*, April 20, 1930, 51; Stewart, *Moonshiners and Prohibitionists*, 218; Larry J. Sprunk, *Historical Resources Mitigation*, vol. 1, *We Remember the Rivers, An Oral History Survey of the River Valleys in the Harry S. Truman Dam and Reservoir Project, Missouri* (Garrison, ND: Historical and Archaeological Surveys, 1980), 274; Brown, *Son of Pioneers*, 176.
49. Perkins, *Hillbilly Hellraisers*, 5; Stephen Strausberg and Walter A. Hough, *The Ouachita and Ozark–St. Francis National Forests: A History of the Lands and USDA Forest Service Tenure*, General Technical Report SO-121 (Asheville, NC: USDA Forest Service, Southern Research Station, 1997), 9–17; "Hilltop Signal," *Buffalo (NY) Commercial*, January 15, 1914, 8; "Sets Fire to Forest," *Batesville (AR) Daily Guard*, April 20, 1915, 3; Catton, *Life, Leisure, and Hardship*, 209.
50. Perkins, *Hillbilly Hellraisers*, 74–95.
51. Grace Hunt Smith, *Buttermilk and Cracklin Bread: An Ozarks Story* (n.p.: n.p., c. 1978), 7–14; Brown, *Son of Pioneers*, 42; Jean Sizemore, *Ozark Vernacular Houses: A Study of Rural Homeplaces in the Arkansas Ozarks, 1830–1930* (Fayetteville: University of Arkansas Press, 1994), 74–78.
52. Ella Lilly Horak, *Good Old Days on the Farm* (n.p.: n.p., 1968), 25–28, 42–43; Julia Parker, *Out of the Past* (Springfield, MO: Empire Printing, 1968), 53; David Denman, "Walnut Street Historic District," NR, State Historic Preservation Office, 1984, 8-3-8-9.
53. Mabel Cogswell Diary, R 517, SHSMR; "Neosho, Newton County, Missouri," *Current Events*, October 1915, 204; Mel H. Bolster, "The Mountain Mind: A Study of Backwoods Americans from 1908 to 1940," *AHQ* 10 (Winter 1951): 309–20; Velda Brotherton, "Virginia Maud Dunlap Duncan," *EOA*, accessed September 6, 2020.
54. Janet Lynn Allured, "Families, Food, and Folklore: Women's Culture in the Postbellum Ozarks" (PhD diss., University of Arkansas, 1988), 2, 13; Howard S. Miller, "Kate Austin: A Feminist Anarchist on the Farmer's Last Frontier," *Nature, Society, and Thought* 9 (April 1996): 189–90, 198–99.
55. Miller, "Kate Austin," 203; Sprunk, *Historical Resources Mitigation*, 139–45; Ronnie Pontiac, "Thomas Johnson: Platonism Meets Sex Magic on the Prairie," *Newtopia*

Magazine, March 19, 2013, https://newtopiamagazine.wordpress.com/2013/03/19/thomas-johnson-platonism-meets-sex-magic-on-the-prairie/, accessed September 8, 2018.

56. Michael B. Dougan, "Elementary and Secondary Education," *EOA*, accessed September 10, 2018; Stephen B. Weeks, *History of Public School Education in Arkansas*, United States Bureau of Education Bulletin No. 27 (Washington, DC: GPO, 1912), 60–61.

57. Kimberly Scott Little, "Missouri Ozarks Rural Schools," Multiple Properties Documentation Form, NR, 1990, E-7; Sherman, *Brief Account*, 6.

58. Thelma S. McManus, *That's the Way It Was: Interviews of Ozark Folk Born in the 1800s* (Morley, MO: Acclaim Press, 2008), 127; Ellen Gray Massey, *A Candle within Her Soul: Mary Elizabeth Mahnkey and Her Ozarks* (Lebanon, MO: Bittersweet, 1996), 68–69.

59. Teaching Notebook, 1911–1912, William A. E. French Papers, R175, SHSMR.

60. Eula Albright, *A History of the Albright Family* (n.p: n.p., 1970), 8.

61. Wayne Clark, *Letters and Diaries of Isaac A. Clarke* (Victoria, BC: Trafford Publishing, 2006), 4, 54, 96, 171, 210–14, 242, 327, 567–71. Among Clarke's students in the late 1860s were nephews of George Washington Baines (great-grandfather of Johnson) and Obediah R. Wright, half brother of Margaret Belle Wright (great-great-grandmother of Obama).

62. Phillips, *History of Education in Missouri*, 54–67; *Fifty-Eighth Report of the Public Schools of the State of Missouri, School Year Ending June 30, 1907* (Jefferson City: Hugh Stephens Printing Company, 1908), 85–119; J. L. Bond, *Biennial Report of the State Superintendent of Public Instruction, State of Arkansas, 1919–1920* (Conway, AR: Conway Printing Company, 1920), 26, 138–42; Dougan, "Elementary and Secondary Education."

63. Dianna Everett, "Dwight Mission," *EOHC*, accessed September 18, 2020; Rose Stauber, "Oaks," *EOHC*, accessed September 18, 2020.

64. Brooks Blevins, "Region, Religion, and Competing Visions of Mountain Mission Education in the Ozarks," *Journal of Southern History* 82 (February 2016): 62.

65. Blevins, "Mountain Mission Schools," 403–405; Peggy Smith Hake, *Iberia Academy and the Town . . . Its History* (St. Elizabeth, MO: n.p., 1980), 5.

66. *Home Missionary*, April 1893, 580–82; February 1896, 525–26.

67. Bruce Barton, "Smith of Iberia," *American Magazine*, December 1916, 42, 76.

68. Michael Kammen, *Mystic Chords of Memory: The Transformation of Tradition in American Culture* (New York: Alfred A. Knopf, 1991), 428; Blevins, "Mountain Mission Schools," 406–408; Blevins, "Region, Religion, and Competing Visions," 82–86.

69. Blevins, "Region, Religion, and Competing Visions," 77–79.

70. Mayme Lucille Hamlett, *To Noonday Bright: The Story of Southwest Baptist University, 1878–1984* (Bolivar, MO: Southwest Baptist University, 1984), 13, 68, 147, 155; Rick Ostrander, *Head, Heart, and Hand: John Brown University and Modern Evangelical Higher Education* (Fayetteville: University of Arkansas Press, 2003), 3–16, 28–55.

71. Phillips, *History of Education in Missouri*, 205.

72. Ibid., 100, 115; Brad Agnew, "Northeastern State University," *EOHC*, accessed August

19, 2020; Jimmy Bryant, "University of Central Arkansas," *EOA*, accessed August 19, 2020; Donald D. Landon, *Daring to Excel: The First 100 Years of Southwest Missouri State University* (Springfield: Southwest Missouri State University, 2004), 48.

Chapter 5. Exposing the Ozarks

1. E. T. Sechler, *Leaves from an Ozark Journal*, vol. 1, 1927–1936 (Springfield, MO: Westport Press, 1969), 33–86.

2. Emmit D. Acklin, *The Wolf Was Never Far Away: Autobiography of Emmit Dolan Acklin* (Norfork, AR: n.p., n.d), 1–17.

3. Ibid., 18–54.

4. Ibid., 10.

5. James West, *Plainville, U.S.A.* (New York: Columbia University Press, 1945), 214, 221.

6. Marvin Lawson, *By Gum, I Made It! An Ozark Arkie's Hillbilly Boyhood* (Branson, MO: The Ozarks Mountaineer, 1977), 105; Tate C. Page, *Voices of Moccasin Creek* (Point Lookout, MO: School of the Ozarks Press, 1972), 108–109, 398, 51.

7. Mark D. Groover, *An Archaeological Study of Rural Capitalism and Material Life: The Gibbs Farmstead in Southern Appalachia, 1790–1920* (New York: Kluwer Academic/Plenum Publishers, 2003), 87, 98; Mary Lee Douthit, Robert Flanders, Barbara Fischer, and Lynn Morrow, *Overview of Cultural Resources in the Mark Twain National Forest, Missouri*, vol. 1, CAR-94 (Springfield, MO: Center for Archaeological Research, Southwest Missouri State University, 1979), 279; Steven D. Smith, *Made in the Timber: A Settlement History of the Fort Leonard Wood Region*, Engineer Research and Development Center/Construction Engineering Research Laboratory Special Report 03-5 (Fort Leonard Wood, MO: Maneuver Support Center, 2003), 127; Dennis Naglich, Stephanie L. Nutt, Steven R. Ahler, Terrance J. Martin, and Michael L. Hargrave, *National Register Eligibility Assessment of Six Historic Sites (23PU278, 23PU395, 23PU742, 23PU755, 23PU757, and 23PU1868) at Fort Leonard Wood, Missouri*, University of Kentucky Program for Archaeological Research Technical Report 683 (Champaign, IL: U.S. Army Engineer Research and Development Center, Construction Engineering Research Laboratory, 2010), 37; Theodore Catton, *Life, Leisure, and Hardship along the Buffalo*, Historic Resources Study, Buffalo National River (Omaha, NE: Midwest Region, National Park Service, 2008), 119; James Lee Murphy, "A History of the Southeastern Ozark Region of Missouri" (PhD diss., Saint Louis University, 1982), 3, 258; Mary Z. Brennan, "Sense of Place: Reconstructing Community through Archeology, Oral History, and GIS" (PhD diss., University of Arkansas, 2009), 85; CB, *Fifteenth Census of the United States: 1930, Agriculture*, vol. 2, part 1 (GPO, 1932), 980–88; CB, *Fifteenth Census of the United States: 1930, Agriculture*, vol. 2, part 2 (GPO, 1932), 1136–41, 1290–95.

8. Walter M. Adams, *The White River Railway: Being a History of the White River Division of the Missouri Pacific Railroad Company, 1901–1951* (Branson, MO: The Ozarks Mountaineer, 1991), 109; Catton, *Life, Leisure, and Hardship*, 211; John Spurgeon, "Drought of 1930–1931," *EOA*, accessed December 10, 2018; Floyd Sharp and Associates, *Traveling Recovery Road: The Story of Relief, Work-Relief and Rehabilitation*

in Arkansas, August 30, 1932, to November 15, 1936 (Little Rock: Emergency Relief Administration, 1936), 119–23.

9.   Richard Mize, "Sallisaw," *EOHC*, accessed December 14, 2018.

10. Omer E. Brown, *Son of Pioneers: Recollections of an Ozarks Lawyer* (Point Lookout, MO: School of the Ozarks Press, 1973), 91–95; Erma Humphreys, *Down on the Farm* (Fort Dodge, KS: self-pub., 1976), 109–125.

11. Ernest J. Webber, *Growing Up in the Ozarks* (Naples, FL: Adams Press, 1988), 125–26; Z. Evalena Pemberton, *Precious Memories of My Arkansas Mother, Edna Pugh Lee* (n.p., 1980), 188–89, 214–16.

12. West, *Plainville, U.S.A.*, 18–29; Leland Fox, *Tall Tales from the Sage of Cane Hill* (Greenfield, MO: Vedette Publishing, 1971), 119–22.

13. Michael Wallis, *Pretty Boy: The Life and Times of Charles Arthur Floyd* (New York: St. Martin's Press, 1992), 97, 109, 328.

14. Wallis, *Pretty Boy*, 170; Larry Wood, *Wicked Joplin* (Charleston, SC: History Press, 2011), 106.

15. Wood, *Ozarks Gunfights and Other Notorious Incidents* (Gretna, LA: Pelican Publishing, 2010), 174–78; David E. Ruth, *Inventing the Public Enemy: The Gangster in American Culture, 1918-1934* (Chicago: University of Chicago Press, 1996), 2; "Held as Gangster at Springfield," *Moberly (MO) Monitor-Index*, September 9, 1930, 10; "Officers Capture Notorious Bandit," *Cassville Republican*, September 11, 1930, 1; Kathleen Van Buskirk, comp., "Outlaw for My Neighbor: The Jake Fleagle Story," *WRVHQ* 7 (Fall 1979): 4–11; Vernon Worthington, "My Recollections of the Cook (Fleagle) Brothers," *WRVHQ* 7 (Fall 1979): 13; "Jake Fleagle," Famous Cases, Garden City, Kansas, Police Department, https://www.gcpolice.org/about-gcpd/history/famous-cases/jake-fleagle, accessed December 18, 2018.

16. Jeff Guinn, *Go Down Together: The True, Untold Story of Bonnie and Clyde* (New York: Simon & Schuster, 2009), 141–70.

17. Ibid., 172–76.

18. Wood, *Ozarks Gunfights*, 194–97.

19. Ibid., 198–200.

20. Ibid., 201–206; Wallis, *Pretty Boy*, 350.

21. Lynne Pierson Doti, "Banking Industry," *EOHC*, accessed December 28, 2018; Richard S. Kirkendall, *A History of Missouri*, vol. 5, *1919-1953* (Columbia: University of Missouri Press, 1986), 133; John A. Dominick, "Banking," *EOA*, accessed December 28, 2018; William L. Silber, "Why Did FDR's Bank Holiday Succeed?" *Federal Reserve Board of New York Economic Policy Review* 15 (July 2009): 19–25.

22. Karr Shannon, *A History of Izard County, Arkansas* (Little Rock: Democrat Printing and Lithographing, 1947), 47; Eugene Oakley, "A History of Grandin and the Missouri Lumber and Mining Company," 1963, booklet at Missouri State University-West Plains Garnett Library, 10.

23. Kirkendall, *History of Missouri*, 5:131–32; William H. Mullins, "Great Depression," *EOHC*, accessed December 28, 2018; Sharp, *Traveling Recovery Road*, 17–18; Smith, *Made in the Timber*, 151.

24. Pamela Salamo, "Harvey Parnell," *EOA*, accessed December 31, 2018; Sharp, *Traveling Recovery Road*, 17; Mullins, "Great Depression".

25. Michael B. Dougan, "Junius Marion Futrell," *EOA*, accessed December 31, 2018; Kirkendall, *History of Missouri*, 5:160–62; Keith L. Bryant Jr., "New Deal," *EOHC*, accessed December 28, 2018; Keith L. Bryant Jr., "Murray, William Henry David," *EOHC*, accessed December 31, 2018.

26. Bryant, "New Deal"; Arrell M. Gibson, *Oklahoma: A History of Five Centuries* (1965; Norman: University of Oklahoma Press, 1981), 156–58; Glen Robinson, "Grand River Dam Authority," *EOHC*, accessed December 28, 2018; Donald Holley, "Carl Edward Bailey," *EOA*, accessed December 31, 2018; Kirkendall, *History of Missouri*, 5:182–183.

27. Jane Brown to Marion Futrell, 1933, FERA Correspondence A-D, Junius Marion Futrell Papers, 1933–1937, Arkansas State Archives, Little Rock; Pearl Christian Brown, *Ozark Mountain Life and Customs: Wood Cook Stove to Microwave* (n.p., 1983), 88; Donald L. Stevens Jr., *A Homeland and a Hinterland: The Current and Jacks Fork Riverways* (Omaha, NE: National Park Service Midwest Region, 1991), 51; "Tells of Social Work with Ozark Destitute," undated *St. Louis Post-Dispatch* clipping, Ozarks Scrapbook, Ozarks Scrapbooks c. 1927–1944, 2007, 167, Southeast Missouri State University Special Collections and Archives, Cape Girardeau; Morris G. Caldwell and Sheila M. Caldwell, "Public Welfare and Social Work Dependency in the Ozarks," *Social Forces* 14 (May 1936): 553; Sechler, *Leaves from an Ozark Journal*, 1:79.

28. Sandra Taylor Smith, "The Civilian Conservation Corps in Arkansas, 1933–1942" (Little Rock: Arkansas Historic Preservation Program, 1997), 7–8; James Denny, "The New Deal, the CCC, and Missouri State Parks," *OzarksWatch* 7 (Spring 1994), 11–13.

29. Steve Illum, "CCC Days at the Shell Knob Camp," *OzarksWatch* 7 (Spring 1994), 28; Smith, "Civilian Conservation Corps," 11.

30. Suzanne H. Schrems, "Civilian Conservation Corps," *EOHC*, accessed January 5, 2019; Denny, "New Deal," 12–14; Smith, "Civilian Conservation Corps," 10–12.

31. Peter W. Nichols and Jeff Patridge, "Stockton Community Building," NR, 1998, 8-2-8-5, https://dnr.mo.gov/shpo/index.html, accessed January 1, 2019.

32. Hope, "Ambition to be Preferred," 11, 22. Unless otherwise indicated, information on WPA/NYA buildings in this and subsequent paragraphs comes from general listings found on the following websites: https://livingnewdeal.org/us/, https://dnr .mo.gov/shpo/index.html, and www. https://www.arkansasheritage.com/arkansas -preservation/properties/arkansas-register.

33. Denny, "New Deal," 13.

34. Gary R. Kremer and Evan P. Orr, "Lake Placid: 'A Recreational Center for Colored People in the Missouri Ozarks,'" in *The Ozarks in Missouri History: Discoveries in an American Region,* ed. Lynn Morrow (Columbia: University of Missouri Press, 2013), 226; "History of Silver Springs, Sequiota Parks in Springfield," *Buffalo (MO) Reflex,* February 16, 2016, buffaloreflex.com, accessed January 7, 2019; "Some Old Schoolhouses Used for Other Purposes," *Tahlequah Daily Press*, April 6, 2015, https:// www.tahlequahdailypress.com/, accessed January 7, 2019.

35. "Putting People to Work," Online Exhibit, Shiloh Museum of Ozark History, Spring-dale, Arkansas, https://www.shilohmuseum.org/exhibits/new-deal-intro.php, ac-cessed January 8, 2019; Webber, *Growing Up in the Ozarks*, 175–77; Evalena Berry,

Time and the River: A History of Cleburne County (Little Rock: Rose Publishing, 1982), 237; Buskirk, "Winds of Change," 4; Sharp, *Traveling Recovery Road*, 93; Humphreys, *Down on the Farm*, 144.

36. Hope, "Ambition to Be Preferred," 14, 36; Robert Cochran, *Vance Randolph: An Ozark Life* (Urbana: University of Illinois Press, 1985), 155–58; "Ozarkers Indignant at 'Copy' Written by WPA Workers in American Guide Book," *Daily Capital News* (Jefferson City, MO), November 3, 1936, 4.

37. "New Deal Agency: Treasury Section of Fine Arts," https://livingnewdeal.org/new -deal-agencies/treasury-department-td/treasury-section-of-fine-arts/, accessed January 19, 2021; Carole Magnus and Roger Maserang, "Fredericktown United States Post Office," 2009, 8-18–8-19, https://dnr.mo.gov/shpo/index.html, accessed January 4, 2019; Allen Du Bois, "Harry Louis Freund," *EOA*, accessed January 9, 2019; Eileen Turan and Keith Melton, "Mike Disfarmer," *EOA*, accessed January 9, 2019.

38. Hope, "Ambition to Be Preferred," 17; Sharp, *Traveling Recovery Road*, 20, 147–49; Clarence R. Keathley, "Reflections on Public Welfare in Washington County, Missouri, 1939–1941," in Morrow, *Ozarks in Missouri History*, 248; Webber, *Growing Up in the Ozarks*, 138–50.

39. Webber, *Growing Up in the Ozarks*, 152; West, *Plainville, U.S.A.*, 30; Larry J. Sprunk, *Historical Resources Mitigation*, vol. 1, *We Remember the Rivers, An Oral History Survey of the River Valleys in the Harry S. Truman Dam and Reservoir Project, Missouri* (Garrison, ND: Historical and Archaeological Surveys, 1980), 252; Brooks Blevins, "Life on the Margins: The Diaries of Minnie Atteberry," *AHQ* 75 (Winter 2016): 297–99.

40. West, *Plainville, U.S.A.*, 14, 84, 216; Julia C. Ehrhardt, *Writers of Conviction: The Personal Politics of Zona Gale, Dorothy Canfield Fisher, Rose Wilder Lane, and Josephine Herbst* (Columbia: University of Missouri Press, 2004), 96, 132.

41. Robert S. Wiley, *Dewey Short: Orator of the Ozarks* (Cassville, MO: Litho Printers and Bindery, 1985), vii, 13–41, 69.

42. Ibid., 133–77, 249.

43. Neal Moore, "A Farm-Labor Alliance in Troubled Times," unpublished paper delivered at the Missouri Conference on History, Columbia, 1987, https://libraries .missouristate.edu/Reuben-T-Rube-Wood.htm, accessed January 11, 2019; Donald R. Deskins Jr., Hanes Walton Jr., and Sherman C. Puckett, *Presidential Elections, 1789-2008: County, State, and National Mapping of Election Data* (Ann Arbor: University of Michigan Press, 2010), 352, 372.

44. West, *Plainville, U.S.A.*, 215; Otto Ernest Rayburn, *Ozark Country* (New York: Duell, Sloan & Pearce, 1941), 343.

45. David M. Kennedy, *Freedom from Fear: The American People in Depression and War, 1929-1945* (New York: Oxford University Press, 1999), 177, 192, 202; *Fifteenth Census . . . Agriculture*, vol. 2, part 1, 1070–1079; *Fifteenth Census . . . Agriculture*, vol. 2, part 2, 1204–1209, 1352–1358.

46. Kennedy, *Freedom from Fear*, 140–41, 204–206; Roger Biles, *The South and the New Deal* (Lexington: University Press of Kentucky, 1994), 38–40; West, *Plainville, U.S.A.*, 134.

47. Sharp, *Traveling Recovery Road*, 100, 119–23; C. Roger Lambert, "The Drought Cattle Purchase, 1934–1935: Problems and Complaints," *Agricultural History* 45 (April 1971): 85; Blevins, *Hill Folks*, 113; Brown, *Ozark Mountain Life*, 133.

48. Biles, *South and the New Deal*, 54; E. F. Chesnutt, "Rural Electrification in Arkansas, 1935–1940: The Formative Years," *Arkansas Historical Quarterly* 46 (Autumn 1987): 226, 231–32, 235, 250, 255–56; Cindy Grisham, *75 Years with North Arkansas Electric Cooperative* (Virginia Beach: Donning Company Publishers, 2016), 21; Stevens, *Homeland and a Hinterland*, 198; E. T. Sechler, *Leaves from an Ozark Journal*, vol. 2, *1937–1946* (Springfield, MO: Westport Press, n.d.), 13; "History of Intercounty Electric," www.ieca.coop/content/history-intercounty-electric, accessed January 21, 2019; JoAnne Sears Rife, interview with author, Springfield, Missouri, December 5, 2012.

49. Biles, *South and the New Deal*, 54; Chesnutt, "Rural Electrification in Arkansas," 226–56; Grisham, *75 Years with North Arkansas Electric Cooperative*, 21; Rife interview; "Lillian Sears Was Early Activist," freepages.rootsweb.com/~dmccamey/genealogy/stories/Lillian.htm, accessed January 21, 2019; "Carroll Electric Cooperative a Mighty Force in Development of Arkansas Ozarks," *OM*, September 1956, 3.

50. Biles, *South and the New Deal*, 52; Brian C. Campbell, "Just Eat Peas and Dance: Field Peas (*Vigna unguiculata*) and Food Security in the Ozark Highlands, U.S.," *Journal of Ethnobiology* 34 (2014): 114.

51. Biles, *South and the New Deal*, 52–57; Kennedy, *Freedom from Fear*, 207, 350–54; Brooks Blevins, *Lyon College, 1872–2002: The Perseverance and Promise of an Arkansas College* (Fayetteville: University of Arkansas Press, 2003), 165.

52. Arrell M. Gibson, *Wilderness Bonanza: The Tri-State District of Missouri, Kansas, and Oklahoma* (Norman: University Oklahoma Press, 1972), 231–45; Lou Martin, *Smokestacks in the Hills: Rural-Industrial Workers in West Virginia* (Urbana: University of Illinois Press, 2015), 1–12; Keathley, "Reflections on Public Welfare," 241–43.

53. Adrianne Finelli, "Men and Dust," loc.gov/static/programs/national-film-preservation-board/documents/men_and_dust.pdf, accessed November 2, 2019; Catherine S. Barker, *Yesterday Today: Life in the Ozarks* (Caldwell, ID: Caxton Printers, 1941), 9, 241, 260; Patsy G. Watkins, "Same People, Same Time, Same Place: Contrasting Images of Destitute Ozark Mountaineers during the Great Depression," *AHQ* 70 (Autumn 2011): 288, 294.

54. Charles Morrow Wilson, "Hemmed-in Holler," *Review of Reviews and World's Work*, August 1935, 58–62.

55. Brooks Blevins, *Arkansas/Arkansaw: How Bear Hunters, Hillbillies, and Good Ol' Boys Defined a State* (Fayetteville: University of Arkansas Press, 2009), 72, 112; Lee Server, *Robert Mitchum: "Baby, I Don't Care"* (New York: St. Martin's Press, 2001), 51; Marguerite Lyon, *Take to the Hills: A Chronicle of the Ozarks* (Indianapolis: Bobbs-Merrill Company, 1941); Barker, *Yesterday Today*; Rayburn, *Ozark Country*.

56. Lennis L. Broadfoot, *Pioneers of the Ozarks* (Caldwell, ID: Caxton Printers, 1944), 16–41, 127–67.

57. Ibid., 49, 25; Vance Randolph, *The Ozarks: An American Survival of Primitive Society* (New York: Vanguard Press, 1931).

58. Rayburn, *Ozark Country*, 54; *Tuxedo Junction*, dir. Frank McDonald, November 25, 1941, Republic Pictures, imdb.com/title/tt0034319/?ref_=ttpl_pl_tt, accessed November 2, 2019.

59. Kennedy, *Freedom from Fear*, 377; Rayburn, *Ozark Country*, 307.

60. Kirkendall, *History of Missouri*, 5:251; Colonel Howard V. Canan, "Career of Paul M. Robinett," https://www.marshallfoundation.org/library/documents/career-paul-m -robinett/, accessed January 24, 2019; Brooks Blevins, "Edward Baxter Billingsley," *EOA*, accessed March 31, 2020; Philip Martin McCaulay, *World War II Medal of Honor Recipients* (n.p.: lulu.com, 2010), 351, 138; "Cole, Darrell S., Sergeant, USMCR, (1920–1945)," Naval History and Heritage Command, https://www.history.navy .mil/our-collections/photography/us-people/c/cole-darrell-s.html, accessed January 24, 2019.

61. Blevins, "Life on the Margins," 300; Rex R. Campbell, *Revolution in the Heartland: Changes in Rural Culture, Family and Communities, 1900–2000* (Columbia: University of Missouri Department of Rural Sociology, 2004), 154.

62. Kennedy, *Freedom from Fear*, 620, 645; Drew Philip Halevy, "World War II," *EOA*, accessed December 28, 2018; Brad Agnew, "World War II," *EOHC*, accessed December 28, 2018.

63. Kirkendall, *History of Missouri*, 5:260–66; Michael Glenn, "O'Reilly General Hospital of Springfield, Missouri, About O'Reilly: A Brief Introduction," https://thelibrary .org/lochist/oreilly/intro.cfm, accessed January 28, 2019.

64. Paul W. Bass, *The History of Fort Leonard Wood Missouri* (Morley, MO: Acclaim Press, 2016), 25–29, 50, 63; John Bradbury and Terry Primas, *Old Pulaski in Pictures: Rivers, Rails, Roads, and Recreation, Pulaski County, Missouri* (Duke, MO: Big Piney Productions, 2012), 55, 95.

65. Kimberly Harper, "'What of the Farmer?' World War II Comes to the Ozarks—The Creation of Camp Crowder," *MHR* 111 (October 2016): 27; Danny Johnson, "Camp Enoch H. Crowder, Missouri," https://armyhistory.org/camp-enoch-h-crowder -missouri/, accessed January 28, 2019; Holly A. Baggett, "The Creation of a Community: A History of Gay and Lesbian Springfield, 1945–2010," in *Springfield's Urban Histories: Essays on the Queen City of the Missouri Ozarks*, ed. Stephen L. McIntyre (Springfield, MO: Moon City Press, 2012), 306.

66. Bass, *History of Fort Leonard Wood*, 54–56; Martha Jo Black and Chuck Schoffner, *Joe Black: More Than a Dodger* (Chicago: Chicago Review Press, 2015), 136–41.

67. Harper, "What of the Farmer?," 42n36, 28–38; Bass, *History of Fort Leonard Wood*, 22–23.

68. Harper, "What of the Farmer?," 25–31; Bass, *History of Fort Leonard Wood*, 9, 51, 62.

69. Smith, *Made in the Timber*, 160–61; "Houses Built at Newburg to Be Transferred to Fort," *Rolla (MO) Herald*, August 14, 1941, 1; Sechler, *Leaves from an Ozark Journal*, 2:66, 80.

70. Kirkendall, *History of Missouri*, 5:265; Glenn Hackett, interview by author, Shirley, Arkansas, August 27, 1993.

71. Zela Rhoads, interview by author, Agnos, Arkansas, October 2, 1998; Pemberton, *Precious Memories of My Arkansas Mother*, 219–23.

Chapter 6. Putting on a Show

1. Information for this and succeeding paragraphs from Kaitlyn McConnell, "Mountain Village 1890, the Town Where History Lives," https://www.ozarksalive.com/mountain-village-1890-town-history-lives/, accessed April 4, 2020; Crystal Payton, *The Story of Silver Dollar City: A Pictorial History of Branson's Famous Ozark Mountain Theme Park*, 2nd ed. (Springfield, MO: Lens and Pen Press, 2007), 51–54, 76–82.
2. Brooks Blevins, *Hill Folks: A History of Arkansas Ozarkers and Their Image* (Chapel Hill: University of North Carolina Press, 2002), 234.
3. Adria English, "Arkansas Haunt: Mountain Village 1890," https://onlyinark.com/culture/arkansas-haunt-mountain-village-1890/, accessed September 21, 2020.
4. *McDonald County Press* (Noel, MO), April 13, 1961, 1.
5. Louis La Coss, "Ozarkians Ready for Tourist Season," *New York Times*, May 24, 1931, E8.
6. W. R. Draper, "Motoring into the Ozarks," *New York Times*, July 20, 1930, XX7.
7. Betty Lou Harper Thomas, "Spavinaw," EOHC, accessed December 31, 2019; H. Dwight Weaver, *History & Geography of Lake of the Ozarks*, vol. 1 (Eldon, MO: Osage Valley Trader, 2005), 13–14; Leland and Crystal Payton, *Damming the Osage: The Conflicted Story of Lake of the Ozarks and Truman Reservoir* (Springfield, MO: Lens & Pen Press, 2012), 115–27; H. Dwight Weaver, *Lake of the Ozarks: The Early Years* (Charleston, SC: Arcadia Press, 2000), 9–28; J. A. Seaburg, "Hydro-Electric Power in the Ozarks," *Scientific American*, August 1931, 94–96.
8. Weaver, *Lake of the Ozarks: The Early Years*, 15; Payton, *Damming the Osage*, 104.
9. John M. Barry, *Rising Tide: The Great Mississippi Flood of 1927 and How It Changed America* (New York: Simon and Schuster, 1997), 407; Mary Suter, "Dammed Arkansas: Early Developments in How Arkansas Came to Be a Dammed State, 1836–1945" (PhD diss., University of Arkansas, 2013), 14–15, 51–62; *White River, Missouri and Arkansas: Letter from the Secretary of War Transmitting Pursuant to Section 1 of the Rivers and Harbors Act Approved January 21, 1927, and Section 10 of the Flood Control Act Approved May 15, 1928 . . .* (GPO, 1933), 153.
10. Glen Roberson, "Grand River Dam Authority," EOHC, accessed January 1, 2020; Suter, "Dammed Arkansas," 62–64; *Report of the Chief of Engineers, U.S. Army, 1942*: part 1, vol. 2 (GPO, 1943), 1967; Rose Fulton Cramer, *Wayne County, Missouri* (Cape Girardeau, MO: Ramfire Press, 1972), 351.
11. J. Blake Perkins, *Hillbilly Hellraisers: Federal Power and Populist Defiance in the Ozarks* (Urbana: University of Illinois Press, 2017), 135–39; Tom Shiras, "Hydroelectric Development in Arkansas," *Popular Mechanics*, April 1922, 574; Suter, "Dammed Arkansas," 93; Sheila Yount, "Clyde Taylor Ellis," EOA, accessed January 1, 2020.
12. *Comprehensive Flood-Control Plans: Hearings before the Committee on Flood Control, House of Representatives, Seventy-fifth Congress, March 30 to April 19, 1938* (GPO, 1938), 780; Mary Yeater Rathbun, *Castle on the Rock, 1881–1985: The History of the Little Rock District, U.S. Army Corps of Engineers* (Little Rock: U.S. Army Engineer District, Little Rock, 1990), 67–73.

13. Evalena Berry, *Time and the River: A History of Cleburne County* (Little Rock: Rose Publishing, 1982), 349–51; Rathbun, *Castle on the Rock*, 74–79.

14. Payton, *Damming the Osage*, 184, 228.

15. "Electricity," U.S. Energy Information Administration, eia.gov/electricity/, accessed January 2, 2020; Blevins, *Hill Folks*, 234; Rathbun, *Castle on the Rock*, 70; R. A. Rogers, *The Premature Graying of the Arkansas Ozarks* (n.p.: 48HrBooks, 2019), 21.

16. Blevins, *Hill Folks*, 194–95; reprinted in Donald Katz, *The Valley of the Fallen and Other Stories* (New York: AtRandom Books, 2001), 152–73.

17. Blevins, *Hill Folks*, 195–99.

18. Ibid., 197–98; Rathbun, *Castle on the Rock*, 73–74; "History of Kimberling City, MO," Table Rock Community Bank, https://trcbank.com/community/home/, accessed January 28, 2020; Steven Teske, "Diamond City," *EOA*, accessed January 28, 2020; Steven Teske, "Holiday Island," *EOA*, accessed January 28, 2020; Lost Bridge Village Community Association, "The History of Lost Bridge Village," lbvca.com/history.html, accessed January 28, 2020.

19. Walter M. Adams, *The White River Railway: Being a History of the White River Division of the Missouri Pacific Railroad Company, 1901–1951* (Branson, MO: The Ozarks Mountaineer, 1991), 83, 151; Scott Branyan, "Bull Shoals Dam and Lake," *EOA*, accessed December 1, 2015; Scott Branyan, "Norfork Dam and Lake," *EOA*, accessed December 1, 2015; Sonny Garrett, "Are There Less Trout in White River?" *Baxter Bulletin*, April 21, 2015, baxterbulletin.com/story/news/local/2015/04/21/less-trout-white-river/26133729/, accessed January 3, 2020.

20. Bryan Hendricks, "Flippin's Wood Dies; Founded Ranger Boats," *Northwest Arkansas Democrat-Gazette*, January 26, 2020, www.nwaonline.com/news/2020/jan/26/flippin-s-wood-dies-founded-ranger-boat/, accessed January 28, 2020; "Flashback: Ray Scott's First Tournament," www.bassmaster.com/slideshow/flashback-1967-beaver-lake, accessed January 28, 2020.

21. "Ranger Boats," *EOA*, accessed January 2, 2020.

22. Savannah Waszczuk, "The Johnny Morris Story," *417 Magazine*, November 2014, 417mag.com/issues/November-2014/the-johnny-morris-story/, accessed January 3, 2020; #181 John Morris, *Forbes*, www.forbes.com/profile/john-morris/#dea239fb517, accessed January 3, 2020.

23. Perkins, *Hillbilly Hellraisers*, 156.

24. Brooks Blevins, *Arkansas/Arkansaw: How Bear Hunters, Hillbillies, and Good Ol' Boys Defined a State* (Fayetteville: University of Arkansas Press, 2009), 112; Suter, "Dammed Arkansas," 94.

25. S.O.S., Inc., "Facts about Table Rock Dam," brochure, folder 36, Wiley Collection, SHSMR; Perkins, *Hillbilly Hellraisers*, 147–50; Jim Clinkingbeard, interview with author, Calico Rock, Arkansas, August 26, 2012; Sara Stone-Parks, telephone interview with author, September 26, 2013.

26. Perkins, *Hillbilly Hellraisers*, 151–55; "Facts about Table Rock Dam"; "Basin Landowners Get 47 Per Cent More for Land in Court Than Offered," *Baxter Bulletin*, May 28, 1943, 1; *Historical Resources Mitigation*, vol. 1, *We Remember the Rivers, An Oral History Survey of the River Valleys in the Harry S. Truman Dam and Reservoir*

Project, Missouri (Garrison, ND: Historical and Archaeological Surveys, 1980), 125, 68; Leland Fox, *Tall Tales from the Sage of Cane Hill* (Greenfield, MO: Vedette Publishing, 1971), 2.

27. Payton, *Damming the Osage*, 215–28.

28. T. Michael Ruddy, *Damning the Dam: The St. Louis District Corps of Engineers and the Controversy over the Meramec Basin Project from Its Inception to Its Deauthorization* (St. Louis, MO: Army Corps of Engineers, St. Louis District, 1992), https://erdc -library.erdc.dren.mil/xmlui/handle/11681/15239, accessed December 29, 2019.

29. James M. Guldin, Greg F. Iffrig, and Susan L. Flader, eds., *Pioneer Forest: A Half Century of Sustainable Uneven-Aged Forest Management in the Missouri Ozarks*, USDA Forest Service General Technical Report SRS-108 (Asheville, NC: Southern Research Station, 2008), 15; *White River, Missouri and Arkansas*, 210–19.

30. Donald L. Stevens Jr., *A Homeland and a Hinterland: The Current and Jacks Fork Riverways* (Omaha, NE: National Park Service Midwest Region, 1991), 200; Will Sarvis, "A Difficult Legacy: Creation of the Ozark National Scenic Riverways," *Public Historian* 24 (Winter 2002): 36.

31. Stevens, *Homeland and a Hinterland*, 201–202; Sarvis, "Difficult Legacy," 40; Statement of G. L. Davis before Senate Committee on Interior and Insular Affairs on Behalf of S. 1381 on July 8, 1961, folder 175, box 6, Drey Papers; Drey to Sen. Clinton P. Anderson (NM), October 20, 1961, folder 202, box 7, Drey Papers.

32. Finding Aid, Leonard Hall Papers, 1946–1983, SHSMR, https://collections.shsmo .org/manuscripts/rolla/r0408/pdf, accessed January 8, 2020; "Current River Development," April 23, 1959, *St. Louis Post-Dispatch* and succeeding Leonard Hall columns, clippings, folder 188, box 6, Drey Papers; Leonard Hall, *Stars Upstream: Life along an Ozark River* (Chicago: University of Chicago Press, 1958); Guldin et al., *Pioneer Forest*, 9–16; Sarvis, "Difficult Legacy," 38–44.

33. Leonard Hall, "Colorful Ozarks Impress Udall," *St. Louis Globe-Democrat*, October 1, 1961, folder 188, box 6, Drey Papers; Minutes, Shannon County Chapter of the Current–Eleven Point Rivers Association, September 28, 1961, folder 210, box 7, Drey Papers; Leonard Hall, "Last Chance for the Current River," *FOCUS/Midwest*, March-April 1963, 14.

34. Bernard Asbell, "The Vanishing Hillbilly," *Saturday Evening Post*, September 23, 1961, 92–95.

35. Ibid., 93–95; Minutes of Shannon County chapter, Current–Eleven Point Rivers Association, October 15, 1961, and "A Question," undated bulletin from the National Park Association, president G. L. Davis, folder 210, box 7, Drey Papers.

36. Steve Kohler, *Two Ozark Rivers: The Current and the Jacks Fork* (1984; Columbia: University of Missouri Press, 1996), 110; Sarvis, "Difficult Legacy," 18; Stevens, *Homeland and a Hinterland*, 202–203; Will Sarvis, "Old Eminent Domain and New Scenic Easements: Land Acquisition for the Ozark National Scenic Riverways," *Western Legal History* 13 (Winter/Spring 2000): 4.

37. Sarvis, "Old Eminent Domain," 18–34.

38. Kathleen Morrison, "The Poverty of Place: A Comparative Study of Five Rural Counties in the Missouri Ozarks" (PhD diss., University of Missouri, 1999), 12; CB, "State

and County Estimates for 2014," https://www.census.gov/data/datasets/2014/demo/
saipe/2014-state-and-county.html, accessed January 10, 2020.

39. Sarvis, "Old Eminent Domain," 34–36; Kelly Fish-Greenlee, "We Are the Horses:
Identity Work in the Southeastern Missouri Ozarks" (PhD diss., University of Kansas,
2009), 15, 69–71, 122–26, 160; Erika Brady, "Mankind's Thumb on Nature's Scale:
Trapping and Regional Identity in the Missouri Ozarks," in *Sense of Place: American
Regional Cultures,* ed. Barbara Allen and Thomas J. Schlereth (Lexington: University
Press of Kentucky, 1990), 60, 73.

40. Guldin et al., *Pioneer Forest,* 18; Jerry W. Venters, "Assails Tactics in Killing Rivers
Bill," *St. Louis Post-Dispatch,* April 1, 1971, folder 151, box 6, Drey Papers.

41. "Arkansas," National Wild and Scenic Rivers System, https://rivers.gov/Arkansas
.php, accessed January 11, 2020; Neil Compton, *The Battle for the Buffalo River: A
Twentieth-Century Conservation Crisis in the Ozarks* (Fayetteville: University of
Arkansas Press, 1992), 23.

42. Theodore Catton, *Life, Leisure, and Hardship along the Buffalo,* Historic Resources
Study, Buffalo National River (Omaha, NE: Midwest Region, National Park Service,
2008), 261–65; Compton, *Battle for the Buffalo,* 52–79, 92–119.

43. Catton, *Life, Leisure, and Hardship,* 266; Compton, *Battle for the Buffalo,* 173–87, 212,
231–59, 281–82.

44. Jim Liles, "The Boxley Valley of Buffalo National River: A U.S. National Park Service
Historic District in Private Hands," *The George Wright Forum* 7, no. 3 (1991): 2–3; Catton, *Life, Leisure, and Hardship,* 266; Compton, *Battle for the Buffalo,* 106–108, 399.

45. Liles, "Boxley Valley," 2–5; Compton, *Battle for the Buffalo,* 43.

46. C. W. Gusewelle, "'A Continuity of Place and Blood': The Seasons of Man in the
Ozarks," *American Heritage,* December 1977, 108; Oral Deaton to Otto Ernest Ray-
burn, February 19, 1957, folder 1, box 13, Otto Ernest Rayburn Collection, UASC;
Virginia Schone, "Peaceful Ozarks," *New York Times,* July 11, 1948, X17; Henry N.
Ferguson, "The Once-Remote Ozarks Are Now Accessible," *New York Times,* De-
cember 11, 1960, XX13.

47. See chapters 7 and 8 of Robert Cochran, *Vance Randolph: An Ozark Life* (Urbana:
University of Illinois Press, 1985); Paul Johns, "The Famous and Sometimes Dubious Ozark Hillbilly Medallion," *Christian County Headliner News,* February 4,
2018, https://ccheadliner.com/opinion/the-famous-and-sometimes-dubious-ozark
-hillbilly-medallion/article_5085ea7c-0844-11e8-a9d7-c76f760a35ca.html, accessed
June 8, 2020.

48. Otto Ernest Rayburn, *Forty Years in the Ozarks* (Eureka Springs, AR: Ozark Guide
Press, 1957), 79–97; Larry Dablemont, "A Gang of Ozark Mountaineers," https://www
.lakeexpo.com/news/lake_news/dablemont-a-gang-of-ozark-mountaineers/article
_ec54f0c4-56a1-11e2-b419-0019bb2963f4.html, accessed May 16, 2020.

49. Blevins, *Hill Folks,* 231–32; James C. Tanner, "Echoes of Appalachia: Poverty-Ridden
Ozarks See a Brighter Future if U.S. Aid Materializes," *Wall Street Journal,* November
13, 1965, 1; Mike W. Edwards, "Through Ozark Hills and Hollows," *National Geographic,* November 1970, 658. Information on articles of 1960s and 1970s derived
from *Readers' Guide Retrospective: 1890–1982,* www.ebsco.com.

50. Donald Van Horn, *Carved in Wood: Folk Sculpture in the Arkansas Ozarks* (Batesville: Arkansas College Folklore Archive, 1979), 59, 62; Celia DeWoody, "Rich Past Carved: Death, Dinosaur, Devil among Tales," *Bolivar Herald-Free Press*, September 13, 2006, https://bolivarmonews.com/home/rich-past-carved-deaths-dinosaur-devil-among -tales/article_29902843-cd2d-5d53-add8-7a9f34c88298,html?mode=jqm, accessed December 27, 2019; Aprille Hanson, "Carver's Artwork Nationally Known," *Arkansas Democrat-Gazette*, December 15, 2011; Payton, *Story of Silver Dollar City*, 62.

51. Clay Anderson, "The Unbelievable Junior Cobb," *OM*, September 1968, 18.

52. Van Horn, *Carved in Wood*, 74, 65, 135.

53. Edwards, "Ozark Hills and Hollows," 658; Weaver, *History & Geography*, 51; Bill Geist, *Lake of the Ozarks: My Surreal Summers in a Vanishing America* (New York: Grand Central Publishing, 2019), 21–24.

54. Geist, *Lake of the Ozarks*, 136–41; Weaver, *History & Geography*, 144; Weaver, *Lake of the Ozarks: The Early Years*, 30; "Musser's Ozark Tavern," Bird Lives: The Life of Charlie Parker Jr., https://birdlives.co.uk/musser-s-ozark-tavern, accessed January 13, 2020.

55. Dan Peek and Keith Van Landuyt, *A People's History of the Lake of the Ozarks* (Charleston, SC: History Press, 2016), 75–81, 109; Weaver, *Lake of the Ozarks: The Early Years*, 8, 38–39; H. Dwight Weaver, *Lake of the Ozarks: Vintage Vacation Paradise*, Images of America (Chicago: Arcadia Publishing, 2002), 49, 62, 84.

56. Peek and Van Landuyt, *People's History*, 112–26.

57. Dan William Peek, *Live! at the Ozark Opry* (Charleston, SC: History Press, 2010), 26–60.

58. Ibid., 107.

59. Vance Randolph and Frances Emberson, "The Collection of Folk Music in the Ozarks," *Journal of American Folklore* 60 (April–June 1947), 119–23

60. Wayne Glenn, *The Ozarks' Greatest Hits: A Photo History of Music in the Ozarks* (Nixa, MO: Wayne Glenn, 2005), 199, 228–29, 269, 166.

61. Glenn, *Ozarks' Greatest Hits*, 131–32, 175–85, 204–208.

62. Ibid., 210–19, 247–49.

63. Ibid., 212, 249, 277–81, 327.

64. Ibid., 227, 264–66, 329–31; Reta Spears-Stewart, *Remembering the Ozark Jubilee* (Springfield, MO: Stewart, Dillbeck and White Productions, 1993), 5–8.

65. Glenn, *Ozarks' Greatest Hits*, 264–65, 329, 378–85; Spears-Stewart, *Remembering the Ozark Jubilee*, 13–24, 60–79, 94–97. The first several episodes of *Ozark Jubilee* were actually broadcast from Columbia, Missouri, as work crews updated Springfield's technological infrastructure.

66. Glenn, *Ozarks' Greatest Hits*, 290, 385–89; Spears-Stewart, *Remembering the Ozark Jubilee*, 97, 22, 124–25; Sara K. Eskridge, *Rube Tube: CBS and Rural Comedy in the Sixties* (Columbia: University of Missouri Press, 2018), 40–41.

67. Glenn, *Ozarks' Greatest Hits*, 379–88; Spears-Stewart, *Remembering the Ozark Jubilee*, 21–38.

68. Glenn, *Ozarks' Greatest Hits*, 382–403; Spears-Stewart, *Remembering the Ozark Jubilee*, 43–57, 88–89, 13–15.

69. Eskridge, *Rube Tube*, 71–77; for seasonal ratings, see *tv-aholic: passion for television* (blog), https://tvaholics.blogspot.com/search/label/Classic%20TV%20Ratings, accessed January 18, 2020.

70. Eskridge, *Rube Tube*, 71–88; Glenn, *Ozarks' Greatest Hits*, 135.

71. Don Richardson Sr., "Junior Cobb of Three Brothers, Ark. Judges 'The Beverly Hillbillies,'" *TV Guide*, July 6, 1963, 8–9; Robert McGill, *Branson's Entertainment Pioneers* (Reeds Spring, MO: White Oak Publishing, 2011), 29; Payton, *Story of Silver Dollar City*, 76–78; Eskridge, *Rube Tube*, 169–72.

72. McGill, *Branson's Entertainment Pioneers*, 15–25; Leland Payton and Crystal Payton, *Branson: Country Themes and Neon Dreams* (Branson, MO: Anderson Publishing, 1993), 40, 75; Aaron K. Ketchell, *Holy Hills of the Ozarks: Religion and Tourism in Branson, Missouri* (Baltimore: Johns Hopkins University Press, 2007), 46–49.

73. Glenn, *Ozarks' Greatest Hits*, 443–54; McGill, *Branson's Entertainment Pioneers*, 32; Payton and Payton, *Branson*, 79; Ketchell, *Holy Hills of the Ozarks*, 38.

74. Glenn, *Ozarks' Greatest Hits*, 312–13, 395–96; McGill, *Branson's Entertainment Pioneers*, 29–39; Payton and Payton, *Branson*, 80–81; Edgar D. McKinney, "Images, Realities, and Cultural Transformation in the Missouri Ozarks, 1920–1960" (PhD diss., University of Missouri, 1990), 179; Spears-Stewart, *Remembering the Ozark Jubilee*, 29, 107; Payton, *Story of Silver Dollar City*, 53–63.

75. Scott Faragher, *The Branson Missouri Scrapbook: A Guide to the New Capital of Country Music* (New York: Citadel Press, 1994), 31; McGill, *Branson's Entertainment Pioneers*, 42–52; Ketchell, *Holy Hills of the Ozarks*, xiv, 230.

76. Faragher, *Branson Missouri Songbook*, 31; McGill, *Branson's Entertainment Pioneers*, 52; Payton and Payton, *Branson*, 98–109; Roy Reed, "Ozark Lollygagging," *New York Times*, March 13, 1988, SMA66.

77. Faragher, *Branson Missouri Scrapbook*, 15; McGill, *Branson's Entertainment Pioneers*, 57.

78. Payton and Payton, *Branson*, 110–30; McGill, *Branson's Entertainment Pioneers*, 57; "Bart on the Road," *The Simpsons*, Episode 20, Season 7, Fox, imdb.com/title/tt0701057/?ref_=tttr_tr_tt, accessed January 20, 2020.

79. McGill, *Branson's Entertainment Pioneers*, 58–59.

80. Ketchell, *Holy Hills of the Ozarks*, xxii; Blevins, *Hill Folks*, 238–41.

81. Jared M. Phillips, *Hipbillies: Deep Revolution in the Arkansas Ozarks* (Fayetteville: University of Arkansas Press, 2019), 59–64; Bethany May, "Eureka Springs," *EOA*, accessed January 29, 2020; Michael Klossner, "The Gospel of Eureka," *EOA*, accessed January 29, 2020.

82. Otto Ernest Rayburn, *Forty Years in the Ozarks: An Autobiography* (1957; Eureka Springs, AR: Wheeler Printing, 1983), 89; Phillips, *Hipbillies*, 3–19; Blevins, *Hill Folks*, 262–69.

83. Blevins, *Hill Folks*, 261–62.

84. Ibid., 263–65.

85. Anthony Harkins, *Hillbilly: A Cultural History of an American Icon* (New York: Oxford University Press, 2004), 124–36; Harold L. Enlow, *Carving Figure Caricatures in the Ozark Style* (New York: Dover Publications, 1975.)

86. Blevins, *Hill Folks*, 245–49.
87. Ibid., 250–51.
88. Ibid., 252–57.
89. *A Report to the Governor and the People of Arkansas from the Arkansas Industrial Development Commission July 1966–July 1967* (Little Rock: AIDC, 1967), 2; *A Report to the Governor and the People of Arkansas from the Arkansas Industrial Development Commission July 1967–July 1968* (Little Rock: AIDC, 1968), 10.

Chapter 7. Farm to Factory

1. Donald Ray Holliday, "Autobiography of an American Family" (PhD diss., University of Minnesota, 1974), 28–38.
2. Ibid., 45–49, 115; Rex R. Campbell, *A Revolution in the Heartland: Changes in Rural Culture, Family and Communities 1900–2000* (Columbia: University of Missouri Department of Rural Sociology, 2004), 195.
3. Holliday, "Autobiography," 84, 120–23, 162–66.
4. Art Gallaher Jr., *Plainville Fifteen Years Later* (New York: Columbia University Press, 1961), 37, 19; Campbell, *Revolution in the Heartland*, 164, 187–88.
5. Walter Severs, interview with author, Ralph, Arkansas, October 18, 2012.
6. Gallaher, *Plainville Fifteen Years Later*, 232–35; CB, *Sixteenth Census of the United States, 1940: Agriculture: Statistics for Counties—Southern States*, vol. 2, part 2 (GPO, 1942), 642–57, 738–53; CB, *Sixteenth Census of the United States, 1940: Agriculture: Statistics for Counties—Northern States*, vol. 2, part 1 (GPO, 1942), 637–61.
7. Theodore Catton, *Life, Leisure, and Hardship along the Buffalo*, Historic Resources Study, Buffalo National River (Omaha, NE: Midwest Region, National Park Service, 2008), 242; *Sixteenth Census . . . Southern States*, 16–22, 224–30; *Sixteenth Census . . . Northern States*, 244–53https://www.census.gov/newsroom/cspan/farming/usda-2-16-2012.pdf, accessed July 5, 2019; Gallaher, *Plainville Fifteen Years Later*, 2.
8. Irene A. Moke, "Canning in Northwestern Arkansas: Springdale, Arkansas," *Economic Geography* 28 (April 1952): 155; Brooks Blevins, *Hill Folks: A History of Arkansas Ozarkers and Their Image* (Chapel Hill: University of North Carolina Press, 2002), 152; Robert Edward Krause Jr., "An Environmental History of the Illinois River Basin in Eastern Oklahoma and Northwest Arkansas" (MA thesis, Oklahoma State University, 2006), 57; Curtis Lanning, "He Still 'Yam' What He 'Yam,'" *Northwest Arkansas Democrat-Gazette*, January 27, 2019, https://www.nwaonline.com/news/2019/jan/27/he-still-yam-what-he-yam-20190127/, accessed July 20, 2019; John Magsam, "Siloam Springs Plant to Close, 238 Jobs End," *Arkansas Democrat Gazette*, September 21, 2017, https://www.arkansasonline.com/news/2017/sep/21/siloam-springs-plant-to-close-238-jobs-/, accessed July 20, 2019.
9. Campbell, *Revolution in the Heartland*, 155; James Ira Breuer, *Crawford County and Cuba, Missouri* (Cape Girardeau, MO: Ramfire Press, 1972), 114; Evalena Berry, *Time and the River: A History of Cleburne County* (Little Rock: Rose Publishing, 1982), 340; CB, *U.S. Census of Agriculture: 1950*, vol. 1, part 23, *Arkansas* (GPO, 1952), 105–10; *U.S. Census of Agriculture: 1950*, vol. 1, part 10, *Missouri* (GPO, 1952), 115–23; *U.S.*

Census of Agriculture: 1950, vol. 1, part 25, *Oklahoma* (GPO, 1952), 112–15; CB, *U.S. Census of Agriculture: 1959*, vol. 1, part 34, *Arkansas* (GPO, 1961), 156–62; CB, *U.S. Census of Agriculture: 1959*, vol. 1, part 36, *Oklahoma* (GPO, 1961), 180–86; Blevins, *Hill Folks*, 152–53.

10. "Retail Distribution of Milk Undergoes Revolution in Recent Years," *OM*, May 1954, 12; C. H. Eckles, "Dairying in the Ozarks," *New York Produce Review and American Creamery*, March 10, 1909, 846; Mike and Cathy Brown, Allen Tatman, and Steven E. Mitchell, "Hosmer Dairy Farm Historic District," NR, 1996, 8-6–8-8, https://dnr .mo.gov/shpo/nps-nr/96000549.pdf, accessed February 6, 2021.

11. Mike and Cathy Brown et al., "Hosmer Dairy Farm," 8-8; *Frisco Employees' Magazine*, May 1932, 19; Robert L. Beck and Stephen F. Whitted, *Missouri Dairy Markets*, part 3, *Southwest*, Research Bulletin 674C (Columbia: University of Missouri College of Agriculture, Agricultural Experiment Station, 1959), 6–8; "Increase Capital Stock," *New York Produce Review and American Creamery*, December 15, 1920, 305; "Missouri Creamerymen Enthusiastic about Cream Grading," *Butter, Cheese & Egg Journal*, October 4, 1922, 4.

12. Beck and Whitted, *Missouri Dairy Markets*, 7–8, 82; J. H. Livingston, "Dairying in the Vicinity of St. Louis," *Frisco Employees' Magazine*, November 1929, 23; Lottie Sedwick Hurley, *History of Mt. Vernon and Lawrence County, Missouri, 1831–1931* (n.p.: c. 1931), 28; *Dairying in the Ozarks*, St. Louis-San Francisco Promotional Booklets, 1925, R816, SHSMR, 9; *Port Arthur Route Agricultural and Industrial Bulletin* (Kansas City, MO), December 1927, 6; Raymond A. Young, *Cultivating Cooperation: A History of the Missouri Farmers Association* (Columbia: University of Missouri Press, 1995), 74.

13. Beck and Whitted, *Missouri Dairy Markets*, 60, 82; "History of Milnot Company," http://www.referenceforbusiness.com/history2/77/Milnot-Company.html, accessed August 15, 2015; "Schreiber Foods, Inc. History," Funding Universe, http://www .fundinguniverse.com/company-histories/schreiber-foods-inc-history, accessed August 15, 2015, *International Directory of Company Histories*, vol. 72 (Chicago: St. James Press, 2005); *Sixteenth Census . . . Southern States*, 44–50, 252–58; *Sixteenth Census . . . Northern States*, 274–83; *Census of Agriculture: 1950 . . . Arkansas*, 81–87; *Census of Agriculture: 1950 . . . Missouri*, 70–79; *Census of Agriculture: 1950 . . . Oklahoma*, 82–88; CB, *U.S. Census of Agriculture: 1959*, vol. 1, part 17, *Missouri* (GPO, 1961), 196–206; *Census of Agriculture: 1959 . . . Arkansas*, 195–98; *Census of Agriculture: 1959 . . . Oklahoma*, 219–23.

14. "We Do Have 'Big Business' in the Ozarks," *OM*, September 1956, 5; "Paul Mueller Company History," *Funding Universe*, www.fundinguniverse.com/company-histories/ paul-mueller-company-history/, accessed May 27, 2019, *International Directory of Company Histories*, vol. 65 (Chicago: St. James Press, 2004); "About Us," Paul Mueller Company, http://uk.paulmueller.com/about-mueller/history, accessed May 27, 2019; Beck and Whitted, *Missouri Dairy Markets*, 49; *Census of Agriculture: 1959 . . . Arkansas*, 195–98; *Census of Agriculture: 1959 . . . Missouri*, 196–206; *Census of Agriculture: 1959 . . . Oklahoma*, 219–23; Gallaher, *Plainville Fifteen Years Later*, 65; Leland Fox, *Tall Tales from the Sage of Cane Hill* (Greenfield, MO: Vedette Publishing, 1971), 169.

15. CB, *U.S. Census of Agriculture: 1964*, vol. 1, part 34, *Arkansas* (GPO, 1967), 316–19; CB, *U.S. Census of Agriculture: 1964*, vol. 1, part 17, *Missouri* (GPO, 1967), 348–55; CB, *U.S. Census of Agriculture: 1964*, vol. 1, part 36, *Oklahoma* (GPO, 1967), 362–67; *Dairy Plants Surveyed and Approved* (Washington, DC: USDA Agricultural Marketing Service, Dairy Division, 1963), https://archive.org/stream/dairyplantssurve5ounit/ dairyplantssurve5ounit_djvu.txt, accessed August 15, 2015.

16. Monett Chamber of Commerce Dairy Show Booklet, 1950, R911, SHSMR; Vearl Rowe, *Sketches of Wright County*, vol. 2 (Hartville, MO: Wright County Historical Society, n.d.), 55; Beck and Whitted, *Missouri Dairy Markets*, 5; *Census of Agriculture: 1959 . . . Arkansas*, 195–98; *Census of Agriculture: 1959 . . . Missouri*, 196–206; *Census of Agriculture: 1959 . . . Oklahoma*, 219–23; CB, *1969 Census of Agriculture*, vol. 1, part 34, *Arkansas* (GPO, 1972), 25–584; CB, *1969 Census of Agriculture*, vol. 1, part 17, *Missouri* (GPO, 1972), 41–920; CB, *1969 Census of Agriculture*, vol. 1, part 36, *Oklahoma* (GPO, 1972), 9–552; CB, *1978 Census of Agriculture*, vol. 1, part 4, *Arkansas* (GPO, 1981), 139–48, 152–54; CB, *1978 Census of Agriculture*, vol. 1, part 25, *Missouri* (GPO, 1981), 146–58, 164–67; CB, *1978 Census of Agriculture*, vol. 1, part 36, *Oklahoma* (GPO, 1981), 139–48, 152–54.

17. CB, *1987 Census of Agriculture*, vol. 1, part 4, *Arkansas* (GPO, 1989), 265–84; CB, *1987 Census of Agriculture*, vol. 1, part 25, *Missouri* (GPO, 1989), 328–57; CB, *1987 Census of Agriculture*, vol. 1, part 36, *Oklahoma* (GPO, 1989), 278–99; CB, *2017 Census of Agriculture*, vol. 1, part 4, *Arkansas* (GPO, 2019), 610–13; CB, *2017 Census of Agriculture*, vol. 1, part 25, *Missouri* (GPO, 2019), 833–37; CB, *2017 Census of Agriculture*, vol. 1, part 36, *Oklahoma* (GPO, 2019), 614–17.

18. *Sixteenth Census . . . Southern States*, 44–50, 252–258; *Sixteenth Census . . . Northern States*, 274–283; *1978 Census . . . Arkansas*, 149–51; *1978 Census . . . Missouri*, 159–63; *1978 Census . . . Oklahoma*, 149–51.

19. Vearl Rowe, *Sketches of Wright County*, vol. 2 (Hartville, MO: Wright County Historical Society, n.d.), 73; Blevins, *Hill Folks*, 105; *Traffic World*, December 4, 1920, 1081; unidentified portion of a Frisco Railroad publication, c. 1920s, "Ozarko," Ozarks Scrapbooks, Southeast Missouri State University Special Collections and Archives, Cape Girardeau; "Springfield Leads in Egg Canning," *Frisco Employees' Magazine*, May 1932, 4.

20. Brent E. Riffel, "The Feathered Kingdom: Tyson Foods and the Transformation of American Land, Labor, and Law, 1930–2005" (PhD diss., University of Arkansas, 2008), 44–48; J. Dickson Black, *History of Benton County* (n.p., 1975), 78; Blevins, *Hill Folks*, 105–106; Benjamin Harvey, "Springdale Poultry Industry Historic District," *EOA*, accessed July 12, 2019.

21. Riffel, "Feathered Kingdom," 55, 46; Blevins, *Hill Folks*, 216.

22. Riffel, "Feathered Kingdom," 66–67; Marvin Schwartz, *Tyson: From Farm to Market* (Fayetteville: University of Arkansas Press, 1991), 3–4; "John Tyson," Walton College Arkansas Business Hall of Fame, https://walton.uark.edu/abhf/john-tyson.php, accessed July 12, 2019.

23. Riffel, "Feathered Kingdom," 69–83; Blevins, *Hill Folks*, 164; CB, *U.S. Census of Agriculture: 1950, Special Reports: Ranking Agricultural Counties*, vol. 5, part 3 (GPO, 1952), 18–20.

24. Riffel, "Feathered Kingdom," 57–63, 97–107.

25. Blevins, *Hill Folks*, 163, 166; Riffel, "Feathered Kingdom," 102.

26. *Sixteenth Census . . . Southern States*, 51–54, 259–62; *Sixteenth Census . . . Northern States*, 284–88; *Census of Agriculture: 1959 . . . Arkansas*, 195–98; *Census of Agriculture: 1959 . . . Missouri*, 196–206; *Census of Agriculture: 1959 . . . Oklahoma*, 219–23; Riffel, "Feathered Kingdom," 22, 82–87, 146–57, 206–231; "The 2017 Top 100 Meat & Poultry Processors," *National Provisioner*, https://www.provisioneronline.com/2017 -top-100-meat-and-poultry-processors, accessed July 13, 2019.

27. Riffel, "Feathered Kingdom," 124, 174–82, 252–66.

28. Ibid., 255, 33–34.

29. Ibid., 220–43, 18, 74–76.

30. Ibid., 75, 173, 119–45, 21.

31. Ibid., 96, 173, 18; CB, *2002 Census of Agriculture*, vol. 1, part 4, *Arkansas* (GPO, 2004), 347–61; CB, *2002 Census of Agriculture*, vol. 1, part 25, *Missouri* (GPO, 2004), 418–41; CB, *2002 Census of Agriculture*, vol. 1, part 36, *Oklahoma* (GPO, 2004), 347–63; *2017 Census . . . Arkansas*, 446–58, 610–13; *2017 Census . . . Missouri*, 557–76, 833–37; *2017 Census . . . Oklahoma*, 446–58, 614–17.

32. "Springfield Stockyards Sells," *Buffalo Reflex*, January 10, 2007, https://buffaloreflex .com/archives/springfield-stockyards-sells/article_b7095591-b0c1-5a86-a5a7- 457647d0dcf3.html, accessed July 9, 2019; Brad Belk, "Joplin Stockyards Thrived dur- ing Great Depression," *Joplin Globe*, August 29, 2009, https://www.joplinglobe.com/ news/local_news/brad-belk-joplin-stockyards-thrived-during-great-depression/ article_098de0ba-e7b6-5a07-8194-606591a89bfb.html, accessed July 9, 2019.

33. "Initiatives and Amendments, 1938–2018," Arkansas Secretary of State, https://www .sos.arkansas.gov/uploads/elections/Initiatives_and_Amendments_1938–2018_1 .pdf, accessed July 18, 2019; Donald L. Stevens Jr., *A Homeland and a Hinterland: The Current and Jacks Fork Riverways* (Omaha, NE: National Park Service Midwest Region, 1991), 205; Gallaher, *Plainville Fifteen Years Later*, 68–70; Blevins, *Hill Folks*, 173–74.

34. Blevins, *Hill Folks*, 172–75; Campbell, *Revolution in the Heartland*, 155; "Southwest Research Center," https://southwest.missouri.edu/about/, accessed July 18, 2019; "Savoy Research Complex," https://aaes.uark.edu/research-locations/savoy-research- complex/, accessed July 18, 2019.

35. *Census of Agriculture: 1959 . . . Arkansas*, 156–62; *Census of Agriculture: 1959 . . . Mis- souri*, 196–206; *Census of Agriculture: 1959 . . . Oklahoma*, 219–23; *1969 Census of Ag- riculture . . . Arkansas*, 25–584; *1969 Census of Agriculture . . . Missouri*, 41–920; *1969 Census of Agriculture . . . Oklahoma*, 9–552; *1978 Census of Agriculture . . . Arkansas*, 139–48; *1978 Census of Agriculture . . . Missouri*, 146–58; *1978 Census of Agriculture . . . Oklahoma*, 139–48.

36. *2017 Census . . . Arkansas*, 393–405, 232–44; *2017 Census . . . Missouri*, 476–95, 232–51; *2017 Census . . . Oklahoma*, 393–405, 232–44.

37. CB, *Census of Population: 1950*, vol. 2, part 4, *Arkansas* (GPO, 1953), 78–82; CB, *Cen- sus of Population: 1950*, vol. 2, part 25, *Missouri* (GPO, 1953), 146–54; CB, *Census of Population: 1950*, vol. 2, part 38, *Oklahoma* (GPO, 1953), 114–19; CB, *1960 Census of*

Population: vol. 1, part 5, *Arkansas* (GPO, 1961), 107–112; CB, *1960 Census of Population*: vol. 1, part 27, *Missouri* (GPO, 1961), 146–54; CB, *1960 Census of Population*: vol. 1, part 38, *Oklahoma* (GPO, 1961), 114–19; CB, *Sixteenth Census of the Population: 1940*, vol. 2, part 1 (GPO, 1943), 418–22; CB, *Sixteenth Census of the Population: 1940*, vol. 2, part 4 (GPO, 1943), 336–42; CB, *Sixteenth Census of the Population: 1940*, vol. 2, part 5 (GPO, 1943), 824–28.

38. Kennard Billingsley, interview with author, Violet Hill, Arkansas, November 10, 1997; *Census of Population: 1950 . . . Arkansas*, 78–82; *Census of Population: 1950 . . . Missouri*, 113–19; *Census of Population: 1950 . . . Oklahoma*, 86–90; *1960 Census of Population . . . Arkansas*, 107–112; *1960 Census of Population . . . Missouri*, 146–54; *1960 Census of Population . . . Oklahoma*, 114–19; *Sixteenth Census . . . part 1*, 418–22; *Sixteenth Census . . . part 4*, 336–42; *Sixteenth Census . . . part 5*, 824–28.

39. See Chad Berry, *Southern Migrants, Northern Exiles* (Urbana: University of Illinois Press, 2000.)

40. Geneva and Steve Emerson, interview with author, Calamine, Arkansas, September 30, 2011.

41. John Grisham, *A Painted House* (New York: Doubleday, 2001); V. R. "Jack" Thomas, *Life in the Heart of the Ozarks* (Kearney, NE: Morris Publishing, 2007), 55–61.

42. Emerson interview; Severs interview; Ray Joe Hastings, interview with author, Doniphan, Missouri, October 13, 2011.

43. Leon Combs, interview with author, Bradleyville, Missouri, February 29, 2012.

44. Combs interview; William Leslie Turner, interview with author, Pond Fork, Missouri, October 4, 2011.

45. Don Keeth and Verna Pemberton, interview with author, Iberia, Missouri, October 7, 2011.

46. Keeth and Pemberton interview; Hastings interview.

47. Combs interview; Greg Hinze, "Take Hold: The Arkansas Migration to North Central Washington, 1935–1960" (MA thesis, Central Washington University, 2010), 73–88; Keeth and Pemberton interview.

48. Cecil Sims, interview with David J. Jepsen, location unknown, February 25, 2005, copy in possession of author.

49. See James N. Gregory, *The Southern Diaspora: How the Great Migrations of Black and White Southerners Transformed America* (Chapel Hill: University of North Carolina Press, 2005.)

50. Hinze, "Take Hold," 75; Combs interview; Joseph F. Singer and J. L. Charlton, *The Socioeconomic Adjustment of Rural Households in the Arkansas Ozarks*, Agricultural Experiment Station Bulletin 767 (Fayetteville: University of Arkansas College of Agriculture, 1971), 75.

51. Greg A. Phelps, "Herbert Richard (H. R.) Gibson," *EOA*, accessed April 27, 2020; Brent E. Riffel, "Walmart Inc.," *EOA*, accessed April 27, 2020; Bethany Moreton, *To Serve God and Wal-Mart: The Making of Christian Free Enterprise* (Cambridge, MA: Harvard University Press, 2009), 8; Blevins, *Hill Folks*, 214–15.

52. Riffel, "Walmart Inc."; Moreton, *To Serve God*, 25–28; "Our History," Walmart, https://corporate.walmart.com/our-story/our-history, accessed August 21, 2020.

53. Moreton, *To Serve God*, 8, 131–32.

54. Ibid., 51–55, 67–80.

55. Brian O'Keefe, "The Man Who's Reinventing Walmart," *Fortune*, June 4, 2015, https://fortune.com/2015/06/04/walmart-ceo-doug-mcmillon/, accessed August 21, 2020; "Our History"; Moreton, *To Serve God*, 251–62.

56. Blevins, *Hill Folks*, 85; Floyd C. Shoemaker, "Madison County: Land of Mines, Forests, Farms, and Factories," *MHR* 53 (October 1958): 7; "Strong Revival of Ozarks Iron Mining," *OM*, March 1957, 3; Jordan and Bender, *Economic Survey*, 17.

57. Department of Community Affairs, *Public Investment Plan for the Missouri Ozarks, 1969* (n.p.: Ozarks Regional Commission, 1969), pp. V-70–V-73; "The History of St. Joe Lead Company," *St. Joe Headframe* (Bonne Terre, MO), Special Edition, Fall 1970, http://sites.rootsweb.com/~mostfran/mine_history/stjoe_history.htm, accessed September 27, 2019; CB, *1980 Census of Population: General Social and Economic Characteristics*: vol. 1, part 27, *Missouri* (GPO, 1982), 407–417; Benjamin Hoste and Romke Hoogwaerts, "Life in Missouri's Fading Old Lead Belt," MSNBC, June 22, 2016, https://www.msnbc.com/msnbc/life-missouris-fading-old-lead-belt, accessed September 28, 2019; Jacob Luecke, "Doe Run—The Lead Belt Heavyweight," *Missouri Business*, June 16, 2015, https://mobizmagazine.com/2015/06/16/doe-run-the-lead-belt-heavyweight/, accessed September 28, 2019.

58. Hoste and Hoogwaerts, "Life in Missouri's"; Eli Chen, "Former Mine in Missouri's Old Lead Belt to Be Reopened for Cobalt Mining," St. Louis Public Radio, July 31, 2019, https://news.stlpublicradio.org/post/former-mine-missouri-s-old-lead-belt-be-reopened-cobal-mining#stream/0, accessed September 28, 2019; Eli Chen, "Mining Company Ordered to Clean Up Lead Contamination in St. Francois County," St. Louis Public Radio, April 4, 2018, https://news.stlpublicradio.org/post/mining-company-ordered-clean-lead-contamination-st-francois-county#stream/0, accessed September 28, 2019; Sarah Haas, "Stream Team Makes Headway on Big River," *Daily Journal Online* (Park Hills, MO), September 19, 2019, https://dailyjournalonline.com/news/local/stream-team-makes-headway-on-big-river/article_32a342d1-b5b2-5cff-af2a-08697d2fe154.html, accessed September 28, 2019; "Superfund Sites," Missouri Department of Natural Resources, https://dnr.mo.gov/env/hwp/sfund/superfundsites.htm, accessed September 28, 2019; Susan Saulny, "Welcome to Our Town. Wish We Weren't Here," *New York Times*, September 13, 2009, https://www.nytimes.com/2009/09/14/us/14kansas.html, accessed September 28, 2019; C. Allan Mathews and Frank D. Wood, "Picher," *EOHC*, accessed September 28, 2019.

59. *1960 Census of Population . . . Arkansas*, 208–213; *1960 Census of Population . . . Missouri*, 291–300; *1960 Census of Population . . . Oklahoma*, 223–28; *Missouri Directory of Manufacturers and Mining Operations, 1969 Edition*, 114–334; *Directory of Arkansas Industries, 1968 Edition* (n.p.: Arkansas Industrial Development Commission, 1968), 19–87; Walter F. Lackey, *History of Newton County, Arkansas* (Independence, MO, n.d.), 223.

60. Robert Massengale, *Black Gold: A History of Charcoal in Missouri* (Bloomington, IN: Author House, 2006), 64, 74, 89, 101–118; Peter Yronwode, "From the Hills to the Grills," *Missouri Resources Magazine*, Spring 2000, https://dnr.mo.gov/magazine/2000-spring.pdf, accessed July 26, 2019.

61. Denise Henderson Vaughn, "Recent Historical Conflicts in Ozark Forests: An Excerpt from a Professional Project" (MA thesis, University of Missouri–Columbia, 2014), 9–25, 35–37, 59; Susan L. Flader, "Missouri's Pioneer: A Half Century of Sustainable Forestry," in *Pioneer Forest: A Half Century of Sustainable Uneven-Aged Forest Management in the Missouri Ozarks*, ed. James M. Guldin, Greg F. Iffrig, and Susan L. Flader, USDA Forest Service General Technical Report SRS-108 (Asheville, NC: Southern Research Station, 2008), 9–30.

62. "Smith Brothers Manufacturing," https://www.theclio.com/web/entry?id=43839, accessed January 22, 2019; Karen Testa, "Big Smith in Fashion Big Time, Industrial Look Makes Missouri Overalls Chic," *St. Louis Post-Dispatch*, May 9, 1996; Michele Newton Hansford, *Carthage, Missouri* (Charleston, SC: Arcadia Publishing, 2000), 70.

63. J. Blake Perkins, "Growing the Hills: The Ozarks Regional Commission and the Politics of Economic Development in the Mid-American Highlands, 1960s-1970s," *MHR* 107 (April 2013): 158; Marilyn Collins, *Rogers: The Town the Frisco Built* (Charleston, SC: Arcadia Publishing, 2002), 110–12; *Missouri Directory of Manufacturers: A Buyer's Guide, 1947 Edition* (Jefferson City: Missouri State Department of Resources and Development, 1947), 398–546; *Missouri Directory: 1969*, 114–334; *Manpower Resources in Missouri* (Jefferson City: Research Section, Missouri Division of Commerce and Industrial Development, 1971), 3.

64. Connie Lester, "Economic Development in the 1930s: Balance Agriculture with Industry," *Mississippi History Now*, www.mshistorynow.mdah.ms.gov/articles/224/economic-development-in-the-1930s-balance-agriculture-with-industry, accessed September 2, 2019; *Report to the Governor and the People of Arkansas* (n.p.: Arkansas Industrial Development Commission, c. 1956), 1–6; *An Industrial History of Arkansas* (n.p.: Arkansas Industrial Development Commission, 1962), unpaginated; Keith Orejel, "Factories in the Fallows: The Political Economy of America's Rural Heartland, 1945–1980" (PhD diss., Columbia University, 2015), 56, 102, 134, 166; Barton A. Westerlund and Roger K. Chisholm, "Arkansas Economic Development Commission," *EOA*, accessed September 2, 2019; *Missouri Existing Business Resource Directory* (Jefferson City, MO: Division of Commerce and Industrial Development, n.d.), 8.

65. Orejel, "Factories in the Fallows," 5–6, 19; *Missouri Existing Business Resource Directory*, 13; Campbell, *Revolution in the Heartland*, 206–207.

66. Republican Coordinating Committee, Task Force on Job Opportunities and Welfare, *Revitalizing Our Rural Areas* (Washington, DC, 1967), quoted in Advisory Commission on Intergovernmental Relations, *Urban and Rural America: Policies for Future Growth* (Washington, DC: Department of Agriculture and Economic Development Administration, 1968), xvi; Orejel, "Factories in the Fallows," 236; data on new and expanding industries gathered from multiple annual reports from the 1960s into the early 1990s published by Missouri's Division of Commerce and Industrial Development and found in box 22, Series New and Expanding Industry/New and Expanding Manufacturers, Research and Planning Program Sub Group, Department of Economic Development RG, Missouri State Archives, Jefferson City.

67. L. Dale Hagerman and Curtis H. Braschler, *Part 1: An Analysis of the Impact of In-*

dustrialization on a Small Town Economy, A Case Study of Ava, Missouri, Research Bulletin 910 (Columbia: University of Missouri College of Agriculture, 1966), 14–36.

68. Ibid., 32–39.

69. Ibid., 39–51, 97–98; *Missouri Directory: Mining, Manufacturing, Industrial Services, Industrial Supplies, 1981* (St. Louis: Informative Data Co., 1981), 320.

70. Charles W. Minshall, John D. Miller, and Allen L. White, *Final Report on Development of a Community Level Target Industry Identification Program to the State of Missouri Division of Commerce and Industrial Development* (Columbus, OH: Battelle Columbus Laboratories, 1976), 114–24.

71. *Missouri Directory: 1981*, 319–433.

72. Ibid.; *Fasco Rewards Distributor Newsletter*, February 2011, https://www.fasco.com/news-events/fasco-newsletters/February-2011-newsletter/, accessed September 9, 2019; Jay Holmes, "Missouri Town Makes Rocket Engines," *Missiles and Rockets*, August 1, 1960, 28–30; Lee Ann Murphy, "Spacetown USA: Neosho's Role in the Apollo 11 Mission," *Neosho Daily News*, July 17, 2019, neoshodailynews.com/news/20190717/spacetown-usa-neoshos-role-in-apollo-11-mission/, accessed September 9, 2019.

73. Stephen L. McIntyre, "Introduction to Part Three," *Springfield's Urban Histories: Essays on the Queen City of the Missouri Ozarks*, ed. Stephen L. McIntyre (Springfield, MO: Moon City Press, 2012), 208; *Missouri Directory: 1969*, 232–38.

74. McIntyre, "Introduction to Part Three," 207–208; *Missouri Directory: 1969*, 232–38; Thomas Gounley, "Springfield's Iconic Solo Cup Being Demolished," *Springfield News-Leader*, January 6, 2015, https://www.news-leader.com/story/news/local/ozarks/2015/01/06/springfields-iconic-solo-cup-demolished/21345557/, accessed September 9, 2019; Thomas Gounley, "Regal Beloit Springfield Plant in Final Days," *Springfield News-Leader*, February 17, 2015, https://www.news-leader.com/story/news/local/ozarks/2015/02/17/regal-beloit-springfield-lant-final-days-property-listed-million/23567113/, accessed September 9, 2019.

75. Tim Knapp, "From Zenith to Nadir: The Story of Springfield's Largest Manufacturing Plant," in McIntyre, *Springfield's Urban Histories*, 214–22.

76. Perkins, *Hillbilly Hellraisers*, 174–84; Ozarks Regional Commission (ORC), *1968 Annual Report* (Washington, DC: Ozarks Regional Commission, 1969), 1–10; ORC, *1976 Annual Report* (Washington, DC: ORC, 1977), 3–19.

77. *Public Investment Plan*, V-52–V-54; Ozarks Regional Commission, *Annual Report, Fiscal Year 1971* (Washington, DC: ORC, 1971), 4–8.

78. Knapp, "From Zenith to Nadir," 230; Charles Storch, "Zenith Moving TV-Assembly Jobs to Mexico," *Chicago Tribune*, October 30, 1991, https://www.chicagotribune.com/news/ct-xpm-1991-10-30-9104070631-story.html, accessed November 4, 2019.

79. Knapp, "From Zenith to Nadir," 233; Peter T. Kilborn, "After the Jobs Went South: A Town Finds Pitfalls in a Retraining Effort," *New York Times*, November 6, 1993, www.nytimes.com/1993/11/06/us/after-the-jobs-went-south-a-town-finds-pitfalls-in-a-retraining-effort.html, accessed November 4, 2019; Kathleen Morrison, "The Poverty of Place: A Comparative Study of Five Rural Counties in the Missouri Ozarks" (PhD diss., University of Missouri, 1999), 14, 21, 221.

80. McIntyre, "Introduction to Part Three," 208–209; Chris Wrinkle, "No. 6 Zenith Clos-

ing," https://sbj.net/stories/no-6-zenith-closing.23635, accessed November 4, 2019; Imani Moise, "Meet the Billionaire behind the New Bass Pro/Cabela's Empire," *Wall Street Journal*, October 3, 2016, www.wsj.com/articles/meet-the-billionaire-behind-the-bass-pro-shops-cabelas-empire-1475517156, accessed November 4, 2019.

Conclusion

1. Kenneth Brower, "The Atolls of Arkansas," *Sierra*, December 27, 2018, https://www.sierraclub.org/sierra/2019-1-january-february/feature/atolls-arkansas-marshall-islands-marshallese, accessed August 11, 2020; Walter F. Roche Jr. and Willoughby Mariano, "A Ray of Hope in Springdale," *Baltimore Sun*, September 17, 2002, https://www.baltimoresun.com/news/bs-xpm-2002-09-17-0209170062-story.html, accessed August 11, 2020.
2. Brower, "Atolls of Arkansas"; Jacqueline Froelich, "Marshallese," *EOA*, accessed August 11, 2020.
3. CB, "QuickFacts: United States," https://www.census.gov/quickfacts/, accessed August 11, 2020.
4. Brent E. Riffel, "The Feathered Kingdom: Tyson Foods and the Transformation of American Land, Labor, and Law, 1930–2005" (PhD diss., University of Arkansas, 2008), 255, 33–34; Perla Guerrero, *Nuevo South: Latinas/os, Asians, and the Remaking of Place* (Austin: University of Texas Press, 2017), 7–10, 114–21, 152–75; Marjorie Rosen, *Boom Town: How Wal-Mart Transformed an All-American Town into an International Community* (Chicago: Chicago Review Press, 2009), 182, 190, 212.
5. Rosen, *Boom Town*, 4, 15, 256; Michel Leidermann, "Latinos," *EOA*, accessed April 1, 2020; https://www.census.gov/data/tables/time-series/demo/popest/2010s-counties-detail.html, accessed September 15, 2020; "District Demographic Data, 1991–2020," Missouri Department of Elementary and Secondary Education, https://apps.dese.mo.gov/MCDS/home.aspx?categoryid=2&view=2, accessed February 4, 2021; "Arkansas School Demographics Databases, 2020–2021," University of Arkansas Office for Education Policy, http://www.officeforeducationpolicy.org/arkansas-schools-data-demographics/, accessed February 4, 2021; Denisa R. Superville, "Q and A: An Arkansas School District's Response to Population Change," *Education Week*, August 19, 2014, https://www.edweek.org/leadership/q-a-an-arkansas-school-districts-response-to-population-change/2014/08, accessed February 4, 2021.
6. Rebecca Mead, "Alice's Wonderland: A Walmart Heiress Builds a Museum in the Ozarks," *The New Yorker*, June 27, 2011, https://www.newyorker.com/magazine/2011/06/27/alices-wonderland, accessed February 5, 2020; Regina Cole, "How a Sleepy Corner of Arkansas Became a Destination for Art Lovers," *Boston Globe*, September 13, 2017, https://www.bostonglobe.com/magazine/2017/09/13/how-sleepy-corner-arkansas-became-destination-for-art-lovers/asWhvHqLbD1lSy5vNM2VaK/story.html, accessed February 5, 2020.
7. Rebecca Solnit, "Alice Walton's Fig Leaf," *The Nation*, February 21, 2006, https://www.thenation.com/article/archive/alice-waltons-fig-leaf/, accessed March 4, 2020; Kriston Capps, "The Rise of Walm-Art," *The Guardian*, April 2, 2007, https://

www.theguardian.com/commentisfree/2007/apr/02/theriseofwalmart, accessed March 4, 2020; Francis Morrone, "Our Priceless Heritage," *New York Sun*, May 19, 2005, https://www.nysun.com/arts/our-priceless-heritage/14066/, accessed March 4, 2020; Lee Rosenbaum, "The Walton Effect: Art World Is Roiled by Wal-Mart Heiress," *Wall Street Journal*, October 10, 2007, https://www.wsj.com/articles/SB119197325280854094, accessed March 4, 2020.

8. Cole, "Sleepy Corner of Arkansas"; Fred A. Bernstein, "A Bold Move," *T Magazine*, March 27, 2012, https://tmagazine.blogs.nytimes.com/2012/03/27/a-bold-move/?scp=2&sq=crystal%20bridges&st=cse, accessed February 5, 2020.

9. Deborah Horn, "Ozark Mountains: Big Business Transforms Land of Hillbillies," *Arkansas Business*, March 15, 2004, https://www.arkansasbusiness.com/article/131255/ozark-mountains-big-business-transforms-land-of-hillbillies, accessed February 18, 2021; Rosen, *Boom Town*, 3; Mead, "Alice's Wonderland."

10. Mead, "Alice's Wonderland"; Eben Weiss, "Bentonville, Arkansas Is Disneyland for Mountain Bikers," *Outside*, November 20, 2019, https://www.outsideonline.com/2405323/Bentonville-arkansas-mountain-biking, accessed February 5, 2020; Sarah Nassauer, "Walmart's Arkansas Hometown Is a Mecca for Luxury-Home Buyers," *Wall Street Journal* (online), March 8, 2018, https://www.wsj.com/articles/walmarts-hometown-has-become-a-mecca-for-luxury-home-buyers-1520521360#:~:text=Walton's%20death%2C%20what%20was%20once,their%20products%20through%20the%20retailer; Timothy A. Schuler, "Black Apple Pocket Community Brings High-Performance Homes to Suburban Arkansas," *Architect Magazine*, December 15, 2015, https://www.architectmagazine.com/technology/black-apple-pocket-community-brings-high-performance-homes-to-suburban-arkansas_0, accessed February 5, 2020; Anne Roderique-Jones, "Why You Should Plan a Road Trip through the Ozark Mountains," *Vogue*, June 16, 2017, https://www.vogue.com/article/Ozark-mountains-travel-guide, accessed February 5, 2020.

11. Roderique-Jones, "Why You Should Plan."

12. Ann Zimmerman, "Arkansas Town Hosts World Championship Squirrel Cook Off," *Wall Street Journal* (online), September 9, 2013, https://www.wsj.com/articles/SB10001424127887324094704579063820643875500#:~:text=Created%20with%20sketchtool.-,The%20Latest%20Tasty%20Treat%3A%20Squirrel!,meant%20to%20keep%20Bentonville%2C%20Ark.

13. CB, "QuickFacts: United States," https://www.census.gov/quickfacts/fact/table/US/PST045219, accessed August 10, 2020.

14. W. Dale Mason, "Indian Gaming," *EOHC*, accessed September 18, 2020.

15. CB, "SAIPE State and County Estimates for 2018," https://www.census.gov/data/datasets/2018/demo/saipe/2018-state-and-county.html, accessed August 10, 2020.

16. Regional Economic Analysis Project, "Arkansas REAP," https://arkansas.reaproject.org/analysis/major-components/per_capita_income/; Regional Economic Analysis Project, "Missouri REAP," https://missouri.reaproject.org/analysis/major-components/per_capita_income/, accessed August 10, 2020. Regional Economic Analysis Project, "Oklahoma REAP," https://oklahoma.reaproject.org/analysis/major-components/per_capita_income/.

17. "SAIPE State and County Estimates."

18. *Marian Days: A Spiritual and Cultural Homecoming*, DVD, directed by Tom Carter (Springfield, MO: Ozarks Public Television, 2019); Ben Kesslen, "Gay-Friendly Towns in Red States Draw LGBTQ Tourists," April 26, 2019, https://www.nbcnews.com/feature/nbc-out/gay-friendly-towns-red-states-draw-lgbtq-tourists-we-re-n998541, accessed March 10, 2020; "Eureka Springs Pride Events," https://www.gayly.com/content/eureka-springs-pride-events, accessed August 12, 2020; Weed Maps, "Arkansas," https://weedmaps.com/learn/laws-and-regulations/arkansas/, accessed March 10, 2020.

19. "LGBTQ-Unfriendly," *Princeton Review*, https://www.princetonreview.com/college-rankings?rankings=lgbtq-unfriendly, accessed February 4, 2021; School of the Ozarks, "Curriculum Overview," https://patriots.cofo.edu/Page/Academics/Classical-Christian-Education/Curriculum-Overview.643.html, accessed March 11, 2020.

20. Dianne Dentice, "Hate Groups," *EOA*, accessed August 24, 2020; Jonathan Ford, "Covenant, the Sword, and the Arm of the Lord," *EOA*, accessed August 24, 2020; Timothy Bella, "In Arkansas, White Town Is a Black Mark," *Aljazeera America*, December 10, 2014, http://america.aljazeera.com/articles/2014/12/10/harrison-arkansas-hategroups.html, accessed August 24, 2020; "Frazier Glenn Miller," https://www.splcenter.org/fighting-hate/extremist-files/individual/frazier-glenn-miller, accessed August 24, 2020.

21. J. Blake Perkins, *Hillbilly Hellraisers: Federal Power and Populist Defiance in the Ozarks* (Urbana: University of Illinois Press), 210–13; Donald R. Deskins Jr., Hanes Walton Jr., and Sherman C. Puckett, *Presidential Elections, 1789–2008: County, State, and National Mapping of Election Data* (Ann Arbor: University of Michigan Press, 2010), 392, 413, 423.

22. Deskins et al., *Presidential Elections, 1789–2008*, 433, 454, 464, 483, 493, 503, 514, 550; Politico, "2016 Presidential Election Results," https://www.politico.com/2016-election/results/map/president/, accessed March 11, 2020.

23. Elisabeth Frances George, "Lesbian and Gay Life in the Queen City and Beyond: Resistance, Space, and Community Mobilization in the Southwest Missouri Ozarks" (PhD diss., University at Buffalo, State University of New York, 2019), 238–42; John Eligon, "A Hideaway Where 'Out in the Ozarks' Has Multiple Meanings," *New York Times*, September 7, 2013, https://www.nytimes.com/2013/09/08/us/a-hideaway-where-out-in-the-ozarks-has-multiple-meanings.html, accessed March 10, 2020; Brooks Blevins, "The Country Store: In Search of Mercantiles and Memories in the Ozarks," *Southern Cultures* 18 (Winter 2012): 53.

24. Lisa Moore LaRoe, "Ozarks Harmony," *National Geographic*, April 1998, 89.

Index

Webster County, Mo., 47, 53, 86
Welch, Fountain T., 90
Wenatchee, Wash., 52, 223
West, Billy, 46
West, James, 137, 140, 154
West Eminence, Mo., 65–66
West Plains, Mo., 143, 193, 228; fruit industry
in, 48–49; markets in, 43, 155
wheat farming and milling, 34–36
Wheatland, Mo., 140
White, John Barber, 66, 73
White River, 103, 135–36, 186; as inspiration
for art and literature, 9, 96; damming of,
20, 80, 97, 172, 174–78; float fishing and
camping on, 5, 22, 94–95; mining in water-
shed of, 80; railroads in watershed of, 11–14;
timber industry in watershed of, 71; tourism on, 89, 167–69, 199
White River Authority, 172
White River Division of the Missouri Pacific
Railroad, 10, 13–14, 75, 94, 96, 138, 142: agri-
cultural promotion by, 34, 53
White River Hills, 6, 119, 136, 203; agriculture
in, 43, 45, 53–55, 58, 205; national forest
in, 123–24; timber industry in, 71–72, 228;
tourism in, 90–91
White River Line. *See* White River Division of
the Missouri Pacific Railroad
White River Railway. *See* White River Divi-
sion of the Missouri Pacific Railroad
Wild, Gilbert, 56
Wild, Gisele, 109
Wild, Herman, 56
Wild, James B., 56
Wild and Scenic Rivers Act, 182–83
Wilder, Almanzo, 29–31, 58, 209
Wilder, Laura Ingalls, 29–31, 153, 209
Wilderness, Mo., 148
Wiley's Cove, Ark. *See* Leslie, Ark.
Wilkins, John, 159
Wilkinson Brothers, 197
Williams, Andy, 198, 199
Williams, H. D., Cooperage Company, 70,
71–72
Williamson, Thames, 2, 135
Willis Shaw Express, 211
Will Mayfield College, 134
Willmore, Cyrus Crane, 188–89
Willow Springs, Mo., 48
Wilson, Charles Morrow, 24–26, 123, 158
Wilson, Clyde "Slim," 191, 192, 197
Wilson, James, 43
Wilson, Joe, 247

Windyville, Mo., 146
Winona, Mo., 65–66
Winslow, Ark., 126, 132
Winter's Bone, 249
Wishon, Isaac Coonrod, 46
Withers, Carl L. *See* West, James
Wolf, John Quincy, Jr., 190, 201
women, role of, 125–27
Women's Christian Temperance Union, 97,
121
Wood, Forrest L. and Nina, 175
Wood, Reuben, 86, 153–54
Woodrell, Daniel, 249
Woodruff, George Washington, 40
Woodruff, John T., 135, 158, 186, 252; feud with
Vance Randolph, 2–6, 98, 150
Woods, Daniel, 118
The Woods Colt, 2, 135
Works Progress Administration, 146, 148–51,
153, 156; Federal Art Project, 150; Writers'
Project, 149–50
World Championship Squirrel Cook Off, 247
World War II, 136, 160–66, 208, 212
Wright, Ethel, 120
Wright, Harold Bell, 2, 5, 20–21, 89; experi-
ences of in the Ozarks, 9–10, 13, 97
Wright, Margaret Belle, 276n61
Wright, Obadiah, 276n61
Wright County, Mo., 42; African Americans
in, 105–6
Wulff, Victor, 228
Wyandotte, Okla., 130
Wyandottes, 104
Wyatt, Newton and Lucy, 108

Yakima Valley, 222
Yellville, Ark., 121, 209; mining in vicinity of,
13, 80, 172
Yocum, Tom, 95
Young, Elbert, 15
Young, Harry, 143–44
Young, Howard I., 80
Young, Jennings, 143–44
Young, Lester, 58
Young, Rose Emmet, 19

Zenith Radio Corporation, 235–36, 238
Zillah, Wash., 222
zinc mining: in Arkansas, 13, 74, 79–80; environmental and health impacts of, 80–82,
157, 227–28; in Tri-State District, 77–80;
unionization in, 157

BROOKS BLEVINS is the Noel Boyd Professor of Ozarks Studies at Missouri State University. He is the author or editor of eleven books, including *A History of the Ozarks, Volume 1: The Old Ozarks*; *A History of the Ozarks, Volume 2: The Conflicted Ozarks*; *Ghost of the Ozarks: Murder and Memory in the Upland South*; and *Arkansas/Arkansaw: How Bear Hunters, Hillbillies, and Good Ol' Boys Defined a State*.

The University of Illinois Press
is a founding member of the
Association of University Presses.

———————————————————

Composed in 10.5/13 Adobe Minion Pro
by Jim Proefrock
at the University of Illinois Press
Manufactured by Sheridan Books, Inc.

University of Illinois Press
1325 South Oak Street
Champaign, IL 61820-6903
www.press.uillinois.edu